Responsible Investment Around the World

Responsible Investment Around the World: Finance after the Great Reset

BY

JULIA M. PUASCHUNDER
Columbia University, USA

United Kingdom – North America – Japan – India – Malaysia – China

Emerald Publishing Limited
Howard House, Wagon Lane, Bingley BD16 1WA, UK

First edition 2023

Reprints and permissions service
Contact: www.copyright.com

British Library Cataloguing in Publication Data
A catalogue record for this book is available from the British Library

ISBN: 978-1-80382-852-7 (Print)
ISBN: 978-1-80382-851-0 (Online)
ISBN: 978-1-80382-853-4 (Epub)

Printed and bound by CPI Group (UK) Ltd, Croydon, CR0 4YY

INVESTOR IN PEOPLE

Contents

1

Introduction

We live in the age of responsible investment. The time for a reset of finance after the 2008 World Financial Recession and the 2020 global pandemic has come. In the aftermath of two major economic crises, the societal call for responsible market behavior has reached unprecedented momentum.

Responsibility is part of the human nature and complements corporate activities and financial considerations. The economic, legal, social and philanthropic responsibilities within the corporate sector are addressed in corporate social responsibility (CSR). Financial social responsibility is foremost practiced in socially responsible investment (SRI). Globalization, political changes and societal trends, but also the current state of the world economy, have leveraged a societal demand for ingraining responsibility into market systems.

The 2008–2009 World Financial Recession set the path for the "age of responsibility." During the US presidential inauguration of Barack Obama on January 21, 2009, his inauguration speech called for a new spirit of responsibility that serves the greater goals of society (The White House, 2009). In the wake of the 2008 financial crisis, past World Bank President Robert Zoellick (2009) addressed the "new era of responsibility" featuring "changed attitudes and co-operative policies" steering responsible corporate conduct and SRI as means of societal progress.

In July 2010, the US Congress approved a sweeping expansion of federal financial regulation in response to the 2008 "the financial excesses" causing the "worst recession since the Great Depression" (Appelbaum & Herszenhorn, 2010). The 2,300-page legislative catalog of repairs and additions to the financial regulatory system reflects the current mistrust in deregulated markets (Appelbaum & Herszenhorn, 2010). The US government sets to ensure responsibility in financial markets and protect from human ethical decision-making failures in this "most important Wall Street reform legislation in 75 years" in the words of the National Economic Council Director Lawrence Summers (*CNBC News*, July 21, 2010). In retrospect, the internal crisis of the banking sector that had steered a worldwide recession also held the potential to create a future built upon renewed attention to social responsibility.

Responsible Investment Around the World: Finance after the Great Reset, 1–8
Copyright © 2023 by Julia M. Puaschunder
Published under exclusive licence by Emerald Publishing Limited
doi:10.1108/978-1-80382-851-020231002

A bit more than a decade thereafter, the novel Coronavirus (SARS-COV-2) hit the world as an external economic shock with widespread implications for finance and economics. During the 2022 World Economic Forum address of US Secretary of the Treasury, Janet Yellen, the post-COVID-19 economic growth was called for inclusive growth in harmony with the environment.[1] Public equality and corporate social justice have – once again – gained unprecedented momentum given the widespread and exacerbated finance versus real economy disparity opened up by the pandemic.

From the mid-twentieth century, human advancements have risen steadily (Puaschunder, 2022). Industrialization, technological advancements, technical inventions and capital accumulation remarkably revolutionized the world (Puaschunder, 2022). Though looking back on an epoch of enormous economic progress in the twentieth century; inequality has grown steadily, quantitatively and qualitatively, sometimes more blatant and in other cases more unnoticingly (Puaschunder, 2022). The overall improvement of living conditions seemed to be granted to only some. Disparity within society, around the world and over time inbetween generations became apparent as the world evolved (Puaschunder, 2022). Relative gains and losses distribution patterns shaped and deepened with economic and external shocks, such as financial liquidity constraints, climate change and COVID-19 (Puaschunder, 2022).

The impact of crises exposed unforeseeable system fragility. Additionally, complex interconnections and transactions in the age of globalization drove inequalities faster and stronger than ever before in history (Puaschunder, 2022). Inequality became the ultimate emergent systemic risk in the wake of an exacerbated connectivity and exchange opportunities during our contemporary digitalized times (Centeno & Tham, 2012; Puaschunder, 2022). What happens in one part of the world today, impacts around the globe and becomes visible and felt instantaneously due to constant communication social online platforms (Puaschunder, 2022). The global interconnectedness lays open blatant gaps in distribution patterns of wealth, access to affordable healthcare, education and a favorable environment (Puaschunder, 2021h, 2022).

The COVID-19 pandemic has vividly outlined the distribution inequalities. The disparate impact, the same large-scale external shock, became felt within society, around the world and over time (Puaschunder, 2022). Inequality arises in the access to quality healthcare that varies dramatically around the world. In addition, climate change requires attention for fairness that the costs of climate change mitigation and adaptation are spread equally within society, between countries and over time inbetween generations (Puaschunder, 2022).

Given all these novel and complex inequalities, the twenty-first century heralded an age of responsible investment. Ethics of finance in harmony with the environmental conditions and natural constraints have become a blatant demand of our times. Obvious inequality creates a need for framework conditions securing parts of the society, the world or generations from negative consequences

---

[1]https://home.treasury.gov/news/press-releases/jy0565

emerging from inequality. A new web of social, ecological and fundamental transfers on a grand and wide-spread scale may ease the discrepancies rising in the twenty-first century. The ongoing COVID-19 crisis stresses the need for securing everyone to overcome pockets of virus-struck areas reinflaming contagion of a deadly and debilitating disease. The post-COVID-19 resilience and recovery period thus holds the potential to underline the strong pledge that until everyone is safe from the virus, no one is safe (Puaschunder, 2021h, 2022).

In the aftermath of the Coronavirus crisis, the world therefore has the potential to benefit from an exacerbated strive for finance in line with societal needs and wants that embrace everyone with lifting and equalizing spirits. Future development methods may bloom to detect disparate impacts and find creative redistribution means to share the benefits and spread the risk alleviation patterns equally within society, around the world and over time (Puaschunder, 2022). Heterodox approaches and novel methods may open eyes for previously unnoticed and less discussed responsible finance solutions in the twenty-first century in order to lead leadership to create equal financial conditions and general economic improvement opportunities for all.

The book starts by studying the emergence of human social responsibility in modern economies. During the last century, markets have leveraged into the most prominent form to distribute scarce resources. Within global markets, international corporations have continuously increased in scale, scope, output and economic influence into the most powerful resource allocation form to spread innovation and prosperity around the world (Chua, 2003; Fitzgerald & Cormack, 2007; Micklethwait & Wooldridge, 2003; Rothkopf, 2008). The ascent of multinationals strengthened the corporate role in society and placed a greater share of social responsibility onto the corporate sector. Throughout recent decades, corporate and financial social responsibility have steadily leveraged into concepts of worldwide recognition in the wake of globalization, digitalization and political and societal trends fostering transparency and ecologic sustainability.

As governmental liberalization trends and globalization led to a progressive deterritorialization of social, political, economic interaction, governmental agencies' ability to protect citizenship rights, fulfill social obligations and avert global crises gradually declined. Global concerns beyond the control of singular nation statues – such as climate change, cybersecurity and global pandemics – imposed new levels of social responsibility onto corporate actors. A societal call for responsible corporate conduct developed in advanced societies, in which the expectations of corporate conduct and market obligations sophisticated. With the information technology revolution providing heightened degrees of easily accessible information, corporate societal impacts became subject to scrutiny to an affluent, internationally focused "Weltgesellschaft" who demanded respect for business ethics around the globe (Nelson, 2004; Sichler, 2006, p. 8; *The Economist*, January 17, 2008; Werther & Chandler, 2006). The emergence of non-governmental organizations further contributed to corporate conduct disclosure and the integration of social responsibility into corporate practices.

As for all these trends, multinational corporate conduct started exhibiting higher levels of responsibility vis-á-vis society. Having gained in economic weight and political power, the majority of corporations tapped into improving the societal conditions by contributing to a wide range of social needs beyond the mere fulfillment of shareholder obligations and customer demands (De Silva & Amerasinghe, 2004; Kettl, 2006). Global players stepped in where traditional governments refrained from social service provision – foremost through privatization or welfare reforms. International corporations also filled opening governance gaps when governments could not administer or enforce citizenship rights, new regulations were politically not desirable, feasible or even when governments had failed to provide social services (Steurer, 2010). By striving to meet citizenship goals, corporate executives integrated responsibility into ethical leadership that served multiple stakeholders by balancing economic goals with societal demands (DeThomasis & St. Anthony, 2006).

Today CSR has leveraged into a pivotal factor to align profit maximization with concern for societal well-being and environmental sustainability. Corporations contribute to social causes beyond mere economic and legal obligations (Elkington, 1998; Lea, 2002; Livesey, 2002; Matten & Crane, 2005; Wolff, 2002). By ingraining economic, legal, ethical and societal aspects into corporate conduct, CSR attributes the greater goal of enhancing the overall quality of life for this generation and the following (Carroll, 1979).

Nowadays almost all corporations have embedded social responsibility in their codes of conduct, introduced CSR in their stakeholder relations and incorporated socially conscientious practices in their management (Crane, Matten, & Moon, 2004; Werther & Chandler, 2006). The emergence of CSR as a corporate mainstream is accompanied by CSR oversight by stakeholders advocating for corporate social conduct.

Under the guidance of international organizations, CSR has developed into a means of global governance and social service provision in innovative public private partnerships (PPPs) that tackle social deficiencies. International organizations thereby bridge the gap between ethical standards and institutionalized ethical corporate conduct.

In line with these trends, CSR has become an *en vogue* topic in academia. Academics investigate innovative PPPs to contribute to social welfare (Moon, Crane, & Matten, 2003; Nelson, 2004; Prahalad & Hammond, 2003).

Concurrent with corporations having started to pay attention to social responsibility, ethical considerations have become part of the finance world. Developing an interest in corporate social conduct, conscientious investors nowadays fund socially responsible corporations (Ahmad, 2008; Sparkes, 2002; *The Wall Street Journal*, August 21, 2008). In SRI, securities are not only selected for their expected yield and volatility, but also for social, environmental and institutional aspects. In the special SRI case of political divestiture, socially responsible investors refrained from contributing to politically incorrect market regimes.

With trends predicting continuing globalization, corporate conduct disclosure and societal crises beyond the control of single nation states, the demand for corporate and financial social responsibilities is believed to continuously rise (Beck, 1998; Bekefi, 2006; Fitzgerald & Cormack, 2007; Livesey, 2002; Scholte, 2000).

In the aftermath of the 2008 World Financial Recession, the call for responsibility within corporate and financial markets grew. The neglect of corporate and financial responsibility in a liberal market climate featured an absence of regulatory and accountability control, which weakened the world economy and caused the real world to face extraordinary liquidity constraints. Media coverage of corporate scandals, fiduciary breaches, astronomic CEO remunerations and financial managers' exuberance perpetuated stakeholders' skepticism in the performance of unregulated, trust-based market systems. The announcement of the recapitalization of the banking system in October 2008 halted worldwide liberalization trends and created a demand for ingraining social responsibility in the corporate and finance world that is regulated by a "watchful eye over the market place" (The White House, 2009).

US President Barack Obama dedicated his inauguration speech to responsibility. The following massive recapitalization of the banking system redefined the roles of governmental, financial and corporate actors in addressing social responsibility (Duchac, 2008). Governmental bail-outs in the wake of corporate bankruptcy contributed to stakeholder pressure and hold the potential to reestablish governmental oversight in the corporate and financial worlds (Greenspan, 2007). The shift of public and private sector forces in addressing social responsibility coupled with regulatory oversight of economic transactions was meant to reclaim trust in markets.

In the aftermath of the 2008 World Financial Recession, transparency of private sector activities, accountability of financial market operations and responsibility of market actors by political and financial leaders grew. Mainstream economic theories started a critique of neoclassical assumptions to demonstrate how markets are largely efficient. Unregulated market forces were proven to sometimes not work towards the best interest of the single market participant and the collective of societal constituents. Financial crisis theories were opened up for socio-psychological notions of economic systems, emotional facets of market participants and their emotional decision-making fallibility imposing risk onto economic systems. As for gaining an accurate understanding of economic markets, heterodox economics research widens the interdisciplinary lens to consider socio-psychological motives in corporate, economic and financial theories and models.

Following a build-up of attention to financial responsibility and socially conscientious investments, the Coronavirus crisis and pandemic outbreak situation since 2019 exacerbated attention to ethics of inclusion and sustainable finance (Puaschunder, 2022). Inequality in the economics and finance realm severed with the COVID-19 crisis. The COVID-19 pandemic rose a finance world and real economy performance gap. The external shock of a worldwide pandemic that changed consumption drastically laid open hidden inequalities. The economic circumstances' disparate impacts require a more in-depth analysis drawing on the power and strengths of the interdisciplinary field of law and economics.

In the post-COVID-19 era, the enormous rescue and recovery aid distributed around the world was often pegged to responsible finance. The massive amount of governmental spending to alleviate the economic impact also brought along unprecedented levels of inflation and low interest rate regimes for an extended period of time. The current inflation alleviation efforts open novel opportunities to enact responsible investment. The US Inflation Reduction Act of 2022 and the US Student Loan Forgiveness are – for example – a critical step forward in making taxation fairer and alleviate inequality.

In the post-COVID-19 era, there is also growing attention to the connection of health and well-being with productivity and welfare. The realization of the connection between health and economic productivity as a financial asset has largely been shed out of the contemporary finance literature. The overall well-being underlying human workforce productivity has become a hidden driver of economic growth in the eye of a global pandemic.

With the growing awareness of long-term implications of COVID-19 – for instance, in COVID-19 long haulers, who have prolonged health impairment after initial infection – but also with climate change pressuring healthy living conditions around the globe, the time has come to peg financial recovery and inflation targeting to higher social and environmental causes that may steer capital toward a pro-social direction. The realization of the deeper connection of health with productivity calls for further attention to health in standard economic growth theories. Health capital should be explored, not only in the personal relation between health and financial outcome but also in the macroeconomic foundation of a healthy population for the overall wealth and development of nation states.

In times when John Maynard Keynes' multiplier is discussed as a way of governmental spending igniting the economy, the quest for governmental investment being focused on social and environmental causes that may multiply, has exalted. The worldwide rescue and recovery aid could serve as the spring feather of SRI in our post-pandemic Renaissance.

Current climate change mitigation and adaptation financing efforts are calling for innovative green investment strategies. Environmental demands for a transition to a green economy are met in most novel attempts - such as the Green New Deal and European Green Deal including a sustainable finance taxonomy.

Responsible Investment Around the World starts by depicting the socio-psychological causes, historic roots and political frameworks of responsibility within corporate and financial markets. Exploring the concept of responsibility within modern market economies will feature historical, socio-psychological, cognitive, political and economic processes that impact on social responsibility within corporate and financial markets.

Socially conscientious finance strengthens trust in responsible market actors and governmental oversight control as vital ingredients for functioning market economies and democratic societies. Real-market responsibility phenomena serve a well-tempered balance of public and private social contributions within modern market economies. In the interplay of public and private responsibility, legislation and regulation as well as socially conscientious leadership serve as favorable structures for social responsibility within the finance sector.

Responsible Investment Around the World addresses the long-term impact of the 2008 World Financial Recession economic transition as well as the widespread and lasting changes implied by COVID-19 around the globe. The book offers a comparative approach to understand the most contemporary responsibility challenges of our time that enact conscientious finance. Fairness and social justice have leveraged into the most pressing ethics demands in the twenty-first century post-pandemic era. Most recent law and economics developments include practical ethical dilemmas arising in justified and democratic access to economic and financial stability within society and in the international compound.

The first part of the book sheds light on the foundations of human responsibility and ethicality (Chapter 2.1) from philosophical (Chapter 2.1.1), economic (Chapter 2.1.2), leadership (Chapter 2.1.3) and behavioral (Chapter 2.1.4) perspectives. Social responsibility within market systems (Chapter 2.2) is the foundation for CSR (Chapter 2.3), which builds on creating value for corporations in close exchange with the community (Chapter 2.3.1). In the international arena (Chapter 2.3.2), corporate and financial social conduct is a culture-dependent phenomenon. As a means of global governance provision (Chapter 2.3.3), CSR contributes to social services in PPPs (Chapter 2.3.4) and serves multi-stakeholder management (Chapter 2.3.5) and conflict resolution purposes. Corporate social conduct has been propagated by the United Nations (UN), foremost in its United Nations Global Compact (Chapter 2.3.6), which offers CSR best practice principles and fosters corporate social conduct as a feature of global governance provision in multi-stakeholder partnerships. The UN has also fostered innovative PPPs that implement social responsibility foremost in the sustainable development goals (SDGs). The COVID-19 pandemic as an external shock (Chapter 2.3.7) has exacerbated inequality around the world (Chapter 2.3.8). Corporate social justice accounts for the newest fortification of CSR in the aftermath of the COVID-19 socio-economic fallout (Chapter 2.3.9).

Financial social responsibility attributes the consideration of CSR in investment decisions, which is the basis for SRI (Chapter 2.4). The most common forms (Chapter 2.4.1) to align financial investments with ethical, moral and social causes are socially responsible screenings, shareholder advocacy, community investing and social venture capital funding. SRI is a multi-stakeholder phenomenon that comprises economic, organizational and societal actors (Chapter 2.4.2). The emergence of SRI in the Western World within recent decades (Chapter 2.4.3) can be traced back to a combination of historical incidents, legislative compulsion and stakeholder pressure (Chapter 2.4.4). As a culture-dependent phenomenon, financial social responsibility features international nuances in SRI conduct (Chapter 2.4.5). The 2008 World Financial Recession has triggered a heightened demand for financial social responsibility (Chapter 2.4.6), which was exacerbated by the economic consequences of COVID-19 even more (Chapter 2.4.7). In the new financial order after COVID-19 (Chapter 2.4.8), inequality in the socio-economic fallout of the COVID-19 external shock (Chapter 2.4.9) became most apparent in the finance performance versus the real economy constraints gap (Chapter 2.4.10). Social volatility and affective fallout propensities in light of the finance versus real economy gap are the socio-economic burdens of the COVID-19 crisis (Chapter 2.4.11). Contemporary high inflation rates in the Western world (2.4.12) coupled with longest-ever low interest rate regimes (Chapter 2.4.13) account for the economic challenges of our times demanding for responsible finance (Chapter 2.4.14). Responsible finance in the twenty-first century can be shaped by disparate impact analyses results that inform targeted rescue, recovery and relief aid (Chapter 2.4.14). The decision on how to allocate recovery funds range from urban–local–regional and national focus (Chapter 2.4.15) to global and future-oriented beneficiaries focus (Chapter 2.4.16). The UN plays a pivotal role in promoting SRI in institutional frameworks for initiatives and actions – foremost enacted in the SDGs (Chapter 2.4.17) and future-oriented finance (Chapter 2.4.18). Financial investment strategies are coupled with political activism in the case of political divestiture (Chapter 2.4.19), which refers to the removal of investment from socially irresponsible markets with the greater goal of accomplishing socio-political changes. Financial social responsibility comprises divestiture of negative market forces as well as positive-screened SRI ventures for conscientious investors (Chapter 2.4.20).

This book captures current trends in CSR and SRI conduct in order to delineate circumstances under which social responsibility is likely to occur in the public and private sectors. Describing UN multi-stakeholder partnerships on the SDGs aims at enhancing the efficiency and minimizing downfalls of public and private global governance provision (Chapter 3). The body of knowledge on political divestiture is outlined in order to draw predictions about the most contemporary efforts to peg political agendas to finance (Chapter 4).

Overall, the book tries to explore innovative ways in which corporations and financial markets create value for society. The research is targeted at investigating potentials and resolving deficiencies in the implementation of corporate and financial social responsibility. The findings derive conclusions for the ongoing adaptation and adoption of CSR and SRI with a special attention to the interplay of public and private contributions. In sum, the book may offer information to help ignite and guide responsible investment to foster the overarching goal of improving the living conditions for this generation and the following.

2

Responsibility

The foundations (Chapter 2.1) of responsibility are found in philosophical roots (Chapter 2.1.1), ingrained in human nature (Chapter 2.1.4) and learned within the societal context (Chapter 2.1.3) given economic realities (Chapter 2.1.2). As a prerequisite for the functioning of market systems (Chapter 2.2), CSR (Chapter 2.3) complements corporate activities with value for society (Chapter 2.3.1) and is considered in financial investments (Chapter 2.4). As a multi-stakeholder phenomenon (Chapter 2.3.5), CSR is of value to various constituents (Chapter 2.3.1) in the international arena, where CSR is practiced in different forms (Chapter 2.3.1). CSR emerged in the Western world and is a culture-dependent phenomenon (Chapter 2.3.1). CSR becomes a feature of global governance (Chapter 2.3.3) in PPPs addressing social service provision (Chapter 2.3.4) and as a multi-stakeholder management means (Chapter 2.3.5). The United Nations Global Compact (UNGC) provides CSR with best practices principles and fosters CSR in PPPs (Chapter 2.3.6). COVID-19 heralds a new finance Renaissance that breeds a climate of responsible investment (Chapter 2.3.7). The COVID-19 external shock induced inequality (Chapter 2.3.8), which drove widespread attention to corporate social justice in the aftermath of the COVID-19 pandemic era (Chapter 2.3.9).

Financial social responsibility is based on considerations of CSR in investment behavior (Chapter 2.4). CSR is the basis for SRI in screenings, shareholder advocacy, community investing and social venture capital funding (Chapter 2.4.1). As a multi-stakeholder phenomenon, SRI comprises economic, organizational and societal constituents (Chapter 2.4.2). The emergence of SRI within the Western world (Chapter 2.4.3) can be traced back to a combination of historical incidents, legislative compulsion and stakeholder pressure (Chapter 2.4.4). SRI is a context and culture-dependent phenomenon featuring different nuances around the world (Chapter 2.4.5). The 2008 World Financial Crisis triggered a heightened demand for corporate social conduct and socially responsible finance (Chapter 2.4.6). The economic impact of COVID-19 (Chapter 2.4.7) heralded a new finance order (Chapter 2.4.8). The disparate impact of the socio-economic fallout of COVID-19 drove inequality around the world (Chapter 2.4.9). The finance performance versus real economy constraints gap (Chapter 2.4.10) created social volatility and affective fallout propensity trajectories, which created silos of inequality within

Responsible Investment Around the World: Finance after the Great Reset, 9–159
Copyright © 2023 by Julia M. Puaschunder
Published under exclusive licence by Emerald Publishing Limited
doi:10.1108/978-1-80382-851-020231004

modern societies (Chapter 2.4.11). Heightened inflation levels (Chapter 2.4.12) and low interest rate regime anomalies (Chapter 2.4.13) are currently offsetting a wave of responsible finance in targeted rescue, recovery and relief aid (Chapter 2.4.14). Disparate impact analyses of law and economics may lead to the decision of how to allocate redistribution between urban, local, regional, national, global and future-oriented beneficiaries (Chapter 2.4.16). Global governance institutions provide an institutional frame (Chapter 2.4.17) for future responsible finance endeavors (Chapter 2.4.18). As a special case of SRI, political divestiture refers to the investment withdrawal from socially irresponsible market regimes with the greater goal of accomplishing socio-psychological changes (Chapter 2.4.19). SRI is also enacted in rational profit maximization considerations of positive-screened market ventures (Chapter 2.4.20).

2.1. Foundations

2.1.1. Philosophical Foundations

Dating back to antique and religious roots, responsibility has been addressed in philosophical, legal and libertarian writings. Ancient Greek philosophers outline responsibility as an essential feature of human commitment and care for others (Reese-Schäfer, 1995 in Sichler, 2006).

Immanuel Kant defined responsibility as an internal moral mainspring for ethicality and duty as a universal privilege of society (Gunkel, 1989 in Sichler, 2006; Kant, 1787/1974, 1788/1974). According to Kant (1787/1974) free, self-determined individuals become responsible when reflecting about others' free will (Berlin, 1969 in Sichler, 2006; Hayek, 1944/2007). Grounding responsibility on self-reflection and social perspective taking, Kant's categorical imperative therefore advises to solely act in ways one wants to be treated by others. Free-willed responsible individuals exhibit pro-social behavior.

In the social compound, collective responsibility therefore fosters an overall trust-based social climate (Luf, 2009; Sichler, 2006). Collective responsible caring breeds the so-called "social glue" – an implicit form of societal order beyond regulations and legal enforcement. The related "Gesellschaftsvertrag" or social contract of socially responsible actors steers social progress and economic stability (Sichler, 2006). Underlying this implicit social compound, responsibility thus coordinates and structures our living.

Legal writings outline responsibility as a feature of ethicality and an expression of natural law (Sichler, 2006). Responsibility is believed to have emerged from the obedience to externally imposed norms into an intrinsic endeavor of a disciplined, modern humankind (Luf, 2009). Post-conventional forms of morality and ethicality attribute individuals to be responsible when they base their individual decision making with respect for others' free will (Auhagen & Bierhoff, 2001; Sichler, 2006).

Based on the ethics of morality, responsibility depicts an internal care for others that stems from altruism – the internal need to benefit others while lowering the level of personal fitness (Trivers, 1971). Underlying motives for altruism are self-fulfillment by contributing to matters beyond the self and the so-called "warm glow" – a positive emotion attributed to caring for and giving to others (Andreoni, 1989; Jenkins, 2007). In an unconscious search for reflective meaning in life and seeking warm glow reinforcement, humans exhibit responsible behavior and ethical decision making (Sennett, 1998). Deciding in line with personal ethics notions is experienced positively as for determining our character to ourselves and others, which grants positive self-worth (Sennett, 1998).

Ethical foundations provide the groundwork for responsibility (Puaschunder, 2013). Philosophical foundations serve to back the demand for sharing the positive and negative consequences of economic actions in a fair manner. With reference to Immanuel Kant's categorical imperative proposing to "not impose on others what you do not wish for yourself" and suggesting to "treat others how you wish to be treated," the ethical imperatives fortify the idea of a common but differentiated responsibility to ensure decent living conditions around the world (Kant, 1787/1974; Puaschunder, 2017b). The need for fairness in the distribution of the global earth and economic well-being benefits among nations is based on Kant's (1788/1974) imperative to only engage in actions one wants to experience being done to oneself. Passive neglect of action on climate mitigation is therein considered an active injustice to others (Chichilnisky, 1996; Chichilnisky, Heal, & Vercelli, 1998; Puaschunder, 2017b).

Potential economic benefits should be distributed around the world, especially in those parts that are in need of development and aid. Since the birth into a nation on earth is involuntary, by birth one may owe a share of the windfall gains acquired simply by the fate of where one was born to those territories. For instance, as outlined by the correlation between greenhouse gas (GHG) emissions and economic climate change gain prospects, those countries that have the prospect of getting economically richer from climate change are also causing the problem (Puaschunder, 2020d). Based on philosophical notions, being born into climate-prosperous regions by fate naturally determines the obligation to distribute some of the climate change-related benefits (Puaschunder, 2017h, 2020d). A higher contribution to the climate change onset and passive neglect to change environmentally harmful behavior should be taken into account when calculating the redistribution transfer payments in relation to other nations (Puaschunder, 2020d).

The German philosopher and New School professor Hans Jonas, a proponent of philosophical biology, addressed the underlying predicament between biological life and economic striving. Jonas (1979) insists on paying tribute to dignity in nature to raise the living human, who only developed within nature. In Jonas' philosophy not only humans are bestowed with freedom but also plants and animals are characterized by their own freedom and striving. Humans thus have to pay tribute to the ethics of human responsibility in relation to nature, which implies an underlying affinity in the relation of human with nature (Jonas, 1979).

Jonas breaks with a long dualistic tradition in philosophical thought that stressed the elevating difference between humans and nature. Jonas is thereby critical of anthropocentric philosophical positions that portray humans independent of nature and self-sufficient in their thoughts. In outlining the alienation from nature prevalent in the philosophy of his time, he established forethinking philosophical leadership on the embeddedness of humans in natural, social, environmental and cultural conditions that become the spring feather of environmentalism, ecological economics but also behavioral insights. The self-realization of humans and their relation to but also dependence on nature creates an obligation or a responsibility to protect and conserve nature. Responsibility includes taking care for the continuous existence and well-being of the related nature.

Jonas builds on Immanuel Kant's categorical imperative but extends the scope of responsibility and ethics to the entire biosphere. Individuals should only act in ways that are in harmony with continuous life and sustainable living conditions on earth. Jonas (1979) advocates for self-realization based on Bildung (education) of humans. Intelligence is pegged to morality and power to responsibility. Bildung in harmony with the overall ecosystem is nurturing a natural inclination toward preservation and enrichment of life of this generation but also future living beings. The connection of life to others and the wider social and environmental communities creates a natural dependency to care for each other and a moral obligation to preserve the life and livelihood of others. Self-realization is naturally transformed into a claim for preservation. The power dominance of humans over nature coupled with self-realization forms a natural responsibility to protect the earth, in which humans are embedded. Who is the strongest also has the greatest ethical obligation to protect the weakest, which includes other humans, the environment and future living and being on earth (Jonas, 1979).

Extending parental care for children, in Jonas' philosophy there is also the future orientation of care for future existence. Ethical considerations also involve the well-being of future generations within environmentally-favorable conditions and the prosperity of humankind. Moral obligations arise from the co-existence but also the mutual care as well as inequality between humans and nature in terms of power and self-awareness.

Jonas is also forethinking the conflict of technological capacities' effect on the biosphere. Technological innovation is assessed and valued in relation to the well-being of humanity and the sustainability of the biosphere. Human knowledge and technological power to affect the condition of the entire biosphere have created a natural responsibility and obligation to protect and conserve. Biosphere is elevated from being just an instrument for human purposes to an end in itself that needs to be cherished, conserved and protected. Human existence and well-being are portrayed dependent on the responsibility to protect whole-roundedly and future-orientedly.

Building on Jonas (1979), Professor Nikulin (2021) pays attention to modern radical changes that lead to an inability to control the future and predict its consequences. Nikulin (2021) stresses that one should act morally and politically in such a way as to make the life of future generations of living beings possible. Nikulin (2021) derives the duty to existence from the right to life. Climate change is considered as a threat to the continuation of a good life and nature's existence thus heralding a call for the ethics of responsibility.

Based on social contract ideas in the tradition of Thomas Hobbes, Jean-Jacques Rousseau and John Lock, John Rawls' (1971) idea of the veil of ignorance is a thought experiment to structure a free, equal and moral society. Principles of justice should thereby be chosen by parties free from consideration of their advantageous or disadvantageous positions in relation to each other. Similar concepts have been argued in Adam Smith (1761/2014) with an impartial spectator, who is not incentivized by market mechanisms.

John Rawls' (1971) veil of ignorance can aid society to agree on supporting ethical efforts without the consideration of the position one may find her- or himself around the world. John Rawls' veil of ignorance suggests that one should not weight in whether being an economic beneficiary or being an agent struggling within the contemporary economic climate when analyzing overall ethical problems. In light of the overall positive and negative implications of economic activities, one should abandon considering the personal gain and loss perspective. A market incentive blind position clearly goes against utilitarian arguments of the rational agents always striving to maximize expected outcomes. The idea of a veil of ignorance over the economic gains of economic activity pays homage to behavioral economics and attempts to bring in ethics and social care into the standard utility function.

Evaluating economic justice problems behind a veil of ignorance leads to the conclusion to engage in redistribution mechanisms that enable decent living conditions around the world. At the same time, shedding light on the economic gain and loss prospects of economic activity and sustainable finance can help find a well-balanced redistribution system that bestows fairness perception to all parties involved. As for redistributing, socially responsible corporate and financial activities are proposed in the following to distribute the benefits but also bear the burdens of economic activity and financial profits in a right, just and fair way within society, around the globe and over time.

2.1.2. Economic Foundations

As for economic foundations, in order to alleviate inequalities in economic impacts, Kaldor-Hicks compensation criteria can guide a prospective redistribution scheme (Law & Smullen, 2008). The Kaldor-Hicks test for improvement potential within a society is aimed at moving an economy closer toward Pareto efficiency (Law & Smullen, 2008). Kaldor-Hicks criteria assume that any change usually makes some people better off and others worse off at the same time. Kaldor-Hicks then tests if this imbalance can be alleviated by winners compensating losers for the change in conditions. In the Kaldor-Hicks criteria both, winners and losers, must also agree that the benefits exceed the costs of redistribution.

The Kaldor-Hicks compensation can be applied to economic constraints in the wake of productive output. As economic gains and losses from production are distributed unequally around the globe, ethical imperatives lead to the pledge to redistribute gains to losing territories in the quest for economic and social justice. Following the rationale of the Kaldor-Hicks compensation and to alleviate injustices, this book will introduce individual motivating drivers for responsibility to be embedded in contemporary financial systems.

In order for the Kaldor-Hicks compensation to work effectively, economic winners and losers must also agree that the benefits of a commonly agreed upon compensation scheme exceed the costs of such action. Governments can work with tax transfers in the present from the winning agents that redistribute by reimbursements to those who cannot compete within financial markets. Governments can also use taxation revenues to protect assets for future generations – for example, which is currently practiced to avoid long-term damages and environmental irreversible lock-ins in regard to climate change. Overall, this tax-and-transfer mitigation policy appears as a Pareto-improving fair solution across the world and among different generations.

Tax-and-bonds transfers could also be used to incentivize industry actors for choosing clean energy. The revenues raised from taxation and bonds would thereby be allocated to subsidize corporations choosing clean energy. This market incentive could shift the general race-to-the-bottom regarding price-cutting behavior and choosing dirty, cheap energy to a race-to-the-top hunt for subsidies for going into clean energy and production.

Climate justice within a country should also pay tribute to the fact that low- and high-income households share the same burden proportional to their dispensable income, for instance, enabled through progressive carbon taxation. Those who caused climate change could be regulated to bear a higher cost through carbon tax in combination with retroactive billing through a corporate inheritance tax to reap benefits from past wealth accumulation that contributed to global warming. Finding the optimum balance between consumption tax adjusted for disposable income through a progressive tax scheme promises to foster tax compliance in the sustainability domain.

2.1.3. Leadership Foundations

Responsibility refers to the human care for others' well-being. Motives for responsible behavior are connected to altruism – as a search for meaning beyond the self – and positive reinforcement of sympathy within society. Responsibility is part of the human nature and is learned within the societal context. Leaders are role models that face an extraordinary obligation to responsibility in balancing multiple stakeholder needs.

Within society, political leaders and institutional role models hold the potential to ignite and strengthen social responsibility. As such, in his historic inauguration speech, the US President Barack Obama openly called for responsibility (Gebert & von Rosenstiel, 1996; Porter & Kramer, 2003; The White House, 2009). Concurrently, World Bank President Robert Zoellick (2009) addressed the "new era of responsibility" featuring sustainable globalization in line with the United Nations millennium development goals (UNMDGs), which became the basis for the currently pursued sustainable development goals (SDGs). In the aftermath of the 2008 World Financial Crisis, both these role models call for responsibility in their public addresses as an underpinning of a vital and modern market economy. In addition to political leaders, academics and intellectual leaders attributed the role of disciplined responsibility in the age of global capitalism (Centeno & Cohen, 2010; Roberts, 2006).

Paying attention to responsible leadership is beneficial for leaders and society: When leadership decisions are subject to public scrutiny, responsibility enhances the constituents' acceptance of their outcomes, which fosters their implementation and in reverse contributes to the success of leaders. For corporate leaders, responsibility is a crucial component of business performance as for strengthening employee motivation and ensuring long-term positive stakeholder relations (Lennick & Kiel, 2007). Financial ethical leadership is an implicit means of reducing the likelihood of fiduciary breaches in principal–agent relations and in the following a prerequisite of economic stability.

Karl Marx was the first to depict responsibility as a central motivating factor in working tasks (Sichler in Weber, Pasqualoni, & Burtscher, 2004). Responsibility leads to the perception of an internal locus of control and helps in identifying working tasks (DeCharms, 1992 in Sichler, 2006). When responsibility is connected to profound reasons that are central to a person's identity, individuals identify themselves with these purposes and feel obliged to act in sync with their values. Social responsibility is a motivating factor in group work tasks (Weber, 1997). Self-imposed responsibility goals become compelling drivers for actions and can leverage into professional endeavors (Damon, Menon, & Bronk, 2003; Gardner, 2007; Sichler, 2003). By stringency of values and actions, responsible working tasks bestow individuals with identity and grant working relations symbolic meaning (Müller, 1990 in Sichler, 2006).

Modern working situations are depicted as for requiring a high degree of responsibility from individuals. Responsibility is a determinant of success and self-worth (Sichler, 2006). This is especially the case with social entrepreneurs and propreneurs, who apply economic acumen to societal causes about which they personally care. Propreneurs are individuals who strive for aligning working situations with personal values, lifestyles and ethical goals (Fischer, 1995 in Sichler, 2006).

In the corporate domain, social responsibility is a feature of business ethics. Business ethics foster the responsibility of corporate actors by setting moral anchors in corporate codes of conduct. Corporate codes of ethics constitute norms of what is right, just and fair that reflect the law and moral convictions of society (Hennigfeld, Pohl, & Tolhurst, 2006). When business ethics match personal responsibility endeavors with the corporate culture, work becomes a self-actualizing motivation factor that fosters productivity (Colby & Damon, 1992; Gerson, 2002; Sichler in Weber et al., 2004). Exhibiting commonly shared social responsibility in line with business ethics strengthens group cohesion and the ability to work harmoniously (Fukuyama, 1995).

In corporate settings, responsible leadership has gained unprecedented importance in the light of the heightened self-regulation of groups featuring an autonomous planning of working times, work relations and high degrees of individual group coordination, decision making and goal accomplishment strategies (Sichler, 2006). An extraordinary obligation to responsibility is attributed to leaders as for serving as role models and incorporating the aspirations of multiple constituents, whose wants and needs leaders balance (Lenk & Maring, 1992; Nelson, 2004). Corporate, financial and political leadership disproportionately impacts the lives of present and future generations (Lennick & Kiel, 2007). In many cases, leadership thus requires a disciplined focus on long-term goals to ensure sustainability (Sichler, 2006). More than others are leaders change agents who can foresee and respond efficiently to future anticipations. In addition, leaders' hierarchical positioning and established power bases grant the opportunity to institutionalize responsibility and bestow subordinates with transformational aspiration of responsibility (Aaronson, 2002; Biermann & Siebenhüner, 2009; De Woot, 2005; Lennick & Kiel, 2007).

2.1.4. Behavioral Foundations

Responsibility refers to the humans care about others' well-being. Motives for responsible behavior are connected to altruism – as a search for meaning beyond the self – and positive reinforcement of sympathy within society. Responsibility is part of the human nature and learned within the societal context. Leaders are role models that face an extraordinary obligation to responsibility in balancing multiple stakeholder needs.

As classic finance theory has blacked out moral and ethical dimensions of investment decision making, the knowledge on socio-economic facets of SRI behavior is limited. Exploratory analyses of demographic and financial SRI correlates are currently complemented by research on socio-psychological SRI motives. A framework of SRI motives is proposed comprising – apart from profitability calculus – socio-psychological motivating factors such as altruism, innovation and entrepreneurship, strategic leadership advantages, information disclosure, self-enhancement and expression of social values of socially responsible investors, who have a long-term focus.

Traditional financial market theory holds investment decisions being based on rationality (Baron, 2000; Carswell, 2002; Michelson, Wailes, van der Laan, & Frost, 2004). Classical portfolio theory depicts investment allocations dependent on profit maximization of expected utility and volatility (Carswell, 2002; Dupré, Girerd-Potin, & Kassoua, 2004; Harvey, 2008; Michelson et al., 2004). Contrary modern experimental economics describes human decision making being "more global in nature" by addressing irrational socio-psychological motives of investment behavior (Becker, 1976, p. 147).

In the first attempt to analyze the reasons for socially responsible market behavior, demographic correlates revealed socially responsible investors to be well-educated and more likely to be female (Hayes, 2001; Rosen, Sandler, & Shani, 1991; Tippet, 2001; Tippet & Leung, 2001). The majority of ethical investors are young to middle-aged (Sparkes, 2002). Socially responsible investors are described as perfectionists serving in caring professions such as medicine, education or social work.

As for investment distributions, 80% of socially responsible investors have mixed portfolios and only 20% exclusively hold onto SRI options (Dupré et al., 2004). No significant levels of materialism, risk propensity and investment performance concerns are found for socially responsible investors, who tend to believe that SRI implies lower returns than ordinary market options (Sparkes, 2002).

A survey of over 1,100 individual investors showed correlations between SRI and socio-psychological lifestyle factors such as post-materialism, self-image enhancement and social attitudes (Lewis, 2001 in Sparkes, 2002). Socially responsible investors are described as liberal pro-environmentalist who are open to exotic cultures. As idealistic altruists, socially conscientious investors are less likely to be self-centered and hold onto traditional gender roles (Ray & Anderson, 2000). At the same time, SRI is connected to religious and moral thoughts (O'Neil & Pienta, 1994; Sproles, 1985; Sproles & Kendall, 1986).

Investors consider SRI options for economic, psychological and social reasons. SRI grants multi-farious utilities to investors – some of them rational, others less in sync with classic homo oeconomicus assumptions. When it comes to SRI, monetary gratification is accompanied by socio-psychological pay-offs and intangible social values (Waldman, Siegel, & Javidian, 2004).

With the current body of SRI studies focusing on the supply side and financial performance, scarce is the understanding of socio-psychological motives for SRI (Cuesta & Valor, 2007; Mohr, Webb, & Harris, 2001). Overall, the reasons for investors exhibiting social responsibility and underlying investor motives to integrate ethicality in their portfolio choice are yet opaque. Exploratory findings on the objectives of socially responsible investors are primarily based on anecdotal evidence (Rosen et al., 1991). As classic finance theories have blacked out moral and ethical dimensions, a descriptive framework for financial social responsibility has yet to be built (Dupré et al., 2004). Investor motives may comprise the intention to maximize profits, altruism as the concern for the societal well-being, need for innovation and entrepreneurship, strategic leadership advantages, need for transparency and information disclosure, self-enhancement through identification and self-consistency, expression of social values and long-term considerations.

The intention to maximize profits: Empirical investigations of the relationship between SRI and profitability offer no stringent, generalizable pattern (Butz, 2003; Hamilton, Hoje, & Statman, 1993). Up to date no clear answer on the performance and efficiency of SRI has been identified (Dixon, 2002; Jones, van der Laan, Frost, & Loftus, 2008; Little, 2008; Mackey, Mackey, & Barney, 2004). While some evidence holds SRI out- (e.g., Kempf & Osthoff, 2007), others under-performing the market (e.g., Fowler & Hope, 2007) and some studies report no difference of SRI to conventional market indices at all (e.g., Abramson & Chung, 2000; Boutin-Dufresne & Savaria, 2004).

Since 1992, the Domini 400 Social Index has outperformed the S&P 500 (Harvey, 2008). Data of the 100 "Best Corporate Citizens" corporations underlined the SRI profitability to outperform the Standard & Poor's 500 (S&P 500) Index – an index of 500 widely held stocks to measure the general market performance (Kotler & Lee, 2005). In addition, a pool of 277 corporations listed on the Toronto Stock Exchange exhibited a positive relation of social responsibility, positive financial return and low volatility from 1996 to 1999.

Sector-specific investigations related corporate environmental responsibility to higher risk-adjusted returns (Cohen, Fenn, & Konar, 1997; Posnikoff, 1997).

In contrast, stocks of 451 United Kingdom (UK) corporations with sound social performance were depicted to significantly underperform the market, while corporations with low corporate social performance were captured to considerably outperform the market (Brammer, Brooks, & Pavelin, 2006). Within the Australian market, ethical funds were significantly undervalued in the market from 2002 to 2005 (Jones et al., 2008). In sync, Wright and Ferris (1997), McWilliams, Siegel, and Teoh (1999), Meznar, Nigh, and Kwok (1994) and Ngassam (1992) reported political divestiture to be associated with shareholder wealth loss.

No difference in the financial performance or volatility rates of SRI to the rest of the market was outlined by Abramson and Chung (2000) as well as Boutin-Dufresne and Savaria (2004).

In closing, there is no stringent answer as to whether SRI is associated with an increase or decrease in shareholder return and volatility (Berman, Wicks, Kotha, & Jones, 1999; Hamilton et al., 1993). Sometimes socially responsible financial market options increase shareholder value, in some cases SRI reduces shareholder profits and sometimes SRI does not deviate from ordinary financial options (Hamilton et al., 1993; Little, 2008; Maux & Saout, 2004).

The inconsistency of findings is attributed to manifold SRI expression forms and measurement deficiencies.

Positively screened SRI funds are more likely to feature information technology and alternative energy industries that attract innovative venture capital providers. Positively screened SRI options tend to be more volatile, yet if successful, grant high profitability – for example, solar energy funds have significantly outperformed the market in recent years and remained relatively stable during the 2008 financial crisis.

As for excluding high-return, high-volatility industries such as petroleum, defense and addictive substances, negatively screened options are more likely to underperform the market, at the same time are robust to overall market changes. Negative screening asset holders are more loyal to their choice in times of crises, which contributes to the stability of these funds. Data on the profitability of political divestiture indicate a potential first-mover advantage for early divestiture.

In a cost and benefit analysis, SRI implies short-term expenditures, but grants long-term sustainable investment streams.

In the short run, screened funds have a higher expense ratio in comparison to unscreened ones – that is social responsibility imposes an instantaneous "ethical penalty" of decreased immediate shareholder revenue (Mohr & Webb, 2005; Tippet, 2001). In addition, for investors, the search for information and learning about CSR is associated with cognitive costs. Screening requires an extra analytical step in decision making, whereby positive screens are believed to be more cognitively intensive than negative ones (Little, 2008). Screening out financial options lowers the degrees of freedom of a full-choice market spectrum and risk diversification possibilities (Biller, 2007; Mohr & Webb, 2005; Williams, 2005).

In the long run, SRI options offer higher stability, lower turnover and failure rates compared to general assets (Dhrymes, 1998; Geczy, Stambaugh, &

Levin, 2003; Guenster, Derwall, Bauer, & Koedijk, 2005; Schroeder, 2003; Stone, Guerard, Gületkin, & Adams, 2001). Being based on more elaborate decision-making processes, once investors have made their socially responsible decision, they are more likely to stay with their choice (Little, 2008). As a matter of fact, SRI options are less volatile and more robust during cyclical changes (Bollen & Cohen, 2004).

SRI measurement deficiencies stem from intangible and time-inconsistent pay-offs as well as measurement errors. SRI studies are methodologically limited as for small sample sizes due to the relative novelty of financial social responsibility, inconsistencies in the short time frames under scrutiny and differing modeling techniques used to estimate investment returns (Jones et al., 2008; McWilliams & Siegel, 1996; Mohr et al., 2001; Ngassam, 1992; Teoh, Welch, & Wazzan, 1999). Most SRI studies do not take externalities on the wider constituency group into consideration, which lowers the external validity of the results and calls for a more whole-rounded examination of SRI (McWilliams et al., 1999).

Altruism as the concern for the societal well-being: A mixture of egoistic and altruistic acts constitutes all human behavior as both are features of human nature (Becker, 1976). Contrary to classical economic assumptions of pure self-interest driving all human beings, behavioral economics attributes altruism as a part of economic decision making (Frank, 2007).

The duality of altruism and egoism in human behavior is addressed as early as in ancient Greek writings. Already Socrates is believed to have connected egoistic individual responsibility to altruism (Sichler in Weber et al., 2004). The predicament of altruism versus egoism is also blatant in Adam Smith's writings (Beinhocker, 2007). In *An Inquiry into the Nature and Causes of the Wealth of the Nations*, Smith (1776/1976) proposes self-interest as the motivating force for any economic activity to enhance societal well-being (Jones & Pollitt, 1998). In *The Theory of Moral Sentiments*, Smith (1759/1976) argues that all human beings are selfishly interested in the well-being of others as for altruistic moral sentiments (Zak, 2008).

Altruism is a state, by which individuals increase the fitness of others at the expense of their own (Wilson, 1975). As one of the most enduring human traits, altruism is evolutionarily explained by the increased survival likelihood of those who are supported by others (Becker, 1976). As a source of value for those who give, altruism is associated with selfish pleasure (Brooks, 2008). Granting mean-ing to the individual beyond the self, altruism contributes to the positive self-perception and well-being of the giver. Short-term intangible gratification of altruism is related to the warm glow – an internally rewarding positive feeling derived from the giver being aware of their pro-social behavior (Brammer, Wil-liams, & Zinkin, 2005; Frey & Stutzer, 2007).

Today classic market fundamentalism is challenged by findings of the roles of altruism in decision making as well as trust and cooperation in market transac-tions (Osnabrugge & Robinson, 2000). Contrary to the classic portfolio theory that holds investments being based on rationality, business ethics describe afflu-ent societies to exhibit altruism in investment choices, which deviate from pure profit maximization (Becker, 2008; Brooks, 2008; Frey & Stutzer, 2007). Market behavior is found to not only be based on striving for competitive fitness, but also to feature pro-social, altruistic endeavors. Within society, altruism breeds cooperation and creates long-term beneficial societal ties. Altruism contributes to collective trust and social capital as implicit prerequisites for any economic market activity and societal prosperity (Brooks, 2008; Frey, 2008).

Behavioral economists introduce altruism and pro-social behavior in financial decision-making analyses. The economic psychology paradigm portrays altruism as a pivotal motivation factor for investment allocations (Brooks, 2008; Csikszentmihalyi, 2003). Investors are attributed altruistic investment motives as for their pro-social concerns (Kirchler, 2011). As socially conscientious investors are found to be willing to sacrifice profits for the sake of altruism, SRI is portrayed as an investment strategy that combines profit intentions with social considerations (Little, 2008).

Extended investors' altruism is expressed in investor philanthropy, which is believed to stem from a utility decline of marginal profits (Holman, New, & Singer, 1985). Investor philanthropy is most common in the United States (USA) due to a combination of financial wealth accumulation, cultural values of giving and tax exemptions for charity. Prominent US investor philanthropists are Warren Buffett – who recently donated over 85% of his fortune to charity – and George Soros, who couples economic investments with philanthropy by holding the Soros Fund Management alongside the non-profit Open Society Institute and Soros Foundation (Bernstein & Swan, 2007; Soros, 1997, 2003).

Need for innovation and entrepreneurship: The concept of innovation is as old as humankind. Innovations emerge from entrepreneurial traits and related behavior in advantageous settings (Drucker, 1985).

Since industrialization innovations are attributed as the mainspring of societal progress and economic prosperity (Schumpeter, 1951/1989). Already Karl Marx described the constant revolution of means of production and diffusion of innovations to spur capitalism. Joseph Schumpeter (1934) attributed profit creation to stem from innovations of entrepreneurs who uniquely combine means of production to generate new products for innovation-seeking market participants. In uniquely and efficiently using resources in an unprecedented, productive way, entrepreneurs spur innovative change. Creative entrepreneurs feature dynamic energy, an extraordinary striving for innovative progress and high levels of risk acceptance (Drucker, 1985; Goleman, 2006; Kirchler, 2011). For entrepreneurs, innovative activities grant excitement. Innovation is related to altruism in the case of social entrepreneurship (Schumpeter, 1951/1989). Social entrepreneurs seek innovative opportunities to alleviate social deficiencies about which they care.

Entrepreneurs are in need of a supportive environment and advantageous societal settings that support their innovative endeavors. While entrepreneurial activities are reported in various historical contexts and exist in almost all cultures, the success of innovative entrepreneurship is dependent on external, culture-related factors such as institutional and regulatory frameworks, investment capital and societal values (Brooks, 2008; De Woot, 2005). As incubators for entrepreneurship, innovative milieus attract entrepreneurs and bring innovations to prosper (Aydalot & Keeble, 1988). Libertarian, open market societies foster innovative milieus as for featuring high levels of economic freedom, a constant investment climate, private property securitization and high levels of social capital (Camagni, 1991; De Woot, 2005; Fromhold-Eisebith, 2004; Rodrik, 2007). Within innovative milieus, knowledge dissemination in sync with collective learning processes and expertise platforms stimulate entrepreneurial activities. In open market societies, entrepreneurial innovations are attributed to drive productivity, create and extend markets and steer economic development (Handy, 2006).

Within the financial market, SRI is an innovative and entrepreneurial investment option (Waldman et al., 2004). As a means of stakeholder activism, SRI allows investors to reward societal progress and innovatively tackle social and environmental concerns. Especially positively screened SRI funds feature innovative corporations that pro-actively administer social responsibility beyond the legal requirements (Aiken & Hage, 1971; Little, 2008). Positively screened environmentally friendly corporations contribute to future-oriented funds that attract innovative and entrepreneurial investors (Blank & Carty, 2002; Coulson, 2002; Meyers & Nakamura, 1980; Russo & Fouts, 1997; Ziegler, Rennings, & Schröder, 2002). In shareholder advocacy, SRI becomes a platform to steer entrepreneurial activities, unprecedentedly influence corporate conduct and address social entrepreneurship within the corporate context (Little, 2008).

As an innovative capital allocation form that attracts entrepreneurial spirits, SRI is preferred by venture capitalists and business angel investors. These future-oriented investors have an interest in innovative market options that instigate societal change and sustainably improve the societal conditions (Schueth, 2003).

Social venture capitalists are prone to screen financial options for entrepreneurial opportunities. Venture capitalists seek to finance social entrepreneurs and early-stage business innovations. Venture funds feature relatively high levels of risk in combination with extraordinary return expectations. Venture capital-backed corporations are prone to astronomic growth of highly valuable market shares. Venture capital serves as an important source for innovative economic growth and international development (Gompers, Kovner, Lerner, & Scharfstein, 2005).

Business angel investors are the oldest, major external entrepreneurial start-up funding source. In the USA, close to three million business angels invest more than US $50 billion in entrepreneurial corporations per year (Little, 2008). Business angels fund 30–40 times as many entrepreneurial start-ups than venture capitalists (Little, 2008). As innovative investors, business angels are attracted to entrepreneurial ideas, willing to take high risks and accept lower returns. Angel investors primarily finance early-stage projects that may require hands-on managerial involvement. As for interests in start-up corporations and early-stage ventures, business angels are less likely to make follow-up investments in the same entities. In the USA, individual angel investors are predominantly male, 35–40 years old – which is significantly older than the average venture capitalist – while their European counterparts are slightly older (Wetzel & Freear, 1996). Business angels are well-educated with 60% holding postgraduate degrees and 13% PhDs in various disciplines. Having more corporate exposure than venture capitalists, around 90% of business angels have prior corporate experience. Business angels tend to be more flexible than venture capitalists and make industry-wide investments. In recent decades, the overall market for business angels has grown quantitatively and qualitatively.

Strategic leadership advantages: SRI implies leadership advantages for investors, when being perceived as distinct, innovative market option related to altruism. Leaders express and distinguish themselves from others by their possessions and in their pro-social activities.

Sociologists outline conspicuous consumption as a means of leadership distinction (Becker & Murphy, 2000; Coleman, 1990; Veblen, 1899/1994). In general, leaders are willing to pay premium prices for trademarked high-end goods and innovative first editions to differentiate themselves from others (Becker & Murphy, 2000).

Related to advantageous power and wealth distributions, leaders are in the position to give to others and those who give distinguish themselves as leaders. Altruistic social responsibility and charitable giving are leadership features. Pro-social behavior of leaders is accompanied by positive feedback and a benevolent climate of subordinates (Brooks, 2008). Giving grants leaders control over their social environment and discourages others from causing harm to givers. In pro-social activities, leaders thereby create strong interpersonal networks that lift their position in hierarchies (Brooks, 2008). As altruism contributes to the social reputation of the altruist, social responsibility serves as a means of status enhancement for leaders (Becker, 1976; Brooks, 2008; Hermann, 2008; Sichler in Weber et al., 2004). Pro-social behavior thereby becomes a source of value for those who give and leads to higher personal standing, leadership effectiveness and ultimately greater success.

SRI implies leadership advantages as for being an innovative, high-end market option that allows investors to distinguish themselves from others and establish and maintain leadership positions. As an innovative entrepreneurial financial market option, SRI implies first-mover advantages and a competitive edge over others. Screenings leverage SRI into high-end, branded products that are related to altruism. Positive image transfer portrays socially responsible investors as pro-social leaders (Ait-Sahalia, 2004). For their charitable giving, socially responsible investors enjoy a positive reputation and related status gains (Ait-Sahalia, 2004; Wright & Ferris, 1997). In this light, SRI serves personal and social interests alike (McWilliam et al., 1999).

Need for transparency and information disclosure: When making consumption choices, individuals seek information. Information about products and corporate performance diminishes uncertainty in purchase situations. Transparency of corporation conduct impacts consumption choices.

Investment decision making depends on information about corporate conduct. Information on corporate social conduct is a prerequisite for investors' trust in corporations, lowered stakeholder pressure and litigation risks. Information on CSR impacts investors' behavior and triggers financial social responsibility (Gill, 2001; Mohr et al., 2001; Myers, 1984; Siegel & Vitaliano, 2006; Williams, 2005).

Investors' access to information about CSR is a prerequisite for SRI. SRI is based on the disclosure of corporate social conduct (Crane & Livesey, 2002;

Little, 2008; Mohr et al., 2001). In general, consumers' knowledge about the CSR performance heightens the positive perception of corporations and triggers investment endeavors.

The basis for shareholder activism is transparency and information disclosure, monitoring of corporate conduct, accountability of the implementation of corporate codes of social conduct as well as internal and external CSR monitoring systems. In the search for trustworthy information on CSR and corporate conduct externalities, socially conscientious investors primarily use corporate track records and shareholder resolutions on social and environmental performances (Graves, Rehbeim, & Waddock, 2001; Little, 2008). Apart from social scrutiny, SRI selections are influenced by information-sharing networks, word-of-mouth knowledge transfer and facial emotional display (Thaler & Sunstein, 2008). Information provision on corporate conduct is triggered by stakeholder pressure and spearheaded by respective security and transparency legislations. Shareholders react positively to governmental transparency demands of CSR conduct and a lack of information on CSR causes investors to refrain from SRI options (Cuesta & Valor, 2007; Williams, 2005). Publicity disclosed unethical corporate behavior leads to divestment and lowered stock prices for a minimum of six months (Dasgupta, LaPlante, & Mamingi, 1998).

In the wake of the 2008 World Financial Recession, corporate governance failures and responsibility deficiencies of market actors have pushed investor calls for transparency of corporate conduct, accountability of shareholder meetings, standardized tracking of proxy votings and accessibility of shareholder meetings. Access to information is believed to lower economic default risks of socially irresponsible corporate conduct and contribute to SRI trends. Financial market disclosure regulations were installed to prevent future economic turmoil due to financial fraud and principal–agent defaults. As a positive externality of the 2008 financial crisis, the drive toward transparency and accountability within financial markets is likely to foster SRI in the future.

Self-enhancement through identification and self-consistency: While socially responsible investors are interested in financial profitability, at the same time they want their portfolio choice to conform to personal opinions and societal norms (Little, 2008; Statman, 2007; Williams, 2005). Socially responsible investors are willing to sacrifice financial returns in order to base their investment allocations on personal and societal values (Statman, 2008).

Financial social responsibility is linked to deontological ethics, which comprise internal obligations to uphold protected values of prescriptive moral rules. When paying attention to protected ethicality, decision makers depart from rationality. Emotional connections to protected values make individuals resistant to economic utility considerations. Forced tradeoffs from deontological ethics result in resistance, anger and denial by wishful thinking. Protected values of ethicality are relatively stable across cultures and hold for public and private conditions (Baron & Spranca, 1997).

Financial social responsibility allows investors to attribute causes that are in line with their beliefs and societal values. SRI combines financial investments with personal values based on societal ethicality (Alperson, Tepper-Marlin,

Schorsch, & Wil, 1991; Frey & Irle, 2002; Sparkes & Cowton, 2004). As a means to integrate ethicality in economic decision making, SRI enables investors to address protected ethicality notions that are in line with their personally held, culturally established social values (Knoll, 2008).

Socially responsible investors fund ethical causes about which they personally care and refrain from ethical infringements. The integration of personal ethics in their portfolio decision making and the perception of the investment decisions being in sync with personal protected values lets investors identify themselves with their choice (Mohr & Webb, 2005). The alignment of beliefs and actions evokes identification with investments that grants investors the notion of self-consistency. Self-consistency triggers positive feelings and contributes to the self-enhancement of socially responsible investors (Frey & Irle, 2002; Schueth, 2003).

Expression of social values: Everyday economic decisions are influenced by social considerations. Social motives underlie financial decision making (Frey & Stutzer, 2007; Hong & Kacperczyk, 2006). Social norms are a prerequisite for financial social responsibility, which enables investors to align personal economic endeavors with social obligations and societal concerns.

In the case of SRI, socially responsible economic activities can leverage into a form of expression of social conformity (Soros, 1995; Statman, 2000). SRI signals culturally endorsed protected values. Socially responsible asset allocations connect the individuals with social reference groups. Thereby SRI becomes a means of expression of accordance of personal values with societal norms and the wider society. The expression of personal values by SRI is attributed to stem from an internal need for conformity of words and deeds with social norms and societal values (Hofmann, Hoelzl, & Kirchler, 2008).

Expressing social norms in their investment behavior empowers socially responsible investors as for the social gratification of their pro-social choice and as an implicit form of influence.

Individuals who care about their pro-social images signal their conformity with societal norms in SRI choices (Huberman, Loch, & Önçüler, 2002). The accordance of market interactions with social norms expresses positive, meaningful social identities. Stemming from the positive image of socially responsible corporations and the social gratification of pro-social behavior, socially responsible investors benefit from reputation and prestige gains (Derwall & Koedijk, 2006; Hong & Kacperczyk, 2006; Schroeder, 2003; Simons, Powers, & Gunnemann, 1972; Stone et al., 2001; Webster, 1975). When paying attention to SRI in their decision making, investors can thus improve their societal status.

SRI is a means of expression for self-determination in the wake of rising levels of autonomy (Sichler, 2006). In quasi-political processes, socially responsible investors use their investments as for expressing their value system by influencing corporate conduct (Dupré et al., 2004; Frey, 2008; Kashyap & Iyer, 2006; Lewis & Mackenzie, 2000). Corporate shares give investors the right to vote at the shareholders' general assembly as well as the possibility to put forward resolutions on corporate governance. Shareholder advocacy allows influencing corporate policies targeted at positive societal implications (Mohr et al., 2001). As a positive externality, the expression of personal values in SRI positively contributes to the overall long-term societal progress.

Long-term considerations: Investment decisions are based on reflections about future prospects. Investment strategies can build on intentions to maximize sustainable financial returns as well as considerations of long-term societal implications of investments (Crowther & Rayman-Bacchus, 2004).

Socially responsible corporate conduct attributes long-term perspectives. Socially attentive corporate conduct features sustainability considerations of corporate executives who are mindful of future risks and social impacts of their decision making. Long-term viability of corporate conduct is ingrained in CSR practices. CSR grants long-term stability of corporate conduct as for creating a supportive business environment and decreasing the likelihood of stakeholder pressure and litigation risks (Little, 2008; Posnikoff, 1997; Sparkes, 2002).

When taking rising CSR trends into consideration, SRI offers long-term financial prospects (Dupré et al., 2004; Little, 2008; McWilliams et al., 1999).

SRI allows investors to support corporations that have a lasting impact on society. Investors interested in "social change" put their investments to work in ways that sustainably improve the overall quality of life. Socially conscientious investors thereby use SRI as a long-term strategy to contribute to society (Knoll, 2008; Schueth, 2003).

From a multi-stakeholder perspective, SRI implies long-term positive societal outcomes (Sparkes, 2002). SRI ensures that corporations are held accountable for any social and environmental impacts and investments are in line with societal values (Sparkes, 2002). By shifting capital from socially disapproved to socially conscientious corporations, SRI fosters corporate social performances. As for being incentivized by first-mover leadership advantages, more and more corporations may pay attention to social responsibility in the future. Accompanied by followers, the rising supply of SRI in combination with a heightened demand for the integration of personal values and societal concerns into financial decision making may prospectively leverage social conscientiousness to become a standard feature of investment markets. In the long run, the integration of SRI into the overall competitive model will further sophisticate social responsibility in corporate conduct (Schueth, 2003; Starr, 2008; Stiglitz, 2003). Financial market demand and supply geared toward SRI will stretch the option range in a more socially responsible direction. In addition, if the majority of investors are socially conscientious, socially responsible corporations will continuously benefit from increasing investment streams. Directed capital flows to socially responsible market options will sustainably contribute to CSR and SRI trends (Dupré et al., 2004). Overall, financial markets attuned to social responsibility will lift entire industries onto a more socially conscientious level (Trevino & Nelson, 2004). As such SRI is attributed the potential to positively impact the financial markets and create socially attentive market systems that improve the overall standard of living and quality of life for this generation and the following.

Hindrances of following through a plan of responsible actions are covered in behavioral insights on bounded ethicality. As a part of the human nature, responsibility underlies fallibility. Responsibility deficiencies arise when moral individuals are not aware that their decision making implies ethical considerations or negative societal externalities. If individuals make moral judgments quickly and intuitively – solely based on their gut feelings of right and wrong – they are prone to believe that their behavior is ethical, yet at the same time fall prey to unconscious biases and accidental unethicality (Haidt, 2001; Puaschunder, 2020a, 2021j).

Based on Simon's concept of bounded rationality – comprising a model in which human rationality is very much bounded by the situation and mental capacity limitations – bounded ethicality attributes human fallibility in ethical decisions (March & Simon, 1958; Murnighan, Cantelon, & Elyashiv, 2001; Simon, 1957). Bounded ethicality describes unintentional deviations from morality and ethical behavior, by which systemic and predictable psychological processes lead people to engage in ethically questionable behavior inconsistent with their conscious ethical notion (Puaschunder, 2020a, 2021j). Since the book *Nudge: Improving Decisions About Health, Wealth, and Happiness* by Richard H. Thaler and Cass R. Sunstein (2008) revolutionized economics, bounded ethicality has become subject to descriptive and experimental scrutiny.

Exploratory evidence describes bounded ethicality to stem from uncertainty and information deficiencies in the way we collect, process and use information in our decision making. Decisions are made behind a "veil of ignorance" of perceivable information (bounded awareness) due to mental capacity limitations and biased cognitions (ethical fading) (Rawls, 1971; Tversky & Kahneman, 1974).

We tend to ignore unethicality cues regarding ourselves (ethical detachment and moral disengagement). As we are prone to adjusting our self-perception to meet our conscious ethical standards (memory revisionism), unethicality can unnoticingly slip into our behavior (slippery slope).

With a focus on the present (availability heuristic), we ignore future generations as potential victims of today's consumption (discounting the future, intergenerational anonymity and temporal trade-off predicaments). Our tendency to reside in the status quo (status quo bias) and adapt our perception and needs to slightly changing conditions (tuning) makes us vulnerable to lurking crises. This is especially crucial in sustainability considerations, in which we tend to underestimate the exponential cost increase of environmental protection and climate change. When refraining from discipline today, we miss opportunities for improving our future conditions (want/should conflicts).

Discounting future events includes perspectives about the future into our everyday economic decision making as a prerequisite for sustainable development. However, if we anticipate the future in discounting, we hold positive illusions (behavioral forecasting errors and positive illusions) and future uncertainty exacerbates this view.

We have misperceptions and biased judgment of others' ethicality. When it comes to others, we unreasonably raise the standards of responsibility (fairness bias) and selfishly claim disproportionate shares of common goods (reactive egoism). In negotiations, we fail to see alternative solutions to ethical predicaments (mythical fixed pie of negotiation).

Collectively shared responsibility gets blurred among constituents (bounded and collective responsibility). Diffusion of responsibility leaves the individual with inefficient rigor to fulfill externally imposed, standardized goals (negative goal attainment). Citizens' public goods detachment and mispriced values of natural resources hinder environmental protection. Organizational command structures and information deficiencies impact subordinates' social responsibility (indirect agency and principal–agent predicaments).

Unnoticed human decision-making fallibility implies responsibility deficiencies for society. As an avenue for change, "libertarian paternalism" currently promises efficient public policy strategies to surmounting bounded ethicality (Thaler & Sunstein, 2008). Libertarian paternalism features policies that account for how people make decisions and invisibly steer decision making in a more socially responsible direction. "Paternalism" thereby stands for manipulating people to act according to the preferences of the policy makers; "libertarian" attributes that changes do not limit the individual freedom. By offering "behavioral nudges," policies influence behaviors within the given institutional framework while upholding personal freedom. Examples of nudges are opt-in and opt-out solutions, in which citizens face either actively or passively framed choices that implicitly influence decision outcomes (Thaler & Sunstein, 2008). This implicit guidance has proved as a successful means to trigger organ donations and financial social responsibility (Thaler & Sunstein, 2008). Bounded ethicality is most crucial when social responsibility deficiencies have economic impacts within market systems.

2.2. Responsibility Within Markets

Within markets, social responsibility is explicitly enforced by governmental regulations and implicitly imbued in commonly held virtues. Responsible market agents foster trust in society as an essential prerequisite for economic stability. In democratic economies, co-existing market forces and governmental regulations complement each other in the provision of social services. Collectively shared corporate social responsibilities can blur the focus on ethicality, which emphasizes the importance of ethical leadership. In the aftermath of the 2008 financial crisis, the call for responsibility in markets grew and with the rising economic disparity during the 2020 COVID-19, market turmoil has reached unprecedented momentum.

Adam Smith (1776/1976) proposed unregulated market forces as the optimum means to propel economies and advance society. Following this notion, libertarianism holds open markets as the most efficient societal system to allocate scarce resources and progress society by the collective striving of self-interested market agents.

Libertarians depict market mechanisms as the optimum means to distribute scarce resources. In the libertarian view, governmental market interference and control of corporate conduct are unnecessary hindrances of free market forces (Friedman, 2002). The individual pursuit of self-interest in combination with unbound market mechanisms is believed to lead to a spontaneous order fostering the overall economic development and societal advancement.

The scenario of self-interested market agents pursuing profit maximization, however, does not address social responsibility (Bekefi, 2006; Simon, 2004;

Soros, 2000). As societies cannot exist without a social compound, governmental social welfare and evolutionary-grown social responsibility notions are essential for human well-being (Rodrik, 2007; Soros, 2000).

As a prerequisite for societal stability, social welfare is guided by democratically enacted governmental control and regulation (De Soto, 2000). Democratic market economies feature a mix of governmental intervention and laissez-faire market forces that complement one another in the provision of social services. Governmental regulations implement CSR in legal frameworks that ensure social responsibility throughout the entire value chain – for example, in the International Organization for Standardization (ISO) and Eco Management and Audit Scheme (EMAS) certifications. Public officials also regulate CSR interactions by multi-stakeholder management means. However, the free choice to engage in social responsibility raises ethical predicaments for decision makers (Taylor, 1988).

In addition to legislative oversight, many market transactions are primarily based on trust (Zak, 2008). Responsible market participants ensure correct business performance and natural rule obedience, which breeds trust in the well-functioning of markets. The collective trust in the responsibility of market actors eases business transactions by replacing the constant need for law enforcement and minimizing contracting, performance and monitoring costs (Andreoni & Miller, 2002; Batson, 1991; Yamagishi & Yamagishi, 1994).

As a means to the end of market efficiency, trust in the responsibility of market actors is a pivotal ingredient of market economies (Newton & Ford, 2008). Trust in the responsibility of market participants is associated with market cooperation (Kramer & Tyler, 1996; Ostrom & Walker, 2003), social capital (Putnam, 2000; Putnam, Leonardi, & Nanetti, 1993), governmental stability (Inglehart, 1999; LaPorta, Lopez-de-Silanes, Shleifer, & Vishny, 1997) and economic growth (Knack & Keefer, 1997; Zak & Knack, 2001). Without trust in market actors' responsible performance, the psychological hesitancy and institutional costs of market transactions would limit economic activities.

Trust, at the same time, implies vulnerability as for the exposure to risks of default in ethical dilemma decisions and bounded responsibility constraints (Kramer, 1999; Mansbridge, 1999). Ethical dilemmas arise as responsible market participants are naturally inclined to self-interest. Personal ethical dilemmas of market decision making can be overcome by concurrently pursuing market profit maximization and altruistic philanthropy. Combining rational market performance with a civilian role is a feature of corporate philanthropists such as, for example, George Soros, who maximizes profits in asset allocations, yet at the same time fosters social welfare in non-profit activities – among others by the Open Society Institute and Soros Foundation.

When individuals who face ethical dilemmas are not aware of decision-making fallibility, their responsibility is bounded. In the corporate setting, ethical predicaments may not become apparent if executives are not trained in responsible decision making. Bounded responsibility also stems from dysfunctional incentives. Corporate goal settings can implicitly shield individuals from perceiving business ethics as a corporate advantage. Organizational command-and-control structures and competitive remuneration systems can accentuate individual profit maximization that counterweights societal concerns. Short-sighted evaluation periods draw attention from long-term perspectives and let managers over-discount the future in environmental sustainability considerations. Information deficiencies lower the degree of social responsibility as for decreasing the possibility to consider the potential future implications of decisions.

As for turning to higher levels of responsibility, ingrained organizational cultural norms, status quo biases and economic sunk costs prevent corporate executives from addressing change. Established power bases, habitual work practices and taken-for-granted managerial command–control hierarchies may cause resistance to reforms, particularly when the outcomes are uncertain.

Collectively shared corporate social responsibilities can blur the focus on ethicality, which emphasizes the importance of ethical leadership. Responsible leadership decisions demand taking multiple perspectives, constituents' needs, social externalities and future anticipations into consideration. Within the organizational context, ethical leadership can be bounded, when leaders face multiple obligations on ethical predicaments that impact their decision-making quality (Puaschunder, 2020a).

Leaders' bounded responsibility bears extraordinary levels of risks as value-based leadership triggers the trust of self-actualized subordinates. Trusting leaders implies exposure to the risk of neglecting useful information, refraining from critical assessments and alternative solution seeking. In group think phenomena, trust in irresponsible leaders lets followers fall prey to leaders' accidental fallibility, which galvanizes the outcomes of decision-making errors (Janis & Mann, 1977; Kramer, 1999; Mansbridge, 1999).

Current knowledge-based market structures and fast-paced market systems increase the risk of leaders' bounded ethicality. The negative impacts of bounded rationality, speedy information and capital transfer are outlined in Paul Krugman's estimations of Austria's bankruptcy likelihood being publicly announced in April 2009. Later found to have been based on erroneous data, the quick information dissemination of his predictions led to a costly foreign investment drain for the Austrian Republic. Finding the optimal balance between value-laden leadership and rational decision making, but also informing leaders and subordinates about decision-making fallibility appear to be essential strategies to minimize negative outcomes of leaders' bounded ethicality in causing societal crises.

Diffusion of responsibility becomes most crucial when corporate executives direct their subordinates to contribute to irresponsible corporate conduct (Darley & Latane, 1968). In this indirect agency, the agents may implicitly be steered toward immoral behavior while being blindfold to the ethical consequences of their action (Cushman, 2008). Agents who recognize moral infringements face trade-offs between command obedience, resistance or whistle blowing.

Today's complex global governance systems shift attention away from individual responsibility. In a currently globalizing world featuring international corporations and a ceasing role of governmental global crises prevention, responsibility can get diffused among anonymous market participants. The tightening of the political, economic and cultural web increases the cognitive load of more and more time-pressured key decision makers who determine the fate of present and future constituents. This tendency may be enhanced as responsibility is a feeling toward a group and less an obligation toward society.

The crucial role of bounded responsibility in triggering societal crises is addressed by the metaphor of predictable surprises. Predictable surprises imply that individuals collectively face obstacles to respond efficiently to avert crises as for neglecting information and anticipating future negative events. Leaders who do not consider the evolving consequences of unreflected unethicality and/ or whose preventive actions are hindered by external constraints can accidentally fall prey to predictable surprises (Winship & Rein, 1999). As such, the 2008 financial crisis was partially triggered by executives who did not foresee the cumulative effects of their singular irresponsible decisions on the overall economic stability and societal condition. Although representatives of financial institutions – such as the International Monetary Fund (IMF) and the European Central Bank – had warned of systemic undervaluation of risks in the years prior to the crisis, no counterweighing actions were taken (Tumpel-Gugerell, 2009). Future risk evaluations and coordinated foresight are meant to prevent future predictable surprises.

Anonymous responsibility diffusion is crucial in principal–agent relations, in which an agent is engaged to responsibly act on behalf of and in line with the best interest of the principal. Agents feature specialized knowledge and skills or overcome physical and temporal constraints within market systems. Information asymmetries between principals and agents in the form of the principal's limited ability to observe the agent's action can result in principal–agent responsibility predicaments.

On an aggregate level, corporate executives face quasi-principal–agent dilemmas in responsibility toward share- or stakeholders. CEO duties typically refer to the best interest of the corporation, but whether this attributes solely to corporate shareholders or a wider range of stakeholders – potentially even future constituents – is not well defined (Cox & Haven, 2003). In 1970, the US economist Milton Friedman held shareholder primacy as the sole responsibility of corporations. As employees to owners, corporate executives were meant to entirely focus on maximizing shareholder equity. This premise was backed up by classic finance theory (Ehrlich, 2005; Fisch, 2006; Friedman, 1970; Renneboog, Horst, & Zhang, 2007; Springer, 1999).

However, the legal basis for shareholder primacy varies throughout national legislations. While the overall judicial records are most often supportive of a duty to maximize shareholders' profits, it leaves room for the possibility that corporations sacrifice in the public interest. Some corporate laws – such as the French – give managers discretion to comply with social norms even if this lowers shareholder profits (Elhauge, 2005). Growing legislations backed up by codes of loyalty and corporate ethics principles promote CEOs' responsibility to a variety of stakeholders and corporate obligations to the larger society (Gabaldon, 2006; Sheehy, 2005). In an attempt to capture the concurrent unstandardized legal foundations within the international arena, in December 2001, the Organization for Economic Co-operation and Development (OECD) held a round table discussion on stakeholder influences on corporations as well as trade-off predicaments between share- and stakeholder responsibilities (Clark, 1986; Nourick, 2001; Simons et al., 1972).

In the finance sector, fiduciary duties imply principal–agent dilemmas. Originated from a person entrusted to another one's property, fiduciaries advise clients on investments or keep custody of client funds. Fiduciaries are individuals who have a fiduciary responsibility that entrusts them to act in the interest of the client without gaining any personal benefit except with the knowledge and consent of the client. Fiduciaries face moral and ethical dilemmas if self-interest conflicts with social responsibility for the client and the wider stakeholder community.

Fiduciary responsibility to a variety of stakeholders is attributed by the US Statement of Investment Principles (Goodpaster & Matthews, 2003). Since the year 2000, trustees have been required to disclose – as a part of their Statement of Investment Principles – the extent to which social, environmental or ethical considerations are taken into account in the selection, retention and realization of investments. This measure was introduced to encourage SRIs in pension funds (Hennigfeld et al., 2006).

Fiduciaries serving anonymous market participants can create a situation of psychological detachment from blurred responsibility. As outlined by the 2008 World Financial Recession, corporate irresponsible conduct and fiduciary responsibility failures in combination with heightened degrees of societal trust without regulatory and accountability controls triggered worldwide financial turmoil. In the aftermath of the crisis outbreak, duties of corporate executives and fiduciaries to share- or stakeholders have become subject to scrutiny (Deegan & Blomquist, 2006; Kotler & Lee, 2005). Obligations to multiple stakeholders are currently foremost ensured by soft-law voluntary corporate and financial social responsibility models that promote to consider the overall stakeholder community in corporate conduct and investment decision making (Rodrik, 2007; Steurer, 2010).

2.3. Corporate Social Responsibility

CSR comprises the economic, legal, ethical and philanthropic responsibilities of corporations toward society. Having leveraged into a mainstream feature of the corporate world in recent decades, today the majority of corporations have embedded CSR in their codes of conduct, incorporated CSR practices in human resources management and ingrained CSR in the stakeholder communication. The rising academic literature on CSR is accompanied by professional audits and reports on corporate social performance. The drive toward CSR stems from globalization, economic and political shifts, societal changes and demographic trends. CSR leveraged in the aftermath of the 2008 World Financial Recession and is believed to continuously rise in the age of social justice (Zheng, 2020).

Today economist Milton Friedman's proclamation of corporations' primary goal being shareholder equity maximization is challenged. Nowadays, corporate conduct increasingly addresses societal and philanthropic responsibilities. As an *en vogue* concept, CSR has gained unprecedented momentum (Livesey, 2002; Matten & Crane, 2005).

Originally drawing upon governmental and political theories that focus on the relationship of the individual to the state, CSR depicts the relationship between individuals and corporations. Based upon business ethics, CSR overlaps corporate philanthropy, corporate citizenship and sustainability. As a "concept whereby companies integrate social and environmental concerns in their business operations and interaction with the stakeholders," CSR comprises the voluntary and pro-active corporate commitment to operate in an economically, socially and environmentally responsible and sustainable manner while balancing the interests of diverse stakeholders (Commission of the European Communities Report, 2001, p. 6; De Silva & Amerasinghe, 2004).

CSR comprises the economic responsibility for the corporation in terms of return on the investment; the legal responsibility to abide by the laws of society as the codification of societal moral commitments; the ethical responsibility to do what is right, just and fair beyond economic and legal obligations; and the philanthropic responsibility to contribute to various kinds of social, educational, recreational and cultural purposes to improve the overall societal quality of life (Carroll, 1979, 1991, 1999).

In the wider sense, CSR can be seen as a quasi-democratic principle to attribute stakeholder demands within the corporate world. CSR is shaped by progressive corporations, societal pressure and partnership-favoring public policies (Steurer, 2010). As a voluntary engagement, CSR activities complement hard-law social regulations. As a form of "mandated self-regulation," CSR rather stems from social pressure than regulatory state power (Bartle & Vass, 2007 in Steurer, 2010).

CSR policies pronounce ethical values and moral goals in the domains of environmental protection, health and safety standards, diversity management and human rights. CSR policy instruments comprise legal (e.g., legal and constitutional acts, regulations on reporting and information disclosure and prohibitions and sanctions for investments), economic (e.g., subsidies, grants, export credits and incentives), informal (e.g., research and educational activities, information resources such as websites, brochures and reports, guidelines and codes of conduct and campaign material), partnering (e.g., networks, partnerships, agreements, multi-stakeholder forums and contact points) and hybrid means (e.g., centers, platforms, programs, labels, action plans, multi-stakeholder initiatives, awards and blacklists, certifications, policy coordination and sustainable and socially responsible procurement) (Steurer, 2010).

CSR is implemented by compliance with discretionary regulations, integration of voluntary norms and ethical principles in leadership models, but also the attention to risks imbued in economic, social and environmental externalities of corporate conduct (Steurer, 2010). CSR social programs and instruments achieve social responsibility goals and weigh social impacts of responsible working practices. In particular, CSR themes feature raising awareness and building capacities for social and environmental causes; improving disclosure and transparency on reliable information on the economic, social and environmental performance of corporations to stakeholders; fostering SRI by considering CSR, social and environmental externalities and ethical criteria in capital allocations; and leading by example regarding socially responsible corporate practices (Steurer, 2010).

In the international arena, CSR pro-actively sets the standards to continuously enhance corporate contributions to economic, social and environmental development (Sachs, 2007; World Development Report, 2005). In this light, CSR is an important forerunner for innovative and future-oriented legislations that help in averting future prisoners' dilemmas in the light of scarce environmental resources.

Within the last decades, CSR has continuously leveraged into a mainstream corporate phenomenon (Wolff, 2002). Today almost all major corporations have embedded CSR in their codes of conduct, incorporated CSR practices in human resources management and embraced CSR in their stakeholder relation. Especially corporations that feature transparent outputs and end-customer contact have integrated CSR into their customer relation. Professional CSR reporting on social, ethical and environmental performance (e.g., standardized ISO norms) serves as a best practice guideline that is accompanied by an emerging stream of academic literature and professional auditing on CSR (Livesey, 2002; Matten & Crane, 2005). Steurer (2010) categorizes the CSR literature to foremost comprise case studies that focus on single CSR initiatives (e.g., Barkemeyer, 2007; Holgaard & Jørgensen, 2005; Konrad, Martinuzzi, & Steurer, 2008); conceptual analyses that capture business–government relations and political aspects of CSR (e.g., Moon, 2002, 2007; Midttun, 2005) as well as exploratory comparative CSR policy analyses (e.g., Crane, McWilliams, Matten, Moon, & Siegel, 2007; Cuesta de la & Martinez, 2004). The disparate ways to address CSR are bundled by respective policy frameworks and initiatives – such as the OECD Guidelines for Multinational Enterprises, the UNGC, the Global Reporting Initiative, AA1000 reports of corporate social impacts, the ISO quality standards and the SA 8000 (Steurer, 2010; Waddock & Graves, 1997). Corporate global governance policies are foremost pioneered at international conventions and conferences – for example, at the World Summit on Sustainable Development, the World Summit on the Information Society and the World Economic Forum.

In recent decades, CSR has risen to prominence in the course of globalization, political and societal trends as well as economic and demographic changes.

In the wake of globalization, the progressive deterritorialization of social, political, economic interaction has leveraged many aspects of societal welfare beyond the power, control and influence of nation states. Global economic interdependence has undermined the capacity of governments to control economies and led to global societal deficiencies out of reach for nation states that demand for multi-stakeholder solutions (Sichler, 2006).

Globalization has heightened the outreach of international corporations and triggered the transnational diffusion of market interactions (Sichler, 2006). Open society trends have expanded markets worldwide. In the wake of outsourcing trends, global players have spread production chains around the world that require social quality control on an international basis (Prahalad & Hammond, 2003; Sichler, 2006). Corporate conduct in politically fragile and ideologically differing territories is challenged by unstandardized regulatory frameworks and culture-dependent business practices. Arising social deficiencies increase the demand for standardized, internationally applicable social norms of corporate conduct which ensure that social best practices are addressed in headquarters and subsidiaries alike. As for facing these challenges, international corporations have grown into social enterprises and global governance entities. Beyond the voluntary fulfillment of corporate social standards, multi-national corporations have become "governmental stand-ins" in the provision of social services in underdeveloped markets (Livesey, 2002, p. 314; Stiglitz, 2003).

Globalization intensified worldwide communication and interaction (Sichler, 2006). Access to information on corporate standards around the globe was fostered by technological revolutions featuring extended media coverage of corporate conduct and peculiarities of production sights (Bonß, 2000 in Sichler, 2006; Waddock & Graves, 1997). The transparency of corporate activities in combination with heightened degrees of autonomous decision making of corporate executives has perpetuated stakeholder activism (Sichler, 2006). Especially corporations operating in competitive international markets with transparent products and/or services are pressured to pay attention to social responsibility (Bagnoli & Watts, 2003).

In the wake of disclosure of corporate failures, non-governmental organizations (NGOs) have evolved. Benefiting from new levels of transparency of corporate activities and access to high-tech media, these voluntary civil society organizations of activist groups monitor corporate operations and disseminate information about CSR. NGOs call for accountability of CSR conduct by taking advantage of Facebook, Twitter and blogs for information dissemination, networking and coordinating activities among stakeholders.

The worldwide corporate expansion has opened governance gaps – implying imbalances between corporations and nation state policies. Global governance gaps are blatant in the human rights domain and applicable to environmental constraints. Gaps open when subsidiary governments refrain from implementing social or environmental protection standards as for the fear of foreign capital flight and losing attraction as low-cost production sites. This has been particularly the case in developing countries in which governments lack the institutional capacity to enforce national laws and regulations against powerful global players doing unethical business within their territory (Ruggie, 2008). The negative impact of multi-national corporations on subsidiary host countries also becomes apparent in agreements between host governments and corporations to freeze social protection as well as foreign investors claiming competitive loss compensations for worker welfare expenditures (Ruggie, 2008). As a remedy, stakeholder-demanded CSR ensures human rights and labor standards as well as sustainability attention in every part of the international supply chain. Problematic oversight deficiencies imply the fact that if infringement cases go to international arbitration, they are generally treated as commercial disputes and thus conducted under closure for the sake of commercial confidentiality (Ruggie, 2008).

Apart from the inability of nation states to manage global governance issues without the help of corporations, CSR emerged in situations when governments retreated from social service provision (Matten & Moon, 2004). Political trends of governmental privatization and market liberalization have steadily lowered the degree of public social welfare. Starting as a policy trend in the 1970s, privatization transferred public services onto the corporate sector (Brown, Potoski, & Van

Slyke, 2006; Van Slyke, 2003). In combination with the stringent deregulation of markets throughout the 1980s and the 1990s – exemplified by Thatcherism and Reaganomics – private actors' social welfare contributions rose continuously.

During the 1990s, new public management introduced private sector market dynamics in public service provision (e.g., by voucher programs) and outsourced state obligations to private contractors (Kettl, 2006). Privatization, welfare reform and outsourcing triggered social responsibility in economic markets. In recent years, CSR – that started out as a neo-liberal concept in the wake of downscaled government regulations – matured into a more progressive approach of societal co-regulation (Steurer, 2010).

Societal trends attributed to CSR feature changed consumption behavior. Post-materialistic consumers who are concerned about human rights and environmental protection want corporate conduct to be in line with legislative frameworks and personal standards of ethics (Sparkes, 2002). Post-materialistic consumers consider CSR in their purchase decision and influence corporate conduct by consumer activism and boycotts (Jones & Pollitt, 1998).

Humanization trends – featuring an increasing autonomy and self-regulation of employees who demand self-determination – fostered responsibility in working situations (Paulus, 1994 in Sichler, 2006). As the core of autonomy, self-determination describes the opportunity to choose processes, control and time frames in fulfilling working tasks (Sichler, 2006). Self-determination is a means to enhance the self-image by fulfilling working tasks responsibly within the social compound (Sichler, 2006). In addition, the rising trend of individualization and participation of an educated workforce and the harmonization of work with lifestyle attitudes have led to the steady growth of CSR (Kettner, 1998 in Sichler, 2006).

CSR-contributing economic trends comprise heightened competition due to a shift from producer- to consumer-dominated markets. The focus on consumer demands has perpetuated social responsibility as a branding feature that fosters corporate competitiveness (Sichler, 2006).

Additionally, technical revolutions have shifted technical work toward high-end cognitive production. In modern work situations, manual demands have become replaced by social responsibility obligations. Coordination, management and planning of future-oriented decision making are nowadays the core of leadership demands (Weber et al., 2004). In combination with heightened levels of autonomy, which leveraged the degrees of freedom of corporate conduct, social responsibility has become a central part of every day's decision making of corporate executives who are responsible to multiple stakeholders (Weber et al., 2004).

Demographic trends of heightened market segmentation raising niche products and services, but also population trends in the Western world are drivers of CSR. Endowed with high levels of purchasing power, the aging baby boomers have leveraged into a high-end, post-materialistic consumption group that pays attention to intangible product features and CSR branding such as eco-labeling. The management revolution in combination with consumer needs-led production has assigned CSR a pivotal feature in today's workforce and production chain.

Today CSR has become an up-to-date issue on the agenda of multi-national corporations operating in the Western world, but also of societies that undergo economic transitions and development. In the light of global problems out of reach for nation states, but also as for the ongoing rise of international joint ventures and strategic alliances; the worldwide importance of CSR is predicted to grow in the following years to come. With a continuously rising role of international corporations in global governance, CSR has become an issue of relevance for a wide range of constituents to whom social responsibility is of value.

2.3.1. The Value of CSR

In the investigation of the relationship between CSR and corporate profitability, no generalizable pattern has been identified yet. This is explained by CSR providing tangible and intangible benefits to various constituents as well as contributing to corporate bottom lines instantaneously, but also on a long-term basis.

Within corporations, CSR fosters attentive resource consumption, strengthens the social capital and motivates the workforce. In the corporate communication with consumers, CSR is a differentiating factor as a means of consumer self-expression. CSR builds stakeholder relations, minimizes litigation risks and attracts investment capital. From a macro-economic viewpoint, social responsibility trends hold the potential to lift entire market industries onto a more socially conscientious level. Downsides of CSR are short-term expenses, risks of corporate mission over-extensions and multi-stakeholder coordination challenges.

Primarily corporations are profitability-dependent entities that increase shareholder return by efficient product and/or service provision (Fullerton & Henderson, 1989). In 1970, the US economist Milton Friedman claimed the sole responsibility of corporations being the shareholder value maximization and managers focusing on any other purpose than profits to neglect shareholder obligations. In Friedman's argumentation social services are solely governmental responsibilities that corporate executives should refrain from as they are neither trained to set and achieve social goals, nor democratically elected to do so (Hennigfeld et al., 2006).

Contrary to Friedman's notion, business ethics feature social and environmental considerations of corporate conduct. The so-called "triple bottom line" advocates for the concurrent corporate pursuit of economic goals, social responsibility and sustainability endeavors (Elkington, 1998). For the last decade, academics and practitioners have investigated the interrelation of corporate profit maximization with social and environmental responsibility, yet no generalizable pattern has been identified yet (Griffin & Mahon, 1997; Waddock & Graves, 1997).

Some empirical evidence finds a positive relationship between CSR and corporate financial performance (CFP) (Kotler & Lee, 2005). Orlitzky, Schmidt, and Rynes (2003) meta-analyzed 52 studies on CSR and CFP featuring a sample of over 33,800 observations and reported a positive relationship between CSR and CFP across various industries for the past 30 years (McWilliams & Siegel, 2001). Some studies show a positive correlation between environmental conscientiousness and economic performance – especially for innovative industries – which is explained by the innovative character and the reduction of litigation risks (Bragdon & Marlin, 1972; Gore, 1992; Holman et al., 1985; Porter, 1991;

Russo & Fouts, 1997; Spicer, 1978). However, whether corporations with better CSR financially outperform because of their social responsibility or whether already extraordinarily profitable corporations are in the position to contribute more to society remains unsolved – thus responsible corporations may be those that can afford CSR based on their overall profitability and market leadership position (Barnett, 2005; Brammer et al., 2006; Hennigfeld et al., 2006; Margolis, Elfenbein, & Walsh, 2007).

Other research outlines no clear connection between CSR and corporate profitability (e.g., Bauer, Koedijk, & Otten, 2005; Cummings, 2000; Fogler & Nutt, 1975; Hamilton et al., 1993; Rockness, Schlachter, & Rockness, 1986; Stone et al., 2001; Tippet, 2001). In 167 meta-analyzed studies on the relationship between CSR and CFP, Margolis et al. (2007) count in 27% a positive, in 58% a non-significant and in 2% a negative relationship between CSR and CFP.

Overall, the current body of knowledge on the relationship between CSP and CFP does not offer a generalizable pattern (Jones & Wicks, 1999 in Orlitzky et al., 2003). The inconsistent relationship between CSR and profitability can be explained by intertemporal costs and benefits of CSR that may cancel out over time and across investigations (Margolis et al., 2007; Reinhardt, 2000). The unsolved relationship between CSR and profitability may also stem from CSR offering multiple tangible and intangible values to various constituents (Clarkson, 1995; Cornell & Shapiro, 1987; Donaldson & Preston, 1995; Freeman, 1984; Mitchell, Agle, & Wood, 1997).

Within corporations, CSR fosters conscientious use of resources, which reduces operating expenses. CSR builds social capital by attracting loyal workers whose social competencies are enhanced (Barney, 1991; Greening & Turban, 2000; Russo & Fouts, 1997). Aligning corporate standards with employees' goodwill motivates employees, in whom CSR builds pride and nurtures self-fulfillment (Moskowitz, 1972; Sichler, 2006; Thomson & Wheeler, 2004). Attention to human rights and safety standards improves the working conditions, which raises human productivity (Hennigfeld et al., 2006; Weinreb, 2004).

Throughout the value chain, attention is paid to CSR. For producers of intermediary goods, meeting CSR and ISO 14000 standards is necessary to attract customers. For end-consumers symbolic CSR brand equity differentiates existing products and services (Kotler & Lee, 2005; Margolis et al., 2007; Puaschunder, 2006). By transporting social values that are in sync with the consumer's worldview, CSR brands trigger consumer–corporation identification processes (Aaker, 1996; Keller, 2003; Matten & Moon, 2004). Beyond the mere act of consumption, purchase decisions allow customers to engage in something that is crucial to their personal lives (Puaschunder, 2006). With goods not only being purchased for primary product features, but also for their emotion-laden symbolic meanings; the strategic alignment of brand images in accordance to individuals' worldviews stimulates corporate sales (Bhattacharya & Sen, 2003).

Access to information about corporate activities helps consumers integrate CSR into their purchase decisions (Mohr & Webb, 2005). Evaluating CSR as an influencing factor in decision making, Puaschunder (2006) surveyed the brand representations of 370 European and North American consumers revealing the influence of CSR on brand preferences. Especially 19–27 years old and internally attributing, self-determined respondents paid attention to CSR.

From a grass-roots perspective, consumers are a driving force for corporate social conduct in their brand preferences. Brand choices can be seen as an additional conduit through which post-materialistic consumers express their world-views in society (Aaker & Joachimsthaler, 2000). Thereby consumption leverages into a personal statement and means of exercising quasi-democratic rights to reward socially responsible corporate conduct (Werther & Chandler, 2006).

In terms of stakeholder relations, CSR determines the relationship between corporations and society. Fostering a socially accepted corporate identity, CSR nurtures a positive reputation of the corporation, improves public relations and decreases the likelihood of stakeholder sanctions (Aaker, 1996; Fombrun, 1996; Keller, 2003). CSR-attentive corporations benefit from strategic partnerships with competitors, suppliers, public entities, non-profit organizations, foundations, NGOs and interest groups that offer support in form of endorsements, expertise, networks, shared distribution channels and human capital. CSR is directly related to pro-social lobbies that advance legislature and policy making regarding social issues of concern and can therefore become a means of political influence. As for positively contributing to society, CSR can be regarded as an indirect long-term investment in a safer and more stable community that serves as a fruitful breeding ground for profitable corporate conduct (Hennigfeld et al., 2006; Windsor, 2001).

Today, a growing body of shareholders factor ethics into investment decisions. Attention to CSR whole-roundedly enhances shareholder satisfaction. Not operating in sync with corporate social standards decreases the possibility to attract investment capital and divestiture (Davis, 1973; Greening & Turban, 2000; Rivoli, 2003; Spicer, 1978).

CSR implies leadership and long-term strategic advantages when triggering corporate innovation and accounting for future risks. As a pro-active stance, CSR can foster early adoptions of future policies and thereby grant first-mover advantages (Kotler & Lee, 2005). Participating in policy dialogues with governmental officials provides opportunities to shape future legislations and adapt to policy regulations early-on. Apart from tax exemptions for socially responsible corporate conduct, CSR decreases the likelihood of regulatory supervision, legislative infringements, litigations and governmental fines. While neglecting CSR raises insurance expenditures, corporate conduct in sync with societal expectations counterweights stakeholder confrontations and sanctions such as purchase boycotts.

From a macro-economic viewpoint, social responsibility trends hold the potential to lift entire market industries onto a more socially conscientious level. Leaders in the field that set corporate social standards enjoy first-mover advantages, customer support and stakeholder relation benefits. Other corporations following CSR patterns may shift entire markets onto a more socially responsible level. In this feature, CSR could offer a "third way" between socialism and capitalism by providing social protection while strengthening a nation's economic competitiveness at the same time (Haufler, 2001 in Steurer, 2010).

As for downsides of CSR, the implementation of social responsibility implies immediate expenses. In addition, positive changes toward social responsibility are long-term processes that must be guided, administered and reviewed (Kotler & Lee, 2005). Partnerships with constituents can bring along time-consuming coordination obstacles. Stakeholder management and multiple goal settings may draw corporate executives' attention away from core corporate obligations (Kotler & Lee, 2005). Serving unfitting causes off track the regular corporate portfolio may raise consumers' skepticism about altruistic corporate activities and harm the overall corporate reputation. When attributing social causes, CSR may at the same time crowd out direct help for social deficiency alleviation – such as charity (Graff-Zivin & Small, 2005). This instance is crucial as CSR remains a second-class corporate obligation with the heightened default risks of corporate bankruptcy. CSR also features accountability limitations. Contrary to governments that are directly enacted by their citizens and governmental responsibility being approved by democratic elections, CSR is subject to lower scrutiny and corporations are only indirectly evaluated for their socially responsible performance by consumers' purchase behavior. Until today one of the major deficiencies of corporate social conduct remains the lack of standardized CSR conduct, which becomes apparent in international comparisons.

2.3.2. International Differences

Cultural frameworks comprise governmental institutions, legislative regulations and societal values that determine corporate conduct. Continental European and Anglo-Saxon CSR models have evolved concurrently. North American explicit CSR practices, developed under low governmental control, foster voluntary, self-interest driven corporate social strategies. Continental Europe is renowned for a more implicit CSR understanding that grew out of an elaborate welfare state structure that assigns corporations a larger share of social responsibility. In Eastern Europe, governmentally backed-up CSR initiatives are raising. Within the developing world, CSR is bound by legal, institutional and democratic challenges.

In today's globalized market economies, corporations expand operations worldwide and feature international production and supply chains. International corporate conduct builds globally comprehensive corporate structures that account for stakeholder demands around the globe (De Sam, Dougan, Gordon, Puaschunder, St. Clair, 2008).

Corporate conduct is inseparably linked to cultural settings (Meyer & Höllerer, 2005; Van Maanen & Laurent, 1993). Cultural frameworks feature specific governmental regulations, legal obligations, managerial practices and societal norms that constitute corporate conduct (Porter & Kramer, 2003; Whitley, 1997). CSR is contextualized by a nation state's legal frameworks and regulations, governmental entities, political landscape, industrial relations, labor conditions, economic circumstances and societal values.

Describing intercultural differences in corporate social conduct based on historical, legislative and regulatory differences allows us to shed light on CSR triggers as well as predictions about current and future trends of corporate social conduct (Kotler & Lee, 2005).

Historically, CSR developed in the Western world hosting the world's largest stock of capital and the most vital economies that feature business ethics and philanthropy (Powell, 2008; Rodrik, 2007). Continental Europe and North America are the main incubators of implicit and explicit CSR notions (Powell, 2008; Rodrik, 2007; Williams & Aguilera, 2006).

European CSR models emerged out of guilds, royal codes of conduct and post-war settlements. First European corporate social conduct traces back to the German guild tradition that required corporations to educate not only for profit maximization, but also for attention to societal well-being. The Hapsburg monarchy stressed consensus among market actors. In 1612, British jurists firstly addressed business ethics in light of social infringements of the East Indian Company (Porter & Kramer, 2003). In the 1790s, first consumer boycotts of slave-harvested sugar were staged in Great Britain. Benevolent capitalism started in the UK around the 1850s and first publications on the fundamentals of corporate citizenship appeared at the turn of the nineteenth century. At the same time, Sweden's constitutional monarchy advocated for stakeholder conflict resolution. Legal writings on sacrificing corporate profits for the sake of public endeavors began in the 1930s (Berle, 1932 in Reinhardt, Stavins, & Vietor, 2008; Dodd, 1932). In the wake of industrialization, the British government developed a regulatory framework and inspectorates to disclose anti-social corporate conduct. During the 1970s and 1980s, philanthropy became popular. In the UK, the impact of the Thatcher era on the British welfare state and the revival of entrepreneurial spirits in the 1980s spearheaded the European CSR movement (Handy, 2006; Moon, 2004). Environmental concerns grew in the wake of the 1989 Exxon Valdez oil spill and steadily rose with attention to climate change. In 1987, the Brundtland Commission channeled the common endeavor to provide an at least as favorable standard of living as enjoyed today in a Sustainable Development Summit. Sustainability became a demand expressed in taxation models, natural resources consumption plans, renewable energy supply but also financial market options. During the 1990s, the first mainstream CSR models emerged as corporate practices complementing philanthropy (Smith, 2003). The increased importance of business ethics was underlined by investors' raising demand for socially screened funds. Consumer boycotts as an expression of stakeholder activism peaked in the wake of the Shell Corporation considering sinking oceanic oil rigs. Continental European legal frameworks started attributing social responsibility to the wider constituency group of corporations. Employment empowerment fostered these endeavors.

In terms of regulatory frameworks, European CSR was originally based on mandatory requirements, which are assigned by the entirety of a country's formal and informal public entities (Matten & Moon, 2004). Corporate boards featuring employee representatives considered corporate impacts on multiple stakeholders (Corfield, 1998; Marinov & Heiman, 1998; Reinhardt et al., 2008). Foremost, the German legislation does not even explicitly obligate to maximize shareholder value, but stresses the role of corporations within society. German

Mitbestimmung laws entitled union representatives' access to corporate supervisory boards. The Austrian voluntary Sozialpartnerschaft emphasized the role of stakeholders in determining corporate conduct. French loyalty codes of conduct obliged corporate executives to care for their employees and included the interest of multiple constituents in corporate decision making (Fanto, 1998).

In contrast to North America, Europe features an elaborate welfare infrastructure that enforces social service provision by taxation. Explicit market controls are accompanied by implicit oversight control of trade unions and industry associations. The European legislation and regulation systems require corporations to take over a significant amount of social responsibility (Strebel, 1980). As a matter of fact, many European corporate activities that account for CSR in North America are not labeled as CSR in Western Europe, as they are mandatory. The resulting implicit CSR understanding features a relatively low salience and absence of outspoken CSR.

During the last decades, however, CSR has become a viable alternative to governmental social welfare provision in Europe. The ongoing Americanization of management concepts in Western Europe created a European explicit CSR notion, foremost visible in the media attention, rise of vanguard organizations, CSR reporting and publicly promoted SRI indices (Crane et al., 2004).

The European Union (EU) plays a pivotal role in building trans-national CSR capacities in networking and partnering approaches as well as economic incentives (Cuesta de la & Martinez, 2004). For the EU, CSR remains a voluntary corporate endeavor. Clear regulations and blacklisting of CSR bad practice, which was discussed at the EU in the early 2000s, never came into effect (European Commission, 2002, 2006 in Steurer, 2010).

European CSR features national implementation nuances. Western European CSR regulations and public policy frameworks are spearheaded in the UK, Denmark and France. In the UK, CSR was already discussed as early as the 1970s (Steurer, 2010). The Thatcher government downsizing the role of the state and cutting regulatory social service provision flourished CSR during the 1980s period of high employment, urban decay and social unrest. The UK regulatory framework was the first to mandatorily require corporate social and environmental conduct disclosure for pension fund trustees (Nelson, 2004). The UK Minister for Competitiveness at the Department for Business, Enterprise and Regulatory Reform launched the European Alliance for CSR as an umbrella network to bring together key CSR constituents to discuss advancements (Moon, 2004).

Since the turn of the millennium, the spread of CSR across Europe was fostered by the Lisbon European Council and the European Commission promoting transparency and convergence of CSR across Europe (Steurer, 2010). The transition of the Commission in 2004, however, halted the pro-active EU CSR policy and re-emphasized business self-regulation on social responsibility (Steurer, 2010). At the EU local level, Western European countries' CSR efforts thus remain national approaches rather than systematically planned and enforced EU matters.

The Nordic region features partnership models in Sweden comprising several national ministries to advocate for human rights, decent labor conditions, environmental protection and anti-corruption in corporate endeavors. Denmark and the Netherlands have established national CSR Centers that coordinate social responsibility activities by promoting dialogues and information exchange in partnerships.

Access to CSR information is ensured by national disclosure and transparency laws. For example, the 2001 French "New Economic Regulations" policy and similar laws in Denmark, the Netherlands, Sweden and Spain require corporations offering publicly traded shares to include information on social and environmental performance in annual reports (Holgaard & Jørgensen, 2005; Steurer, 2010). However, the accuracy of the information provided remains unchecked. In sync, positive examples of CSR disclosure are more often awarded than negative examples are blacklisted (Steurer, 2010). Certified labels (e.g., Blue Angel and EU Eco-label) are a pivotal instrument to foster corporate transparency as for combining access to information with economic incentives for corporations (Steurer, 2010).

Within Eastern Europe, CSR is growing and has foremost been implemented by expanding international corporations. For Eastern European transforming economies, CSR grants foreign investment perspectives, international partnerships and corruption prevention. Eastern European governments regulate CSR policies, endorse privately led social initiatives and monitor fairly regulated corporate compliance. Awareness for CSR and transparency is fostered by awards and information campaigns (Steurer, 2010). Challenges in Eastern Europe comprise information deficiencies and misperceptions – for example, a survey of 475 Bulgarian, Croatian and Romanian corporate managers revealed that CSR is understood as a means to solely abide by governmental control and CSR is still undermined by corruption (World Development Report, 2005).

In the USA, the Quakers addressed social responsibility and value-based corporate conduct since the seventeenth century. Already Tocqueville (1835/1959) described corporate social conduct. In the 1950s, the Supreme Court removed legal restrictions that limited corporate social involvements and legislators intentionally incentivized policy gaps to be filled by non-governmental social service provision (Carroll, 1999; Moon, 2005; Steurer, 2010). In the 1960s, stakeholder activism increased US corporations to exhibit social responsibility, which led to the widespread establishment of corporate in-house foundations and charity programs. Academics paid attention to CSR when the United Student Against Sweatshops (USAS) movement demanded manufactured goods to publicly disclose the names and addresses of production sites (Roddick, 2001). Within the USA, CSR is more popular in Democratic than Republican-led states, which is explained by CSR compliance in order to please pro-social-stakeholders and conservative US administrators ignoring CSR (Aaronson, 2002; Liston-Heyes & Ceton, 2007 in Steurer, 2010; Mathis, 2008).

Since the breakdown of communism, predominately Anglo-American management models have been adopted throughout the world (Hennigfeld et al., 2006). Under the guidance of international organizations – such as the United Nations (UN), World Bank, IMF and the World Trade Organization (WTO) – democratic, open market society values exported corporate social standards on an international basis (Chua, 2003; Friedman, 2002). Featured by the largest and most powerful nation state economy for centuries, today the USA has established itself as an innovative forerunner in CSR management practices as a means of global governance. Concurrently a trend toward financial social responsibility featuring socially attentive securities has emerged.

The US legal framework is based on the Anglo-Saxon Common Law that emphasizes shareholder demands. The Canadian Common Law legislature requires corporate executives to act in the corporate interest with respect for shareholders (Reinhardt et al., 2008). The Australian Corporate Law holds CEOs to make decisions in the best interest of the corporation, yet a statutory business judgment rule grants considerable discretion to serve the greater good (Corfield, 1998). As a European Common Law country, the UK's legislation permits corporate managers to engage in philanthropy as long as acting in the interest of shareholders (Lynch-Fannon, 2007).

North American regulatory frameworks are significant for a tradition of low governmental oversight and social welfare. In combination with hosting the most powerful corporate sector that accounts for a relatively large percentage of the nation's economic productivity, North American corporations feature sophisticated CSR conduct (Palazzo, 2002; Smith, 2003). In North America, CSR is much more a discretionary issue with the government mainly offering incentives through negative tax exemptions. As for a tradition of participation and self-help, in North America, high levels of civic participation have led to CSR being directly enacted by mostly voluntary corporate policies which are openly promoted as CSR. The respective explicit CSR features self-interest driven corporate strategies to address societal deficiencies. As for low levels of oversight and unstandardized quality control, corporations have flexibility in fulfilling self-imposed social responsibilities.

In the developing world, CSR conduct is still bound by emerging, weak or absent legal frameworks, unenforceable legislations, democracy infringements and corruption. Governance gaps and CSR failures are likely to occur in overseas subsidiaries of multi-national corporations that feature a lack of compliance with local laws and regulatory as well as oversight challenges (Reinhardt et al., 2008).

While CSR emerged out of neo-liberal concepts that facilitate the downscaling of governmental regulations, in recent years, CSR has matured from a philanthropic idea to a more comprehensive concept of a pro-active strategic management move that engages in global governance around the world (Steurer, 2010). As of today, CSR initiatives around the globe already tackle a wide range of global problems out of reach for single nation states. With more and more transnational corporate conduct and an ongoing rise of international joint ventures and strategic alliances, this trend is believed to continue.

Overall, CSR remains a politically dependent concept that varies from culture and time (Steurer, 2010). As for the future, the optimum balance of social responsibility provision in between the public and private sectors given respective national and international frameworks is yet to be determined. While liberalization trends have led to a rising importance of corporate social contributions, governmental bail-outs and recapitalizations of the corporate sector in the wake of the 2008 financial crisis have re-established governmental control over corporate social conduct. Already building up in the previous decade, rising awareness of climate change heightened sustainability concerns in corporate conduct. During the COVID-19 pandemic, health and well-being became subject to corporate scrutiny and part of corporate governance as never before in the history of industrialization and globalization (Gelter & Puaschunder, 2021). Sustainability and being productive in harmony with the ecological limits have become vital parts of corporate decision making and economic growth. Corporate leadership has become interested and engaged in traditional global governance goals.

2.3.3. Global Governance

Global governance advances societies by enhancing social responsibility in market systems and improving governmental efficiency. CSR becomes a feature of global governance when corporations provide social welfare, but also when CSR serves a multi-stakeholder conflict resolution means in PPPs. Governments foster corporate social service provision as this flexible, soft-law approach benefits from comparatively low resistance. Under the lead of international organizations, the contributions of CSR to global governance have foremost been institutionalized by the United Nations Global Compact (UNGC).

The UNGC sets basic and transparent principles for the engagement of the private sector in global governance. In a multi-stakeholder approach, the UNGC distinguishes CSR principles of action for the corporate world. In the interaction between the UN and the private sector, the UNGC initiatives help in moving toward a universal consensus on the minimum standards of corporate social conduct in the areas of labor standards, human rights, poverty reduction, health and workplace safety, education and community engagement. The participation of corporations in the UNGC is foremost ensured through PPPs. Multi-stakeholder partnerships target at leveraging the quality of corporate commitment to UN principles.

Derived from governmental public management, global governance strengthens international societal progress by enhancing social responsibility in market systems, improving governmental efficiency and complementing governmental social service endeavors.

CSR contributes to global governance in social service provision and as a multi-stakeholder conflict resolution means in (PPP) solutions. PPPs incorporate social responsibility into the business agenda and combine public and private forces in providing social services as an innovative and flexible global governance form. Partnering endeavors build on different constituents' interest in pursuing shared social objectives by mutual resource exchange (Steurer, 2010). PPPs feature voluntary information sharing and regulatory flexibility, which are key for solving transnational social constraints. Rising economic and institutional cross-linking lets PPPs appear as a viable means of flexible social service provision.

Throughout recent decades, corporate executives increasingly paid attention to tackle international problems out of reach for national entities. Various political and societal trends have increased corporate contributions to global governance.

The decline of nation state social service provision in the wake of the reinventing government idea gave market actors a greater role in establishing social welfare services. Innovative public management concepts – such as outsourcing, networked governance and multi-stakeholder partnerships – have leveraged social responsibility into corporate obligations and let CSR become part of corporate conduct.

As corporations gained ground in global governance, nowadays corporate and governments attribute social responsibility in PPPs. CSR has become an essential component of international social service provision and leveraged international corporations into global governance entities. Global governance provided by CSR opened a new frame of reference on which to evaluate corporate impacts on society. Corporate goal setting became an opportunity to address societal concerns and promote CSR to quasi-democratic constituents.

In response to the CSR trend, governments have become interested in flexible corporate social service provision as these voluntary business efforts redistribute corporate resources to public causes. From the governmental perspective, CSR complements hard regulations with a visionary soft-law approach benefitting from comparatively low resistance (Moon, 2007 in Steurer, 2010). For the public sector, PPPs offer flexible and efficient social responsibility provision. PPPs address governance gaps and foster international development. Governments therefore assist and stimulate corporations to raise the voluntary social performance beyond minimum legal requirements (Liston-Heyes & Ceton, 2007 in Steurer, 2010). Governmental CSR initiatives form a cross-sectoral policy field that is based on voluntariness and collaboration of public and private sector entities.

The novelty of PPPs brings along an absence of standardized legislative or regulatory frameworks that guide disparate entities administering global governance. Multi-stakeholder constituents feature conflicts of interest hindering agreements on policy ratifications and implementations. Expertise imbalances can counterweight effective dialogues and multi-stakeholder solution finding (Ruggie, 2008). As a remedy, CSR serves for multi-stakeholder management and conflict resolution between multiple PPP constituents that contribute to global governance.

Under the guidance of international organizations, CSR in PPPs fosters the harmonization of cooperative regulatory reforms and trust between multiple stakeholders (Ruckelshaus, 1996). Since the 1950s, PPPs have been institutionalized under the guidance of international organizations. International organizations bring together multiple constituents in addressing global governance. In a multi-stakeholder approach, public–private multi-stakeholder partnerships create flexible networks for addressing social deficiencies and providing social welfare. Bringing together national representatives to constitute international agreements, international organizations promote the standardization of social and environmental policies. International organizations foster transnational consortia advocating for global social policies and provide a framework for implementation strategies to nation states with respect for national interests and corporate endeavors. International organizations guide the harmonization of national endeavors and contribute to global governance by PPP on-ground capacity-building and technical assistance.

Seeking institutionalized solutions, the UN provides legislative or regulatory frameworks to govern the activities of multiple public and private representatives in addressing global governance. Foremost, the UNGC guides CSR in enhancing PPPs and multi-stakeholder global governance. As an example of a global governance PPP, the UN fosters PPP in the implementation of the SDGs.

2.3.4. Public Private Partnerships

Globalization bringing along societal problems out of reach of nation state control has leveraged the demand for global governance. An emerging global governance trend features PPP social service provision. Under the guidance of international organizations, PPPs connect the corporate world with governments on societal concerns. Global governance PPPs reduce social deficiencies and foster international development. As flexible governance structures, PPPs ingrain multi-stakeholder expertise and resources in public management. For corporations, innovative PPPs grant first-mover advantages and public relations management. With continuing globalization and worldwide corporate expansions, international organizations are believed to increasingly attribute PPPs as a means for enhancing societal prosperity. Challenges of PPPs are the establishment and maintenance costs as well as the novelty and complexity of multi-stakeholder approaches.

Globalization has leveraged the demand for global governance. As of today, international deficiencies out of reach for nation states have risen due to industrialization, global trade, international corporate expansions, environmental challenges and economic frictions of interconnected financial markets (Mathiason, 2007). An emerging trend in global governance provision features the combination of public and private sector forces in PPPs. With the rise of international problems and global crises beyond the scope of nation states, PPPs have developed into innovative and flexible means to tackle societal deficiencies, avert global crises and foster societal welfare (Hart, 1995).

For global governance, the combination of public and private sector forces in PPPs builds political, economic and judicial infrastructures in addressing societal challenges. PPPs bring together the leaders of business and government for mutual knowledge exchange and expertise enhancement on social welfare provision and crises prevention. In multi-stakeholder approaches, governmental agencies and business practitioners attribute social responsibility to the greater goal of improving societal progress. Innovative hybrid partnership models feature expanded partnering with trade unions, academia, financial institutions, philanthropists and the civil society.

The establishment of Bretton Woods Institutions such as the UN, the World Bank, the IMF, but also the WTO has increased the administration of global governance by PPPs (Mathiason, 2007). International organizations promote PPPs as for supporting international development throughout the world. International organizations provide a combination of regulatory frameworks, technical assistance, training, mentoring and evaluation of contributions to partnerships.

With continuing globalization and worldwide corporate expansions of corporations, international organizations are believed to increasingly foster PPPs for development (Beck, 1998; Levitt, 1983; Livesey, 2002; Scholte, 2000).

In connecting the forces of business, society and government, PPP creates multiple values for society. In the public sector, PPP improves public management by knowledge transfer. As multi-stakeholder attempts, partnerships offer flexible access to key resources and strengthen public institutions in their regional, national and international management and public administration endeavors.

In the corporate world, PPPs imbue social responsibility into the corporate agenda and align CSR with corporate goals (Bekefi, 2006). PPPs build a stable business climate by bringing together various constituents to reflect upon the corporate role in society. Partnerships with governments, donors, NGOs and community organizations strengthen multi-stakeholder relations (Nelson, 2004). In the integration of overseas markets, partnerships broaden corporate value chains and corporate distribution networks. PPPs build relations with public sector entities and engage corporate officials in public policy dialogues.

As for the early attention to future regulations and adoption of innovative corporate practices, PPPs grant first-mover advantages to corporations (Prahalad & Hammond, 2003).

For society, PPPs solve long-term societal problems out of reach for national entities. Partnerships build flexible framework conditions for good governance and responsible corporate conduct around the world. In the developing world, PPPs spread the benefits of open market societies and drive economic growth with respect for posterity. As for long-term business opportunities, corporate partners make sustainable development contributions to communities such as basic infrastructure and access to social welfare (Bekefi, 2006; Kanter, 2003). Innovative PPPs expand economic opportunities to un(der)served segments and provide financial services in an economically viable manner (e.g., Grameen banking).

Downsides of PPPs are transaction costs of the establishment and maintenance of partnership relations. Multiple stakeholders administering global governance can imply conflicting interests. In the international arena, intercultural differences, expertise imbalances and differing access to resources can counterweight an effective dialogue of multiple stakeholders (Ruggie, 2008). The relative novelty of multi-stakeholder global governance provision brings along an absence of legislative frameworks for administering partnerships and no regulation on standardized PPP conduct. As a remedy, CSR serves as an innovative PPP management approach. As a multi-stakeholder participation framework, CSR brings together diverse constituents in their attempts to address global governance. As a co-regulatory arrangement, CSR guides corporations and governments in their pro-social endeavors (Moon, 2002). As a management practice, CSR reduces the complexity imposed onto various PPP constituents and alleviates conflicts between multiple PPPs contributing to global governance. By providing tools, standards and means for corporate social conduct, CSR – as a multi-stakeholder management means – harmoniously coordinates the multiple partners' views on social service provision (Ruckelshaus, 1996).

2.3.5. CSR as a Multi-stakeholder Management Means

CSR comprises economic, organizational and public constituents, who demand corporate value creation with respect for social and environmental responsibility. As a corporate means to account for a variety of constituents, total responsibility management (TRM) addresses multiple stakeholder concerns. As a feature of TRM, CSR allows managing various stakeholders' demands for the greater goal of according multiple constituents' viewpoints and reducing conflicts.

Originally the word "company" derives from the Latin 'cum panis' – meaning to break bread together – which attributes the role corporations play in society (Werther & Chandler, 2006). In recent decades, corporate endeavors have leveraged from a primary shareholder-value focus to a broader variety of stakeholders. Corporations engage in mutually beneficial ways with society and touch on multiple actors. As "any group or individual who can affect, or are affected by, the achievement of the organization's objectives," corporate stakeholders comprise economic (e.g., shareholders, customers, creditors, suppliers and competitors), organizational (e.g., CEOs, managers, executives and employees) and public stakeholders (e.g., representatives of international organizations, governments, trade unions, NGOs and non-profits) (Freeman, 1984, p. 46).

The recent trend toward PPPs has widened the spectrum of corporate constituents. Tackling social, economic and societal deficiencies in multi-stakeholder approaches, PPPs comprise various constituents and engage corporate entities with multiple stakeholders. Multi-stakeholder partnerships are complex combinations of diverse actors that may hold differing interests, goals and perspectives as well as represent counterweighing power regimes.

Primary stakeholders – such as CEOs, managers, employees – are prone to focus on profit maximization and enhance competitive advantages and corporate growth. Corporate owners demand return on investments by efficient and profitable corporate conduct in line with legislative and regulatory obligations. Employees are interested in remuneration and care for safety, health standards and human rights. Suppliers attribute fair trade and continued business relations.

Secondary stakeholders are institutional representatives that shape corporate conduct and set best practice standards. Governmental agencies emphasize anti-corruption and compliance with legal and regulatory boundaries. NGOs and activists advocate for corporate social performance in triple-bottom-line reporting. Related communities want corporate conduct to be in line with societal norms and environmental protection. Customers demand products and services in sync with their preferences and values.

In general, multi-stakeholderism raises the likelihood of goal ambiguity and dissenting views on goal achievement strategies. Multiple stakeholders may feature power differences – for example, international organizations have a different standing than NGOs within the international arena. Varying cultural contexts imply differing social, political, historical and economic circumstances impacting PPPs that accentuate conflicting interests and communication barriers between constituents (Meyer & Höllerer, 2005; Van Maanen & Laurent, 1993; Whitley, 1997). Countries, in which governments traditionally have assigned corporations to take over a significant amount of social responsibility by mandatory regulations, feature a relative low attention to CSR, which draws attention from decreasing partnership challenges.

To balance the needs and interests of multiple constituents of PPPs, corporations feature total responsibility management (TRM) (Waddock & Graves, 1997). TRM stakeholder approaches address a wide range of constituents. TRM multi-stakeholder analyses depict partner contributions and differing standpoints on multiple goal settings to overcome principal–agent predicaments (Freeman, 1984). In this feature, TRM implicitly protects corporate stakeholders from contributing to negative externalities of corporate conduct.

As a feature of TRM, CSR brings together various constituents on social responsibility matters. Enhancing the relationship between corporations and stakeholders, CSR aligns corporate activities with constituents' demands. In harmoniously according multiple stakeholders, CSR serves as an implicit stakeholder management and conflict prevention means (Risse-Kappen, 1995). In addition, CSR signals interest in stakeholder demands and corporate engagement in public matters. CSR pays attention to the needs and wants of multiple constituents with the greater goal of increasing the social value of corporations and lowering the downsides of corporate conduct within society.

As for the novelty of TRM, there is no standardized framework of the best practice to implement CSR, which impacts the effectiveness of PPPs. The most sophisticated institutional attempt to standardize disparate CSR endeavors is provided by the UNGC.

2.3.6. The UNGC

Global governance provision evolved under the guidance of international organizations. The UN brings together corporate actors with governmental entities and civil society in multi-stakeholder partnerships for addressing international challenges. The UNGC advocates for considering UN principles in corporate conduct with respect for human rights, labor standards, environmental sustainability and anti-corruption. The UNGC thereby serves as a framework for CSR and PPP administered global governance provision.

Globalization, the rise of international corporations and global governance trends connected the corporate sector with society. In recent decades, corporations have steadily become key actors in the provision of global governance administered through CSR and PPPs. Institutionalized CSR was first promoted by the International Chamber of Commerce and advanced in the OECD Guidelines for Multinational Enterprises as well as the ILO's Tripartite Declaration of the Multinational Enterprises and Social Policy. The UN Declaration of Rights addressed corporate social and environmental responsibility for the achievement of the UNMDs and the subsequent SDGs (Kettl, 2006).

The UNMDGs focused on (1) eradication of extreme poverty and hunger, (2) achievement of universal primary education, (3) promotion of gender equality and empowerment of women, (4) reduction of child mortality, (5) improvement of maternal health, (6) combating HIV/AIDS, malaria and other diseases, (7) ensuring environmental sustainability and the (8) developing global partnership for universal development.

In 1999, UN Secretary General Kofi Annan presented the UNGC to define the relationship between the UN and the corporate world, regulate CSR endeavors and strengthen partnerships for the achievement of UN goals. The UNGC advocates for corporate contributions to global governance and provides a framework for voluntary social engagement.

The UNGC has become the world's largest and most renowned PPP global governance initiative by featuring thousands of corporations and civil society partners.[1] In a multi-stakeholder approach, the UNGC embraces a growing network of corporations and international stakeholders with the binding goal of fostering a more sustainable and inclusive world economy. The UNGC comprises representatives of the UN, governments, corporations, labor unions, civil society and academia.

The UN is the main UNGC umbrella organization that supports the UNGC being represented by a GC Leader Summit, Board, Office and Local Networks and Inter-Agency Teams working closely with governments and corporations. Corporations contribute to PPPs that foster the UN vision of a more sustainable and inclusive marketplace. Corporations are expected to align their operations, work practices and codes of conduct with the UNGC principles. Corporations should operate in sync with UNGC principles that are ingrained in the corporate strategy, culture and day-by-day operations. Corporate executives are invited and trained to consider environmental, social and governance (ESG) goals in corporate decision making. CSR best practice transfer in networking, dialogue, learning and partnering mainstreams CSR to replicate the UNGC principles within the corporate world. PPPs engage corporate stakeholders to accomplish the SDGs.

Corporate executives are advised to publicly advocate for the UNGC in press releases, speeches and annual reports. For corporations, the UNGC is an entry point to the UN agenda, a means to benefit from public sector outlooks and innovative stakeholder management tool. Corporations that engage in the UNGC experience social and environmental governance as long-term strategies.[2] Paying attention to the UNGC and demonstrating active participation in societal issues provide the best practice leadership advantages. Corporate conduct in line with the UN principle attracts a loyal workforce and enhances consumer identification. Embracing the UNGC improves the corporate reputation and lowers stakeholder pressure.

---

[1]The United Nations Global Compact Office. (2007, June). Enhancing partnership value: A tool for assessing sustainability and impact. Retrieved from http://www.unglobalcompact.org/docs/news_events/8.1/Partnership_value.pdf

[2]The United Nations Global Compact Office. (2007, July). The Global Compact. Annual review. Leaders Summit. Retrieved from http://www.unglobalcompact.org/docs/news_events/8.1/GCAnnualReview2007.pdf

Civil society and labor organizations represent stakeholder communities. The civil society implicitly sets the social standards for corporate social conduct. Labor organizations are driving forces in the implementation of the UNGC and provide accountability control.

Academia strengthens the theoretical advancement of business ethics and disseminates information about the UNGC. Academics influence corporate leaders through research, business education, management development, trainings and advocacy. Academics independently monitor the effectiveness of UNGC partnerships, measure their impact and provide accountability control. Academic teaching educates in business ethics.

The UNGC raises awareness for the corporate role in global governance. As a platform for exchange, the UNGC motivates corporations to connect with society. The UNGC Learning Forum offers a network of experts and practitioners to exchange knowledge on CSR best practices. In disseminating CSR case studies, the UNGC fosters interdisciplinary learning on business ethics. In regular conferences and summits, leaders from the business and governmental world are brought together to align in the alleviation of global governance problems.

In an attempt to regulate CSR, the UNGC sets specific rules, norms and conventions to be implemented by the corporate sector with respect for legal foundations, ethics standards and moral values. As a frame of reference, the UNGC provides universal corporate principles with respect for human rights, labor standards, environmental protection and anti-corruption to create sustainable benefits for corporations and society.

The UNGC Principles comprise attention to human rights, labor standards, environment and anti-corruption. The UNGC principles provide a leadership model of CSR corporate conduct. The UNGC participating parties are meant to align their policies and work practices according to the Ten Principles. The UN endeavors should be attributed in corporate policies, stakeholder dialogues, corporate learning and networking partnership projects.

To ensure quality control, the UNGC features systematic impact assessments and evaluations of corporate performance. Quality control is made transparent by UNGC statements of continued support, in Communication on Progress in the achievement of the UNGC principles as well as public commitment statements.[3] Corporate CSR and partnership commitments are also monitored in periodic letters of support. In addition, an UN ombudsperson and contact points for complaints on social and environmental violations are in place. The UNGC output indication metrics serve as leadership best practice models and public accountability control for pro-social engagement of the corporate sector. The UNGC paves the way for CSR as a successful contribution to PPPs in the accomplishment of the SDGs.

---

[3]The United Nations Global Compact Office. (2007, July). The UN Global Compact operational guide for medium-scale enterprises. Retrieved from http://www.unglobalcompact.org/docs/news_events/8.1/Operational_guide_ME.pdf

The SDGs were incepted in 2015 by the UN with the intention to achieve substantial progress by 2030 on poverty, hunger, health and well-being, education, gender equality, clean water and sanitation, affordable and clean energy, decent work and economic growth, industry, innovation and infrastructure, reduced inequality, sustainable cities and communities, responsible consumption and production, climate action, life below water, life on land, peace, justice and strong institutions as well as partnerships for the goals. The UN facilitates monitoring and public visualization of progress toward the goals, for instance, in the SDG Tracker, an online tool to make data on SDG accomplishments accessible to the wider public. The COVID-19 pandemic had a major influence on all SDGs.

2.3.7. COVID-19 Pandemic External Shock

The new Coronavirus crisis (COVID-19) is an infectious disease that was first diagnosed in Wuhan, China, in December 2019. The majority of those infected with COVID-19 only develop mild symptoms such as fever, cough, difficulty breathing and tiredness as well as loss of smell and taste, but also rashes and other diffuse symptoms. Depending on age and pre-existing conditions, COVID-19 can also lead to acute complications such as organ failure, cytokine loads, blood clots and septic shock. Prevalences, such as obesity and diabetes, but also the general status of the immune system, are crucial determinants of whether COVID-19 is of danger to the individual. Prevention and holistic medicine play an important role in whether the disease turns out to follow a trajectory of severe or only mild symptoms.

The novel Coronavirus SARS-CoV-2 that first emerged in 2019 accounts for the most unexpected globally widespread external shock to modern humankind. In January 2020, the World Health Organization declared a state of emergency with international relevance over COVID-19, and in March 2020 a global pandemic. COVID-19 changed behavioral patterns around the world dramatically and will have a lasting impact on society (Baldwin & Weder di Mauro, 2020).

As of the fall of 2022, over 600 million recorded infections have caused over 6 million documented deaths in almost all countries and territories around the globe (Worldometer Coronavirus Cases, 2021). Coronavirus cases count includes multiple infection counts but excludes undercounts. According to estimates, the actual number of infections is a multiple of around 4 up to 13 of the reported and recorded case numbers (Aizenman, Carlsen, & Talbot, 2021; Mandavilli, 2021; McPhillips, 2021).

Early scientific estimates predicted that about 80% of the world population would get infected with the virus in densely populated areas in one form or another at a point in their life without considering the multiple variants that emerged subsequently (BBC News Scotland, 2020; Noh & Danuser, 2021). With the initial virus being replaced by different variants, epidemiologists increasingly believe that all human beings will have some touchpoints with COVID-19 at a certain point in their lives (Zhang, 2021).

Over the course of the spread of the novel Coronavirus, people around the world have become aware that taking preventive measures can limit the spread of the deadly and debilitating virus – including social distancing and social contact tracking, collective and individual hygiene, preventive healthcare and foresighted nutrition as well as vaccination and medication (Britt, 2020; Harrison, 2021; Puaschunder, 2021a; Rubin, 2020; Sachs et al., 2020; WebMD, 2020).

The further the COVID-19 healthcare crisis deepened, the more it became apparent that in some previously infected individuals the virus lingers to the point of debilitation and often changes health conditions long term. From 10% upwards to more than 50% of those previously infected people with COVID-19 develop long-term symptoms of the disease, which are often diffuse, come in waves and – to this day – are not well understood (Hart, 2021; Searing, 2021). Some of these ongoing long-haul patients seem to recover completely, but simply take more time to do so than the average estimated 14-day recovery period. While other patients still struggle a long time after their initial infection – potentially due to pockets of remaining viral loads, an immune system reaction and an overactivation of the body's unspecific immune system and/or an awakening of an auto-immune disease or other previous infections causing complications to recover (Drbeen Medical Lectures, 2021; Fernandes Maia et al., 2021). With this broad-based and long-term impact on the status of health of society in mind as a driver of societal well-being and productivity, and with no direct cure against the long-term implications of COVID-19 at hand yet, we can say that COVID-19 will be the most impactful external shock triggering lasting change in our lifetimes (Coleman, 2021; *The Economist*, 2021b).

The large-scale dimension of COVID-19 infections around the world is underscored by an estimated 10–50% of those previously infected with COVID-19 facing some kind of longer-term or long-term health impact and/or chronic debilitation that is currently not well understood by the medical profession (Hart, 2021; Searing, 2021). Given the worldwide spread of the virus and that the demographic likelihood to become a COVID-19 Long Hauler peaks in the 30-50 years of age bracket, we can predict a large-scale, long-term and global impetus of COVID-19 long-haul induced change.

From the history of humankind and the knowledge about previous diseases, we can draw the inference that crises have very often been turning points and the ultimate spring feathers of lasting societal development (Ecowellness Group, 2020; Schmelzing, 2020).

With reference to historical precedents of the past, generation COVID-19 long haul partially being recognized as a disability may result in increased pressures to reform social, healthcare and retirement systems on a large scale. Especially when considering the relatively young age of COVID-19 long-hauling onsets, which is currently estimated to peak around the ages of 30–50, the long-term impetus of this usually highly productive part of society being slowed and/or weakened will be substantial when considering the expected decline in tax revenue from this age group's working income.

In its entirety, COVID-19 has the potential to dominate future individual, political and corporate decisions directly or indirectly, but certainly profoundly. The widespread and long-term impacts of COVID-19 will likely transform the law, economics and governance of our world and modern society lastingly.

Corporate conduct has never been as focused on collective health and well-being before, while financial social responsibility addresses widening inequality gaps.

2.3.8. COVID-19 Induced Inequality

The COVID-19 external shock created economic disparity between nations, industries and societal groups. Rising inequality trends in healthcare, economics and finance, education, digitalization and environmental conditions exacerbated during the global COVID-19 pandemic. Cutting-edge innovations of our lifetime target at bringing affordable quality healthcare to all, bridging the finance world and real economy inequality gap, fostering global access to quality education in harnessing digitalization advancements and but also equality in connectivity and tech-skills development and a favorable environment to overcome unforeseen inequality in the shadow of COVID-19.

On an interconnected globe with a highly mobile twenty-first century population and a most contagious virus, common health and well-being are as internationally interdependent as never before in the history of modern humankind. The endeavor of a commonly healthy world with attention for precaution against pandemics is challenged by nowadays unprecedentedly blatant healthcare inequality around the world. Access to affordable quality medicine and precautionary prevention of widespread diseases depend on economic prosperity and freedom from corruption. Modern healthcare being technologically advanced also requires digitalization and innovation market financialization for modern preventive and precautionary medical care.

The COVID-19 external shock created economic disparity between nations, industries and societal groups. The Union Bank of Switzerland (UBS) described the lagest economic gap between world economies for at least 40 years during the onset of the pandemic (*The Economist*, 2020a, 2020b, 2021a). In contrast to earlier economic turmoil stemming from system-inherent crises creating liquidity constraints, the external COVID-19 shock caused "social volatility" – a collectively depressed mood that largely dampened consumption. The difference to previous systemic recessions becomes apparent in the rapid recovery of well-managed financial funds – for example, the S&P 500 recovered 50% of its pre-COVID-19 value within the first three months after the crisis and reached an all-time highs-trend from August 2020. Deutsche Bank recorded rising earnings after the onset of Coronavirus crisis in Europe, especially the investment bank branch of 43% or €2.4 billion (Smith, 2020). The clear distinction between COVID-19 profit and loss industries made it possible for today's highly flexible financial world to quickly exchange weakened market segments – such as oil, public transport and aviation, face-to-face service sectors such as international hospitality and gastronomy – with above-average market options – such as pharmaceutical companies and emergency medical devices for healthcare, digital technologies, fintech, artificial intelligence (AI) and big data analytics industries, online retail, automotive and interior design industries.

Inequality has increased in society since the 1990s as a result of the wave of US financial market deregulation (Piketty, 2016). The financial world performance began to diverge massively from the real economy in 2008–2009 and experienced the greatest divergence so far with the Coronavirus crisis that widened the gap between top performance of financial markets and negative fallout in the real economy (*The Economist*, 2020a, 2020b). The strong contrasts between COVID-19 winners and losers as well as the deep gap between strongly positive financial market developments and the negative performance of the real economy induced by lockdowns, which is currently exposing the real economy to a wave of private bankruptcies and liquidity bottlenecks, therefore call on governments around the world to reboot financial markets to return to be a service industry – to serve the real economy.

In the overall economy, the COVID-19 crisis with lockdowns and urgent healthcare needs has produced a major consumption shift that led to winning and losing industries. The finance world has largely been able to avoid harm by diversifying and flexibly replacing winning for losing industries in well-managed portfolios, as well as by shorting and hedging of industries with a prospective loss during the crisis. At the same time, the real economy has often been hit by bankruptcy and liquidity constraints that played out in harmful choices and negative socio-psychological fallouts. All of this has widened an exacerbating finance performance versus real economy gap.

In the post-COVID-19 era, corporate and political power dynamics may shift in light of long haulers' relation to work and their appreciation of a healthy environment to be productive. Employers will likely face pressure to create a safe and secure working environment. Employers may also have rising tort liability risks that may be mitigated by hiring health consultants. Pro-active care for maintaining a healthy workforce and the overall long-term well-being of employees, including preventive care in teams, will become an essential corporate feature to attract qualified labor, whose bargaining power increases in the eye of labor shortages in human-facing industries and positions (Whelan, 2021).

Government bailout packages are likely to be financed over the long term by the historically lowest, never-so-long-low key interest rates. Low key interest rates will continue to allow the capital market to flourish. But this is based on the cost of a weakening of the potential of the interest rate as a monetary policy tool, which John Maynard Keynes (1936/2003) already described as a "liquidity trap." The low interest rate policy brings along long-term external financing of past ideas, which impairs the flexibility of investors to finance future-oriented innovations and may hold back societal progress. Low interest rates on savings accounts in the real economy keep people trapped in the debt financing of past dreams (Arora, 2020). Household debt traps are causing massive psychosocial burdens, a so-called "deaths of despair" trend is already noticed in the USA for mid-career death spikes induced by alcoholism, drug use and suicide (Case & Deaton, 2020).

One clear winner industry of the pandemic is the current market transitioning to digitalized economies. Already before the outbreak of the pandemic, AI, algorithms, robotics and big data entered healthcare with booming health self-tracking devices and preventive medical care enhanced by big data insights. Today's cosmopolitan luxury shifted into virtual online spaces as COVID-19 has also perpetuated the online tech world. Physically distant, we came closer digitally than ever before. Worldwide data traffic exploded on a flat digital globe. An online multi-tasking workforce gained global reach, while technology reduced bureaucracy. Digitalization kicked in all industries.

Other industries booming in the wake of the COVID-19 pandemic are healthcare precaution. Concrete wellness and healthcare trends were proliferating in the wake of the pandemic. COVID-19 peaked attention for hygiene, pharmaceuticals and emergency medicine. COVID-19 healthcare apps now estimate individual contagion risks and derive large-scale health trends from big data. Digitalized healthcare heightens the demand for privacy protection of vulnerable patients and anti-discrimination based on health status. Bluetooth-cartography of medical devices helps overcome bottlenecks and prevents fraud while protecting privacy. Telemedicine cures remotely all over the world. With pre-existing prevalence, such as obesity and diabetes, but also the immune system influencing the COVID-19 disease trajectory, preventive care and whole-rounded lifestyles gained unprecedented attention.

COVID-19 triggered a de-urbanization in the USA – a trend to move to environmentally pleasant surroundings. Given the contagion risk in crowded metropolitan areas and air purification being challenged in city skyscrapers with closed ventilation and elevators, corporate headquarters moved to remote work or suburbs. Retail shifted online to lower fixed cost of real estate and health risks. Hygiene and health leveraged into core business of contemporary city scaping – as visible in the New York public transport cleanup and consumer trends to own personal cars or bikes. Art and culture events scaled down to more rural communities or were re-curated for social distanced performances or even were staged in virtual luxury worlds. Gastronomy orderings and shared virtual eating experiences are socially distanced service sector innovations. The sharing economy started offering workspace closer to nature. Moving to cheaper suburbs now allows a remote workforce to build wellness cocoons with attention to healthy living embedded in nature. The environment is also represented in biophilic architecture trends that resembles nature. One of the innovations for broad-scale environmental change was addressed during the Conference of the Parties COP 26 in sustainable clothing lines made out of natural material. For instance, fungus clothing offers a carbon-negative organic alternative to fast fashion. Hygienic antibacterial surfaces for cleanability and technologically enhanced kitchens are booming. With precise online retailing and people spending more time at home, minimalism is trending as people are getting rid of unnecessary items at home. The de-urbanization is yet not a ruralization, as people are not giving up the luxuries of metropolitan areas, such as exchange of goods, services and ideas in highly specialized markets with diverse market actors.

As North American universities faced high revenue losses from international students staying away and closed campus housing, universities were exploring hybrid education in larger international network consortia. Students from all over the world could thereby flexibly take courses in large international education hubs with participating institutions being far spread out over the world. Without relocation costs and visa requirements, students will also be free to study longer.

Education of the future could thus become truly global, individually specialized and life-long. Global access to online education could become an international development transformation game changer. Overall expected price adjustments for education in the USA may lift the education debt burden in the USA that has already curbed large-scale consumption of the generation internship since the beginning of the millennium.

With the digitalization disruption, however, come along novel inequalities. Inequality in internet connectivity, tech-skills and digitalization-affinity, leverages AI–human compatibility as competitive advantage. Digital online working conditions that make individual living conditions transparent emphasize social hierarchies in our educational and work-related interactions. On a global scale, problems arise from a dominance of digital innovations and online communication tools being centered in the USA, which imposes data deficit, revenue losses and problems to enforce the European privacy protection.

Never before in the history of humankind have environmental concerns in the wake of economic growth heralded governance predicaments as we face today. Global warming is having an extraordinary impact on the economic, social and eco-system effects of market economics. In the financing of climate change mitigation and adaptation efforts, the most recent the United Nations COP26 on climate change revealed the need for climate justice (Sachs, 2021). Climate change presents societal, international and intergenerational fairness as challenge for modern economies and contemporary democracies all over the world. The economics and politics of climate change recently gained the attention of economic gains and losses in a warming climate being distributed differently throughout the world rising inequality concerns (Puaschunder, 2020d; Sachs, 2021).

In today's climate change mitigation and adaptation efforts, high- and low-income households, developed and underdeveloped countries as well as overlapping generations are affected differently (Puaschunder, 2016b). To address the economic effects of climate change, individual decision making and discounting offer insights into environmental impacts and framework conditions. Current empirical trends and international efforts to combat climate change have also shed attention to the role of financing climate change mitigation and adaptation efforts (Sachs, 2021). Climate change induced inequalities are proposed to be alleviated with a climate taxation-bonds strategy that incentivizes market actors to transform the energy sector and mitigate as well as adapt to climate change. In the financialization of climate policies, fair climate change benefits and burden sharing within society, inbetween countries all over the world but also over generations are currently introduced in sustainable finance.

2.3.9. Corporate Social Justice in the Aftermath of the COVID-19 Pandemic

COVID-19 has shown rising inequality trends and opened eyes for previously unnoticed discrepancies within society, around the world but also over time. Social justice pledges have gained unprecedented momentum in the eye of unequal access to health, capital, education, digitalization and environmentally favorable conditions. In the shadow of inequality, ethical imperatives arise from the humane-imbued care for inclusion and access to equal opportunities. Inequalities drive the demand for creative inequality alleviation strategies that have the potential to bestow the post-COVID-19 era with the notion of a new Renaissance.

In light of the multi-faceted inequality that opens widespread qualitative and quantitative gaps, social justice has become a blatant demand. We are entering the age of corporate social justice and inclusive societies (Zheng, 2020). Ethics of inclusion as a forerunner to inclusive rights and privileges opened to everyone are natural behavioral ethical laws that could herald a post-COVID-19 novel Renaissance.

The COVID-19 crisis represents the most unforeseen external shock for modern economies. Drastic downturns for trade, human mobility and international service industries demanded unprecedented governmental intervention (Gössling, Scott, & Hall, 2020; International Monetary Fund, 2020a, 2020b; Puaschunder, Gelter, & Sharma, 2020a, 2020b; Sachs et al., 2020; United Nations, 2020; World Bank, 2020). Overall, the COVID-19 global recession is estimated to be the deepest since World War II (WWII), with the largest fraction of economies experiencing declines in per capita output since 1870 (Kose & Sugawara, 2020). The economic external shock seems to have ended globalization and international exchange if considering the World Bank expecting the sharpest decline in remittances in recent history (World Bank, 2020).

While the recession did not last as long as originally expected and reverted to growth in 2021, it is still likely to have a persistent worldwide impact when considering the substantial quantitative easing and monetary control the saving of the global world economy has taken (Congressional Research Service, 2021; National Bureau of Economic Research, 2021a, 2021b). All these measures resemble the onset of a lasting economic crisis with fundamental changes in society (International Monetary Fund, 2020a, 2020b). The unprecedented size, scope and dimensions of COVID-19 rescue and recovery plans have also sparked discourse about the potential negative consequences of inflation and urge to reflect on the disparate negative impacts on marginalized groups (Brunnermeier Academy at the Princeton Bendheim Center for Finance, 2021).

In its uprooting disruption, the crisis also holds enormous potential as governments around the globe have embarked on a course to avert the negative impetus of the COVID-19 pandemic economic shock. These measures resulted in the most concerted long-term international, governance and governmental changes funded by unprecedentedly large rescue packages and recovery aid (Cassim, Handjiski, Schubert & Zouaoui, 2020; The White House of the United States of America, 2021a, 2021b, 2021c, 2021d). The short-term impact of COVID-19 has triggered massive financial flows of economic rescue and governance recovery aid around the world already. Coupled with behavioral changes and abrupt shifts in consumption patterns in addition to governmental legal and governance regulatory innovations, one starts imagining the once-in-a-lifetime potential of COVID-19 for a lasting "reset" of the world (Monck, 2020).

In the international arena, central banks of all major world economies and the European Central bank coordinated to lower the price of US Dollar (USD) liquidity swap line arrangements in order to foster the provision of global liquidity (Alpert, 2021; European Central Bank, 2020a, 2020b, 2020c, 2020d; Federal Research of the United States of America, 2020a, 2020b). The IMF and the World Bank issued economic stimulus and relief efforts in the range of around US $260 billion with the majority of relief aid being distributed in the developing world (Alpert, 2021; International Monetary Fund 2020c; World Bank, 2020).

Throughout the evolving crisis, all major economies responded to the economic fallout of COVID-19 in financial terms. In light of the ongoing COVID-19 crisis, governments around the world have rolled out economic assistance packages or recovery releases that by mid-2020 already amount to a total of over US $10 trillion (Cassim et al., 2020; The White House of the United States of America, 2021c). Given the long-term impetus of the societal consequences of COVID-19, the economic rescue and recovery aid is of historic momentum. (Puaschunder, 2021c).

Across countries, economic stimulus responses to the COVID-19 crisis vastly outsize those to the 2008 financial crisis (Cassim et al., 2020; The White House of the United States of America, 2021c). The qualitative and quantitative stimulus, rescue and recovery aid packages have surpassed all other programs of this type in human history (Alpert, 2021). The cost of saving the global economy is estimated to have been US $834 million per hour for 18 months, including almost 4 trillion rescue funds spent by the United States Federal Reserve alone (Thomasson & Hirai, 2021).

Economic COVID-19 stimulus and relief efforts mainly comprise international fiscal and monetary stimulus and relief efforts but also direct rescue bailout packages. These are often coupled with publicly administered healthcare and labor regulation, such as *Kurzarbeit* schemes limiting the number of work hours per worker in order to keep workers employed (Congressional Research Service, 2020; Eurostat, 2020; Jones, Palumbo, & Brown, 2020; Mayhaw & Anand, 2020; Organisation for Economic Co-operation and Development (OECD), 2020; *The Economist*, 2020a, 2020b).

The size, scope and dimension of COVID-19 rescue and recovery plans account for the historically largest concerted action to avert the negative economic fallout to a worldwide external economic shock. In confronting the crisis and evaluating international and governmental rescue efforts, the size of rescue and recovery aid has gained widespread attention, foremost because of fear of inflationary pressure (Blanchard, 2021; Brunnermeier Academy at the Princeton Bendheim Center for Finance, 2020).

These unprecedentedly large amounts of governmental stimulus, economic bailout and rescue funds hold opportunities in financing a great reset (The World Economic Forum, 2021). In strategically setting economic incentives and stimulating societal advancement in the post-COVID-19 era, society is hoped to emerge stronger out of a crisis (Brunnermeier Academy at the Princeton Bendheim Center for Finance, 2020). The socio-economic trends of our currently emerging generation COVID-19 long haul have the overall impetus to enhance society's potential for building resilience vigilantly.

Acknowledging the rising inequality levels around the world, the unprecedentedly large and widespread rescue and recovery aid could be used to steer positive change in a post-COVID-19 new renaissance. How to align economic interest with justice and fairness notions is the question of our times when considering the massive challenges faced in terms of environmental challenges, healthcare demands and social justice pledges. Already now attempts exist to peg the governmental rescue and recovery aid to noble causes of inequality alleviation. For instance, the USA proposed the Green New Deal that offers a possibility to make the world and society more equitable in the domains of environmental justice, access to affordable healthcare and social justice excellence.

The Green New Deal (GND) is a governmental strategy to strengthen the US economy and foster inclusive growth. The GND is targeted at sharing economic growth benefits more equally within society. Ethical imperatives and equity mandates lead the economic rationale behind redistribution in the GND as social peace, health and favorable environmental conditions are prerequisites for productivity. The GND offers hope in making the world and society but also overlapping generations more equitable and thus to bestow peace within society, around the world and over time. In answering the question if the GND is equitable, one has to acknowledge that the GND is a fairly novel phenomenon with international variations and diverse implementation strategies.

The European pendant of the GND is the European Green Deal (EGD) and the European Sustainable Finance Taxonomy. All these programs are large-scale endeavors with a long-term impact to make the world a more inclusive place. The goal of these deals is to improve the current and future management of outputs, outcomes and impact that works toward creating a more just and inclusive society, economy and future world.

The success of these long-term large-scale endeavors will depend on future conditions. Monitoring and evaluation can currently only give a short-term assessment of the performance of projects, institutions and programs by governments, international organizations, NGOs as well as social media campaigns. In the continuous assessment of programs, more and more younger generations and the most diverse stakeholders should be included as all these projects grant insights for the controlled evolution of large-scale transformation to a more inclusive world. In the end, to the young and the diverse groups within society and around the world but also over time, the relevance, effectiveness, efficiency and impact of all these endeavors will matter lastingly if SRI is employed with a future-oriented discounting outlook.

2.4. Socially Responsible Investment

The consideration of CSR in investment decisions is the basis for SRI. SRI is an asset allocation style, in which securities are not only selected for their expected yield and volatility, but foremost for social, environmental and institutional aspects. The most common forms to align financial investments with ethical, moral and social facets are socially responsible screenings, shareholder advocacy, community investing and social venture capital funding (Chapter 2.4.1). SRI is a multi-stakeholder phenomenon that comprises economic, organizational and

societal constituents (Chapter 2.4.2). In recent decades, SRI experienced a qualitative and quantitative growth in the Western world (Chapter 2.4.3) that can be
traced back to a combination of historical incidents, legislative compulsion and
stakeholder pressure (Chapter 2.4.4). SRI is a context and culture-dependent
phenomenon (Chapter 2.4.5). The 2008 World Financial Recession drove SRI
demand (Chapter 2.4.6).

The contemporary post-COVID-19 economic fallout (Chapter 2.4.7) has
heralded a new finance order (Chapter 2.4.8). In order to alleviate inequality
in the socio-economic consequences of COVID-19 (Chapter 2.4.9), a deeper
understanding of the finance performance versus real economy constraints gap
is needed (Chapter 2.4.10). Social volatility and affective fallout propensity distribution within society (Chapter 2.4.11) should be reflected upon with special
attention to the high inflation rates (Chapter 2.4.12) and historically longest low
interest rates (Chapter 2.4.13).

Responsible finance in the post-COVID-19 era features targeted rescue and
recovery relief aid (Chapter 2.4.14) with a redistribution focus on the urban,
local, regional, national (Chapter 2.4.15), global and international levels (Chapter 2.4.16). The UN plays a pivotal role in institutionally promoting SRI in guide-
lining principles and PPP initiatives Chapter 2.4.17) providing a future outlook
in redistribution finance (Chapter 2.4.18). Political activism finds expression in
financial markets by political divestiture, which refers to the removal of stocks
from socially irresponsible markets with the greater goal of accomplishing social
and political changes (Chapter 2.4.19). Positive-screened funds are SRI ventures
of the future addressing climate stabilization financialization and climate wealth
redistribution mechanisms (Chapter 2.4.20).

Today social responsibility has emerged as an *en vogue* topic for the corporate
world and the finance sector. Contrary to classic finance theory that attributes
investments to be primarily based on expected utility and volatility, the consideration of social justice and responsibility in financial investment decisions has
gained unprecedented momentum (*The Economist*, January 17, 2008; *The Wall
Street Journal*, August 21, 2008; Zhang, 2021).

Financial social responsibility is foremost addressed in SRI, which imbues personal values and social concerns into financial investments (Schueth, 2003). SRI
thereby merges the concerns of a broad variety of stakeholders with shareholder
interests (Steurer, 2010).

SRI is an asset allocation style, by which securities are not only selected on
the basis of profit return and risk probabilities, but foremost in regard to social
and environmental contributions of the issuing entities (Beltratti, 2003; Williams,
2005). SRI assets combine social, environmental and financial aspects in investment options (Dupré et al., 2004; Harvey, 2008).

Through the last decades, financial social conscientiousness grew qualitatively
and quantitatively. As of today, SRI has been adopted by a growing proportion
of investors around the world. The incorporation of social, environmental and
global governance factors into investment options has increasingly become an
element of fiduciary duty, particularly for investors with long-term horizons that
oversee international portfolios. Most recent regulatory advancements include
the US GND and EGD as well as the Sustainable Finance Taxonomy.

Socially responsible investors allocate financial resources based on profit maximization goals as well as societal implications. Pursuing economic and social value maximization alike, socially responsible investors incorporate CSR into financial decision making (Renneboog et al., 2007; Schueth, 2003; Steurer, Margula, & Martinuzzi, 2008). Socially conscientious investors fund socially responsible corporations based on evaluations of the CSR performance as well as social and environmental risks of corporate conduct. Thereby, SRI becomes an investment philosophy that combines profit maximization with intrinsic and social components (Ahmad, 2008; Livesey, 2002; Matten & Crane, 2005; Wolff, 2002).

SRI allows the pursuit of financial goals while catalyzing positive change in the corporate and financial sectors as well as the international political arena (Mohr et al., 2001; Schueth, 2003). In the case of political divestiture, socially responsible investors use their market power to attribute global governance goals. Through foreign direct investment flows, SRI relocates capital with the greater goal of advancing international political development (Schueth, 2003; Starr, 2008).

As of today, SRI accounts for an emerging (Chapter 2.4.3) multi-stakeholder phenomenon (Chapter 2.4.2) with multi-faceted expressions (Chapter 2.4.1). SRI practices differ throughout the international arena (Chapter 2.4.5) as SRI emerged out of several historic roots (Chapter 2.4.4). The 2008 World Financial Crisis has heralded the call for responsible finance around the world (Chapter 2.4.6). The current economic fallout of the COVID-19 crisis (Chapter 2.4.7) has exacerbated socio-economic disparities and inequalities (Chapter 2.4.9).

The new finance order in the aftermath of the COVID-19 pandemic (Chapter 2.4.8) should leverage responsible finance as a means to alleviate the finance performance versus real economy gap (Chapter 2.4.10). The different affective fallout propensities disparately distributed within society create social volatility (Chapter 2.4.11). High inflation (Chapter 2.4.12) and longest-ever low interest rate regimes (Chapter 2.4.13) dominate the call for responsible finance that targets rescue, recovery and relief aid (Chapter 2.4.14). Urban, local, regional or national foci (Chapter 2.4.15) as well as global and future-oriented beneficiaries of governmental recovery aid (Chapter 2.4.16) are potential recipient targets. Institutional... frameworks may ground recovery aid (Chapter 2.4.17) with a long-term future-oriented sustainability vision (Chapter 2.4.18). To align various SRI notions, the UN builds institutional frameworks in respective initiatives (Chapter 2.4.17). Political divestiture features capital withdrawal from politically incorrect markets – for example, such as the foreign investment drain from South Africa during the Apartheid regime and the capital flight from Sudan as for the humanitarian crisis in Darfur or the search for clean energy and market reaction to Russia's accession attempts (Chapter 2.4.19). Positive-screened SRI ventures are future prospective drivers of change to finance and implement the UN SDGs on a large scale (Chapter 2.4.20).

2.4.1. Forms

The most common forms to align financial investments with ethical, moral and social considerations are screenings, shareholder advocacy, community investing and social venture capital funding. Screenings integrate the evaluation of corporate financial and social performances into portfolio selections. Positive screenings target at corporations with sound social and environmental responsibility. Negative screenings exclude entities featuring morally and ethically irresponsible corporate conduct. Shareholder advocacy is the active engagement of shareholders in the corporate management by voting, activism and dialogue. The majority of shareholders exercise their voting rights by proxy resolutions, in which a third party has the right to advocate for the shareholders before the corporate board. Negative shareholder activism comprises political lobbying, consumer boycotts, stakeholder confrontation and negative publicity. Community investing describes ear-marks of investment funds for community development, but also features access to financial products and services to un(der)served communities. Social venture capital supports pro-social start-ups and social entrepreneurs for the greater goal of increasing the social impact of financial markets.

SRI features various forms and foci to align financial considerations with ethical, moral and social endeavors. The most common are socially responsible screenings, shareholder advocacy, community investing and social venture capital funding (Steurer et al., 2008).

Socially responsible screenings are "double bottom line analyses" of corporate economic performance and social responsibility. In screenings, financial market options are evaluated based on economic fundamentals as well as social features and corporate conduct externalities (Schueth, 2003). In addition to the traditional scanning of expected utility and volatility, screenings include qualitative examinations of intra- (e.g., corporate policies and practices and employee relations) and extra-organizational (e.g., externalities on current and future constituents) features of corporate conduct (Schueth, 2003). In general, screenings are based on corporate track records of societal impacts, environmental performance, human rights attribution and fair workplace policies as well as health and safety standards outlined in CSR reports. Consequentially screening leads to the inclusion or exclusion of corporations from portfolios based on social, environmental and political criteria.

Positive screenings feature the selection of corporations with sound social and environmental records and socially responsible corporate governance (Renneboog et al., 2007). Areas of positive corporate conduct are human rights, the environment, health, safety and labor standards as well as customer and stakeholder relations. Corporations that pass positive screenings meet value requirements expressed in their social standards, environmental policies, labor relations and community-related corporate governance.

Negative screenings exclude corporations that engage in morally, ethically and socially irresponsible activities. Pro-active negative screenings refrain from entities with corporate conduct counter-parting from international legal standards and/or implying negative social externalities (Renneboog et al., 2007). Negative screenings may address addictive products (e.g., liquor, tobacco and gambling), defense (e.g., weapons and firearms), environmentally hazardous production (e.g., pollution and nuclear power production), but also social, political and humanitarian deficiencies (e.g., minority discrimination and human

rights violations). Specialty screens feature extraordinary executive compensations, abortion, birth control, animal testing and international labor standard
infringements (Dupré et al., 2004). In 2005, the most common screenings in
the USA targeted at tobacco (US $159 billion in total net assets, approximately
28%); liquor (US $134 billion, 25%); gambling (US $41 billion, 7%); defense/
weapons (US $34 billion, 6%); community impact (US $32 billion, 5%); labor
concerns (US $31 billion, 5%); environmental issues (US $31 billion, 5%); consumer safety (US $28 billion, 5%); workplace diversity and equal employment
opportunity (US $27 billion, 5%); faith-based objections (US $12 billion, 2%);
adult entertainment (US $12 billion, 2%); human rights (US $11 billion, 2%);
animal testing (US $10 billion, 2%) and abortion, healthcare, biotechnology,
medical ethics, youth concerns, anti-family entertainment and excessive executive compensation (US $5 billion, 1%).

Post hoc negative screening implies divestiture as the removal of investment
capital from corporations and/or markets. Divestiture is common to steer change
in politically incorrect regimes, but also used to promote environmental protection, human rights, working conditions, animal protection, safety and health
standards (Broadhurst, Watson, & Marshall, 2003; Harvey, 2008; McWilliams &
Siegel, 2000).

In the wake of historical and political events, socio-political pressure can
evolve that triggers corporations to divest politically incorrect markets. The
impact of socio-political events on financial considerations is attributed to political divestiture – the act of removing funds from politically fractionated markets.
Political divestiture triggers foreign investment flight from politically incorrect
markets based on CSR information (Steurer, 2010). Political divestiture targets at
forcing political change by imposing financial constraints onto politically incorrect regimes that counterpart from international law resulting in war, social conflict, terrorism and human rights violations. Prominent cases are South Africa
during the Apartheid regime; governmental human rights violations in Burma
as well as the humanitarian crises in Sudan's Darfur region or Yemen's crisis,
the middle east political tensions or the invasion attempts of Russia in Ukraine.
Environmental political divestiture is mainly concerned with clean energy supply
and sustainability as well as human rights attention throughout the production
value chain.

The majority of socially screened funds use multiple screens and sometimes
complement screening with shareholder advocacy, community investing and
political interests.

Based on transparent and accountable corporate policies and procedures,
shareholder advocacy is the active engagement of shareholders in corporate
policy making, managerial practices and corporate social conduct (Little, 2008).
Shareholder advocacy comprises shareholder activism and dialogues as well as
active endowments.

In their role as corporate owners, socially conscientious investors target at
positively influencing corporate conduct in shareholder activism (Schueth, 2003).
Shareholder activism refers to shareholder groups engaging in "coordinated
action to utilize their unique rights to facilitate corporate change" (Sparkes &
Cowton, 2004, p. 51).

Positive shareholder activism implies advocating for socially responsible corporate conduct in shareholder meetings. Shareholder resolutions provide formal communication channels on corporate governance among shareholders, management and the board of directors. Resolutions can request information from the management and ask for changes in corporate policies and practices. In resolutions, shareholders use their voting right as a means to influence corporate behavior and steer corporate conduct in a more socially responsible direction (Little, 2008). In the USA, shareholder resolutions are managed by the US Securities and Exchange Commission. Shareholders who wish to file a resolution must own at least US $2,000 in shares in a given corporation or 1% of the corporate shares one year prior to filing proposals. Resolutions appear on the corporate proxy ballot, where they can be voted on by all shareholders or their representatives either electronically, by mail or in person at the annual meeting. The vast majority of shareholders exercise their voting rights by proxy. Proxy resolutions grant third parties rights to vote for shareholders on matters before the corporation (Little, 2008). Proxy resolutions on social issues and corporate governance generally aim at improving corporate policies and practices as well as encourage management to exercise good corporate citizenship with the goal of long-term shareholder value increase. Current trends comprise transparent and accountable proxy voting policies to support social and environmental responsibility. For example, mutual fund proxy disclosure regulations target at making corporate records publicly available.

Negative shareholder activism exerts activist influence and ranges from political lobbying, consumer boycotts and confrontations geared by negative publicity to pressure corporations into socially responsible corporate conduct (Sparkes & Cowton, 2004).

Parties engaging in shareholder dialogues seek to influence corporate policies and practices without introducing a formal resolution on their concerns. The corporate management is attentive to shareholder dialogues as for avoiding formal proxy resolutions and investment withdrawal.

Active endowments emerged from academics establishing procedures for integrating social responsibility in university endowments. SRI campus advisory committees issue proxy-voting guidelines as recommendations on proxy ballot votings.

Community investing started in the 1970s with direct investment for unserved communities. Community investing involves investor set-asides and ear-marks of investment funds for community development, but also features access to traditional financial products and services ranging from credits, equity and banking products to low-income and at-risk communities (Schueth, 2003). Community development banks focus on lending and rebuilding lower-income segments. Community development credit unions grant access to credits to unserved communities. Community development loans provide credit for small businesses with focus on sustainable development and resource conservation, but also sponsor community services. For individuals, community loans open avenues to affordable housing, education, child and healthcare (Little, 2008; Schueth, 2003). Financial empowerment of micro-enterprises helps disadvantaged minorities by financial education, mentoring and technical assistance.

Social venture capital funding finances socially responsible start-ups and social entrepreneurs to foster the positive social impact of capital markets. Community development venture capital funds provide capital for small start-ups with growth potential in traditionally un(der)developed regions. The very many forms of financial social responsibility expression embrace a wide range of SRI stakeholders and entities.

2.4.2. Stakeholders

SRI is a multi-stakeholder phenomenon that comprises economic, organizational and societal actors. SRI stakeholders represent the financial and public sectors as well as academia and media. Primary SRI constituents are banking executives, fiduciaries, institutional and private investors, governmental and non-governmental representatives, labor union members, officials of international organizations as well as academics and media correspondents. To overcome socio-economic losses implied by the various stakeholders' SRI notions, stakeholder dialogues integrate multiple parties to align differing viewpoints and priorities in common goals.

Due to various forms of expression, SRI is a multi-stakeholder phenomenon. Building the relationship between the financial world and society, SRI comprises multiple stakeholders. Corporate, financial and public constituents are economic (e.g., institutional and private investors), organizational (e.g., labor union representatives, banking executives and fiduciaries) and societal (e.g., representatives of international organizations and NGOs, governmental officials, public servants, non-profits, media representatives and academics) actors.

Banking executives at the managerial level are promoting SRI options to clients. In this function, bankers are the key information agents on SRI to financial decision makers.

The largest segment of screened accounts comprises private and institutional portfolios managed by fiduciaries. Fiduciaries (e.g., private equity executives, fund managers and investment managers) are financial professionals. As opinion leaders in the field, fiduciaries are key players in promoting financial options and advocating for SRI.

Institutional investors (e.g., universities and governments) range from public pension funds to small non-profit organizations and can include corporations, state and municipal governments, religious organizations, hospitals and healthcare plans, college and university endowments, foundations, trade unions and other entities with social and environmental endeavors.

Private investors (e.g., shareholders) are individuals who choose SRI as for efficiency considerations in combination with altruistic and social responsibility notions. For private investors, SRI can be connected to the need for innovation, self-enhancement and self-expression. Private investors may view SRI as a long-term competitive leadership advantage.

International organizations play an important role in promoting responsible investment. The UNGC and the UN Environment Programme (UNEP) Finance Initiative launched the Principles for Responsible Investment (PRI) in April

2006 at the New York Stock Exchange (NYSE) to ingrain social responsibility in investment decision making of asset owners and financial managers. The UN Conference on Trade and Development spearheaded the "Responsible Investment in Emerging Markets Initiative" in 2008. The UN launched the MDGs and is currently pursuing the SDGs.

Public pressure and governmental control to enhance financial accountability and market transparency trigger SRI. Governmental policy makers craft regulations that foster accountability and transparency of financial assets and operations – for example, the freedom of information legislation. Governmental regulations fortify institutional investors to adopt socially responsible criteria in their investment decisions.

NGOs promote transparency and accountability within the financial sector. NGOs have become vital forces to monitor corporate conduct and sophisticate shareholder activism – all of which are important prerequisites for SRI (Mohr et al., 2001; Williams, 2005).

In recent decades, labor unions have paid attention to SRI as a means to imbue social responsibility into financial markets – foremost in the areas of human rights, labor conditions and minority empowerment.

Within recent decades, SRI has emerged as a prominent investment option. From the beginnings, the ascent of SRI was backed up by the academic community. Foremost academic financial experts, behavioral economists, sociologists and social psychologists have increasingly paid attention to social responsibility within economic market systems.

The public opinion on SRI is partially created by media representatives who gather, select, process and disseminate information on socially responsible corporate conduct and financial social responsibility.

As a novel multi-stakeholder phenomenon, SRI is driven by a variety of internal and external forces. Financial social responsibility touches on diverse interests of the various stakeholders. Diverting stakeholders' SRI notions and differing, underlying interests and motives of SRI constituents imply multi-stakeholder predicaments. As a means to reduce the complexity of the phenomenon, stakeholder management concepts depict the various engaged groups and study their view on SRI (Freeman, 1984). To overcome socio-economic losses implied by various SRI notions and stakeholder approaches to administer financial social responsibility, stakeholder dialogues create common goals by integrating adverse opinions that have evolved in the wake of the rise of SRI over the last decades.

2.4.3. Emergence

Due to qualitative and quantitative growth in the Western world within recent decades, SRI emerged as an investment philosophy adopted by a growing proportion of financial practitioners. Key indicators for the ascent of SRI are the increasing number and diversity of SRI options. The rise in SRI is accompanied by the upcoming of stock exchange rating agencies, social responsibility impact measurement tools, social reporting and certifications, which the European Sustainable Finance Taxonomy currently tries to categorize. Today, the range of shareholder engagement possibilities is more sophisticated than ever and trends forecast a further maturation of SRI.

SRI originally emerged from a niche market option that was offered by a small number of specialist retailers. In the wake of the rising trend toward financial social responsibility, SRI grew qualitatively and quantitatively (McCann, Solomon, & Solomon, 2003; Solomon, Solomon, & Norton, 2002; Sparkes, 2002).

In recent decades, SRI options have increased in size, number and scope (McCann et al., 2003; Solomon et al., 2002; Sparkes, 2002). Over the past two decades in the new millennium, assets involved in social investing have risen faster than other professionally managed investment options in the USA and Europe (Cui, 2008; Knoll, 2008; Social Investment Forum Report, 2006).

Pre-2008 World Financial Recession, SRI was a growing segment of the US financial services industry that controlled around US $2.5 trillion – accounting for about 20.7% of the US market – in professionally managed assets in 2005 (Schueth, 2003; Williams, 2005). Of these assets, screenings were the dominant SRI form (with US $1,802 billion in assets), followed by shareholder advocacy (US $703 billion) and community investing valuing for US $20 billion. In the first decade of the new millennium, screenings were accompanied by a rise in community investing and shareholder advocacy. In the USA, screened funds were available in more than 370 classes that represented US $1.8 billion in net total assets in 2005. The majority of SRI assets comprise socially screened separate accounts that are managed for individual and institutional clients. SRI separate accounts have increased more than 20-fold from US $40 billion to US $1.79 trillion in the decade from 1995 to 2005. Assets in socially screened mutual funds and other pooled products rose from US $151 billion in 2003 to US $179 billion in 2005.

The post-2008 World Financial Turmoil Era saw a deepened interest in financial market stability, which drove the idea of responsibility as a prerequisite for functioning and sustainable markets (Connaker & Madsbjerg, 2019). With the turn of the millennium also the impacts of climate change became more and more apparent in all parts of the world and the substantial risk imbued in environmental degradation, irreversible tipping points and terminal lock-ins (Puaschunder, 2020d). Increasing interest in ESG criteria in investment decision perpetuated the demand for SRI. In the beginning of 2018, US $11.6 trillion of all professionally managed assets in the USA were pursuing some sort of ESG strategy, which equals approximately one-fourth of the market (Connaker & Madsbjerg, 2019).

Institutional investors: The largest segment of screened assets comprises the combined publicly – on behalf of institutions – or privately managed institutional portfolios. Institutional investors feature corporations, state and municipal governments, religious entities, hospitals and healthcare facilities, college and university endowments, foundations, trade unions and other institutions that are engaged in financial markets. Institutional investors of insurance corporations, depository institutions and investment entities issue pension, mutual and endowment funds (Harvey, 2008). In the USA, institutional investors range from public pension funds with socially screened assets to small non-profit organizations.

Shareholder advocacy: Over the decades, shareholders were raising ESG topics in corporate dialogues. In 1995, US $473 billion in institutional assets involved shareholder advocacy expressed in resolutions or formal proxy-voting guidelines on social issues (Social Investment Forum Report, 2006). From 2003 to 2005, shareholder resolutions on social and environmental issues increased from 299 to 348 shareholder proposals, of which 177 reached a proxy vote (Social Investment Forum Report, 2006). With the Securities and Exchange Commission increasingly promoting the integration of shareholders' environmental and social proposals in most recent years, more than 566 environmental- or social-related shareholder resolutions have been filed by early 2022 and substantially more proposals are getting onto ballots, already 343 proposals were pending for votes by the end of March 2022 (Nani & Beyoud, 2022).

Commercial SRI funds: Several commercial SRI funds account for financial social innovations in products, measurement indices and accountability control. One of the market leaders, KLD Research & Analytics, holds the oldest SRI performance measurement index. As one of the largest social responsibility indices, the US Domini 400 Social Equity Fund started in May 1990 and recently launched the Domini European Social Equity Fund (Little, 2008). The large-cap growth fund Calvert offers the Calvert Social Index comprising 641 corporations that have been screened for social, economic and environmental purposes (Farzad, 2007). As a large-cap growth fund, Vanguard features the FTSE4Good US Select Index, which holds 425 screened options. Most recent decades have featured an explosion of green bonds and sustainable finance options that are currently categorized in the Sustainable Finance Taxonomy.

In terms of sector-specific distributions, SRI is geared toward finance products, information technology, consumer goods and healthcare. Vanguard offers innovative finance options, while Calvert primarily comprises finance and information technology entities (Little, 2008). Calvert and Vanguard hold more than two-thirds of their investment in the healthcare, finance and information technology sectors. In comparison to the general S&P 500 Index, SRI options tend to refrain from the energy sector (e.g., petroleum).

The ascent SRI has been accompanied by a change in the qualitative nature of social investments. The current SRI notion is very different from the earlier "ethical investment" based on negative screenings (McCann et al., 2003). Although a moral touch remains, the establishment of SRI retail funds and the adoption of SRI by institutional investors have leveraged SRI into a pro-active positive screening option and tapped into green bonds and environmental sustainability ventures.

Today, the SRI market has reached unprecedented diversity featuring a wide range of sophisticated SRI activities and a variety of stakeholder engagement possibilities. Financial social responsibility comprises commercial SRI retail to the public in socially screened separate accounts, mutual and pension funds, bonds and community development as well as hybrid instruments that undergo financial and ethical value tests (Mathieu, 2000; Rosen et al., 1991; Sparkes & Cowton, 2004). The establishment and advancement of SRI retail and the adoption of SRI by major institutional investors have matured SRI from a margin to a mainstreamed asset allocation style that is backed by governance (e.g., in green bonds helicopter funding of global governance institutions), governments (e.g., in institutional investor activities), shareholders (e.g., in voting preferences) and stakeholder pressure (e.g., fortified on social media online platforms that exacerbate transparency of corporate conduct impacts along the entire value chain) (Mathieu, 2000; Rosen et al., 1991; Sparkes & Cowton, 2004).

The growth of financial social responsibility expressions has leveraged SRI into an investment philosophy adopted by a growing proportion of investment firms and governmental agencies around the world (Knoll, 2008; Mohr et al., 2001; Sparkes & Cowton, 2004). The sophistication of socially responsible shareholder engagement has triggered an upcoming of social and environmental stock exchange rating agencies, SRI impact measurement tools, corporate social and environmental reporting and certifications (Steurer et al., 2008). SRI has proliferated as a prominent term in the financial literature with business professionals and analysts monitoring and reporting on social, ethical and environmental corporate performance (e.g., Dow Jones Sustainability Index, FTSE4Good Index and OeSFX). This trend is captured in the European Finance Taxonomy endeavors, goes hand in hand with practitioners and academia studying financial social responsibility as well as stakeholders commenting on social, environmental and ethics impacts of corporate endeavors on social media.

The most recent SRI innovations comprise improved disclosure standards, benchmarking of CSR and SRI codes of conduct, screening for biotechnology as well as environmental funds paying attention to climate change. Future forecast trends are the growth in screened funds, active SRI ownership models and community investing innovations in combination with a focus on the SDGs (Little, 2008; Social Investment Forum Report, 2006). The variety and ascent of SRI options can be traced back to the historic roots of financial social responsibility.

2.4.4. Historical Background

SRI can be traced back to ethical investing of religious institutions and societal attention to social, environmental and political deficiencies. In the 1960s, shareholder activism of civil rights campaigns and social justice movements drove SRI. Since the 1980s, positive screenings identified corporations with respective CSR policies. Political divestiture became prominent in the case of South Africa's Apartheid regime. Environmental catastrophes in Chernobyl and Bhopal as well as the Exxon Valdez oil spill triggered environmentally conscientious investment.

SRI was propelled in the wake of the micro-finance and cooperative banking revolution. In 2006, a UNGC division launched "The Principles for Responsible Investment (PRI)" in collaboration with the NYSE. In the wake of the 2008 World Financial Recession, SRI was attributed the potential to re-establish trust in financial markets. Stakeholder pressure and changing financial market regulations enhancing accountability and transparency perpetuated SRI. The COVID-19 external shock brought about an unprecedented concerted wave of governmental aid and recovery packages, which were oftentimes pegged to socio-ecological agendas. The impact of the widespread financing of social and environmental causes in the US GND and the EGD but also market regulatory action fostering sustainable development is expected to be long-term and substantial.

Historically SRI can be traced back to ethical investing of religious institutions. Already in medieval times, Christianity imposed financial restrictions based on the Old Testament. The Catholic Church prohibited usury as early as 1139. Judaist writings praised ethical monetary policies. Methodism urged people to not engage in "sinful" trade and profit maximization from exploitation (Cuesta & Valor, 2007). In the seventeenth century, the Quaker Society of Friends refrained from weapons and slave trade. The UK Methodist Church advocated for the avoidance of unethical corporate conduct. The Christian Pioneer Fund was the first official exclusion of "sin stocks." Until today, Islamic banking restricts adult entertainment and gambling (Renneboog et al., 2007).

The early beginnings of modern SRI are attributed to social responsibility concerns emerging from an attention to social, environmental and political market deficiencies. The demand for financial social responsibility became blatant in the wake of humanitarian, social and environmental crises (Williams, 2005).

Until the end of WWII, the financial industry was strictly regulated with very few financial shares being traded over the counter and the range of financial options being limited (Soros, 1998). The post-war years featured a gradual lifting of financial market restrictions, which gave leeway for an individualization of financial asset allocations. During the post-war period, SRI was propelled by stakeholder pressure in connection with legislative and policy compulsion. Legislative information disclosure reforms coupled with governmental encouragement of trustees to develop social responsibility drove SRI (Solomon et al., 2002; Sparkes & Cowton, 2004).

In the late 1960s, modern SRI evolved in the wake of shareholder activism. Civil rights campaigns and social justice movements opposed college endowments to fund warfare. Minority empowerment, consumer rights activism and environmentalist movements leveraged the sensitivity for financial social responsibility (Renneboog et al., 2007; Sparkes, 2002). Since 1969, the Council on Economic Priorities rated corporate social and environmental performance. In 1970, SRI was introduced to academic discourse at a conference at Yale University. Subsequently, many universities established committees to advise trustees on social investment. In the 1970s, the Investor Responsibility Research Center and the Interfaith Center on Corporate Responsibility were launched to promote shareholder advocacy and proxy resolutions (Social Investment Forum Report, 2006). In the 1960s, anti-Vietnam War institutional investors sold Dow Chemical shares as for producing napalm (Biller, 2007). In 1971, the first modern SRI mutual fund – the PAX World Fund – was created by a group of US Methodist clergy that aimed at divestiture from Vietnam War supporting corporations (Broadhurst et al., 2003; Renneboog et al., 2007). The Dreyfus Third Century Fund opened the following year to avoid "sin stocks" and raise labor standards. The subsequent Domini 400 Social Index screened corporations for environmental and social performance. In 1972, activists criticized Harvard University for owning shares in petroleum corporations. Around the same time, political divestiture was firstly discussed in the case of the Angolan repressive government (Alperson et al., 1991). By the mid-1970s, a significant number of governments had enacted shareholder rights to address corporate activities that caused "social injury" and many universities had established committees to advise trustees on SRI and shareholder rights. In 1976, Reverend Leon Sullivan – a civil rights activist and director of General Motors – developed the Sullivan Principles to foster equal remuneration and workplace opportunities to empower minorities (Voorhes, 1999). During the 1980s, political divestiture became prominent in the case of the South African Apartheid regime featuring racial segregation and economic discrimination against non-European groups (Merriam Webster Dictionary, 2008). By 1979, a majority of universities had established advisory committees on South African investments followed by a widespread divestiture trend of socially concerned investors, churches, cities and states to end Apartheid in South Africa (Schueth, 2003; Voorhes, 1999). By the end of the 1980s, billions of dollars had been divested from South Africa backed by governmental statutes – such as the 1986 US Comprehensive Anti-Apartheid Act – which impacted the South African economy. In the 1980s, catastrophes in Chernobyl, Bhopal and the Exxon Valdez oil spill triggered antinuclear and environmental concerns of stakeholders. Political libertarian movements rose ethical considerations in financial investment decisions (Soros, 2008). With the desire to set standards for corporate social and environmentally conscientious conduct, social investors started to use positive screenings to identify and support corporations that pay attention to human rights standards, equal opportunities, labor relations, environmental protection, consumer safety and community concerns. Positive screenings outlined corporations that meet or exceed certain social and environmental standards based on information from social and environmental records. In 1981, the American Social Investment Forum was formed as a professional body for individual and institutional SRI constituents (Broadhurst et al., 2003). In the beginning of 1990s, the Domini 400 Social Index was created as the first socially screened index of corporations listed by the S&P Index. In the 1990s, SRI was perpetuated by the micro-finance revolution and the co-operative banking system (Brenner, 2003).

Since the turn of the century, financial markets were attributed a rising share of global governance. Institutional investors increasingly used their clout to influence corporate conduct (Solomon et al., 2002; Sparkes & Cowton, 2004). Socially conscientious investors became active in demanding corporate governance reforms impacting on societal causes. SRI emerged in the wake of heightened information disclosure on corporate social conduct in combination with governmental encouragement of trustees to develop SRI. As for all these trends, the UNGC division launched the "PRI" in collaboration with the NYSE in 2006. This PPP initiative was set up to increase the number of socially responsible investors and steer SRI by creating models for positive change within the investment community.

2.4.5. International Nuances

SRI is a context and culture-dependent phenomenon featuring international differences. North America, Europe and Australia account for the most vital SRI markets. In the USA, SRI is mainly promoted by independent organizations and regulatory institutions that use proxy statement disclosure to rate corporations on their social and environmental performances and impacts. Based on the US model, since 2006, the Canadian Securities Administrators have mandated mutual funds to publicly disclose their proxy voting. In Europe, SRI booms in Northern and Central European countries, yet is relatively slow to take off in Southern Europe.

Within the EU, institutionalized and governmentally administered SRI rose in recent decades. In the UK, SRI was perpetuated by governmental legislations encouraging shareholder votings and formal consultations with funds' holders on the adoption of social, ethical and environmental policies. Similar regulations are currently considered by the European Parliament and have been passed in Australia, Germany and Sweden. In German-speaking countries, SRI propelled during the 1970s green wave. The 2002 Australian Financial Service Reform Act introduced social responsibility disclosure statements for financial services followed by the Australian Securities and Investment Commission issuing SRI disclosure guidelines. Emerging SRI markets are Latin America, South Africa and Japan with prospective extensions to Taiwan, Singapore and Hong Kong. Brazil, South Africa and Asia exhibit a special attention to micro-finance and community investing.

As a context and culture-dependent phenomenon, international differences in SRI conduct stem from differing market practices, governmental and institutional frameworks, societal values and moral obligations that impact on financial market behavior. While Anglo-Saxon capital market systems (such as the USA and UK) feature private share- and stockholder investments, European financial markets are significant for governmental and institutional banking.

Today financial social responsibility is booming in the Western world. SRI has foremost been adopted in Central Europe and Anglo-Saxon countries (Sparkes & Cowton, 2004). North America, Europe (especially the UK) and Australia account for the most vital SRI markets. Most recent developments comprise the United States GND and European Union Green Deal, which promise to steer finance in a more socially conscientious direction. The Next Generation EU and the European Finance Taxonomy are attempts to classify and categorize industries based on the social, economic and ecologic contributions. In the sustainability domain, green bonds are currently at the forefront to finance climate change mitigation and adaptation efforts.

North America. The USA: Prior to the 2008 financial crisis, the USA was home to half of the world's capital and publicly traded corporations. Hosting 7,000 self-made millionaires and 170 billionaires, the US political and legal systems disproportionately reward capital allocation talent. The USA features the most liberal market economy in the world coupled with a comprehensive set of market transparency rules, a vigorous, free media and highly educated market actors (Roberts, 2006). The US Constitutional Law endows with substantive rights of freedom of speech, assembly or association, press and religious exercise as well as property securitization. The USA is renowned for explicit CSR combined with a competitive market system and low governmental social welfare.

Having grown out of niche market options for value-led investors, SRI is attributed to have prospered in the USA due to shareholder activism, shareholder participation and independent financial entities' efforts. In recent decades,

US shareholders have increasingly gained access to proxy statements for the sake of disclosure on social and environmental externalities of corporate conduct. Since 2004, various corporate scandals led to legislations addressing funds disclosure of proxy votes, which leveraged shareholder resolutions to become the mainstream track record for socially responsible corporate conduct (Little, 2008). The so-called "Wall Street Rule" implicitly captures the role of shareholder activism as a soft-law market regulation (Lydenberg, 2002).

Today, the USA features the widest variety of SRI options and socially responsible performance measurement indices. In 2005, US \$2.5 trillion assets were attributed as socially responsible funds accounting for growing 20.7% of total US investments (Williams, 2005).

In Canada, SRI was officially introduced by the Ethical Growth Fund in 1986 (Williams, 2005). Since 2001, the Canadian shareholder resolution rules were based on the respective US model leading to a rise in SRI (Sparkes & Cowton, 2004). The Canadian Institute of Chartered Accountants introduced disclosure guidelines in 2001 combined with a mandatory disclosure obligation since 2004 (William, 2005). Since 2006, the Canadian Securities Administrators have mandated mutual funds to publicly disclose their proxy voting records and policies. SRI is foremost organized by the Social Investment Organization (SIO) which is renowned for regular SRI surveys and conferences (Williams, 2005). Recently, SRI and foremost community investing have grown significantly in Canada (Social Investment Forum Report, 2006).

Europe. The EU features institutionalized and governmentally administered SRI. From 2003 to 2006, the European SRI market grew by 36% (Steurer et al., 2008).[4] In 2005, 375 green, social and ethical European funds were identified with €24.1 billion. According to Eurosif, responsible investments by European institutional investors (excluding the Nordic region) comprised €1.138 billion in 2006. In 2008, SRI funds accounted for up to 18% of the market share.[5] The UK lead the SRI movement with €8.0 billion in total assets, followed by Germany with €6.7 billion, Austria with €5.3 billion, France with €3.1 billion, Switzerland with €2.9 billion, Italy with €2.7 billion and Sweden with €2.5 billion in 2005 (Social Investment Forum Report, 2006). While SRI booms in Northern and Central European countries, the movement is slower to take off in Southern Europe. Community investing is more frequent in Latin countries – foremost Italy, France or Spain – than in Nordic regions.[6]

Within Europe, the UK leads in socially responsible assets under management (Sparkes, 2002). First UK Victorian concerns about employment conditions shed light on corporate social conduct. Ethical banking was established

---

[4]European Social Investment Forum Report. (2009, January). Retrieved from http://www.eurosif.org/.
[5]European Social Investment Forum. (2009, January). Retrieved from http://www.eurosif.com/publications/sri_studies.
[6]European Social Investment Forum Report. (2009, January). Retrieved from http://www.eurosif.org/.

by the Mercury Provident in 1974 and introduced to retail banking in 1992. In 1997, a group of university affiliates launched a campaign for ethical and environmental investment of pension funds, which led to Sustainable and Responsible Investment policies in 2000 (Williams, 2005). Since 2000, the UK law requires all occupational pension funds to formally consult the adoption of social, ethical and environmental policies (Sparkes & Cowton, 2004; Williams, 2005). The UK government regulations reassure pension funds to declare the extent to which environmental, social or ethical considerations are taken into account in the selection, retention and realization of investments (Steurer et al., 2008; Sparkes, 2002). Similar regulations have been passed in Germany and Sweden and are currently being considered by the European Parliament.

Political divestiture was enacted by the Belgian government in 2007 by forbidding Belgian investors to finance anti-personnel mines and cluster munitions (Steurer, 2010). The enforcement of the law, however, is problematic as disclosure requirements for professional investors are low and sanctions are not foreseen (Steurer, 2010).

Sweden's 2000 Public Pension Fund Act required all Swedish National Pension Funds to address environmental and social topics in the report of investment activities and management of the funds (Steurer, 2010). While the law gives leeway to what extent funds comply with the law, it helped in providing access to information and raising awareness for SRI. In addition, a Joint Ethical Council offers investment recommendations for stakeholders (Steurer, 2010). The Dutch Green Funds Scheme grants information on tax exemptions for SRI (Steurer, 2010). The French Pension Research Fund offers insurance plans in line with SRI principles. In German-speaking countries, SRI was propelled in the wake of the 1970s green wave that focused on environment protection and peace movements. The "Gemeinschaftsbank" as well as the "Ökobank" became the first SRI traders (Williams, 2005). Major influences are attributed to Green Parties, the 1991 Renewable Energy Act as well as tax exemptions and information campaigns for green funds (Williams, 2005).

The Pacific Rim and Asia. In Australia, direct share ownership leads to a heightened number of pro-active SRI screenings of individual investors (Williams, 2005). The first Australian ethical investment movement began in the early 1980s, which formulated the Australian Ethical Investment Trust in 1989 (Cummings, 2000). The Ethical Investment Association (EIA) emerged throughout the 1990s to launch first SRI benchmarking reports in 2001 and create a SRI symbol as a seal of approval for SRI products (Williams, 2005). The Financial Service Reform Act 2002 introduced ethical product disclosure statements for financial services. In 2003, the Australian Securities and Investment Commission (ASIC) issued SRI disclosure guidelines (Williams, 2005). From 2001 to 2004, SRI activities raised by over 100% from AUS $10.5 billion to AUS $21.5 in 2004 (Williams, 2005). From 2004 to 2005, managed SRI portfolios increased by around 70% from AUS $4.5 billion to AUS $7.7 billion – making SRI the fastest growing investment segment (Jones et al., 2008).

Emerging Markets. In emerging markets, SRI promotes international development. Even in countries where screening and shareholder advocacy are relatively limited, the impacts of community investing, micro-finance and enter-prise development have been substantial (Social Investment Forum Report, 2006). Newly emerging and rapidly growing SRI markets are Latin America (foremost Brazil), South Africa and Asia reaching US $2.7 billion in total SRI assets. Japan remains Asia's leading market for SRI with more than 100 billion yen in over 10 SRI funds. More than 12 screened funds are available in the Islamic banking territories of Malaysia, Taiwan and Singapore. Hong Kong has been identified as a ripe market for an Asian SRI expansion. Micro-finance and community investing continue to play a significant role for Asian low-income social entrepreneurs and developing communities. Barriers to social investors in emerging markets are the lack of accountable CSR practices, standardized SRI market options and access to financial markets. In the international arena, international organizations' global governance sets the institutional framework for SRI.

2.4.6. 2008 World Financial Crisis

In the beginning of 2008, CEOs of world-leading corporations agreed on the diminishing power and influence of nation states in providing global governance. Globalized capitalism was praised as the triumphing market system and an upcoming financial market hegemony was forecast (Ahmad, 2008). Rising levels of social venture capital in international development led to predictions about the emerging influence of financial markets in providing social welfare. Given the worldwide outreach of financial markets in social and political affairs, financial social responsibility was attributed as an innovative means of global governance.

The 2008 financial crisis put a new perspective on the role of financial markets in addressing global governance. The impact and influence of the 2008 World Financial Recession on economic markets, global policy making and society is undoubtable. The crisis has caused what Alan Greenspan called a "once in a century credit tsunami" featuring governmental takeovers and bailouts, a "lock-up" of credit markets and inter-bank lending, a 25% drop in financial market indices per month and two almost bankrupt European countries (Duchac, 2008).

Multi-faceted contributing factors ranging from demographics, political influences, financial exuberance and over-confidence in innovative and deregulatory financial markets are believed to have caused the crises: demographic trends of the baby boom generation's peak in purchasing power fueled financial market and real estate bubbles. September 11, 2001 in combination with other political events created collective uncertainty that was met by the US Federal Reserve's aggressive interest rate cutting, which increased the amount of circulating capital to nurture bubbles and triggered a refinancing boom with subprime borrowers. Financial lending practices of securitizations propelled capital flows from investors to subprime borrowers creating an illusion of wealth, which attracted speculators who further fueled bubbles. Deregulation in the wake of the 1999 Financial Service Reform Act repealed the Glass-Steagall Act, which removed legal separations of commercial and investment banks and exposed an interconnected market system to higher risk levels. In principal–agent dilemmas, mortgage brokers focused on short-term self-interests. In addition, trust in financial modeling techniques caused irrationally low default estimates. Credit rating agencies publishing optimistic ratings led to overconfidence causing financial turmoil (Duchac, 2008).

Overall, the social, political and economic risks exposed during the 2008 World Financial Recession propelled the interest in crisis-robust sustainable finance solutions in SRI (Trevino & Nelson, 2004). As an implication of the crisis, citizens have become more attentive to social responsibility within market systems. Media coverage of financial fraud, fiduciary responsibility breaches, astronomic CEO remunerations and financial managers' exuberance are increasing stakeholder calls for the inclusion of transparency and accountability control in financial markets.

To avoid a recurrent scenario in the future, enhanced transparency and accountability of investment options and ethicality of responsible market participants became blatant demands. Corporate governance, information disclosure and monitoring within the corporate and financial world leveraged into central issues of concern of shareholders, policy makers and civilians.

As direct implications of the crisis, corporate executives were increasingly forced by stakeholders to pay attention to financial social responsibility. SRI featuring concern for corporate accountability and transparency in screenings, resolutions and stakeholder dialogues seemed as a remedy to re-establish trust in corporate and financial market conduct (Social Investment Forum Report, 2006). The 2008 financial crisis leveraged SRI into a more common financial investment option.[7]

Accompanied with the rise of SRI in practice was heightened academic and public debate on the influence of public and private actors in administering social responsibilities within market systems. In the aftermath of the crisis, stakeholders re-discussed the role of economic and financial markets in providing and administering global governance (Little, 2008). The manifold expressions of the interplay of governmental, corporate and financial market forces in addressing social responsibility and attributing global governance become apparent during the COVID-19 pandemic.

2.4.7. Economic Impact of COVID-19

The novel Coronavirus SARS-CoV-2 imposes the most unexpected external economic shock to modern humankind, triggering abrupt consumption and behavior pattern shifts around the world with widespread socio-economic impacts. In order to alleviate unexpected negative fallouts from the crisis, attention to governmental bailouts and recovery packages gained unprecedented momentum.

In confronting the crisis, economic bailout and rescue packages are oftentimes targeted with attention to inequality imbued in our COVID-19 shock era.

---

[7]Spiegel Online. (2009, January). Retrieved from http://www.spiegel.de/spiegel/0,1518,589895,00.html.

Inequality heightened in the COVID-19 economic fallout in abruptly changed economic demand patterns that have resulted in economically gaining and losing industries, which widened an unexpected economic performance gap between the finance sector and the real economy. Systemically differing liquidity in the finance sector and the real economy during the crisis implies sector-specific affective fallout propensities.

Currently experienced longest-ever low interest rate regimes foster capital flow for innovation in the finance world, while disincentivizing household savings decreases private consumers' resiliency, which exacerbates negative emotional consequences in the real economy with households facing a narrowing of liquidity constraints. Industry-specific inflation patterns as well as urban-versus-rural disposable income differences should be considered in the wake of ambitious bailout and recovery plans when choosing bailout and recovery beneficiaries and targets. The potential focus of bailouts and recovery ranges from urban–local and national to even global and future-oriented beneficiaries, as pursued in public investments on climate stabilization in the GND or EGD or the Sustainable Finance Taxonomy.

The COVID-19 crisis represents the most unforeseen external shock for modern economies. Starting from the beginning of 2020, the novel Coronavirus caused a dramatic downturn for trade, human mobility and international service industries (Gössling et al., 2020; Puaschunder et al., 2020a). From April 2020, more than half of the world's population faced some sort of lockdown and/or consumption constraints and economic shortages, which disrupted economic productivity substantially (International Monetary Fund, 2020a, 2020b). These lockdowns led to a slump in general consumption and reduced trade by an estimated 10% (*The Economist*, 2020a). In the first half of 2020, global foreign direct investments plummeted by 49% and were even around 75% suppressed in the developed world (United Nations Conference on Trade and Development, 2020). All the human social interaction constraints in all major world economies coupled with a halt of human transport and trade shortages around the globe spilled over into an unprecedented international economic decline (Sachs et al., 2020; United Nations Conference on Trade and Development Committee for Coordination of Statistical Activities, 2020). The global economy is estimated to have contracted by an estimated 3–5% of general world economic output in 2020, which is six times the economic magnitude of the 2008–2009 world recession (International Monetary Fund, 2020a, 2020b; World Bank, 2021). The IMF measured that the world economy, as measured by real gross domestic product (GDP), shrank by as much as 3.5% in 2020 (Alpert, 2021). Rising poverty levels put an additional 150 million children at risk worldwide (UNICEF, 2020).

The COVID-19 global recession is the deepest since WWII, with the largest fraction of economies experiencing declines in per capita output since 1870 (Kose & Sugawara, 2020). The economic external shock seems to end globalization and international exchange if considering the World Bank expecting the sharpest decline in remittances in recent world history (World Bank, 2020). All these measures resemble the onset of a lasting economic crisis with fundamental changes for society (International Monetary Fund, 2020a, 2020b; Puaschunder & Beerbaum,

2020a, 2020b). Global governance institutions and governments around the globe have set out on a course to avert the negative impetus of the COVID-19 pandemic economic shock (Cassim et al., 2020; The White House of the United States of America, 2021b, 2021c).

2.4.8. COVID-19 New Finance Order

The outbreak of the COVID-19 crisis triggered the world's largest-ever wave of governmental rescue and recovery aid that is oftentimes pegged to social, environmental and ethical causes that enact public responsibility. Central banks of all major world economies – such as Australia, Brazil, Canada, Denmark, Japan, New Zealand, Singapore, South Korea, Sweden, Switzerland, the UK, the USA – and the European Central Bank coordinated to lower the price of USD liquidity swap line arrangements in order to foster the provision of global liquidity (Alpert, 2021; European Central Bank, 2020a, 2020b, 2020c, 2020d; Federal Reserve of the United States, 2020a, 2020b). The IMF and the World Bank issued economic stimulus and relief efforts in the range of around US $260 billion with the majority of relief aid being distributed in the developing world (Alpert, 2021; International Monetary Fund, 2020c; World Bank, March 3, 2020, March 17, 2020, April 22, 2020).

As of May 2021, all major economies responded to the economic fallout of COVID-19. In response to the ongoing COVID-19 crisis, all major economies around the world have rolled out economic-assistance packages or recovery releases that by mid-2020 already were summing up to over US $10 trillion and with continuous prospects of renewal and further development (Cassim et al., 2020; The White House of the United States, 2021b, 2021c).

Across countries, economic-stimulus responses to the COVID-19 crisis outsize those to the 2008 financial crisis (Cassim et al., 2020; The White House of the United States, 2021c). The qualitative and quantitative stimulus, rescue and recovery aid have surpassed any other similar attempt in human history (Alpert, 2021). Economic COVID-19 stimulus and relief efforts mainly comprise international fiscal and monetary stimulus and relief efforts but also direct rescue bailout packages (Alpert, 2021).

COVID-19 response, rescue and long-term monetary aid started in China. In the early days of the detection and outbreak of the novel Coronavirus, the China Monetary Response was first a US $506 billion stimulus package short-term aid, followed by US $732 billion in discretionary fiscal measure and US $198 billion additional support and long-term monetary interest rate lowering (Alpert, 2021).

Hong Kong adopted three major fiscal stimulus and relief packages totaling over US $30 billion with additional smaller stimulus measures following (Alpert, 2021).

Three stimulus packages were launched in Japan with the highest share of GDP and additional plans to boost liquidity totaling up to US $1 trillion in liquidity plus fiscal spending bills increased for business loans (Alpert, 2021; Bank of Japan, 2020; Szmigiera, 2021).

India started with interest rate lowering and an injection of almost US $100 billion into the financial system and facilitated market loans loosening bank lending restrictions (Alpert, 2021; Reserve Bank of India, 2020). The ongoing COVID-19 pandemic in India triggered additional monetary stimulus packages of US $266 billion and fiscal spending of US $27 billion (Alpert, 2021; Saha, 2020). Additional relief spending was promised in the range of US $50–100 billion and is on its way to boost consumption by direct payments and tax incentives (Alpert, 2021; Kazmin, 2020; *The Hindu*, 2020).

South Korea cut interest rates, enacted financial stability and liquidity packages in the range up to US $10 billion, also operated via bonds and fiscal stimulus, recovery and relief packages of over US $100 billion (Alpert, 2021; Bank of Korea, 2020a, 2020b, 2020c, 2020d, 2020e, 2020f; Hana, 2020; Hyunjung, 2020; *The Straits Times*, 2020).

Australia entering a recession for the first time in almost 30 years subsequently lowered its interest rate broad-based and launched three relief packages worth a total of around US $300 billion (Alpert, 2021; Karp, 2020; Martin, 2020; Murphy, 2020; Reserve Bank of Australia, 2021).

Brazil tackled the COVID-19 economic fallout with statutory limitations on its fiscal spending, lowered the benchmark interest rate and added around US $300 billion liquidity to credit markets, including a fiscal stimulus package (Alpert, 2021; Ayres, 2020; Central Bank of Brazil, 2020; Geist-Benitez, Valenzuela, & Walsh, 2020; Government of Brazil, 2020).

Russia and the Gulf Region faced a drop in oil and gas exports revenues, which were answered in Russia by lowered interest rates (Alpert, 2021; Bank of Russia, 2020a, 2020b, 2020c, 2020d, 2020e, 2020f, 2020g). The Bank of Russia allocated financial aid around US $70 billion through direct aid plus additional lending programs to stimulate the economy (Bank of Russia, 2020a, 2020b, 2020e; *The Moscow Times*, June 2, 2020).

Canada's dependence on dropping oil and gas prices but also halted raw material exports challenged the Canadian economy, which the Canadian government stabilized with a US $75 billion relief package including unemployment insurance and wage subsidies (Alpert, 2021). Canadian Monetary Policy included three cuts of the Canadian benchmark interest rate plus inflation targeting and liquidity banking lending facilitation backed by bonds and mortgages (Alpert, 2021; Bank of Canada, 2020a, 2020b, 2020c, 2020d, 2020e; Canada Mortgage and Housing Corporation, 2020).

The EU had a concerted Eurozone monetary policy administered by the European Central Bank that faced constraints due to an already low interest rate regime (Alpert, 2021; European Central Bank, 2020a, 2020b, 2020c, 2020d). Recovery plans included the pandemic emergency longer-term refinancing operations, currency swaps, increased lending and Euro-denominated liquidity for central banks outside the Eurozone to provide market stability and financial liquidity partially enacted via bonds in the US $128 billion range (Alpert, 2021; European Central Bank, 2020a, 2020c, 2020d).

The Pandemic Emergency Purchase Programme issued US $800 billion in bonds and commercial papers throughout the year 2020 that were expanded up to a total of US $1.5 trillion until the end of June 2021 in order to reach a total target of US $2.24 trillion (Alpert, 2021; European Central Bank, 2020d). The EU concerted action to avert the economic downturns of the COVID-19 pandemic in a common fiscal stimulus proposal funded by Eurobonds triggered the Next Generation EU bringing member states closer together in a fiscal union and stability solidarity pact (Alpert, 2021; Nagarajan, 2020; Stevis-Gridneff, 2020; Strupczewski & Abnett, 2020).

In addition to concerted EU action, the national governments of the Eurozone countries passed fiscal and monetary policy acts in line with directives from the European Central Bank. Germany enacted the – by far – largest fiscal stimulus and Economic Stabilization Fund within the Eurozone with liquidity constraint relief summing up to around US $950 billion (Alpert, 2021; Anderson et al., 2020; Benoit & Fairless, 2020; German Federal Ministry for Economic Affairs and Energy, 2020; German Federal Ministry of Finance, 2020; Reuters, 2020). Similar European Central Bank-conducted monetary and fiscal policy measures were performed in France, Italy, Spain, Austria and the Nordic countries with several subsequent stimulus and relief packages as the COVID-19 economic crisis unfolds (Alpert, 2021). European aid tends to strengthen the relatively more public administered healthcare system and union-protected workers throughout Europe – for instance, when thinking about the *Kurzarbeit* model that provides governmental funds for the industry to not lay off workers during the pandemic but shorten their worktime (Gelter & Puaschunder, 2021). In addition, Europe tends to support households directly, alongside granting business liquidity and social security aid (Gelter & Puaschunder, 2021).

The UK faced economic turmoil due to Brexit and trade re-negotiations during the onset of the pandemic. The Bank of England cut its benchmark interest rate twice to 0.1% and issued governmental and non-financial, investment corporate bonds in the range of US $567 billion (Alpert, 2021; Bank of England, 2020a, 2020b, 2020d, 2020e, 2020f, 2020g, 2020h, 2020i). Lending and asset-purchasing programs of the Bank of England aid to extend credit during the crisis, especially to small and medium-sized enterprises, with collaterals for the central bank (Alpert, 2021; Bank of England, 2020a, 2020b). For instance, the British Covid Corporate Financing Facility sets out to purchase commercial paper and counter-cyclical capital buffers to aid liquidity in the banking sector (Alpert, 2021; Bank of England, 2020c, 2020d, 2020e; Jones & Milliken, 2020). The UK fiscal stimulus comprises six packages totaling up to 18% of the UK GDP (Alpert, 2021; Szmigiera, 2021).

The US economy fell into recession in February 2020 in the wake of the news over COVID-19 and a worldwide evolving pandemic (Alpert, 2021; National Bureau of Economic Research, 2021a, 2021b). The US unemployment rate rose as high as 14.8% in April 2020, the highest since the Great Depression (Alpert, 2021; United States Bureau of Labor Statistics, 2020). As of August 2021, the unemployment rate was 5.4%, which was 1.9% above the 3.5% in pre-pandemic February from the previous year (Alpert, 2021; Statista, 2021). The US economy, as measured by real GDP, fell by 3.5% year-over-year (YOY) in 2020 exhibiting a shrinking trend for the first time on an annual basis since 2009 (Alpert, 2021; Federal Reserve Bank of St. Louis, 2021).

The US Federal Government responded to the crisis in the most extensive fiscal stimulus packages and emergency relief. The US Congress passed four special appropriations laws for the Federal Government to use in relief efforts, of which the largest was the Coronavirus Aid, Relief and Economic Security (CARES) Act, which provided approximately US $2.08 trillion in all-time-highest aid in North American history.

Governmental efforts were coupled with the Federal Reserve taking monetary stimulus measures to stabilize and boost the economy in incremental interest rate cuts and discount rate drops down to 0.25% and Federal Reserve repurchase agreement interest rate to 0% (Cox, 2021). Lending programs, loans and asset purchases as part of a US $700 billion quantitative easing plan and repurchasing options, as well as bonds financing and regulation changes, are meant to stabilize the market and foster liquidity (Alpert, 2021; Federal Reserve of the United States, 2020b; Smialek & Irwin, 2020). The ongoing direct aid programs sum up trillions of USD, of which US $2.56 trillion were spent by the US Federal Government as of March 31, 2021 (USASpending.Gov, 2021). A total of four laws included an estimated total of US $3.92 trillion funding for credit, loans and loan guarantee programs (USASpending.Gov, 2020).

The size, scope and dimensions of COVID-19 rescue and recovery plans are unprecedented and account for the historically largest concerted effort of action to avert the negative economic fallout to an external economic shock. In confronting the crisis and evaluating international and governmental rescue packages, the size of rescue and recovery aid has gained widespread attention for potential negative consequences, such as long-term debt and inflation. For instance, the quantitative dimensions and largess of governmental financialization of aid has led to star-economists Lawrence Summers[8] and Paul Krugman[9] arguing over the right size of the governmental intervention in economic stimulus (Brunnermeier Academy at the Princeton Bendheim Center for Finance, 2021; Coy, 2021). Summers points out at the sheer amount of stimulus that could set off inflationary pressures – a concern shared by other economists, such as Olivier Blanchard, a macro-economic expert on inflationary pressure (Blanchard, 2021; Schneider, 2021).

In the evaluation and monitoring of these unprecedentedly large amounts of governmental stimulus, economic bailout and rescue packages, socio-economic attention should also be paid to inequality in our COVID-19 shock era. COVID-19 has become the ultimate inequality accelerator due to changed demand patterns having resulted in economically gaining and losing industries. Sophisticated

---

[8]Harvard Economics Professor, former Vice President of Development Economics, Chief Economist of the World Bank, Senior US Treasury Department Official throughout US President William Clinton's administration, and former Director of the National Economic Council for US President Barack Obama in the 2008–2009 World Financial Recession.

[9]Nobel Prize winning Professor of Economics and columnist for *The New York Times*.

financial market tools have enabled finance experts to gain from shorting COVID-19 losing industries but also exchanging COVID-19 losing for pandemic winning industries in well-monitored funds and asset allocation options. In addition, the finance industry can use diversification of portfolio components but also hedge against COVID-19 losing industries. The real economy is stuck with less flexible obligations than financial assets. All these features widened an unexpected economic performance gap between the finance sector and the real economy that exacerbates an already prevailing trend of inequality between finance and real economy productivity and resiliency.

Systemically differing liquidity in finance and the real economy implies sector-specific affective fallout propensities. Currently experienced, longest-ever low interest rate regimes foster capital flow for innovation in the finance world, while disincentivizing household savings decreases private consumers' resiliency. Debt burdens and liquidity constraints in private households bring along negative behavioral aspects and destructive propensities, such as malnutrition, socio-psychological impairment, drug intake and suicidal considerations.

Industry-specific inflation patterns as well as urban-versus-rural disposable income differences in the wake of ambitious bailout and recovery plans should be considered when choosing bailout targets. The economic lens needs legal insights to adjust to unproportionally heavy and disparately severe impacts on certain populations, which should become the main focus of governmental rescue and recovery in short-term emergency aid. The potential focus of bailouts and recovery ranges from urban–local or national to even global and future-oriented beneficiaries, as pursued in public investments on climate stabilization in the GND or EGD or the Sustainable Finance Taxonomy (Puaschunder, 2022).

2.4.9. Inequality in the Socio-economic Fallout of COVID-19

The UBD identified the largest economic gap between world economies for at least 40 years during the outbreak of the COVID-19 pandemic 2020a, 2020b). Inequality is rising in terms of the quantitative output gap. Already now it also becomes apparent that the COVID-19 crisis is an accelerator to already existing inequality patterns. The COVID-19 external shock heightened economic disparity between nations, industries and societal groups that often have already existed prior to the crisis, but are now more accentuated – for instance, such as in access to corruption-free quality healthcare, subsidized preventive medicine and healthy nutrition but also in terms of access to digitalization benefits reaping within society and around the world (Puaschunder & Beerbaum, 2020a, 2020b).

While COVID-19 created significant health and security risks as well as economic costs, the pandemic also brought about unanticipated opportunities for specific market segments (Puaschunder et al., 2020a, 2020b). Some industries actually profited economically from the pandemic due to a heightened demand – for instance, such as hygiene producers, medical care facilities, pharmaceuticals including vaccination and medical supply chain providers and the medical professions curing widespread COVID-19 symptoms and chronic diseases arising from COVID-19 long haulers (Agrawal, Ahlawal, & Dewhurst, 2020; Lerner, 2020; Monck, 2020).

From an economic perspective, COVID-19 is an external shock that has accelerated ongoing digitalization trends (Puaschunder & Gelter, 2019). In light of the enormous potential to digitally monitor and track healthcare statuses worldwide and over time, big data offers enormous potential to detect the outbreak of pandemics early on but also the possibility to capture widespread health trends and general reactions to novel occurrences. In the medical sector, the individual condition can be put into perspective with other larger groups in order to derive inferences about the individual health status and outcome perspective of medical conditions. The digital age in its feature to detect information real-time in combination with unprecedented data storage opportunities and computation power in Bayesian analytics has created the most innovative advancements to improve human lives with digitalization. As never before in the history of humankind, individuals are now monitoring their health status in real time and find themselves online to evaluate medical goods and services together. Bluetooth technology tracking of medical devices helps with bottleneck allocation problems and combats fraudulent misuse of resources.

As the fear of a virus contagion through human contact led to lockdowns in all major economies around the globe, the power of digitalization became the source of touchpoint-less contact with the social compound during the pandemic. Because of widespread lockdowns, social distancing and increased home office work in many industries, social scientists have observed a more widespread acceptance of instant communication tools, social engagement and entertainment platforms (Corlatean, 2020). Robotics aided in patient care or have taken on everyday tasks of shelving groceries, administering checkouts or delivering items with drones.

Fear of attending hospitals or seeking medical aid in transmission points has broken a wave of telemedicine and healthcare information exchange online. Especially in the long hauler segment with novel, diffuse and often unclarified symptoms that come in waves, laypeople have turned to fast and easy information exchange in online social media self-help groups as visible in the Facebook Long Hauler Survivor Corps group – an open forum to discuss potential unfamiliar long haul COVID-19 symptoms and their fast remedy. These citizen scientists meet online to discuss their pressing symptoms and crowdsource information on currently evolving trends in medical, patient and personal care to then inform scientists based on their amalgamated narrative data (Dockser Marcus, 2021). Robotics and automated computer systems also promise to help COVID-19 long haulers navigate through a complex world during times of weakness and debilitation (Dockser Marcus, 2021). AI now offers amazing remedy opportunities to aid long haulers in dealing with information overload when waves of fatigue set in unexpectedly and somewhat unpredictably.

Overall, algorithms, robotics and big data have thus experienced an unprecedented use and widespread acceptance within society in the wake of COVID-19 addressed as the digitalization disruption of our new age renaissance (TU The Top Alumni Club Event, 2020). Digitalization accounts for the number one revolution winner in the wake of the COVID-19 pandemic.

Yet at the same time, digitalization brought along novel inequality determinants. The workforce is now more divided than ever on skills pegged to digitalization and AI–human compatibility skills. Those with better access to internet connectivity and AI–human compatibility (i.e., computer and AI literacy and related skills) have growing competitive advantages, which clearly accentuates the already pre-pandemic unprecedentedly growing gap between skilled and unskilled workers based on compatibility with novel technologies (Puaschunder, 2017d, 2017e, 2017i, 2019i, 2019k).

Talking about Coronavirus economic disparate impact, the COVID-19-induced lockdowns and workplace closures have also saved corporations on safety and security costs, maintenance and rent or leases (Ecowellness Group, 2020, 2021). While certain firms and industries have benefited from the pandemic, others have suffered from the expenses and burdens of COVID-19 (Bartik et al., 2020; Dua, Ellingrud, Mahajan, & Silberg, 2020; Kwak, 2020; Price, 2020). What differed from previous financial turmoil and economic crises was the fact that the economic fallout was not caused by financial constraints and economic fundamentals, but came out of an external shock that dampened the real economy activity and shifted demand extremely (International Monetary Fund, 2020a, 2020b; Lee, 2021; Ngai, 2020). Unprecedentedly clear inequality arose based on individual preconditions, social stratification and work parameters that shaped the outcome in meeting the pandemic. The crisis created a great divide between winning and losing market actors, societal groups, industries, nations and potentially also generations (Espitia, Rocha, & Ruta, 2020; World Bank, 2021). While we are still in the midst of the economic recovery and governmental market aid determining the economic outcome of the crisis, already now it has become apparent that the crisis appears to have widened the gap between financial market performance and real economy liquidity constraints.

2.4.10. *Finance Performance Versus Real Economy Constraints Gap*

Inequality between financial markets and real economy activities has already increased in society since the 1990s, in the USA in the aftermath of financial market deregulation (Chetty & Brunnermeier, 2020; Milanovic, 2016; Piketty, 2016). The financial world performance began to diverge massively from the real economy in 2008–2009 and experienced the greatest increase so far with the Coronavirus crisis that widened the gap between top performance of financial markets and negative socio-economic fallout in the real economy (*The Economist*, 2020a, 2020b). From the first economic shock during the Coronavirus crisis developed a striking and unexpected unequal financial market performance versus the real economy outcome that exacerbated during the recovery.

While the finance world seized its opportunity to benefit from the COVID-19 shock winning opportunities, the real economy experienced a liquidity crunch induced by lockdowns and halted consumption opportunities triggering waves of private bankruptcies and liquidity bottlenecks. Starting from the beginning of 2020, the novel Coronavirus caused a dramatic downturn for general consumption and service sector industries. Mobility, trade and tourism including gastronomy plummeted (Gössling, et al., 2020; Puaschunder et al., 2020). In the real economy, COVID-19 caused "social volatility" – a collectively depressed mood that largely cuts consumption and opportunistic spirit. Social distancing led to corporate temporal closures accompanied by massive layoffs – particularly in the service sector gastronomy and tourism industries. Employment fell below 70% in the mid-career segment of these industries. About 5% of European workers were on short-work schemes. Unemployment rose thanks to widespread *Kurzarbeit* labor protection plans, which encouraged firms to reduce work hours instead of laying off or furloughing workers (Jones et al., 2020). According to the OECD and Bloomberg, 19% of workers were furloughed in Great Britain, 23% in Germany and 41% in France (Jones et al., 2020; Mayhaw & Anand, 2020; Organisation for Economic Co-operation and Development (OECD), 2021). In more market-oriented territories, the impact was more severe.[10] For example, in Great Britain unemployment jumped from 3.8% to 5.4%, and in the USA from 3.7% to 8.9% (Congressional Research Service, 2020; Jones et al., 2020). Coupled with individual households being under lockdowns, consumption decreased by 46% in China, 97% in Germany and 20% in the USA, as well as 78% in Great Britain in the early months of the pandemic (Jones et al., 2020).

While the real economy faced economic constraints, the clear distinction between COVID-19 profit and loss industries made it possible for today's highly flexible financial world to quickly exchange weakened market segments – such as oil, public transport and aviation, face-to-face service sectors such as international hospitality and gastronomy – with above-average market options – such as pharmaceutical companies and emergency medical devices for healthcare, digital technologies, fintech, AI and big data analytics industries, online retail, automotive and interior design industries. Financial portfolio managers could simply diversify risks and exchange market losing segments for Coronavirus winning industries in well-managed funds and diversified flexible market options. Financial managers could use sophisticated techniques to short or hedge against an obvious decline in the price of clear COVID-19 losing industries.

The finance world was thus enabled to turn market losses into gains in their favor. Finance professionals were in a quicker-and-easier-to-regain position once the crisis hit and certain consumption propensities became apparent. Whereas the real economy just started to adapt to changing conditions as in most cases real economy agents were more bound in long-term obligations. Just imagine the difference in capital mobility between a portfolio investment and being a restaurant owner with complex long-term leases, on-the-job-trained employees and locked-in order contracts.

As clear difference to the previous financial market system – inherently caused recessions – such as the 2008–2009 World Financial Recession that mainly stemmed from turmoil in the finance sector and banking liquidity constraints – the

---

[10]Economy, Eurostat. Retrieved from https://ec.europa.eu/eurostat/web/covid-19/economy.

external COVID-19 shock surprised with an overly rapid recovery of well-managed financial funds. For instance, the Financial Times Stock Exchange Group, Dow Jones Industrial Average and Nikkei plummeted in the first quarter of 2020 drastically (Jones et al., 2020). At the same time, Deutsche Bank recorded rising earnings after the onset of Coronavirus crisis in Europe. Especially the investment bank branch saw rising earnings of 43% or €2.4 billion in the third quarter of 2020 (Smith, 2020). The S&P 500 recovered 50% of its pre-COVID-19 value within the first three months after the crisis, regained pre-pandemic levels by June 2020 and reached all-time high trends since August 2020.[11] Not to mention cryptocurrencies and crowdfunding options' unexpected unprecedented market performance.

In all these features, the strong inequality between COVID-19 winners and losers widened an already existing financial market versus real economy gap. Deep socio-psychological divides opened between strongly positive financial market developments and the negative socio-economic fallout that increased harmful lifestyle propensities of the real economy world.

2.4.11. Social Volatility and Affective Fallout Propensities Spread

Volatility is a measure of the amount of randomness in a financial quantity at any point in time (Lee, 2021). Volatility stems from the notion of fleeting and describes transitory market movements (Lee, 2021). As an indicator of financial well-being, volatility is a basis for evaluating the overall market climate and stock performance (Lee, 2021). Implied volatility is the market estimation of future volatility, which is associated with unpredictable market changes and an overall economic uncertainty (Lee, 2021).

While standard neoclassical theory defines volatility as a "standard deviation of stock prices" or "statistical dispersion of returns for a given security or market index," political, social and cultural influences also shape volatility (Lee, 2021). Social volatility adds a social dimension to this rational account of market uncertainty. Departing from notions that trading is purely based on financial rational calculus, the concept of social volatility captures collective interpretations of market performance (Lee, 2021). Imbuing a subjective element to probability estimations of events and their occurrences, social volatility thereby has a direct effect on economic outcomes, culture and society.

Social volatility stems from social affect and collective moods of emotional market actors, who react to information flows. Affect has a tremendous impact on the collective mood intensity and the quality of judgment around market conduct (Bergson, 1911, 1913; Deleuze & Guattari, 1987). Emotions, desires and passions play a role in breaking waves of economic trends. The popular imagination and expectation thereby create a buzz or steer that drives or crunches market actors' behavior (Lee, 2021). Weighing on one's beliefs and desires in the reflection of information provided about markets shapes individuals' intentions and actions.

---

[11]Ycharts. Retrieved from http://www.ycharts.com. Accessed on April 10, 2021.

Affective choices may lead to collective trends and sometimes to suboptimal economic outcomes (Lee, 2021).

Affect adds a qualitative dimension to volatility, which is missing in the belief–desire model of decision making under uncertainty (Bergson, 1911, 1913; Deleuze & Guattari, 1987). The belief–desire–intention model as the framework to analyze action and communication in markets explains market phenomena, such as herd behavior, panic selling and irrational exuberance around expectations creating bubbles (Akerlof & Shiller, 2009; Keynes, 1936/2003). Affect theory thereby offers an expandable understanding about the emotional sensibilities of collective information flow guiding individual decision making and the subsequent economic outcomes and societal propensities.

The importance of affect for market reactions and finance outcomes is prominently described in John Maynard Keynes' (1936/2003) notion of "animal spirits," capturing the collective irrational force that can underlie economic outcomes. George Akerlof and Robert Shiller (2009) build on the idea of collective moods influencing overall market performances. The New School Professor Benjamin Lee accounts the work of Giles Deleuze, Henri Bergson and Baruch Spinoza as the most important philosophical influences on the development of contemporary affect theory (Deleuze & Guattari, 1987; Lee, 2021). Brian Massumi explicitly used Spinoza, Bergson and Deleuze to create the theoretical parameters for affect theory and connected emotionality research to the finance world (Lee, 2021; Massumi, 1995, 2015).

The belief–desire model and moral philosophy notions influenced behavioral economics and behavioral finance theories (Puaschunder, 2020a). Affect also adds to behavioral economics, which is primarily based on the study and description of mental shortcuts that often lead to suboptimal choices. The behavioral economics empirical validation of affective decision making to impact individual economic choices started with Daniel Kahneman and Amos Tversky (1974, 1979, 2000). Behavioral economics experiments and empirical fieldwork discovered that individuals systemically do not behave rationally as for being tainted by heuristics, framing and affective biases (Kahneman & Tversky, 1974, 1979, 2000). Belief–desire models were introduced in Daniel Kahneman's flow model that attributed affect as an influence on decision making (Kahneman & Tversky, 1974, 1979, 2000). Behavioral choice models also integrated unconscious biases and social volatility based on time prospects and money use (Kahneman & Tversky, 1974, 1979, 2000).

The belief–desire model and decision making under uncertainty became the dominant framework for subjectivity in quantitative finance. Affect theory rose to prominence out of the wish to understand irrational group behavior in the wake of the 2008–2009 World Financial Recession and market sentiments tainted by Brexit (Lee, 2021).

Today's affect theory in economics and finance proponents are Laura Berlant and Sianne Ngai – in her most recent book *Gimmick* – both authors connect affective fallouts to finance prospects and derive subsequent behavioral response propensities (Berlant, 2011; Ngai, 2020). Ann Case and Angus Deaton provide evidence for the negative emotional consequences of economic disparate impacts and rising inequality in the American society (Case & Deaton, 2020; Ngai, 2020; Piketty, 2016).

Social volatility levels and emotional fallout to economic crises differ drastically within society. Different emotionality propensities in the eye of market communication about the overall economic state are grounded in different opportunity conditions and flexibility degrees of freedom that vary between different social groups. The intensity and nature of emotionality propensities changed dramatically during the COVID-19 pandemic between those invested in financial markets and those who derive income from real economy labor activities, especially in the service sector or professions with large crowd entertainment. The emotional ebbs and flows during times of crises vary by a professional challenge. The extent and intensity of sensations about contemporary events create a gap between capital and labor. The same events are experienced in differing emotional states due to high market profits for financial gains and liquidity constraints imposed in the real economy.

Csikszentmihalyi (2003) found high-skilled individuals indulging in high challenges, while low-skilled individuals are more likely to experience work stress. In Csikszentmihalyi's *Flow of Everyday Experience*, highly skilled individuals grow on challenges, which are experienced as "flow" moments that create positive reinforcement loops via enjoyable emotions, while low-skilled workers are facing apathy, worry and anxiety alerts, stresses and depressions when hitting constraints (Csikszentmihalyi, 2003). Csikszentmihalyi (2003) suggests that being "in the zone" and "in flow" occurs when there is an optimal alignment of goals and abilities. People then get positively absorbed by a task.

In light of the current economic situation, the ebbs and flows of affective intensities thereby form certain decision-making qualities and affectual propensities that draw silos of experiences, which differ between societal classes. This prepares the argument that flow underlines the distinguishing factor between those who can afford long-term considerations in markets whereas others become negatively emotional in their decision making under tight constraints.

Time plays a crucial role in the social division of affectual propensities. Financial market proponents or capitalist-industrialists appear to have more long-term possibilities and constant financial streams in light of the unprecedentedly long and large rescue and recovery efforts than consumption-constraint individual consumer-workers. The finance world is specialized in discounting future value and can thereby maintain longer-term planning, whereas real economy agents are more prone to depend on a constant salary stream, which is required to consume and maintain a standard of living. Volatility is thereby grounded in a flow model driven by affect that creates a differing sense of time. Different societal groups face different propensities to be holders of opportunities and to have a long-term view in personal finance and opportunities to derive personal gains from overall market losses. Other distinguishing factors are the turnover time and need of capital as well as the obligation to pay for production and consumption goods of workers in the real economy.

It is therefore assumed that financial analysts are the ones prone to rational thinking capacity during times of economic upheaval. In the real economy, employees and workers are bound to work for a salary in order to fulfill their day-to-day needs and wants. The holders of the means of production – for instance, factory owners and service sector managers – are likely facing long-term contracts and obligations that they cannot exit or ward off easily.

The ones engaged primarily in capital gains have the luxury of flexibility to exchange losing for winning stocks in well-managed funds or diversify their portfolio. They are the ones who can wait out and suspect the implied volatility of underlying market options as better estimators of future market performance. And the finance world can turn market downers into profits in shorting and hedging options over time. For all these flexibilities, the finance world stays detached from emotionality given the possibility to hedge, short against and spread risks via diversification of more fungible assets that are not needed to be liquidated to cover day-to-day expenses.

The anthropologist Caitlin Zaloom (2006) describes the riding on the ebbs and flows of socially shared affects constructing economic up and down swings (Lee, 2021). Instincts of traders and market actor's engagement in capital for investment determine the better understanding and profiting from natural rhythms of financial fluctuation (Lee, 2021; Zaloom, 2006). Dynamic traders can thereby outperform the market in an understanding of collective moods bleeding into collective action influencing market outcomes (Ayache, 2008; Lee, 2021). Surfing volatility thereby becomes a skill of those using money to make money (Csikszentmihalyi, 1990; Lee, 2021; Zaloom, 2006).

While the finance world experiences a confidence boost thanks to diversification, shorting and hedging potential during economic frictions triggering rescue and recovery aid during the Coronavirus outfall, the real economy suffers from closeness to real-world experiences and real-world salary stream dependency. Real economy proponents have real skin in the economic game as their everyday life expenses are more likely to depend on salaries. Facing a propensity to a loss of confidence during a pandemic in the eye of real-life constraints, real economy dependent market actors have therefore a propensity to negative emotional fall-outs during economic crises. Real economy dependent producers and workers are more likely to react emotionally negatively given their constraint budgets and perceived lack of degrees of freedom. Industrialist-capitalists enjoy a longer time horizon but are also more likely stuck in long-term obligations and constraint by budget lock-ins.

The problem of a gap between the finance world and the real economy highlights a distinction of classes within society. The propensities of classes in markets determined by either being a finance world agent or real economy worker are either emotionless or filled with affect in the eye of a pandemic. These two classes that either gravitate toward wealth and relaxation flow or poverty and negative excitement during crises determine either ego-boosting or self-depleting behavioral response propensities during a crisis. While economic crises are absolved by awareness and relatively less emotional content in the finance world, the hypervigilance and tension of the real economy due to real world constraints and inflexible obligations create an unequal emotional outburst that is related to certain patterns of involuntary reflexes and behaviors. The real economy seems to suffer from loss of confidence with personal affective states in times of crises given their threats to well-being, while the finance world has a powerful anti-affective force of crisis gain potential that invigorates flow in control of the situation. The affective reconstruction of the reality varies between the two worlds of finance with hope and real economy facing loss and risk aversion during a crisis. These two propensity trajectories and narratives exist concurrently in experiencing a common crisis together.

Affective states taint the conditions of life and how decisions play out in the lived time. The affective moments saturate the cognitive processes that lead to different subjectivities of reality and guide different behaviors. A common historical moment thereby appears as a diverse visceral moment in assessing the diverse opportunities and risk prospects of different professional groups. A shared atmosphere of a cluster of opportunities determines a pattern of navigating in markets. The different patterns of affective responses thereby leverage into the structural divide in economies struck by an external shock (Nassif-Pires, de Lima Xavier, Masterson, Nikiforos, & Rios-Avila, 2020; Nikiforos, 2020). The convergence between the affective response and economic differences creates zones of inequality in society inherent in external shocks and subsequent crises' differing outfall (Nassif-Pires et al., 2020; Nikiforos, 2020).

The inequalities of contemporary capitalism lie in the emotional state of the real economy and the rational mastery of the finance world that gets exacerbated in the dynamic relations of social crowds and clans. While the finance world is more likely to be detached from real world financial constraints, the real economy suffers from a collective trauma in the face of threats and catastrophes in their everyday lives and the higher risk propensities of precarity.

The slow death of despair analogy refers to the emotional fallout in the eye of time and money constraints of the real economy working class (Berlant, 2011; Case & Deaton, 2020). Slow deaths occur due to the emotional mindset of the working class, who are more prone to lack peace of mind for reproduction and/or preventive care in exercise or healthy food intake during an economic crisis (Berlant, 2011; Case & Deaton, 2020; Ngai, 2020; United States Centers for Disease Control and Prevention (CDC), 2020). Consumption and self-medication are more likely to become the stress relief mechanism in order to cope with the difficulty of contemporary life, which varies between different professional groups. Real economy profit extraction of workers exhausts the workers' bodies and feeds the affect to give in to impulsive everyday pleasure consumption, which can amalgamate to slowly growing diseases or chronic debilitating conditions (Berlant, 2011; Case & Deaton, 2020).

This socio-economic fragility also plays out in novel digital media handling divides. In today's unprecedentedly digitalized world, online media consumption and affect elicited through online virtual media news on insecurity and uncertainty may have a profound impact on individual's lives and determine the individual's consumption patterns. Collective moods created online in instant and global information sharing constituting social volatility are a sign of our globalization time, in which reflexive communication on social media tools has created novel socio-economic pressures (Harvey, 1990; Lee, 2021).

As the internet offers unprecedented opportunities to blast information instantaneously and truly globally, there seems to be volatility introduced by digital technologies in the contemporary culture and politics of finance (Lee, 2021). The internet with its social media and search engine information flow has steadily increased the turnover time of information (Lee, 2021). Lee (2021, p. 70) therefore concludes that the "fractal butterfly effects become increasingly commonplace." The overflow of "availability cascades" has become the norm rather than the exception (Lee, 2021, p. 70). Digital technologies speed up the widespread transmission of information about volatility. Social contexts then echo the collective sensual activity in light of events that get transmitted and reinforced in social media. Affective scenarios are emphasized in social discourses via instant messaging within social bubbles and group-specific silos that reciprocate emotions and feelings about the economic outlooks and cultivate social norms sector-specifically. The representation and transmission of positivity or negativity about the same event are constantly updated in real-time within different societal groups. So while the overall narrative may be similar – such as an external shock in a pandemic – the different social groups may create differing social representations that are laden by a set of different emotions that echo in social online platforms about them (Puaschunder, 2021a). Emotions and moods thereby build up in large mass cultures and subgroups via new technologies that are constantly and reflexively scanned for news and information and that change on a periodic basis. Instant communication media thus proliferates world realities about the current state of the world in our common modes of living. The financial traders notice implied volatilities and can use it for their favor in their long-term vision; while the real-world dependent worker gets emotionally laden and is turned to self-destructive choices. This kind of novel social volatility, and also the class divide in those who can handle social volatility more relaxed versus emotional, account for an increasing phenomenon as digital technologies unfold around the globe exponentially and information transfer speeds up unprecedentedly. Inequality of emotionality accounts for the most rising social trend of our pandemic times, which is almost not captured in the standard economics and finance literature but has vast impacts on individual behavior determining collective well-being and hence welfare of society (Puaschunder, 2021a). The emotional fallout propensities are exacerbated by a disparate impact of inflation and low interest rate regimes on different groups within society as discussed in the following.

2.4.12. Inflation

"Inflation is the decline of purchasing power of a given currency over time" (Fernando, 2021). This sustained increase in the general level of prices for goods and services in a country occurs when a national money supply growth outpaces economic growth (Fernando, 2021). Inflation, measured as an annual percentage change, indicates that a unit of currency effectively buys less than it did in prior periods (Fernando, 2021). In inflation, prices of goods and services rise over time, purchasing power decreases and people are incentivized to spend money, which boosts the circulation of money and thereby market activities and subsequently economic growth.

Inflation is widely considered to have an inverse relation to unemployment (Armstrong, Glyn, & Harrison, 1991; Brenner, 2003). The Fisher effect outlines the inverse relation between interest rates and inflation (Hayes, 2020). Central banks around the world engage in the monetary tool of inflation targeting to hold inflation at a certain level, most likely around 2–3% per year, to ensure a continuous standard of living for all market actors (Jahan, 2021). Especially in regard to lead currencies – such as the USD, the Eurozone Euro, the UK Pound Sterling, the Swiss Franc and the Australian Dollar – inflation can have vast impacts on the affordability of goods and services in countries that are pegged to these lead currencies.

Our current economic time features prevalent macro-economic drivers of inflation in the prevailing central bank money supply boom, demand pull, cost push and monetary debasement (Crescat Capital, 2021). Around the world, central banks and governments are lowering interest rates to produce liquidity across the globe. By far all-time-high global central bank assets creation reached US $31 trillion for the first time in 2021 (Crescat Capital, 2021). The US issuance of treasury bonds hit unprecedented high levels, while the US Federal Reserve continued monetizing debt through large quantitative easing programs creating excess money supply adding to inflation (Crescat Capital, 2021).

Inflation is caused by an oversupply of money in the economy. Just like any other commodity, the prices of money are determined by supply and demand. If there is too much money supply, the price of money goes down and its purchasing power decreases, leading to the prices of everything else priced getting more expensive.

Built-in inflation may trigger a wage–price spiral, which occurs when workers demand higher wages to keep up with rising living costs. This in turn causes businesses to raise their prices in order to offset their rising wage costs, leading to a self-reinforcing loop of wage and price increases (Crescat Capital, 2021). Demand-pull inflation refers to situations where there are not enough products or services being produced to keep up with demand, causing their prices to increase (Crescat Capital, 2021). Currently, demand is expected to skyrocket after household savings peaked throughout the end of 2020 coupled with consumer spending unleashed throughout 2021 (Crescat Capital, 2021). Trends already project 7.5 times higher the historical average annual spending adjusted for inflation for 2021. Prices surged with the grand re-opening of the economy after the Coronavirus crisis and hightened interest rates then tamed inflation, which remained sticky as for supply chain members continuing on a higher price regime (Crescat Capital, 2021).

Inflation is also likely caused when corporate costs of production increase, forcing businesses to raise their prices to maintain their profit margins. Production during pandemic constraints has likely increased costs including wages, taxes and natural resources, imports and safety of labor. Supply shortages occurred during lockdown. Production disruptions and consumption patterns shifted abruptly in the beginning of the external shock of COVID-19 (Helper & Soltas, 2021). Labor shortages also occurred in key qualified frontline workers as well as professions with a vast array of human touchpoints (Whelan, 2021). Pro-active care for maintaining a healthy workforce and the overall long-term well-being of employees, including preventive care in teams, will become an essential corporate feature to attract qualified labor, whose bargaining power increases in the eye of labor shortages in human-facing industries and positions (Ghilarducci, 2021; Whelan, 2021). The COVID-19 long haul prospect and prolonged COVID-19 pandemic have risen US job openings to historic highs and the share of US corporations not being able to fill positions has increased to 15%, which accounts for a record highest rate ever measured (Ghilarducci, 2021; Whelan, 2021). At the same time, more workers are quitting with the job quits rate at 2.7% in June 2021 (Whelan, 2021). In addition, the US retail inventory to retail sales ratio has been at an all-time low and labor-management conflicts are expected to rise with the widening of the finance market versus real economy gap assumed to become even more accentuated in the future (Crescat Capital, 2021).

Monetary debasement is another driver of inflation that currently adds inflationary pressure to the US economy featuring a twin deficit of 25% of the nominal GDP (Crescat Capital, 2021). Corporate debt has grown to near all-time highs while bond yields remain near all-time lows (Crescat Capital, 2021). Excess liquidity in the market has created one of the most speculative investment environments of all times with cryptocurrencies and social online media playing a peculiar, novel role in overheating markets. At the same time, commodities, such as food and beverage, which already had elevated price levels since 2000 and experienced a significant rise during the 2008–2009 World Financial Recession that has not adjusted to previous levels, have exhibited vertical price spikes throughout the pandemic (Cox, 2021). Adding to commodities price explosions, the aggregate free cash flow for the top 50 gold and silver miners is now growing exponentially (Cox, 2021). With growing concerns of monetary debasement emerging, investors continue to bid up commodity prices, leading to higher consumer prices (Cox, 2021). In addition, the S&P 500 earnings yield adjusted for the consumer price index (CPI) is now at its most negative level in 30 years, which has been attributed to as an understated measure of true inflation (Cox, 2021).

Understanding the role of the exponential rise in prices for the stability of the underlying economy is key when trying to avoid historical examples of the past, such as the hyperinflation during the interwar period of the first quarter of the twentieth century (Hayes, 2021). International transmissions of inflation are discussed in historic examples to build adaptive expectations on information about current and past experiences with inflation (Hall & Soskice, 2001; Soskice, 1978). Disequilibrium inflation occurs when the actual rate of inflation is greater than the expected followed by social unrest and industrial conflict (Hall & Soskice, 2001; Soskice, 1978). As a more recent positive example, during the 2008–2009 World Financial Recession, the US Federal Reserve dropped its interest rate target to close to zero, and then was forced to use unconventional monetary policy tools including quantitative easing as an emergency measure to stimulate the economy and prevent it from tumbling into a deflationary spiral (Cox, 2021; Federal Reserve Bank of St. Louis, 2015). Treasure bonds issuance was used in order to avoid a free fall inflationary price drop (Federal Reserve Bank of St. Louis, 2015). Due to the treasury bonds issuance and trust in the US economic performance, the

US government remained intact as the economy continued an overall productive pace during the period of the Great Recession and only saw very modest increases in inflation (Cox, 2021; Federal Reserve Bank of St. Louis, 2015).

A potential wage–price spiral – such as the one in the 1970s – is likely to be followed in the decades to come, driving investment in raw materials, real-estate and innovative finance options, such as cryptocurrencies (Crescat Capital, 2021). The number of companies mentioning inflation in earnings calls and people searching for the term "inflation" on Google is growing at a pace as never before, which feeds into the general population not feeling confident to hold cash or save money in the bank accounts (Crescat Capital, 2021). This kind of behavior spurs large-scale investment and/or highly risky myopic growth consumption – such as in investments in cryptocurrencies – fueling further bubble build-up potential. All these developments shape economic booms and busts. The underlying market behavior, however, is hardly understood or covered in the standard economic or finance literature (Crescat Capital, 2021; Keynes, 1936/2003; Puaschunder, 2017g). Yet, information about the economy is key in shaping collective moods that determine individual market actors' propensity to consume or invest, which leads to specific underlying economic long-term cycles and their positive or negative socio-economic fallout propensities.

While economics offers multiple accounts on the relationship of inflation with interest rate dynamics and purchasing behavior shifts in various inflation rate scenarios, less is known about inflationary effects on different social strata. Inflation affects different people in different ways, with some benefiting from its effects at the expense of others who relatively lose out. Inflation therefore can be viewed positively or negatively depending on the individual viewpoint and rate of change.

Obviously, creditors (the lenders of funds) are in a less favorable position when it comes to the value of money than debtors (the borrowers of funds) economically if considering the overall purchasing power of creditors declines over time, while the overall debt burden for the borrower declines with time. Higher inflation thus harms savers because it erodes the purchasing power of the money they have saved in their accounts and benefits borrowers because the inflation-adjusted value of their outstanding debts shrinks over time (Fernando, 2021). But this effect is a rather economic mechanism, in which creditors lose degrees of freedom over time by decreasing the purchasing power of the funds they expect to receive back. Higher inflation can trigger two scenarios: for one, inflation encourages spending, as consumers will aim to purchase goods quickly before their prices rise further. Savers, on the other hand, could see the real value of their savings erode, limiting their ability to spend or invest in the future (Fernando, 2021).

What is missing in economic writing is attention to the psychological account of debtors, who often cannot afford purchases on their own, lock themselves in debt repayment prisons and lower their purchasing power freedom to reallocate funds over time. Never having the financial means to finance large-scale choices flexibly but constantly having to pay back old debt puts individuals in a backward-looking prison of constant debt repayment of past needs and wants. When people are facing to spend in the real economy on debt, they create a debt burden. With debt burdens, they live financing shadows of their past consumption choices.

Then life somehow goes backwards and rests in the yesterday. Capital being the withheld consumption today grants future flexibility of consumption. Consumption that does not result in debt may grant peace of mind rather than imposing emotionality in the face of long-term constraints (Csikszentmihalyi, 2003). Money at hand thus is psychic energy released at the holder's discretion giving the ultimate freedom of future-oriented choice (Csikszentmihalyi, 2003).

In the international arena, inflation is a double-edged sword for import and export industries. Inflation declines a national currency's value, which benefits exporters by making their goods more affordable when priced in the currency of foreign nations. Inflation at the same time harms importers by making foreign-made goods more expensive (Fernando, 2021). Thus, inflation is neither good nor bad – it more depends on if your revenue or purchasing power is based on imports or exports.

Inflation hits metropolitan populations harder than rural populations, not only in the general price levels but the relative income spent on living expenses. The currently found economic Doughnut effect speaks about richer metropolitan segments having moved out of cities to live in suburbs (hence the Doughnut) during the COVID-19 pandemic, while poorer individuals, who cannot afford relocation costs remain in the city and are more likely to have lost the income sources stemming from richer populations' purchasing power (Ramani & Bloom, 2021).

Inflation effects also depend on whether inflationary changes are anticipated or unanticipated. For instance, when considering that the re-negotiation of contracts may take a certain period of time. The question here is not whether inflation occurs but who has the flexibility to renegotiate salaries and other transfer payments for living expense conditions at what pace. People living off a fixed-income or social welfare payment beneficiaries – such as those on food stamps, governmental welfare programs, retirees and annuitants, see a sticky – hence hardly or slowly change over time, or non-renegotiable decline in purchasing power that is likely not adjusted for inflation fast enough or at all. People being able to renegotiate their terms or – again – people with savings that can wait out negotiations benefit more from inflation than those who are constraint and pay off old mortgages under tight budget constraints, resulting in decreased negotiation power and likely facing high costs for refinancing or a personal bankruptcy, which may lead to social misery and self-harming choices.

Those with tangible assets – like property or stocked commodities – benefit from moderate inflation as these asset holdings' values are likely to increase with inflation (Cassim et al., 2020; Passy, 2021; The White House of the United States of America, 2021b, 2021c). People holding cash may typically prefer no inflation, as it erodes the value of their cash holdings (Fernando, 2021). Homeowners and landlords rather benefit from inflation, especially if homeownership is built on a fixed-interest or no mortgage. Housing prices tend to rise in inflationary markets and homeowners are able to raise the rent each year or lease term (Cassim et al., 2020; Passy, 2021; The White House of the United States of America, 2021b).

So the discussion of our time should not be about whether the size of the quantity of money established to aid and back economic recovery will likely cause inflation but to whom transfer payments should be redirected in order to offset the negative disparate impact of inflation. It is thus not to label inflation good or bad per se but to rather educating people about their own personal situation and aid in their decisions to navigate in the jungle of finance more strategically in a fast-paced and ever-changing world.

2.4.13. Interest rate

Government bailout packages are partially financed via debt and a historically lowest, never-so-long-low key interest rate for savings after the COVID-19 pandemic to spur (Blanchard, 2017; Puaschunder, 2021c). The USA, but also other major economies around the world faced historically low interest rates for savings below growth rates (Blanchard, 2017; Puaschunder, 2021c).

Low interest rates allow investors and industry professionals to borrow money for innovative corporate and financial endeavors, which will overall boost the economy and provide a vital liquidity stream for the finance sector (Keynes, 1936/2003). Falling interest rates lubricate the spread of capital across the globe and foster innovative activities by heightening the prospect of a net rate of profit. The economist John Maynard Keynes (1936/2003) described the underlying subjective and objective factors of aggregate consumption patterns and factors that influence individual savings propensities. Subjective factors are the desire to save for future consumption and contingencies, to use passive and speculative investment to expand future income, to amass wealth, and for some, even to enjoy miserliness (Keynes, 1936/2003). Objective factors include windfall gains or losses, taxation, price controls, expectations and changes in the interest rate (Shaikh, 2016). Institutional and organizational factors shape and channel all such factors.

In Keynes' (1936/2003) General Theory, the interest rate is subjective and interest rates are linked with each other by maturity (Shaikh, 2016). Keynes (1936/2003) postulates the interest rate being determined by subjective preferences and the price of a commodity is based on the cost of its production (Shaikh, 2016). In Keynes (1936/2003), prices and the interest rate are based on expectations of how the market will perform (Puaschunder, 2019h, 2019i; Shaikh, 2016). The government can step in by reducing the interest rate to override the fall in confidence through investment stimulus (Keynes, 1936/2003; Shaikh, 2016). A low interest rate regime may crowd out capital accumulation and spur financial investment flows (Keynes, 1936/2003; Shaikh, 2016).

At the same time, a cut in interest rates also fuels international bubbles in finance and real estate as well as leads to consumers being incentivized to spend rather than save, which puts them at risk of lowered resilience in times of crises (Passy, 2021). Excessive borrowing may also imply that corporations and governments become excessively indebted, which raises liquidity constraints and market risks. When investing stops and elevated debt levels become endemic, banking liquidity and governmental credit decreases and the economy will enter a system-inherently-induced recession, such as the market downturn in 2008–2009. When savings interest rates are low and public debt accumulates, social welfare costs arise in debt rollovers, which crowds out capital accumulation and implies missed welfare opportunities in the future (Blanchard, 2017).

Low key interest rates will continue to spread the inequality gap of the finance world versus the real economy performance. Low interest rates and access to capital will allow the capital market to flourish based on incentivized liquidity and access to venture capital. Long low interest rate regimes will – at the same time – weaken the potential of the interest rate as a monetary policy tool of central banks. The macro-economic ineffectiveness of lowering an already low interest rate even further was first described by Keynes (1936/2003) as a "liquidity trap" at the beginning of the twentieth century during the Great Depression. The blasé consumer sentiment over a marginal decline of an already low interest rate was also discussed by Ben Bernanke during his term as the Chairman of the Federal Reserve during the 2008–2009 Financial Recession.

From the hardly captured socio-psychological standpoint, a low interest rate promotes a rise in consumer debt. With falling interest rates and credit being made easier, consumers and other spending continue to rise. A low interest rate policy thereby brings along long-term external financing of past ideas, which impairs the flexibility of investors to allocate liquidity to future-oriented innovations and may hold back societal progress and thus actually decrease general welfare in the long run (Blanchard, 2017). A rising tide of debt also increases the likelihood of real economy constraints and subsequently financial market crashes if people realize that endemic debt levels are no longer sustainable.

The Austrian School of Economics describes excessive issuance of bank credit as a driver of crises in banking systems (Schumpeter, 1934, 1943/1976, 1949, 1989). Excessive issuance of bank credit is exacerbated if central bank monetary policy sets interest rates too low. The resulting expansion of money supply causes a boom, in which resources are misallocated because of artificially low interest rates and inflation rise. This unsustainable boom is followed by a bust, in which malinvestments are liquidated below their original costs and the money supply contracts and then the financial market system collapses.

Different groups in society may have different outlooks on the same information. While financially versed parts of the population may experience the COVID-19 economic fallout as an opportunity – given modern finance tools and methods such as shorting, derivatives and diversification – the real economy may hit stronger feelings in the eye of uncertainty given the lower levels of degrees of freedom fueled by low interest rates (Lee & Martin, 2016; LiPuma & Lee, 2004). What is new to this argument nowadays, is the fact that we are seeing massive socio-psychological burdens in private households these days in the middle class of the USA (Case & Deaton, 2020). Consumer debt tends to create lurking social misery in the long run that has a socio-psychological propensity fallout for sub-optimal choices, decisions with negative overall impact over time and self-destructively harmful behavior. A so-coined "deaths of despair" trend is already noticed in the USA for mid-career population segments that face death spikes induced by alcoholism, drug use and suicide – all problems that have been exacerbated during the COVID-19 pandemic (Case & Deaton, 2020; United States Centers for Diseases Control and Prevention, 2020). Low interest rates on savings accounts in the real economy keep people trapped in the debt financing of past aspirations (Arora, 2020). Private household debt traps differ from public or governmental debt as the Ricardian equivalent points out in intergovernmental entities' ability to issue bonds and roll over debt to future generations in comparison to private household entities (Blanchard, 2017). Financial managers may therefore currently benefit from the low interest regimes in access to capital at the socio-psychological fall-out expense of the real economy and in the eye of an overall market insecurity risk implied in low interest rate regimes in the long run.

One related theory that was brought forward recently was the idea of Sianne Ngai's (2020) Gimmicks that give a tableau of illusions that do not add up to reality (Case & Deaton, 2020). Gimmicks include the camouflage of unequal expansion of capitalist gains and economic opportunities by mass media, literature, television, film, video and art to social media online that procreates cultures of aspirations that actually make people unhappy in the long run (Ngai, 2020). Good life fantasies and lifestyle aspirations in a low interest rate climate may create prisons of debt for indebted consumers who spend their whole life paying off bills of previous choices based on past aspirations. Their consumption patterns and financial flows psychologically go backwards in time. This cruelty in the optimism portrayed in media created by capitalist machineries may be associated with the so-called "death of despair" – rising numbers of self-induced deaths in the young middle class through such means as alcohol, drug intake and suicide noticeable in today's capitalist society (Berlant, 2011; Case & Deaton, 2020; Ngai, 2020; United States Centers for Disease Control and Prevention, 2020).

2.4.14. Responsible Finance: Targeted Rescue, Recovery and Relief Aid

The trends of abruptly changed demand patterns having unexpectedly widened the economic performance gap between the finance sector and the real economy, differing flexibility and liquidity potentials between finance and the real economy implying sector-specific affective fallout propensities but also the currently experienced longest-ever low interest rate and industry-specific inflation patterns all lead to the quest for a closer analysis of the disparate impact of the COVID-19 pandemic in the distribution decision of rescue and recovery funding. Governmental rescue and recovery aid should be informed by the results of the analysis of the diversified impact of economic variables on specific societal groups. When contemplating on the targeted rescue and relief efforts of governments and public institutions, the focus of the aid should be guided by a whole-rounded effect analysis.

Economic crises in the wake of pandemics are intensified situations with extensive threats to survival, economic resilience and heightened risk of social upheaval. The distribution of funds thus highly depends on the geopolitical and biopolitical locations as well as the socio-economic starting ground. The distinction into social classes of crises is structural and should include the role of affect – which materializes in emotional excitement caused by crises in some parts of the population and emotionless rational response in others that determines health and well-being whole-roundedly and over time.

As a first start in a stratified economic impact analysis, governmental officials currently face decisions whether to target funds and policy aid on the local versus rural versus urban level, national versus international prospect as well as the immediate versus the long-term beneficiaries, as pursued in public investments on climate stabilization efforts underlying the GND or EGD or the Sustainable Finance Taxonomy (Barbier, 2009; Earthworks, 2019; European Commission, 2019; Pargendler, 2020).

2.4.15. Urban–Local–Regional and National Focus

In the decade prior to the COVID-19 pandemic, globalization already slowed. From 2010 onwards, a trend called "slowbalization" depicted stagnant or declining international trade, finance and profits abroad (D'Urbino, 2019). The rising "glocalisation" of consumers meant that purchasing decisions were more focused on the local production (Abe, 2020; D'Urbino, 2019; Gertz, 2020; Lighthizer, 2020; McDonald, 2020; Shalal, Alper, & Zengerle, 2020; Theodosopoulos, 2020). CSR pledges had gotten informed and environmentally conscientious consumers supported their communities in leveraging shopping as a quasi-democratic and personal choice act (Puaschunder, 2017g). As the internet online window to the world sheds light on production conditions abroad, in many developed jurisdictions, firms felt increasingly compelled by political pressure to re-shore production and localize global value chains (Ryan, 2019). Contagion risks became apparent as shadows of the invisible hand vividly outline in the 2008–2009 World Financial Recession financial spill-overs. Food insecurity emerging out of commodity prices' international interdependence and global health safety risks in spreading diseases in an increasingly mobile population are additional globalization negative externalities and risks (Centeno, Cinlar, et al., 2013).

Newest trends that gained prominence during the COVID-19 lockdowns couple architecture with being close to nature and living in harmony with the local community. People have become more local than ever before in the history of modern technologies. Agri-hoods spread all over the world as organized communities began to integrate agriculture into a residential neighborhood. These closed eco-systems are communities that facilitate local food production and consumption as well as provide shared recreational facilities for its local community members (Ecowellness Group, 2021). Agri-hoods are extraordinarily popular with millennials, who master global mindsets online with having grown up using the internet and instant communication tools more than any other generation before (Agritecture, 2021; Garden Destinations, 2021). In their real lives though, millennials seem to long for supporting a local, non-complex world, in which they like to enjoy harmony with the given nature around and their local community. As of May 2020, there were already 90 agri-hoods in the USA and another 27 are planned. In their own living spaces, individuals tend to enjoy closeness to nature (New Hope Village & Farm, 2021). Biophilia designs have skyrocketed during the pandemic. Biophilic designs resemble nature within the private living space – such as in cork or wood but also fungus and plants around (Pearlman, 2021).

Since 2016, nationalism emerged in homeland-first and EU-exit sentiments (Profita, 2019). The ongoing Coronavirus crisis exacerbated these trends of slowing globalization by putting an abrupt halt to global mobility and migration (Puaschunder, 2020c, 2021d). Currently economic arguments for nationalism are experiencing a renaissance (Gelter, 2021). Foreign direct investments already declined even in the decade prior to the Coronavirus era (D'Urbino, 2019). Governmental ownership to defend against takeovers and large-scale governmental bailout packages to rescue struggling industries have gained unprecedented momentum in the wake of the crisis. All these signs point to nationalism having become a focus of governmental attention for distributing bailouts and recovery funds. COVID-19 has strengthened nationalist impulses and outlines that protectionist policies are not always detrimental (Gelter, 2021). Infant-industry protectionism but also our times of the pandemic crisis recovery arose that the idea of nationalism appears somewhat favorable (Gelter, 2021). Benefits of a local regional and national focus of attention are to keep foreign political influences but also international competitors that establish market dominance out of one's own territory. International competition on national soil can be harmful to breeding a country's own innovation (Chang, 2002). Just contributing to a part of the production chain may crowd out learning-by-doing at work and erode the social compact (Chang, 2002).

A protectionist view allows to first focus on allocating funds solely to one's own territory and work with the existing talent pool and resources, which hones skills that may trickle down in multiplier effects into the own economy (Keynes, 1936/2003; Mazzucato, 2013). In crisis mode, firms can benefit from being embedded into local business networks and a close relationship with the respective government that helps them to become more resilient (Gelter, 2021). Since the economic disturbances from the pandemic are not disappearing entirely and further economic shocks are likely to recur, it may be beneficial for countries to establish resilient structures for firms on one's own grounds that help them to survive crises, even if they come at the expense of traditional efficiency goals in corporate governance (Gelter, 2021). The local or domestic network simply offers a smaller, easier to control regulatory focus – especially when the world and interactive effects appear highly complex in a fast-paced changing pandemic crisis climate.

2.4.16. Global and Future-oriented Beneficiaries Focus

The COVID-19 external shock that released the largest and most widespread economic recovery aid and rescue packages worldwide came at a time of global attention to rising inequality around the world (Piketty, 2016). As the crisis unfolded, global inequality in access to affordable medical care but also preventive healthcare became apparent (Puaschunder & Beerbaum, 2020a, 2020b). The Coronavirus crisis truly challenged leaders around the world to argue for economic systems to become equitable and share the benefits of economic prosperity and scientific advancement equally around the globe (Puaschunder & Beerbaum, 2020a, 2020b). Global governance has taken a leading role in arguing for access to affordable vaccinations around the world (Puaschunder & Beerbaum, 2020a, 2020b).

The crisis has also drawn attention to novel social inequalities within society and sharpened our senses for the disparate impact of policies of prevention and recovery for different societal groups. More than ever before in the history of modern humankind are leaders urged to place their policy programs in line with social justice pledges. How to align economic interest with justice notions has leveraged into the most important question of our times.

The crisis also came during a time when ecological limits had been reached and climate change was on the minds of the global community (Puaschunder, 2020d). The worldwide and long-term impact of CO_2 becoming apparent in rising temperatures around the globe changing living conditions massively, drove the need for concerted action on climate stabilization (Puaschunder, 2020d). Around the world, global public and private sector entities are nowadays working on a broad variety of climate change mitigation and adaptation and climate stabilization efforts. Like no other concern of our lifetime, the solutions and accomplishment of climate stabilization goals will determine the lives of many generations to come. More than ever are leading law and economics scholars currently trying to imbue the idea of environmental justice in a greening economy (Armour, Enriques, & Wetzer, 2021; Broccardo, Hart, & Zingales, 2020).

COVID-19 rescue and recovery aid echoes all these contemporary concerns in being pegged to green economy efforts and social justice pledges. This is foremost the case in the USA with the US President Biden administration fostering the GND but also the EU Commission sponsoring the EGD and a Sustainable Finance Taxonomy (Barbier, 2009; Earthworks, 2021; Pargendler, 2020; Puaschunder, 2021b, 2021g; The United States Congress, 2019). These ambitious acts and plans account for the most vibrant and large-scale developments in our lifetime if considering the massive amount of funds involved but also the widespread impact of energy transition.

The GND is a governmental strategy to strengthen the US economy and foster inclusive growth (Puaschunder, 2021b, 2021g). The GND directly targets at sharing economic benefits more equally within society (Puaschunder, 2021b, 2021g). The GND thereby addresses the most pressing concerns of our times in the quest to align economic endeavors with justice and fairness. Concrete central areas of development tackle environmental challenges, healthcare demands and social justice pledges (Puaschunder, 2021b, 2021g). Ethical imperatives and equity mandates lead the economic rationale behind redistribution in the GND. Social harmony, access to affordable quality healthcare and favorable environmental conditions are thereby pursued in an understanding of their role as prerequisites for productivity (Puaschunder, 2021b, 2021g). In all these endeavors, the GND offers hope in making the world and society but also overlapping generations more equitable. As a large-scale and long-term plan, the GND offers to bestow peace within society, around the world and over time (Puaschunder, 2021b, 2021g).

To determine if these efforts will be successful, we have to acknowledge that they are fairly novel and include the most complex variety of actions that will have to be performed for a longer time horizon than simple economic recovery after system-inherent recessions would require. The multiple implementation facets and various agents involved but also the contested theoretical foundations and long-term implications will need more time to monitor and evaluate the effectiveness and equitable growth accomplishments than regular rescue and recovery efforts, such as the 2008–2009 World Financial Recession bailout and recovery packages. Tracking the success of these endeavors will be a long-term goal by itself, mainly due to the diversified projects, long-term impetus and the stratified impact of large-scale economic changes. While it is thus too early to tell how successful these projects will be in the grand scheme of complex issues tackled and over time in light of history, already now it is becoming apparent that teaching law and economics with a focus on ethics of inclusion honing a disparate impact lens will become key to ensure our common sustainable development and human progress of the future.

2.4.17. Institutional Framework

Today business leaders tend to contribute to the creation of economic and societal progress in a globally responsible and sustainable way by means as never before experienced. Corporations that join the PRI report concomitant tangible (profit gain, efficiency, product innovations and market segmentation) and intangible (reputation and employee morale) benefits.

The United Nations Environment Programme Finance Initiative (UNEP FI), the Equator Principles, The Green Bond Principles and the various corporate reporting led initiatives such as Global Reporting Initiative and Integrating Reporting. The key constituents are stock exchange and financial analyst communities as future SRI drivers to support the UNGC goals. In addition, NGOs are invited to advance financial market transparency and accountability.

For the future, the world's leading Stock Exchange Commissions seek to further support the PRI and to consider innovative ways how to partner with the UNGC. Sustainable development impact reporting can thereby highlight sustainable development criteria such as environmental and social standards. For instance, the United States' Overseas Private Investment Corporation uses about 30 development indicators to evaluate job creation and human capacity-building, sustainability effects as well as impacts on environmental and community benefits and their reach (World Investment Report, 2015).

In addition, specific sustainable development outcomes could be screened by finding if funds are in line with industrial development strategies and regional economic cooperation. Monitoring could comprise an ombudsperson and facilitator to help ensure a vital sustainability climate. In light of the rising climate change awareness and demand for an economically efficient transitioning into renewable energy, the UN-led Earth League most recently incepted the Climate Risk and the Finance Sector working group in partnership with UNEP FI, the World Resources Institute and the Global Challenges Foundation. The UNEP FI is a global partnership between the UNEP and the financial sector. Over 200 institutions, including banks, insurers and fund managers, work together with the UNEP to capture the mutual impacts of environmental and social considerations on financial performance. At the Third Conference on Financing for Development in July 2015 in Addis Ababa, and at the global summit on the Sustainable Development Goals in New York City in September 2015, external financing for development was proven as a key driver of developing economies.

In the wake of the 2015 inception of the UN SDGs, a report was published by UNEP FI in cooperation with the PRI, UNEP Inquire and the UNGC that aims at elucidating debates surrounding ESG issues in the light of fiduciary duty. The report is meant to foster investors' understanding and consideration of ESG issues in their investment decision making. The research stresses the point that a failure to consider long-term investment value drivers, which include ESG issues, in investment practices is a failure of fiduciary duty. The report also touches on the implementation of sustainable finance and impact investment in order to propose practical action for institutional investors, financial professionals and policy makers to embrace sustainable development. Given the pressing demand for sustainable development, the need for an introduction of political divestiture as a means to implement the SDGs is blatant.

In a climate of corporate governance and global challenges beyond the control of singular nation states, the idea of promoting political divestiture as a sustainable development incentive and conditionalities tool has reached unprecedented momentum. Departing from narrow-minded, outdated views of responsibilities of corporations only adherent to making profit for shareholders and abiding by the law (Friedman, 1970), corporate executives nowadays are more prone to act responsibly in meeting the needs of a wide range of constituents. Apart from avoiding unethical societally harmful behavior, such as bribery, fraud and employment discrimination, corporate executives currently pro-actively engage in corporate governance practice with a wider constituency outlook, including the needs of future generations.

The UN plays a pivotal role in promoting SRI. In 2004, the UN invited a group of leading financial institutions to form a financial responsibility initiative under the wing of the UNGC. The PRI were launched as part of the UNGC to encourage institutional investors to embrace SRI. This initiative develops guidelines and recommendations on how to integrate environmental, social and corporate governance in financial markets and how financial investment banks and fiduciaries can implement social responsibility goals as a risk management tool. In February 2008, the UN Conference on Trade and Development (UNCTAD) launched the "Responsible Investment in Emerging Markets" initiative, which enhances transparency of emerging financial markets. SRI and in particular green investments have been at the forefront in financing causes at the heart of the SDGs.

From a global governance perspective, the UN plays a pivotal role in promoting SRI. In January 2004, the UN attributed the key role of the financial sector in meeting the UNGC's objectives. Subsequently, a group of leading financial institutions was invited to form a joint financial sector initiative under the guidance of the UNGC Board. This forum was set up to discuss ways in which financial investment banks and fiduciaries can consider and implement social responsibility as a risk management tool.[12] In associated research units, the initiative developed guidelines and recommendations on how to integrate environmental, social and corporate governance in asset management and securities brokerage services.

To advance financial social responsibility, the UN launched "The Principles for Responsible Investment" (PRI) at the NYSE in April 2006. The PRI are supported by the UNGC Conference Board, the chief executive officers of 20 global corporations, the International Finance Corporation of the World Bank Group, the Swiss Government, Columbia University and the UNEP Finance Initiative. Under the auspice of the UNGC and the UNEP Finance Initiative, the PRI invite institutional investors to consider SRI and mobilize chief executive officers of the world's largest pension funds to advance SRI on an international level. The principles are designed to place financial social responsibility into the core of investment decision making of financial managers and asset owners of pension funds, foundation assets and institutional endowments. At the one-year anniversary of the PRI, more than 170 institutions representing approximately US \$8 trillion in assets had committed to the PRI. Corporations that join the PRI report concomitant tangible (profit gain, efficiency, product innovations and market segmentation) and intangible (reputation and employee morale) benefits.

In February 2008, the UNCTAD launched the "Responsible Investment in Emerging Markets" initiative at the Geneva PRI office. This PPP targets at fostering transparency and disclosure of emerging financial markets. The key constituents are stock exchange and financial analyst communities as future SRI drivers to support the UNGC goals. In addition, NGOs are invited to advance financial market transparency and accountability. For the future, the world's leading Stock Exchange Commissions seek to further support the PRI and to consider innovative ways how to partner with the UNGC.

Global governance institutions play a crucial role in implementing the proposed relative economic climate change gains redistribution scheme with plurilateral summit capabilities. Comprising all nations of the world, global governance entities have the capacity to instigate the idea of a "Global GND," (GGND) which could globalize ideas of the GND and the EGD to enact a binding taxation-and-bonds solution for climate change. Empirically driven redistribution schemes could thereby build the support of all international actors involved and imbue a notion of economically driven rationality in fairness that could win countries to act and comply. Global governance institutions, such as the World Bank, IMF, or the UN, could act as norm entrepreneurs and action catalysts of a GGND that redistributes the unequally distributed relative economic gains of a warming earth to places that face economically declining economic prospects.

---

[12]The United Nations Global Compact Office. (2007, November). Who cares wins: Connecting financial markets to a changing world: Recommendations by the financial industry to better integrate environmental, social and governance issues in analysis, asset management and securities brokerage. Retrieved from http://www.unglobalcompact. org/docs/news_events/8.1/WhoCaresWins.pdf.

The important role that global governance institutions can play in supporting and implementing a GGND targets at redistribution to overcome global inequalities in regard to climate change. Global governance institutions can shape the conduct and array of international actors to contribute to a commonly agreed global scheme. Economically driven indices could aid in taking the political nature out of redistribution politics and historically laden international relations. Drawing attention to the need for future research on this nexus will serve as a first step in finding economically driven redistribution schemes.

In the world compound historically, the advanced countries have gained welfare through environmental extraction, while the developing countries have not and appear nowadays as the most burdened with the environmental disasters, for instance, in regard to climate change. In the aftermath of the United Nations Climate Change Conference COP26 meeting, it has been argued that the advanced countries have an obligation and responsibility to finance the adaptation to global warming of the low-income countries through direct transfers and credit guarantees (Sachs, 2021).

A most recent World Bank Report calls for fair climate taxation and bonds mix worldwide (Semmler, Braga, Lichtenberger, Toure, & Hayde, 2021). While the World Bank Report presents a global overview of the current state of climate taxation and climate bonds' usage around the globe, it calls for more macroeconomic models that enact climate bonds and tax strategies concurrent use coupled with redistribution and burden-sharing (Semmler et al., 2021). In addition, *The New York Times* most recently discussed the disparate impact of climate policies and climate protection attention disparities (Flavelle, 2021a, 2021b). Literature emerges on how the world's richest people are driving global warming (Roston, Kaufman, & Warren, 2022).

In the aftermath of the COP26 annual climate meeting of the UN, Jeffrey Sachs put forward an idea of funds for climate change mitigation and adaptation that should be raised by climate tax-funded grants provided by some countries as transfer payments, while other countries should be recipients of green bonds granted to low-income countries (Sachs, 2021). While Sachs (2021) argues that half of the funds raised should be grants (transfers) and half green bonds that help transition to renewable energy in low-income countries, global governance regimes could refine prioritizing which countries should be grantors and which recipients based on data-driven criteria. A country's starting ground on the relative economic climate gains and losses spectrum, a country's climate flexibility and a country's CO_2 emission contributions to production and consumption levels, as well as a country's CO_2 emission level changes and the bank lending rate, could determine or whether a country should be on the taxation regime for funding mutual climate stabilization or whether a country should be on the receiving end of climate bond solutions. Pegging the country's situation to the initial starting levels on rational grounds and relations to each other allows for turning the general price-cutting competitive race-to-the-bottom into a race-to-the-top for the mutual climate fund allocations. Integrating the CO_2 emission level changes over time imbues incentives to change harmful behavior to this common climate fund solution.

An international climate change fund could be based on five indices that integrate the relative country's initial position on the relative economic climate change gains and losses index spectrum, and a country's climate flexibility understood as the future climate wealth of nations trading assets in combination with CO_2 emissions production and consumption levels as well as changes in CO_2 emissions over time and the bank lending interest rate per country (Puaschunder, 2022).

An overall redistribution key could be introduced to determine per country transfers based on the relative climate change economic windfall gain reaper or victim status and climate flexibility as well as the contribution to the climate change problem measured per country and over time by CO_2 emissions of production and consumption as well as CO_2 emission changes and the bank lending rate per country. For the redistribution scheme to work, those countries with climate change losing prospects and low ranges of climate flexibility, CO_2 emissions in production and consumption, decreasing CO_2 emissions and high bank lending rates could be granted climate bond prospects with high bond yield rates that are financed by countries that have relative economic climate change winning prospect and high ranges of climate flexibility as well as high CO_2 emissions in production and consumption, increasing CO_2 emission trends and low bank lending rates via taxation. Countries in the middle of the original climate change winners and losers index spectrum with medium climate flexibility levels as well as medium rates of CO_2 emissions in production and consumption or non-changing CO_2 emission rates and medium bank lending rates should have a mixed strategy of taxation and bonds with moderate bond yield rates. Those countries that are relatively high climate change economic windfall gain reapers on the winners and losers index spectrum that have high climate flexibility as well as have high rates of CO_2 emissions in production and consumption and increasing CO_2 emission levels as well as low bank lending rates should issue bonds funded by taxation that offer high bond yield rates in countries with climate change losing prospects and low ranges of climate flexibility, low CO_2 emissions in production and consumption and decreasing CO_2 emissions as well as high bank lending rates.

The idea of differing climate bond regimes is also extendable to sector-specific bond yield interest rate regimes. On a country level, high CO_2 emitting industries could face a climate taxation in order to set market incentives for a transition to renewable energy. The revenues generated from the taxation of carbon-intensive industries should be used to offset climate change losses and subsidize climate bonds. Within a country, the bonds could be offered by commissioning agents, such as local investment banks, who could install industry-specific premium bond payments and maturity bond yields based on the environmental sustainability of an industry, for example, as measured by the European Sustainable Finance Taxonomy. The more sustainable an industry performs, the higher bond yield should be granted in sector-specific interest rate regimes within a country. This strategy should set positive market incentives via subsidies. Funding industries for not polluting could change the traditional race-to-the-bottom price-cutting behavior driving CO_2 emitting energy supply to have industries compete over subsidies for using clean energy. In this way, bond yield differences between industries could set positive market incentives for transitioning to renewable energy and sustainable productivity solutions.

An in-between country regime could enact fairness on the different starting grounds of countries as relative economic climate change windfall gain reapers or victims coupled with incentivizing countries and/or corporations to compete over better bond conditions. Incentives could thereby target at lowering CO_2 emissions or subsidizing corporations to move production to places that are climate victims in order to help revitalize economies that have a shrinking prospect under climate change.

The effectiveness of policies will depend on the national circumstances, the design, interaction and stringency in the implementation (Kato, Mittnik, Samaan, & Semmler, 2014; Semmler, 2021). Integrating climate policies into broader development agendas will also require to be attentive to the local regulations and standards, the prevailing tax regime and carbon consumption charges, tradable permits and financial incentives but also voluntary agreements, information instruments and future research and development (Semmler, 2021). Especially the improvement of new technologies will be essential for transforming the energy sector for a broad-based renewable energy sector establishment (Mazzucato, 2013; Semmler, 2021). Government initiatives to fund and subsidize the transition to renewable energy via research and development enhanced innovations are needed (Mazzucato, 2013). The respective technologies are expected to become more efficient and less cost-intensive over time (Braga, Fischermann, Semmler, 2020; Heine et al., 2019; Mazzucato, 2013; Semmler et al., 2021).

The recent World Bank Report on green bonds and climate taxation (Semmler et al., 2021) outlines that carbon pricing and green bond initiatives are growing but still concentrated in high-income countries (especially Europe) and China (classified as upper-middle income). A tax-and-bonds strategy, in which relative climate change gains are redistributed could open the market and motivate even internationally developing parts of the world to participate in order to be funded for their low CO_2 emissions production and consumption levels in comparison to advanced countries. To this day, most green bonds tend to be project-specific and a new infant market operation (Semmler, 2021). Governance on green bonds and the current experience with sustainability and resilience financing in the GND, EGD and the Next Generation EU will determine the future of green energy in learning-by-doing of sector-specific but also long-run outcomes (Semmler, 2021).

Most recently green bonds have been promoted as an innovative climate stabilization strategy (Puaschunder, 2017a, 2018c, 2018d, 2020d, 2021f; Sachs, 2014; Semmler et al., 2021). Green bonds are, in most cases, governmental bonds. Issuance of a bond is taking a loan or getting credit to be repaid in the future. The issuer of bonds establishes the bond for bond buyers. Investors who purchase bonds can expect to make a profit as the bond matures.

The bond pricing and yields of bonds depend on the underlying cause and/or asset risk. An issuer of bonds that show high yields indicates that the fund carries high risks of being repaid. Borrowing money can only be issued by paying a risk premium, which entails the yield containing a risk premium. Risk can also mean negative externalities that others have to pay sometimes in the future, which is already internalized in the bond yield today.

In green bonds, borrowers issue securities to secure financing for projects with positive environmental impact, such as climate stabilization and a transfer to renewable energy solutions. Green bonds are mainly issued by central banks, which identify qualifying assets or loans which meet sustainability criteria. Tax benefits are often granted for investing in green bonds. In climate bonds, funds with high risk are often those with uncertain outcomes of climate protection, new green energy innovations, disaster risk, etc.

Financing climate change mitigation and adaptation will have different targets – while mitigation has global effects, adaptation is more focused on overcoming the adverse local impacts of global warming, such as disasters that tend to be more regional. Climate bonds can reduce global climate risk and contribute to the overall economy, for example, in environmental protection and de-risking the economy (Bolton et al., 2020; Braga, Semmler, & Grass, 2020). Green bonds can also be used for transitioning to a clean energy economy or funding innovation (Puaschunder, 2016a). For example, green bonds can kick-start ideas representing green energy and/or avoiding disasters, thus carrying a high yield and reward in the long run.

The effectiveness of the finance and markets for this transition to a low carbon economy depends on attracting investors and removing financial market roadblocks (Lichtenberger, Braga, & Semmler, 2022). While many recent studies find yield differentials between green bonds and conventional funds, Lichtenberger et al. (2022) highlight that green bond returns might be mixed with conventional bonds. Lichtenberger et al. (2022) emphasize that green bonds protect investors from oil price and business cycle fluctuations as well as stabilize portfolio returns and volatility. In the long run, green bonds benefit the economy and generate positive social returns even if these assets currently may only have lower yields (Lichtenberger et al., 2022). Green bonds can thus be justified not only from the point of view of climate protection and climate disasters avoidance but also by endogenous growth theory (Aghion & Howitt, 1992, 1998; Arrow, 1962; Lichtenberger et al., 2022; Kaldor, 1961; Lucas, 1988; Romer, 1986, 1990; Uzawa, 1965; Vitek, 2017).

Another approach to raising funds for a transitioning to a green economy takes a closer look at the macro-economic impacts and economic growth prospects under global warming. Effects of climate change vary around the world and are likely to impose considerable economic prospect changes, which will increase over time as global temperatures increase (Lomborg, 2021). Global warming will likely cause relative economic gains and losses, distributed unequally throughout the world and over time (Lomborg, 2021; Puaschunder, 2020d).

Economic research has elucidated the economic impact of climate change on the world and found stark national differences (Burke, Hsiang, & Miguel, 2015; Puaschunder, 2020d). Burke et al. (2015) estimate how climate change will affect GDP per capita. In addition, the IMF conducted a cross-country analysis of the long-term macro-economic effects of climate change and found country inequalities in global warming effects (Kahn et al., 2019). One translation of climate change gains and losses in burden-sharing contribution schemes is usually defined in Nordhaus' Regional Integrated model of Climate and the Economy model (RICE model). This regional, dynamic, general-equilibrium model of the economy integrates economic activity with emission levels as the primary driver of human-made climate change (Orlov, Rovenskaya, Puaschunder, & Semmler, 2018).

Puaschunder (2020d) measured the GDP prospect differences under climate change worldwide and found exacerbating climate inequalities. Puaschunder (2020d) introduced a climate change winners and losers index, representing relative economic climate change windfall gain reaper and victim countries, based on the economic prospects under climate change around the world and over time. The model assumes that there are relative economic climate change reapers that have a windfall gain from a warming globe while other relative economic climate change victims face immediate disadvantages due to global warming. The model primarily focuses on shedding light on the inequality in countries and regions of the world exacerbated by climate change determining economic prospects. The index attributed relative economic gain and loss prospects based on the medium temperature per country and the optimum temperature for economic productivity per GDP agriculture, industry and service sector, and the GDP sector composition per country to determine how far countries are deviating from their optimum productivity levels on a time scale (Puaschunder, 2020d). It is to note that the "relative economic climate change windfall gain reapers and victims" are categories on a spectrum, that the gain and loss perspectives addressed are only concerning GDP growth and that the gains/losses distribution are windfall/victim categories that countries did not accomplish or chose willingly. Gains and losses are somewhat random distributions throughout the world. It is sheer luck in the birth lottery where one falls into. But the behavior around the world differs drastically when it comes to climate change causing CO_2 contribution, which should also be addressed in redistribution strategies insofar as those who cause global warming also have a higher responsibility to protect the earth from climate change.

Climate justice addresses inequalities inherent in global warming with a mandate to alleviate imbalances and enact fairness regarding climate benefits and burden-sharing. To alleviate inequalities in climate change impacts between countries, ethical imperatives of Immanuel Kant's (1783/1993) categorical imperative and John Rawls' (1971) veil of ignorance but also economic calculus as put forward in Kaldor-Hicks' compensation criteria guide redistribution schemes.

Following ethical considerations of Immanuel Kant's (1783/1993) categorical imperative and John Rawls' (1971) veil of ignorance, the climatorial imperative was formulated to advocate for the need for fairness in the distribution of the global earth benefits among nations (Kant, 1783/1993; Puaschunder, 2020d). Based on Kant's imperative proposing to "Act only according to that maxim whereby you can at the same time will that it should become a universal law," no climate harm should be done to any country independent of a country's position on the relative economic climate change gains windfall reapers and victims' spectrum (Kant, 1783/1993, p. 30). Passive neglect of action on climate mitigation is an active injustice to others based on the climatorial imperative (Puaschunder, 2020d).

Moral and ethical guidelines may be enhanced with the Kaldor-Hicks Compensation Criteria. The Kaldor-Hicks test for improvement potential within a society aims to move an economy closer toward Pareto efficiency (Law &

Smullen, 2008). Kaldor-Hicks criteria assume that any change usually makes some people better off and others worse off at the same time and tests if this imbalance can be alleviated by relative economic climate change windfall gains reapers compensating climate change victims for the change in conditions. Applying the Kaldor criterion in the context of taxation and bonds would serve as an example by which the economy moves closer to Pareto optimality if the maximum number of gainers are prepared to pay the losers and to agree that the change is greater than the minimum amount the losers are prepared to accept. In the Kaldor-Hicks criteria, both sides must also agree that the benefits exceed the costs of such action. The fungibility of compensation (money will always be there) while there are irreversible lock-ins and tipping points in environmental degradation (climate may be irreversibly locked in and degrade living conditions in a non-linear trajectory) demand for action against climate change at the expense of repayable monetary costs.

The Kaldor-Hicks compensation can be applied to environmental constraints regarding climate change. As economic gains and losses from a warming earth are distributed unequally around the globe, ethical imperatives lead to the pledge to redistribute gains to losing territories in the quest for climate justice. Climate justice comprises fairness between countries but also over generations in a unique and unprecedented tax-and-bonds climate change gains and losses distribution strategy. Climate change winning countries are advised to use taxation to raise revenues to offset the losses incurred by climate change. Climate change victims could be incentivized to receive bonds that have to be paid back by future generations.

Regarding taxation within the winning countries, foremost, the gaining GDP sectors should be taxed. Those who caused climate change could be regulated to bear a higher cost through carbon tax combined with retroactive billing through a corporate inheritance tax to map benefits from past wealth accumulation that potentially contributed to global warming. A corporate inheritance tax could raise funds if there is a merger and/or acquisition or a takeover of a corporation, which would allow quasi-retroactive taxation of past corporate activities that may have caused GHG emissions. Climate justice within a country should also pay tribute to the fact that low- and high-income households share the same burden proportional to their dispensable income, for instance, enabled through progressive carbon taxation and a carbon consumption tax.

For the Kaldor compensation to work effectively, the relative economic climate change windfall gain reapers and climate change victims must also agree that the benefits of a commonly agreed-upon compensation scheme exceed the costs of such action. International cooperation and/or significant participation are crucial ways to internalize global externalities, avert climate change and agree upon a commonly pursued rescue and resilience plan (Nordhaus, 1994; Puaschunder, 2022; Semmler, 2021). Aside from free-rider problems and penalties for non-compliance, this chapter will introduce a novel climate taxation-and-bonds strategy to redistribute climate change gains and raise widespread momentum for a transitioning to a zero-carbon global economy based on the notion that the redistribution is fair.

A novel policy recommendation for enacting climate justice entails a taxation funding strategy coupled with a climate bonds repayment based on the following influence factors: (1) the country's initial position on the relative economic climate change windfall gains and losses index spectrum; (2) a country's climate flexibility as a broad economic degree of freedom spectrum and future trade benefit; (3) the country's human-made contribution to climate change as measured by CO_2 emissions; (4) the ability and willingness of a country to change its CO_2 emissions in relation to others; (5) the estimated lending rate of bonds in that country as well as (6) the consumption-based, trade-adjusted CO_2 emissions of a country. These six drivers in five proposed indices determine a higher or lower burden on carbon taxes (abatement costs) to finance climate bonds to be repaid later.

As Puaschunder (2020d) found in a worldwide dataset over all countries, being a relative economic climate change gain windfall reaper country and emissions are related. The relation between GDP growth prospects in light of climate change and the percentage of GHG emissions for ratification was investigated based on the total and percent of GHG emissions communicated by the Paris COP21 Parties to the Convention retrieved in their national communications and displayed in GHG inventory reports as of December 2015. Over a sample of 181 countries globally, a highly significant correlation between a relative economic climate change gain windfall reaper country and the self-reported percentage of GHG emissions for ratification was found. As a cross-validation check, the percentage of GHG emissions for ratification was significantly positively correlated with self-reported GHG emissions per country. This result leads to the conclusion that those countries that emit more GHG are the ones with a positive GDP prospect on the warming earth until 2100. The more time countries seem to have a favorable production climate, the more likely they are to emit GHG and contribute to global warming (Puaschunder, 2020d). All indices build on the insights that relative economic climate change windfall reaper countries are more likely responsible for human-made climate change. Diversified financing of common green bonds with a unique incentive scheme for carbon reduction is a new method to share the burden and the benefits of climate change within society in an economically efficient, legally equitable and practically feasible way.

Since 2007, there has been a steady rise in carbon taxation and green bonds issuance (Flaherty, Gevorkyan, Radpour, & Semmler, 2017; Heine et al., 2019; Semmler et al., 2021). Throughout the world, some countries engage primarily in carbon pricing, some in green bonds. Foremost the USA, Europe, China, Australia, South Africa and the Southern parts of Latin America feature a mixture strategy comprised of carbon pricing and green bonds (Semmler et al., 2021). Portfolio and hedge fund managers strive to reduce risks to the overall portfolio with green bonds in the short and long run (Braga, Semmler, et al., 2020). Capital markets can expedite green investments by de-risking innovative green finance (Braga, Semmler, et al., 2020). The financial benefits of green bonds include a de-risking of investor portfolios and a diversification strategy against market volatility (Semmler, 2021).

Lichtenberger et al. (2022) find that empirical beta pricing and yield estimates reveal some public involvement in the green bonds market, especially for long-maturity bonds. Investment options – based on renewable energy – can reduce the risks and political dependencies on commodities associated with non-renewables (Gevorkyan & Semmler, 2016). Renewable energy, therefore, appears as a crisis-stable market option, also as for being chosen based on ethical values (Puaschunder, 2019g, 2019h). Climate bonds incentivize a transition to renewable energy solutions (Semmler, 2021). Subsidies and carbon taxation can complement the role of the de-risked interest rates and expedite the energy transition (Lichtenberger et al., 2022).

Green bonds have substantial revenue-raising opportunities to fund climate policies (Semmler, 2021). Bonds can serve as a hedging instrument against oil price fluctuations in portfolios, particularly low fat-tail correlations (Semmler, 2021). Green bonds are fixed-income securities usually certified by a third party to have the funds for climate stabilization. Green bonds are thus predestined for low capital cost green projects and instruments for funding green counter-cyclical investment (Semmler, 2021). Green bonds unlock the necessary funding for the investment in sustainability projects, such as clean energy, low-carbon transport and green buildings (Flaherty et al., 2017; Semmler, 2021).

Green bonds are safe and crisis-robust long-term assets as they are often financed via quantitative easing and backed by the state (Semmler, 2021). The investment grade for green bonds appears to be equal to or greater according to S&P rating (Semmler, 2021). The standard duration for green bonds is greater than 10 years, which predestines green bonds for long-term intergenerational burden-sharing strategies (Semmler, 2021). Green bonds enable intertemporal burden-sharing of climate change mitigation and adaptation (Orlov et al., 2018; Sachs, 2014).

Climate bond issuing agencies comprise public and private sector entities. Public sector green bond providers include international institutions, central banks, governments and municipalities (Semmler, 2021). The World Bank but also the IMF as well as central banks and municipalities have played a leading role in the development and utilization of green bonds over the last few years (Semmler, 2021). The IMF is also playing the lead role in helping national governments to build their capacity to address climate challenges and share the risk of climate-related disasters in bonds, loans and trusts (Georgieva & Tshisekedi, 2021). Based on information derived from the Bloomberg Terminal, Semmler et al. (2021) outline that bonds are heterogeneous in terms of issuer, duration, counry, currency and sectors. Most green bonds are issued by banks, real estate, power generation, utilities, governments, supranational entities and the energy sector.

An international intermediary financial institution could manage and guarantee loans in a common taxation-bonds strategy spanning over the entire world. International banks – such as the World Bank and the IMF – but also central banks are the main climate bond issuing authorities (Braga, Semmler, et al., 2020; Heine et al., 2019; Semmler et al., 2021). The World Bank issued the first green bond in 2007 (Braga, Semmler, et al., 2020; Semmler, 2021). International organizations like the World Bank, IMF, or the UN have the global governance strength to support international green fund climate change mitigation and adaptation efforts and incentivize countries to transition to renewable energy. Global governance institutions are already serving as intermediaries for redistribution efforts.

Similar models exist, for instance, in the EU. The European Investment Bank acts as an intermediary for credit demand by low-income countries and a credit supply backed by taxes of advanced countries. For instance, the European Investment Fund under the European Guarantee Fund finances developing economies to help with the fall-out of the COVID-19 pandemic. In addition, the European Investment Bank has funded large-scale infrastructure development projects with a sustainable edge – for instance, by issuing a European Guarantee Fund most recently for infrastructure investment and development in Poland and Lithuania (European Investment Bank, 2022a, 2022b). According to the European Investment Bank, the "Pan-European Guarantee Fund (EGF) was created by the European Investment Bank Group (EIB and EIF) and European Union Member States as a community response to the COVID-19 pandemic." This bond "aims to increase access to credit for businesses in the wake of the economic effects of lockdowns and restrictions to contain the COVID-19 outbreak" (European Investment Bank, 2022a, 2022b). The fund strives to boost those communities of the EU economy that have been hit by the pandemic the worst (European Investment Bank, 2022a, 2022b).

First ideas in green global governance exist in the GGND, which features a concerted plan of a policy package to instigate global change (Boyle, Leggat, Morikawa, Pappas, & Stephens, 2021; O'Callaghan & Murdock, 2021). The GGND was first proposed by the United Nations Environment Programme (UNEP, 2009). The UNEP describes the GGND as a policy package to revive the world economy, reduce carbon dependency and further sustainable growth (UNEP, 2009). The UNEP GGND focuses on economic stimulus, domestic regulatory reform and international cooperation. State-led economic stimulus fosters decarbonizing carbon-intensive sectors of the economy – such as energy, transport, buildings and agriculture (UNEP, 2009). Domestic policy reform includes eliminating environmentally harmful subsidies and strengthening environmental legislation (UNEP, 2009). International cooperation advocates for changes to the policy architecture governing international trade, aid, global carbon markets and technology transfers (UNEP, 2009).

Via a GGND international agreement, global governance institutions could generate global social norms that foster a domestic implementation of a green stimulus. Policy measures may thereby be pegged to COVID-19 recovery efforts, such as in the US GND and the EGD plans (European Commission, 2019; The United States Congress, 2019; The United States Congress, 116th Congress, 1st Session, House Resolution 109, 2019; The White House of the United States, 2021a, 2021b, 2021c; United Nations, 2020; United Nations General Assembly, 2020, Art. 47; Vivid Economics, 2021; World Trade Organization, 2020, 2021). A global governance approach – as pursued in the GGND – could shape the conduct of an array of international actors and identify emerging trends in the global governance of system dynamics on climate stabilization efforts.

The implementation of the financing of climate change mitigation and adaptation efforts could become a concerted action of multiple entities: first, mitigation is likely to be tackled on an international level by global governance institutions. Adaptation is expected to be more prevalent on a country level. Financing climate mitigation and redistribution of climate change economic windfall gains to economically losing territories in the wake of climate change could become the central focus of international entities, such as the UN, the World Bank and the IMF. Redistribution of climate gains to territories that have a decreasing GDP prospect in light of global warming could be accomplished via taxation and bonds if international entities support such a plan concertedly. For instance, the UN could target a binding climate agreement between countries during their COP meetings. All UN joining nations would then sign up for implementing a climate gains redistribution via taxes and bonds. Alternatively, or complementary, the World Bank and/or the IMF could work out a redistribution scheme via their existing contributions key and loan programs. While the UN features a democratic "one-country-one-vote" voting system, the World Bank and IMF have voting schemes that also weigh in the national financial contributions of all participating entities. As a universal dispute resolution for non-compliance with the outlined plans, prospectively the World Trade Organization (WTO) or International Law Commission of the UN in New York could serve as panels for oversight, monitoring and evaluation control. Governments and multilateral organizations are also essential to support the issuance of green bonds as private funds show higher yields, volatility and beta prices (Braga, Semmler, et al., 2020).

As for climate change adaptation funding, central banks could become intermediaries for issuing country-specific and industry-specific bonds on the national level. Country-wide bonds could feature an interest rate bandwidth around the universal bank lending rate for climate bonds determined by international entities. Within the bandwidth, central banks could offer green bonds with specific premium bond payments for industries based on the industry carbon emission levels. Industry-specific interest rates could turn the traditional price-cutting behavior that drives corporations to seek for cheap and often non-renewable energy sources to opt-in for a competitive race-to-the-top for beneficial interest rates that gratify choices for renewable energy solutions. A beneficial industry shift could also be fortified by COVID-19-rescue and recovery packages that are in line with the GND program in the USA and the EGD in Europe (European Commission; United Nations, 2020; United Nations General Assembly, 2020, Art. 47; The United States Congress, 2019; The White House of the United States, 2021a, 2021b, 2021c; Vivid Economics, 2021; World Trade Organization, 2020, 2021). The GND and the EGD, in combination with the European Sustainable Finance Taxonomy, are the most widescale efforts to marry the idea of economic growth in line with the natural resources pool and with respect for environmental limitations.

Problematic may be the largess of funds needed that may exceed the capacity of funding agencies within smaller nations. The lending capacity remains a political problem internationally and nationally. On the international level, questions arise about the power dynamics of interest groups that may influence the agenda of the World Bank, the IMF and central bank grantors. Collective action problems may drive the political pressure on different constituency groups. Transfer funds will be challenging to achieve. Potential incentive mechanisms may be discussed, such as bonus systems. But also, socio-psychological motives may be elicited in nurturing an awareness that countries that are first-and-foremost victims of climate change deserve a guaranteed repayment for damage and losses. A politically neutral international tax-and-bonds-scheme should primarily focus on redistribution fairness aside from historical or political agendas. Lastly, also the Coronavirus crisis serves as a vivid example of collective action problems around the world to contain a life-threatening virus, of which no one is safe, until everyone is safe.

Climate change mitigation and adaptation are currently financed by a climate taxation and green bonds strategy. Green bonds have become fundamental pillars for raising funds for a transition to renewable energy (Puaschunder, 2016a). Solar power and wind turbines, eco-friendly infrastructure and more research and development in clean energy and green technology are all investments for averting climate change funded by bonds (Puaschunder, 2016a).

Public entities, such as the World Bank or the IMF, or governmentally backed bonds, such as municipal governments investing in renewable energy projects, are primary green bond issuers. Asset-backed securities are similar to traditional bonds, but their debt repayment is financed by a particular revenue stream, such as tolls or surcharges on energy use (Semmler, 2021). Covered bonds are a type of asset-backed security that are also guaranteed by the issuing agency (Semmler, 2021). The repayment mechanism of green bonds depends on which of these categories the bond falls into. The strategic bundling of bonds but also tax-and-bonds strategies are currently debated in science and policy contexts. The financing of climate justice is estimated to comprise 5–7% of the contemporary world GDP, accounting for US $5–6 billion (Braga, Semmler, et al., 2020; Flaherty et al., 2017).

Green bonds could fund all these endeavors and are currently pegged to governmental aid in the post-COVID-19 crisis recovery aid. Governments can also bring back the financial world in the service of improving and stabilizing the real economy in a stricter separation between investment and consumer banks, which already began in the course of the regulations following the 2008–2009 World Financial Recession. Central banks, on behalf of the World Bank or the IMF, could take the lead in offering differing bond regimes on a global scale.

The European Taxonomy for sustainable activities creates an EU standard to classify assets and investments according to their climate benefits, following the new technological trends and indicators of the European Union Technical Expert Group on Sustainable Finance (2020). Organized by sector and technology, the European Sustainable Finance Taxonomy provides references to classify climate change mitigation and adaptation activities, including environmental objectives (European Union Technical Expert Group on Sustainable Finance, 2020). Broad-based climate stabilization through bonds and credits could thereby finance climate change mitigation efforts, while global warming adaptation funding would address the impact of climate change on its local effects, such as regional disasters. The European classification of industries' contribution to climate change in the European Sustainable Finance Taxonomy could become the basis for setting positive market incentives to change market dynamics via differing bond regimes.

Inbetween countries, global governance could determine climate change transfer grantors and beneficiaries of climate bonds in a climate tax-and-bonds strategy.

The transfers could be based on the relative economic climate change windfall gain reapers and victims index but also the climate flexibility of a country and the willingness and ability of a country to change its CO_2 emissions and the CO_2 emissions production and consumption levels as well as the bank lending rates. All these factors could serve as parameters for whether a country should be using more of a climate taxation strategy to grant the common climate bonds endeavors or be a recipient of a favorable climate bonds regime with high bond premium and maturity rates. Being a relative economic climate change windfall gain reaper or victim could be integrated into an index based on the CO_2 emissions per country in relation to other countries. On a yearly basis, countries already determine their GHG emission levels, hence the relative country contribution to the climate change problem. The factors of being a relative economic climate change windfall gain reaper or victim country and having climate flexibility as a country but also the current CO_2 emissions and the CO_2 emissions production and consumption levels and the bank lending rates for credits could determine a key to estimating the transfer need and country responsibility to contribute to a common plan.

Climate bonds could thereby feature a combination of climate justice between countries and over time. Indices could inform about a redistribution scheme, in which the relative economic climate change windfall gain reaper and climate flexible countries finance the climate bonds by taxation. In countries that already face declining economic prospects due to climate change and that are naturally climate-constraint, the interest rate regime for climate bonds should be more favorable compared to relative economic climate change windfall gain reaper countries. High CO_2 emitting countries that are contributing more to the problem should be financing climate bonds via a tax regime that pays for their establishment and maintenance. Lower CO_2 emitting countries should be beneficiaries of transfer payments via climate bonds with a higher interest rate premium for common green bonds. This will incentivize territories that gain economically from climate change in the short run to curb harmful emissions and move towards renewable energy. Climate fund transfers should also pay attention to CO_2 emission production and consumption differences. Accounting for international trade disparity could address how countries compare CO_2 emissions production and consumption levels. In addition, redistribution schemes could also pay attention to historically grown bank lending rate differentials. All these redistribution measures could enact climate justice between countries in a given year.

The diversified climate bonds should also depend on the CO_2 emission changes of countries over time. In order to ensure that countries are incentivized to keep their CO_2 emissions at a low level and compete over a transition to renewable energy, countries should have the prospect of shifting from being a climate bond grantor (those countries that pay for the fund with climate taxation) to become climate bond beneficiaries (those countries that receive climate bonds for favorable market conditions subsidized by payments of the climate bonds grantors). The prospect of gaining from global warming for lowering CO_2 emissions could enact climate justice action over time, if the index that determines where a country falls onto the climate bonds-grantor or climate bonds-beneficiary spectrum also includes CO_2 emission changes from year to year.

In addition, the bank lending rates of a country could determine whether a country should be granting the climate bonds via taxation or be a beneficiary of favorable climate bonds-enacted transfer payments. Countries with bank lending rates, in which industries have ample access to market capital, should work toward a transition to renewable energy and thus operate with the taxation of industries with high CO_2 emission levels. Countries facing high bank lending rates should be climate bond transfer payment beneficiaries partially funded via the tax revenues in countries with low bank lending rates. In high bank lending rate countries, the climate taxation-and-bonds solution could also be financed via debt paid back by future generations, who receive a favorable climate in lieu. This will enable the implementation of climate justice over time between generations.

Future scientific investigations could learn from previous examples of green bonds for sustainable development focusing on climate.[13] A multilateral organization such as the IMF, the World Bank, the UN but also the EU rescue and recovery funds have already worked out specifications for similar bond solutions (Semmler et al., 2021).

In the future, global governance institutions are believed to play an increasing role as "global society" leaders to tackle large-scale complex problems – such as climate change but also COVID-19 alleviation – that create global social norms to sustainably implement global public policies by identifying change agents on the national level (Barnett & Sikkink, 2011). Future research should pay attention to emerging trends in global redistribution models to alleviate climate inequalities and enact climate justice worldwide and over time. Broader issues, specifications and institutional arrangements might need to be addressed to move the idea of climate-related redistribution patterns forward. Global governance institutions could further build on research-driven inequality parameters to derive concrete policy implementation solutions of global equity norms via global taxation-and-bond-schemes (Boyle et al., 2021; O'Callaghan & Murdock, 2021).

Future writings could also investigate the underexplored role of global governance institutions in changing country-level dynamics according to international world power resolutions. The global governance research literature could be fortified by insights into the dynamics of modern relations of global societies as dense networks of states with shared values and agreed-upon principles (Barnett & Sikkink, 2011). How powerful global governance institutions could help the legitimacy and lead in a cascading of social norms internalized in a network of change agents on the local levels should be explored (Finnemore & Sikkink, 1998). As for concrete redistribution plans, different means of transfer should be investigated in future studies, ranging from taxation models, direct or indirect transfers, credit guarantees, bonds issuance and conventional repayment schemes.

Future studies on climate change impacts may address the different tipping points and disaster drivers of temperature rise, weather extremes and sea-level rise, as this current model only considered temperature as the primary determinant of economic growth (Dietz, Rising, Stoerk, & Wagner, 2021). The simplistic

---

[13]https://treasury.worldbank.org/en/about/unit/treasury/ibrd

model of only prospecting the impact of temperature on GDP growth was chosen as a first starting point to sketch out the potential of a relative climate change economic windfall reaper or victim countries' models for redistribution for inequality alleviation strategies. Future theoretical work may define and clarify climate argumentations, which served as the basis of the indices. Future index sophistications could feature additional influence factors, such as disaster effects and historical inequalities to refine the redistribution schemes proposed.

Future index extensions could also address the CO_2 emission levels per capita and emission changes per citizen. The current state of this chapter will hopefully set the stage for future research that refines the variegated impact of climate, weather and coastal risks as a future economic determinant in order to lead toward a more just balance of economic gains and losses around the world, also per capita on the most granular level.

Future comparative studies could compare the costs and effectiveness of various tax and bond designs not only in a cost-effectiveness analysis but also in terms of political feasibility and legal impetus. Forecasting studies should tackle potential obstacles and contingency planning if there are unintended outcomes that raise problems for compensation compliance or if there is a pushback in future generations, or if the plan of redistribution over time does not work. Philosophical problems of bonds should be addressed in future generations not having caused the climate problem but being indebted for stabilizing the climate in the past. Counter argumentations of money being fungible and always there but a stable climate and natural resources' finite character could be underlined. As for future research on implementing the proposed redistribution plan, political economy insights may inform about bargaining and the role of cartels in reaching favorable common goods allocation outcomes. Historical examples of previous world leaders' negotiations (e.g., after World Wars or revolutions) may lead to analyzing contemporary negotiation strategies and outcome risk estimate forecasting.

Future law and economics extensions should particularly pay attention to the disparate impact of climate policies on marginalized and vulnerable societal groups. In a heterodox opening of the macro-economic aggregate production and consumption functions, the disproportionately hard effect of policies on gender, race and other vulnerable populations must be addressed with special heterodox attention.

For the legal community, the proposed tax-and-bonds strategy is a concrete commitment bond strategy application (Armour et al., 2021; Ayres & Abramowicz, 2011; Bishop, 2019; Omarova, 2021). Corporate legal scholars may add information about the practicality of green bonds and how to avert negative downsides, such as greenwashing, through clear and concrete contracts, economic incentives and sanction mechanisms.

2.4.18. Finance after the Great Reset

The post-Coronavirus crisis era offers the unique historical potential to peg all-time-high governmental rescue and recovery packages to environmental long-term causes (Puaschunder, 2021c). The US GND, as well as the EGD and Sustainable Finance Taxonomy will grant unprecedented opportunities to scale up green investments through green bonds as part of a fiscal program to move out of the COVID-19 economic hangover (Semmler, 2021). While there has been a macro-economic debate about the monetary size of the current governmental rescue efforts and if the largess of governmental aid may trigger inflation and unbearable debt levels, the heterodox need for a diversified view and disparate impact of inflation and longest-ever, lowest-ever interest rate regimes becomes apparent at the same time (Brunnermeier Academy at the Princeton Bendheim Center for Finance, 2021; Puaschunder, 2021c). Future work could address the normative implications of the developed insights. For instance, in future research, the European Taxonomy for sustainable activities could serve as the basis of CO_2 emissions per industry measurements and thereby lead to a respective redistribution key between countries based on the industry contributions to the climate change problem (European Union Technical Expert Group on Sustainable Finance, 2020).

As for methodological avenues for future research, redistribution criteria could be sophisticated. For instance, the nature and rate of GDP growth over the following decades, the distributional impacts of funded green projects by income class in countries paying off loans, assessment of climate change windfall gain reapers, and who should pay taxes to pay off bonds but also climate victims and their risks estimates could follow. Different scenarios of net benefits by income class in relative economic climate change windfall gain reaper and victim countries over time with probability estimates would be a grand future endeavor.

Additional layers of inequality should be explored in future Law and Economics analyses of the problem, for instance, in disparate impact studies but also international law and development angles, for example, in the different levels of resilience watch of moving coastlines between the developed and undeveloped nations. Migration as a coping mechanism in regard to climate change may offer additional future prospective research avenues and index parameters to be added in future extensions of the presented model.

Future open research questions are the economic validation and measurement of positive and negative externalities of all these endeavors over time and a disparate impact assessment, which can be granted by a truly heterodox viewpoint (Woo, 2021). Methodological heterodoxy could open the spectrum of macro-economic models with a more comprehensive treatment of preferences, the climate sensitivity of infrastructure, as well as different technologies' impact on the success of climate mitigation and adaptation policies (Mazzucato, 2013; Semmler, 2021). The overall contextual influence should be explored in post-Keynesian analyses of the presented problem to estimate the political salience of the presented solutions.

Future behavioral research could be dedicated to shifting from a climate change windfall gain reaper ability-to-pay to a voluntary-driven willingness-to-pay, which would also crowd out the negative externalities of greenwashing. Climate change imposing a highly complex collective action problem with political reality constraints and burden of debt for future generations in the climate bonds solution solutions are future complicated yet fertile research grounds to be studied that deserve attention.

Overall, introducing the idea of climate taxation and green bonds in an incentives-driven tax-and-bonds strategy is a new heterodox method that establishes green bonds as a possible macro-economic policy aimed at ensuring to share the burden but also the benefits of climate change over time, between countries and markets but also within society in an economically efficient, legally equitable and practically feasible way.

2.4.19. Political Divestiture

The influence of financial markets in global governance becomes apparent in political divestiture. Political divestiture refers to the removal of investments from socially irresponsible markets with the greater goal of accomplishing social and political change. A prominent case for political divestiture is the capital flight from South Africa during the Apartheid regime featuring racial segregation policies connected to economic discrimination against non-European South African groups. Anti-Apartheid activism began in 1965 and led to the guided divestiture of US corporations since 1978. The enactment of the US Comprehensive Anti-Apartheid Act in 1986 backed up political divestiture from South Africa. During Apartheid, international socio-political pressure and foreign investment flight were accompanied by cultural restrictions and UN international trade sanctions. By 1990, South African President de Klerk began dismantling the Apartheid system accompanied by an Apartheid reform process. As of today, political sanctions are imposed on the Sudanese government in response to related terrorist activities and the humanitarian crisis in Darfur. The Sudanese Divestment Task Force (SDTF) publicly outlines Sudan's dependence on foreign direct investment (FDI) and the governmental vulnerability to political divestiture.

Divestiture is an act of removing stocks from a portfolio to screen out socially irresponsible corporations based on social, ethical and religious objections (McWilliams & Siegel, 2000). In the case of political divestiture, investments are withdrawn from politically incorrect markets in the wake of stakeholder pressure and global governance sanctions. Sanctions are economic or military coercive measures to put pressure on governments that depart from international law. By cultural neglect and economic trade restrictions, such as tariffs, sanctions yield to adjudication with the greater goal of triggering positive political and societal change (Merriam Webster Dictionary, 2008).

Divestiture became a global governance means in the case of the South African Apartheid regime during the 1980s. Current political divestiture sanctions have been imposed on the Sudanese government as for implying a humanitarian crisis in Darfur.

One of the most prominent cases of political divestiture has been the capital flight from South Africa during the Apartheid regime. The Apartheid system came into effect in South Africa in 1948 when the National Party gained parliamentary majority leading to repression, censorship, majority disenfranchisement and racial separation. Apartheid refers to political and social policies of racial segregation connected to economic discrimination against non-European groups in the Republic of South Africa (Merriam Webster Dictionary, 2008).

India became the first country to take action against South Africa by imposing an export embargo followed by a range of economic, social and political sanctions. The first wave of US anti-Apartheid activism began in 1965, when members of "Students for a Democratic Society" protested at the Wall Street Chase Bank headquarter against loans to the South African government (Crawford & Klotz, 1999). Throughout the late 1960s and early 1970s, students urged university endowment administrators to divest South African holdings. The Sullivan Principles became a basis for political divestiture advocating for investors' social responsibility (Voorhes, 1999). By the late 1970s, it became apparent that the National Party would not abandon the Apartheid system for fear of losing political power to the African National Community (Zeff & Pirro, 1999). In the international arena, social and political pressures on public pension funds to restrict or eliminate investments in corporations engaging in business and trade with South Africa grew.

Coordinated divestiture of US corporations from South Africa began in 1978. Political divestiture became legally backed up by the enactment of the US Comprehensive Anti-Apartheid Act in November 1986 (Ngassam, 1992). In the decade from 1978 to 1988, the number of US publicly traded firms with operations in South Africa fell from 274 to 175 – featuring prominent multi-nationals such as Exxon, Xerox, Coca-Cola, General Motors, Honeywell and Citicorp. In 1986, South African trade plummeted by 15% with Britain, by 25% with Germany and by 40% with the USA in 1987. By the mid-1990s, more than 200 US corporations had either totally or partially disinvested from South Africa on a voluntary basis and new investments in South Africa were scarce (Alperson et al., 1991). All these activities impacted the South African economy, led to an overall decline in the living standard of South Africans and triggered emigrations from South Africa (Alperson et al., 1991). Attempts of the National Party to tighten its hold on South Africa resulted in racial killings, religious bombings and steering the so-called "black on black" violence. These atrocities triggered waves of anti-Apartheid activism in the international arena (Zeff & Pirro, 1999). The student-led "South African Catalyst Project" coordinated anti-Apartheid action across the USA and investment communities adopted total divestment policies (Voorhes, 1999).

However, during the 1970s and 1980s, high gold, diamond, metal and mineral prices let some traders turn a blind eye to South Africa's Apartheid policies (Zeff & Pirro, 1999). South Africa was often successful in replacing trade partners, to whom it sold raw materials for an "Apartheid discount" (Zeff & Pirro, 1999). For example, while the USA, Denmark and France prohibited imports of South African coal in 1985, South Africa became the major supplier of coal imports to the European Economic Community in 1986. As trade never completely stopped with South Africa, the anti-Apartheid movement became criticized as a patchwork of voluntary and mandatory prohibitions undertaken by only some market actors.

By the mid-1980s, increasing international, social and political pressure to end Apartheid was backed up by UN trade sanctions. By the end of the 1980s, a multitude of international corporations had pulled out of South Africa and the end of the Cold War eased the strategic need for minerals, which lead to falling prices of commodities. South Africa was unable to trade in the international markets and had become a pariah nation, cast out of the UN and the Commonwealth and isolated from international sporting activities (Zeff & Pirro, 1999).

The end of Apartheid is dated in February 1990, when President F.W. de Klerk announced Nelson Mandela's release and slowly began to dismantle the Apartheid system. In 1992, a referendum approved the Apartheid reform process. On April 27, 1994, the first democratic elections in South Africa, wherein all races were allowed to vote, led to Nelson Mandela becoming the first native President of South Africa. Political divestiture in combination with respective cultural and economic sanctions is attributed as a contributing factor to the end of Apartheid in South Africa (Zeff & Pirro, 1999).

A timeline of the actions against Apartheid from 1946 to 1998 featured concerted action of global governance institutions as well as financial markets. As a chronology of political divestiture and sanctions against South Africa, from 1946 on the UN addressed South African domestic discrimination. In 1948, the UN adopted the Universal Declaration of Human Rights as an international legal basis against Apartheid. In 1962, the UN General Assembly called for diplomatic, economic and military sanctions against South Africa for its Apartheid system. Shortly thereafter, the UN Security Council adopted an arms embargo for South Africa and the USA ended military supply trade with South Africa. The African Union also excluded South Africa and supported sanctions against the country. International organizations rejected South Africa as a member. By 1964, Great Britain banned arms exports to South Africa and Japan froze FDIs in the country. The UN established a Trust Fund and education programs for South Africa to not stop positive progress in 1965. In the USA, students protested at Manhattan's Chase Bank headquarters against loans to South Africa, which started the first wave of controlled divestiture. Throughout the 1970s, major banks and governments continued to ban investments and loans to South Africa. The 1972 book *The Ethical Investor* promoted political divestiture leading to numerous institutional investors divesting from South Africa. Arab oil embargos and boycotted South African art and culture celebrations in New York City follow. By 1974, the UN General Assembly suspended South Africa. In 1976, international banks and governments raised loan restrictions on South Africa. Nuclear technology transfers and general arms embargo for South Africa were backed by the UN Security Council. South Africa got excluded from the International Atomic Energy Agency governing board of the UN in 1977. Additional US student protests against Apartheid triggered continuous institutional investor boycotts of South African market options. The Sullivan Principles and European as well as Canadian corporate conduct opposed operations with South Africa. The USA tightened restrictions on military support of South Africa. The UN General Assembly called on the Security Council to consider preventing South Africa from developing nuclear weapons in 1979. Shortly thereafter the UN General Assembly advocated for a cultural boycott of South Africa. In 1982, the US state of Connecticut became the first US state to legislate a South Africa divestment policy for pension funds. Subsequently, in 1983, the US Congress passed the Gramm Amendment, blocking the IMF loans to Apartheid-practicing states.

In the same year, the UN General Assembly adopted a Program of Action against Apartheid that halts nuclear technology transfer, nuclear cooperation as well as the delivery of reactors and fissile material to South Africa. The Free South Africa Movement was launched at the South African embassy in Washington DC in 1984, while the UN Security Council expanded the military boycott to ban South African imports. By 1985, as the Chase Bank and other international banks refused to roll over their loans, the South African government declared a partial moratorium on repayments of commercial debt. The 1985 UN Security Council resolution 569 urged all member states to prohibit nuclear-related contracts with South Africa. Subsequently, Australia banned trade of South African arms, weapons and computer equipment. In the same year, the Commonwealth passed economic sanctions against South Africa in October, including a ban on purchases of South African uranium and Commonwealth exports of enriched uranium and nuclear technology. The US Corporate Council on South Africa was formed to oppose Apartheid. The third and most intensive wave of US student anti-Apartheid activism features groups of university presidents to promote sanctions against South Africa and increase divestment activities. Several US cities adopted selective contracting provisions to foster sanctions. The USA, the European community and other countries implement additional sanctions on South Africa. By 1986, France banned weapons trade with South Africa and the Commonwealth adopted additional economic sanctions. The European community and Japan banned imports of South African goods including iron and gold. General Motors' divestiture from South Africa was followed by a flood of US corporations leaving the country. Barclays Bank ended loans to South Africa in response to consumer pressure in May 1986 and withdrew from South Africa by November sparking other banks to follow. The US Congress enacted the Comprehensive Anti-Apartheid Act in October 1986 and students protested against South African conduct. By 1987, US retirement funds' shareholder resolutions targeted at withdrawing South Africa and university and municipal divestment policies flourished. The US government removed the tax exemption status from corporations operating in South Africa by 1987. By 1989, Exxon Mobil and Goodyear – the largest remaining corporations – withdrew from South Africa. From the 1990s, the governmental approach toward Apartheid shifted. Sanctions were lifted gradually from the beginning of the 1990s. By 1993, Nelson Mandela called to end economic sanctions against South Africa and by 1994 Nelson Mandela became the first democratically elected President of South Africa. Trade embargos ended. US institutional investors returned to invest in South African funds. South Africa rejoined international organizations, re-established diplomatic ties around the world and got reinvited to contribute to international arts and culture events.

Up to now, the effects of negative screenings on corporations and whether divestment is associated with an increase or decrease of shareholder value are unclear. Unanswered remains the question if political divestiture grants first-mover advantages for early withdrawing entities as politically fractionate markets lead to long-term economic decline (Posnikoff, 1997). Empirical investigations of political divestiture are primarily based on event studies. This methodology is limited as for refraining to take externalities on the wider constituent group into consideration, relatively short time frames under scrutiny, small sample sizes and the irreplicability of unique political events (McWilliams et al., 1999; Teoh et al., 1999). In the wake of historical and political events, stakeholder pressure can trigger divestment from politically incorrect markets. Since the start of political divestiture in the 1970s, the connection between politics and investments has been subject to scientific scrutiny, yet comparative results are scarce. This deficiency was attributed to the following meta-analysis. Drawing from the field of SRI, the evaluation analyzed the body of research on political divestiture from South Africa during Apartheid.

Most of the studies of political divestiture feature the event study methodology, which describes the effects of socio-political events on markets (Peterson, 1989). Event studies examine how the release of specific information impacts stock prices and corporate values during a particular time (Harvey, 2008). The event "time window" under scrutiny comprises the period immediately before, during and after the event of interest (Peterson, 1989). Six evaluation studies of political divestiture from South Africa during the Apartheid were meta-analyzed as for finding a pattern of stakeholder pressure, political divestiture and corporate endeavors (Puaschunder, 2015c). The meta-analysis covered the question if corporations divesting politically incorrect markets are more likely to experience an increase, decrease or no change in market value and found varying results – some studies suggest a positive effect, others a negative impact and even no overall performance pattern of political divestiture and corporate value was reported (Puaschunder, 2015c). The study also detected a research gap on the impact of political divestiture on corporations operating in politically fractionate markets (Puaschunder, 2015c).

The instringent results are attributed to stem from methodological limitations (Puaschunder, 2015c). Political divestiture is captured by the event study method which was evaluated for validity threats (Puaschunder, 2015c). Internal validity limitations of event study designs stem from confounding and contaminating history occurrences, sample selection biases and inappropriate time frames (Puaschunder, 2015c). Insider trading information leakage but also industry-specificities imply additional validity drawbacks (Puaschunder, 2015c). The external validity is challenged by geographically limited and time-targeted studies as well as non-typical samples that feature a lowered replicability and generalizability of the findings (Puaschunder, 2015c). Future research may compare the values of divesting corporations with those operating in politically incorrect markets.

Another historical example to outline the case of divestiture is the Sudan divestiture during the 1990s. First international trade restrictions on the Sudanese government originated as a response to alleged support of international terrorist organizations. Since 1997, the US imposed sanctions against Sudan prohibiting import and export of goods and technology exempt humanitarian aid. In addition, the financial support of the Sudanese government projects was limited. Multiple US states, local entities, universities and institutional investors pursuing a divestment strategy against Sudan triggered an international FDI drain from Sudan.

In 2003, atrocities and genocide committed against the population of the Darfur region by the Sudanese government raised an international call for political divestiture. Since July 2004, the international community recognized the fighting in the Darfur region as a response to genocide and humanitarian infringements. In the absence of direct military intervention, financial activists and socially responsible investors seek an end to the politically incorrect regime in Sudan.

Key political events that put pressure on international corporations to divest Sudan started by the fall of 2004. Political pressure on European corporations operating in Sudan started when the former German Development Minister Heidemarie Wieczorek-Zeul spoke in favor of sanctions against Sudan.[14] The German Minister reported that contradictory promises from the Sudanese government had counterweighted ending the genocide and humanitarian infringements in Sudan's troubled Darfur region.[15] Wieczorek-Zeul recommended an arms and oil embargo along with freezing Sudanese foreign financial assets.[16]

In 2005, New Jersey adopted a divestment law, which required all state pensions and annuity funds to phase out investments in corporations supporting the Sudanese government exempt from humanitarian aid.[17] The 1997-imposed US sanctions against corporations that operate in Khartoum were renewed by President Bush in 2005. Public pension fund holders were informed to re-consider shares of corporations conducting operations in Sudan that may indirectly support a genocide regime. As divestiture from Sudan unfolded in 2006, the Sudanese Government paid close to US $1 million for an eight-page supplement *New York Times* advertisement advocating for investments praising for a "peaceful, prosperous and democratic future."[18] In response, Sudan activists flooded the *New York Times* with demands for an apology. California state pension funds banned Sudan followed by the US Congress passing a bill to sanction the Sudanese government in 2006.[19] Fidelity advocated for divestiture from 2007 in Sudan.[20] Major investment firms, such as Citibank, JP Morgan Chase, Merrill Lynch, Morgan Stanley, T. Rowe Price, Wells Fargo, passed shareholder resolutions for divesting Sudan.[21] On December 20, 2007, human rights groups and value-based investors

[14]Deutsche Welle, September 13, 2004.
[15]Deutsche Welle, September 13, 2004.
[16]Deutsche Welle, September 13, 2004.
[17]Retrieved from http://www.sudanreeves.org/Article14.html 21. Accessed on March 2008. Retrieved from http://www.sudanreeves.org/Article14.html. Accessed on March 2008.
[18]Retrieved from http://www.democracynow.org/2006/3/27/blood_money_as_divestiture_movement_heats. Accessed on March 2008.
[19]Retrieved from http://sudanwatch.blogspot.com/2006/09/uss-schwarzenegger-signs-pensionfund.html. Accessed on March 2008.
[20]Retrieved from http://fidelityoutofsudan.googlepages.com/fidelity'smay15secfiling. Accessed on March 2008.
[21]Retrieved from http://www.sudandivestment.org/home.asp. Accessed on March 2008.

advocated on Wall Street for divestiture from Sudan.[22] A coalition of leading human rights organizations, six major banks and financial institutions as well as other corporations announced the filing of shareholder resolutions on divestiture from Sudan with a special attention to petroleum corporations.[23] The overarching goal was to promote divestiture from Sudan on Wall Street in order to end the violence in Darfur.[24] By 2008, a Sudan shareholder resolution campaign took off and the SDTF announced the first Sudan-free index and provided tools to calculate indices that exclude Sudan investments from standard ratings.[25] Institutional investors – such as US state and local entities, universities, cities and states – were triggered to divest Sudan.[26] In general, divestment campaigns targeted at industries that fund or indirectly support the Sudanese government. Corporate divestment strategies comprised international corporations operating in the petroleum (70% of petroleum revenues are used to fund military action), energy and defense industries. Other divestment strategies aim for corporate activities that fund or support the Sudanese government or refrain from providing goods and services to the disadvantaged populations of Sudan.[27] Notable corporations having left Sudan trade in the hope to change the Sudanese government's actions are 3M, Xerox, Baker Hughes, Siemens AG, Berkshire Hathaway, Weatherford International and Marathon Oil.

The newest political divestiture advancements are targeted at accomplishing sustainable development. Political divestiture in the sustainability domain calls for sustainable development leadership that steers intentional finance executives' actions to benefit the stakeholders and should-do care for political concerns alongside financial considerations. Not simply considering to avoid unethical behavior by political divestiture, but also adopting a positive and pro-active ethics lens through green investments, become an ueberethical corporate sector drive to consider the interests of a wider range of stakeholders (Puaschunder, 2011a, 2011b, 2015a, 2015c). Sustainability concerns of the finance world thereby directly reach out to a wider constituency group. Stretching the constituency's attention to future generations is based on voluntary sustainability with respect for future generations' needs to ensure the long-term viability of society.

---

[22]Retrieved from http://www.amnestyusa.org/document.php?id=ENGUSA20071220 001&lang=e. Accessed on March 2008.

[23]Retrieved from http://www.amnestyusa.org/document.php?id=ENGUSA20071220 001&lang=e. Accessed on March 2008.

[24]Retrieved from http://www.amnestyusa.org/document.php?id=ENGUSA20071220 001&lang=e. Accessed on March 2008.

[25]Retrieved from http://www.sudandivestment.org/docs/msci_indices_press_release_ 1_7_07.pdf. Accessed on March 2008. Retrieved from http://www.sudandivestment. org/home.asp. Accessed on March 2008.

[26]Retrieved from http://www.sudandivestment.org/divestment.asp. Accessed on March 2008.

[27]Retrieved from http://www.sudandivestment.org/divestment.asp. Accessed on March 2008.

Surpassing state-of-the-art ethical corporate leadership quests on ethically com-
pliant behavior and avoidance of unethical corporate conduct, incorporating
sustainable development into contemporary SRI models may extend the idea of
"positive political divestiture" – that is outdoing legal and ethical expectations –
with respect for UN SDGs. Going beyond mere compliance involves actions
that pro-actively promote social good, beyond what is required by law, political
divestiture for sustainable development extends SRI as a broader social contract
between business and society over time.

Financial leadership on sustainable development of the future will foster social
responsibility beyond mere compliance. Political divestiture helps corporations to
also contribute to societal progress in a responsible and sustainable way. As a
broader definition of corporate responsibility beyond the avoidance of negative
downfalls, the call for political divestiture as a sustainable development implementation tool in the corporate world stresses the obligation to not only with-
draw funds from politically incorrect regimes but to contribute the newly released
funds towards options that steer societal progress with respect for the needs of
future generations. Defining novel responsibilities with a broader social contract
between finance and society embraces discretionary activities that contribute to
sustainable societal welfare. Political divestiture thereby provides a broad range of
corporate, social and societal advantages. Socially responsible funds offer crisis-
stable market options, as being less volatile and influenced by cyclical changes and
whimsical market movements. Especially negative screenings are extremely robust
in times of uncertainty – as socially conscientious investors remain loyal to values
(McLachlan & Gardner, 2004; Puaschunder, 2011a, 2011b).

As for this track record of stability during times of societal and economic
downturns, political divestiture nowadays appears as a favorable market strategy
for lowering emergent risks and ingrain sustainability in economic market systems (Centeno & Tham, 2012; Puaschunder, 2015a, 2015c).

Potential obstacles in the implementation of political divestiture include regulations that appear to be lagging behind when considering novel challenges in the
eye of interdependent economic, institutional and political networks determining financial market moves. New risks are imposed onto corporate and financial
actors by fast-paced information flows that increase the complexity of decision-
making contexts and the cognitive overload of fallible financial leaders.

Globalization and a quickening of information flow about corporate conduct
around the world have placed social and environmental concerns on financial
managerial agendas to an increased extent while more and more financial managers operate in a global environment. The future conceptualization of sustainable
and responsible managerial behavior may embrace the wider constituency range
and stretch the concept of political divestiture from FDI withdrawal to pro-active
voluntary sustainable development funding. An extended stakeholder view on
political divestiture may not only stop at funds withdrawal but consider a broader
set of constituencies.

Future targets in financial decision making may impact the social performance
and long-term viability of society. A broader, social contract between finance and
sustainable development can be enacted by discretionary activities that are not

expected of the finance world and their leaders in a moral or legal sense but directly contribute to sustainable development. This suggests that there is a need for a broader definition of financial social responsibility that goes beyond compliance and in particular political divestiture to encompass the obligation to contribute to societal progress in a responsible and sustainable way. Finance leaders thereby pro-actively outperform legal and ethical expectations regarding the rights and needs of future generations. This positive CSR drive refers to an ueberethical enhance-ment of societal welfare beyond the narrow scope of the current generation.

In the age of globalization, multidisciplinary and multilevel research approaches may investigate the comparative and cross-national dimensions of political dives-titure and their implications for leadership decision making and behavior in the global arena. Interdisciplinary and multilevel research approaches could feature scientific collaborations with researchers based in different countries to embark on contemporary political divestiture studies and investigate the comparative and cross-national dimensions of political divestiture impacting corporations, eco-nomic markets as well as society (Puaschunder, 2015a, 2015c, 2016f). Sustain-ability development representing agents from different disciplinary backgrounds (economics, business, psychology, etc.), research fields (e.g., strategy, organiza-tional behavior and international and cross-cultural management within the field of business), methodological approaches (both qualitative and quantitative) and regional expertise (in-depth knowledge of North-American, European and Asian business systems and institutional environments) may engage on the description of political divestiture as a pro-active finance choice that does not rest at "pun-ishing" politically incorrect markets but rather promote political divestiture as a sustainable development tool to create positive societal change.

International studies of financial world investment reports should be targeted at deriving a sophisticated conceptualization of "responsible behavior" in the political divestiture domain that is applicable to all cultural groups and stake-holders. International research on political divestiture could unravel drivers of sustainable development and responsible financial managerial behavior. Cross-national, multi-level analyses could thereby retrieve influence factors on the adop-tion of globally responsible SRI and political leadership and financial practices that trigger sustainable development. Knowledge of contextual factors that pro-mote political divestiture decision making with regard to sustainability could include favorable characteristics of the organization and aspects of the broader institutional and cultural contexts in which firms are embedded that automatically trigger sustainable development concerns. Thereby the antecedents of sustainable and responsible management at multiple levels (individual, group, organization, national context, supranational bodies) but also the interlinkages among vari-ables should be investigated. Institutional contexts within which companies and their managers operate determine executives' responsible choices. Differences in corporate governance and legal contexts but also the nature of regulation and the likelihood of enforcement shape business ethics as well as expectations of what is considered good governance and ethical conduct in a country. Manag-ers' responsible leadership may therefore vary across institutional contexts in the international arena.

What may be considered as political practice in one part of the world may not be ethical state-of-the-art in another. As a consequence, corporate leaders embedded in different national systems may exhibit different political concerns and sustainable development standards. Cross-national variations in political practices and socially responsible divestiture could be captured in order to derive implications for financial decision makers on how their political divestiture activities could steer sustainable development. Adopted SRI strategies and political divestiture cases may be scrutinized for globally standardized, locally adapted and transnational factors to delineate globally consistent as well as locally oriented political divestiture approaches to support sustainable development. With the underlying premises of exhibited behavior being a function of both – the person and the environment in which that behavior takes place – future research may also unravel political divestiture under situational constraints that the broader cultural and institutional environment imposes on the adoption of sustainable and socially responsible practices.

Cross-culturally operating institutions may face challenges for political divestiture stemming from local differences in financial practices and social ethical norms as well as differing thresholds to sustainable behavior. For instance, challenges arise if corporations or even nation states of the industrialized world outsource financial decision making or sustainable development practices into territories with weaker law enforcement and public scrutiny. These findings emphasize the need for sensitivity to local conditions, transparency of financial decision making as well as stakeholder expectations monitoring when conducting business in different contexts.

Future research may also address ethical dilemmas faced by financial managers in the global arena and their coping strategies. The insights gained promise to enable leaders operating in the global arena to balance global and local considerations in making responsible decisions. As an implication, international political divestiture and sustainable development practices should be locally oriented and emphasize sensitivity to local conditions when conducting financial contributions and practicing political divestiture in different cultural contexts.

Financial executives with foreign subsidiaries should gain training to adapt to specific sustainable development needs and circumstances of local sustainability customs to address sustainable development meaningfully. In the international arena, external influences have shaped the practice of financial social responsibility. National legislations, policy frameworks and cultural landscapes have brought out differing SRI forms as governmental forces and institutional incentives either curb or perpetuate specific financial social considerations. With no stringent legal international basis, in some parts of the world, SRI activities are mandated by national, federal, state or local laws and regulations. In others, the judicial record leaves room for investors if and how to allocate resources in a socially conscientious way.

Until today our insights on external forces shaping SRI customs, however, remain rudimentary. SRI practices are still inconclusive in the global arena leading to disparate SRI notions throughout the world. Capturing the current state of SRI around the world will give a more conclusive picture of the role of financial social responsibility for sustainable development. Analyzing financial social considerations on a global scale through a prism of legal setting and institutional customs will help in finding mutually shared contents of financial social investment. Paying attention to international differences in SRI options will also serve as a first step to harmonize differing financial social responsibility practices in the ongoing SRI adaptation around the globe. Enabling a more harmonious discourse on SRI will reduce the complexity of SRI and diminish socio-economic losses imbued in the ambiguity of this multi-stakeholder phenomenon. Studying the manifold SRI expressions resulting from the various interplays of governmental, corporate and financial market forces will also allow drawing inferences about a positive political divestiture framework and boundary conditions of financial social conscientiousness for sustainable development. International SRI descriptions will thus offer insights on financial social responsibility triggers and repeatable patterns as a basis for successful SRI policies for sustainable development.

Another possibility would be to develop new approaches to international investment law and policy making for promoting sustainability and inclusive development. When investigating the role of the finance sector in sustainable development, a holistic viewpoint on financial social responsibility must be taken. Innovatively coupling individual decision-making research findings with insights on external influences on social responsibility promises to help in managing financial market social responsibility risks for society.

While micro-behavioral economists may in particular unravel human socially responsible cognition in the search for human-imbued ethicality nudges; macroeconomists may explain how individual social responsibility can shape collective market outcomes. General investigations of the perception of SRI in the wake of the inception of the SDGs could determine in what way the financial crisis has changed the financial community's view of economic markets' social responsibility obligations. Once-in-a-century-available information on the social representations of financial social conscientiousness in the time of climate change action should be reaped as a unique source on societal perceptions of financial market reforms for a pro-active stakeholder engagement. Studying investors' cognition on SRI in this unique transition point in time also provides an innovative snapshot of the current crises' potentials to ingrain ethicality in competitive market systems. Concurrent multi-stakeholder analyses may attribute the newly defined role of public and private constituents in social contributions and search for the optimum balance of deregulated market systems and governmental control in providing sustainable development. Capturing real-market social responsibility phenomena could thereby not only help in finding well-tempered PPP networks to support sustainable development. Oversight accountability could also present information on corporate and financial social conduct that will lead academics, technocrats and practitioners to reflect deeper about responsibility within market systems and rethink their roles in backing socially favorable finance flows.

While ingraining social conscientiousness in the financial market appears as a panacea to avert future economic crisis, behavioral economists may contribute their insights on the human natural laws of social responsibility (Puaschunder,

2011a, 2011b). Behavioral ethics specialists may inform on the role of political and financial decision making for sustainable development. Behavioral economics laboratory experiments could thereby shed light on human ethicality to help reducing cognitive barriers on moral dilemmas and alleviate potential financial-social decision-making predicaments (Puaschunder, 2015b). Evolutionary psychologists may explore the emergence of ethicality in human beings by investigating what aspects of social responsibility are ingrained in human traits and the constitution of mind and which ones are nurtured by external factors. Organizational behavior scholars may add by attributing how goals can stipulate ethicality in the finance world. Unpacking social responsibility incentives but also goal settings with positive externalities appear as interesting research avenues. In the case of financial markets, short-term goals can lead to critical trade-offs from long-term societal endeavors (Puaschunder & Schwarz, 2012; Shilon, 2011).

Future research on the fallibility of human decision makers and external, global influences on social responsibility may help deriving recommendations on how to steer socially conscientious behavioral patterns in the finance world. All these endeavors are aimed at fostering financial social responsibility as a future guarantor of economic stability and sustainable social progress throughout the world. This piece hopefully contributes to a future rise of social responsibility in our currently globalizing, economically transforming and environmentally fragile world, in which we should feel responsible.

The newly emerging CSR and SRI phenomena also open avenues for future research with on social responsibility trends. Academic institutions should nurture the financial community's ethical sense. Business schools and think tanks could support SRI research and offer financial ethics education. Financial economists are advised to integrate socio-economic factors into standard economic profit maximization models. Concurrently behavioral economists should aim at explaining human decisions-making fallibility on responsibility considerations and ethicality perceptions.

Future research may study SRI in a qualitatively and quantitatively nested approach. Qualitative interviews on the social perception of SRI will help resolving societal losses imbued in the novelty of the phenomenon and aligning incoherent viewpoints on SRI. Exploratory studies may capture predicted SRI trends with attention to socio-economic success factors of financial social responsibility and stakeholder-specific SRI nuances. Quantitative market assessments may feature the event study methodology as the state-of-the-art analysis technique for measuring the impact of political divestiture with a sustainable development focus on corporate success. Financial market experiments may complementarily test micro-economic effects of divestment behavior.

Research on bounded decision making could reveal implicit and accidental financial social irresponsibility and may validate the proposed socio-psychological SRI framework to distinguish moderator variables of investors' willingness to trade off financial profits for social gratifications. The findings will reduce cognitive barriers of decision-making predicaments and lead to educative means for steering behavioral patterns in a more socially conscientious direction. Research-based transparency campaigns could promote political divestiture as a more risk-free market option during times of crisis throughout the financial community and thereby raise the stakeholders' confidence in pro-social political divestiture sustainable development.

The role of supranational factors that influence responsible leader behavior provides further insight into the propensity to engage in sustainable development. With supranational institutions – such as the UN – having turned to the codification of the triple bottom line in the UNGC, managers are increasingly respected for their accountability and responsibility. Insights on the influence of supranational regulatory measures and institutions (e.g., NGO activism and the enactment of the UNGC) on financially responsible managerial behavior may shed light on success factors in the adoption of sustainable development in the finance world.

International institutions should set priorities on the political divestiture for sustainable development implementation agenda. Quantitative metrics based on standardized evaluation frameworks could help coordinate a global monitoring and impact assessment of the role of the finance sector in sustainable development implementation. The IMF conditionalities could serve as a role model for lasting sustainable development impact and the positive funds allocation monitoring and due diligence quality assurance. In addition, indices of local, national, regional and global financial sustainability endeavor will help building PPP synergies but also shed light on positive and negative externalities and trade-offs of political divestiture steering sustainable development. Independent governance institutional evaluation frameworks will help streamline social, economic and environmental goals through cost-benefit analysis, life cycle cost discounting and social equality programs. PPPs will aid the adaptability and flexibility in collaborations between governments, the finance sector and academia. International organizations' emergent risk and crises prevention frameworks will aid reform political divestiture endeavors to imbue a sustainability focus and how multiple actors' divestiture strategies could be streamlined and synchronized. Differences in business systems, legal context, the nature of regulation and the likelihood of enforcement and punishment modes therefore have to be scrutinized when shaping the political divestiture agenda in the global arena.

Academic research can spearhead temporal perspectives in contemporary SRI research. In particular, a macro-economic model of political divestiture impacts over time could study intertemporal transfers from the finance sector to sustainable development with special attention to public and private sector contributions as well as benefit and burden sharing (Puaschunder, 2016a, 2016e, 2017b). Based on the triple bottom line, social, environmental and economic sustainable development contribution potentials of the finance world could be explored. Cross-cultural differences could be outlined by cross-sectional regression analyses on a global scale. Avenues of future research could also enhance our understanding of how the finance world and other stakeholders can effectively promote socially responsible behavior for sustainable development.

A wider conceptualization of political divestiture leadership based on comparative cross-cultural research will help detect sustainable development antecedents. Interdisciplinary, multilevel research will allow outlining drivers of sustainable development in the investment community and situational influence factors on sustainable development in the international financial sector. The organizational-, situational-, societal- and supranational-level determinants of responsible financial managerial behavior can be influenced by top management teams, policy makers, educators and external regulators. Best practice studies in this area could shed light on how financial companies can systematically design and utilize human resource management practices and leadership development programs to promote responsible investment behavior.

Prospective findings may thus enhance our understanding of how finance companies and other stakeholders can effectively prevent, manage and control the finance sector risks associated with politically fragile markets but also go beyond to explore innovative ways how SRI can contribute to sustainable development around the globe. Capturing the impact of external factors on financially socially responsible decision making and coping with the ethical dilemmas in leadership challenges may serve as a basis for training and development activities on using political divestiture for accomplishing positive societal change. The implementation of political divestiture for sustainable development could further be solicited through building financial cultures that enhance an ethical climate. In line with the mere exposure effect, access to information on sustainable development fosters the integration of environmental and social governance in financial decision making (Frey & Irle, 2002). Information disclosure about the stability and effectiveness of political divestiture, when attributed to sustainable development, will help in driving consumer confidence in pro-social political divestiture acts.

With the rising importance of transparent financial social responsibility and financial institutions integrating ESG issues into investment analysis; social investment criteria should become a standard part of the fiduciary duty of trustees, financial advisers, asset managers and intermediary institutions. To strengthen these trends, financial institutions and experts are encouraged to consider environmental and social responsibility in a variety of ways. Information on positive political divestiture should become part of financial market operations. Media reports may inform asset managers and financial analysts about the link between political divestiture and sustainable development. Supervisory bodies could help promote the inclusion of socio-ethical political criteria in financial management. Accounting entities, rating agencies and index providers should adopt environmental and social governance standards as a basis for evaluation criteria that guarantee the concurrent financial and ethical performance. Stock exchange advisors can help by communicating the importance of environmental and social responsibility governance to listed corporations. Asset managers should encourage brokers to conduct SRI screenings with a political and sustainable development focus.

Investors are recommended to request information on SRI and develop political proxy voting strategies. Pension fund trustees can help by considering environmental and social criteria in the formulation of investment mandates. Consultants and financial advisers should incorporate environmental and social corporate governance in their portfolio allocation strategies and accept social responsibility as a state-of-the-art of fiduciary obligations. Financial analysts will then assess market opportunities with respect to social contributions and actively participate in ongoing voluntary responsibility initiatives.

As the basis for stakeholder engagement and monitoring, transparency and accountability are key for advancing corporate and financial social market behavior. Novel SRI options that fulfill unmet responsibility needs will open the market for socially responsible economic growth while bringing societal change.

Future research may also connect the individual experience to social responsibility in order to unravel ethicality nudges. Common goal compliance can thereby be modeled by contexts that automatically nudge corporate decision makers in a sustainable development direction. Internationally validated political divestiture for sustainable development models will elucidate intercultural, national and regional differences in sustainable finance impact. Findings will help imbue efficiency measures on political divestiture for sustainable development through real-world relevant means following the greater goal to provide fruitful corporate contributions for a sustainable humankind. Cross-national sustainability solutions and interculturally sensitive political divestiture business practices may help imbue sustainable development concern in corporate conduct in the global arena.

On the financial corporate incentive level, sustainable development may be implemented through performance management and reward systems to hold managers accountable for politically irresponsible behavior as well as creating psychological incentives to think about future consequences of current corporate conduct and financial support of irresponsible markets. Best practices studies on political divestiture will serve as corporate risk management tool to help build a culture of positive SRI and foster a corporate design that pays tribute to ethical financial leadership. In building a cadre of sustainable development leaders in the finance world through corporate trainings and team building development but also financial social responsibility performance measurement and political-conscientious decision-making reward systems, sustainable development in the finance sector will be advanced.

At the organizational level, when recruiting, selecting and promoting financial managers, it is essential for organizations to understand how individual-level variables – such as personality traits, motives and values – may predict managers' propensity to engage in ethical behavior. For example, firms can use personality tests and integrity tests, along with interviews and assessment centers, to help determine which employees might be more likely to act politically responsibly. They can also assess applicants' attitudes and values to decide whether they will match the corporate culture, with the assumption that candidates' formal qualifications and job-related skills may not be the best predictors of responsible behavior on the job. Studying personality traits but also motives and values that steer financial managers' propensity to engage in politically conscientious financial decision making will allow to set up assessment centers that reveal which individuals are more likely to act irresponsibly and if the managerial ethics will likely match the corporate culture on the sustainable development dimension. Sustainable development can also be imbued in financial activities by creating and enforcing financial company policies and codes of conduct, supporting training and development initiatives which are aimed at increasing moral awareness regarding political conditions of the operating markets. Once the individual has joined the organization, induction programs, individual coaching by the supervisor, training and development programs and other socialization practices could ensure that newcomers learn values, expected behaviors and social knowledge that are necessary to become politically conscientious financial managers and leaders.

In terms of communication and control systems, top management teams and government officials may actively promote responsible behavior and discourage irresponsible behavior by communicating ethical integrity messages. Regarding the specific case of political divestiture, future behavioral decision-making studies may target unraveling the decision to divest, asking whether corporations were pressured into divestment by shareholders, customers or other stakeholders. First-mover advantage effects may be investigated alongside general SRI questions such as the authenticity of divestiture.

Future investigations may also pay attention to the generalizability of former punishment political divestiture cases such as the divestiture from Sudan, capital flight from Burma, the ongoing capital drain from Iran, the arms embargo of the Israel–Palestine region and the contemporary trend toward positive political divestiture fossil fuel divestment and reallocation toward green funds. Special attention could be paid to developing countries which are most dependent on FDI for aid and especially vulnerable to political infringements, humanitarian crises and sustainable development needs. Comparison studies with different divestment sectors could derive a common theory on the corporate implications of divestiture and financial impact in accomplishing SDGs.

Most recent political divestiture developments include the divestment from non-renewables, foremost oil and gas. Climate change presents specific risks and challenges associated with system failure. The very logic of increasing globalization carries problems that demand for a re-designing of governance structures and institutional arrangements that reduce the probability of such dangers arising (Centeno, Cinlar et al., 2013). Carbon divestiture is an innovative means to fund climate stabilization burden sharing and an implicit climate change mitigation and adaptation means to overcome future socio-economic losses and avert irreversible tipping points. Carbon divestiture thereby instigates a transition to renewable energy and funding mitigation and adaptation policies (Puaschunder, 2017c).

In the current implementation of carbon divestiture, deriving recommendations on how to use carbon divestiture as a market mechanism to transition to renewable energy could be based on historical examples. Future research must analyze climate change risks inherent in global environmental conditions (Puaschunder, 2018c). Future exploratory climate change literature analyses could clarify what contemporary notions of climate change risks are associated with carbon industries in order to retrieve a real economy-based climate change risk definition to be used for carbon divestiture acts. In the future, international academic and practitioners' literature on climate change risk, climate mitigation and adaptation as well as climate justice should be reviewed. A thorough literature analysis will form a foundation of knowledge on climate change, climate mitigation and adaptation as well as climate justice approaches on an international scale to be integrated to a framework of carbon divestiture. A stakeholder-nuanced review of corporations with carbon-intensive activities but also unnecessary carbon footprint should cover public and private, organizational and societal stakeholders to retrieve notions on global warming risks and climate change mitigation and adaptation stemming from carbon industries.

In the international arena, a stakeholder analysis should also hold a special focus on climate funding as well as bond solutions. The results could guide a descriptive analysis of climate change mitigation and adaptation strategies based on carbon divestiture. The theoretical insights gained could also lead to a final semi-structured interview guide to explore climate risk notions based on carbon-intensive industries and success factors to avoid climate change by fossil fuel divestment and gain climate justice by a transition to renewable energy and climate bonds solutions.

Practitioners' bond market actors and finance stakeholders may be recruited comprising of very many stakeholder groups such as banking executives (e.g., financial executives, managers and bank officials); fiduciaries (e.g., private equity, mutual funds and investment managers); institutional investors from central banks, governmental and rating agencies, universities; private investors (e.g., shareholders, etc.) from financial trade agencies; public policy specialists of global governance networks; labor union representatives; NGOs (e.g., NGO executives) contacted online; international organizations (e.g., UN, World Economic Forum and Open Society Institute); academics (e.g., professors, assistants and PhD candidates) and media representatives (e.g., journalists and reporters). These activities could be oriented toward producing an interdisciplinary consensus on global climate change risks stemming from carbon-intensive industries and formulating guidelines for future research on climate change mitigation and adaptation support by carbon divestiture.

Subsequent exploratory descriptive and qualitative data collection on climate change mitigation and adaptation should clarify how climate change risks are defined and perceived by various stakeholder groups in order to retrieve a stakeholder-specific climate change risk definition with focus on climate justice, mitigation and adaptation. Contemporary notions and strategies of climate change risk mitigation will draw a real-economy relevant climate change risk mitigation strategy based on divestiture. What factors contribute to the success of carbon divestiture should be clarified in order to derive success factors of climate change risk mitigation and adaptation means and prospectively favorable interdependencies of divestiture and subsequent clean energy investment.

Future research may combine theoretical and empirical research featuring qualitative and quantitative methodology. After a literature review of climate change risk, climate justice and climate change mitigation and adaptation strategies, quantitative research should target at gaining an in-depth understanding of climate change risk mitigation and climate change stability implementation and climate adaptation in the international arena through divestiture. Quantitative market analyses aim at capturing international climate change mitigation and adaptation interdependencies regarding divestment. The field-specific perspectives include a nomenclature creation, literature reviews, quantitative and qualitative methods and public policy information of experts and institutions.

The first research endeavor should develop our understanding of climate change risk through the analysis of specific climate threats. The task will be approached by case studies and expert interviews with the goal of developing a multidisciplinary methodological analysis of global climate risks to be proposed to be alleviated through divestment and reinvestment in clean energy solutions as well as recommendations of harmonious climate change mitigation and climate adaptation strategies.

Preliminary research should therefore aim at better understanding the structure, nature and challenges of these complex interaction and feedback systems of climate, climate change mitigation and adaptation choices and elaborate how it can be funded through refinancing strategies away from carbon-intensives to clean energy.

The complexity and number of interactions will also require a qualitative analysis on the challenges of climate policy funding. In this context, it is also important to capture and map what regulatory and policy solutions exist and have been developed in response to climate crises in the financial sector. Academic studies should target climate change monitoring, inspection and surveillance as well as climate change adaptation policies as the basis for further modeling of how to respond with an ethical imperative on market transactions.

In the climate change burden sharing model building, the underlying research question is what would be sustainable financing methods of climate change financing in order to assist the implementation and management of climate stabilization via carbon divestiture? In deriving information on climate change mitigation implementation and management strategies, the question should be answered what institutions could issue and what sustainable finance regimes could manage climate change bonds funded by carbon divestiture. This information is essential in order to craft institutional climate change management strategies and define feasible market structures and policies to support climate change bonds.

All these endeavors will help in following the greater goal to derive viable intertemporal policy strategies based on real market mechanisms. In addition, the fiscal sustainability of climate change bonds over time should be evaluated in order to estimate real world relevant climate change mitigation market strategies in the finance sector based on future bond prospects funded by fossil fuel divestiture.

Future research endeavors should survey the current scholarship on contemporary climate policies and their funding (e.g., cap & trade, carbon tax and green energy). Here also climate change mitigation and adaptation strategies should be gathered in order to prepare the modeling and methodologies of systemic climate risk and climate stabilization based on carbon divestiture. Intergenerational climate change burden sharing through intergenerational fiscal policies and sustainable finance methods could be delineated in order to introduce carbon tax and climate bonds as a novel approach to implement intergenerational climate justice. Comparisons of climate change risk reduction means on the international level will help derive insights for global governance experts on how to implement climate justice: climate change mitigation and adaptation study efforts should investigate how climate change is mitigated on the international level in order to derive international climate change prevention strategies. The adaptation efforts should be scrutinized on a global level in order to unravel interdependencies of climate change mitigation and adaptation based on carbon divestiture on a world-wide basis. This may be done by economic market analyses featuring externality predictions and cross-market comparisons coupled with social network analyses. Community research will present field-specific perspectives on systemic risk mitigation in the finance sector. Expert interviews will allow an understanding of aspect of climate change bond strategies that stakeholders find most relevant. Case studies on global climate risk mitigation will portray climate change abatement with attention to particular stakeholder perspectives in order to retrieve a real-world relevant climate strategy.

Overall, all these endeavors will strengthen the research and design of climate, encourage interdisciplinary exchange on the contemporary complex climate agenda in strategic partnerships, as well as raise awareness and engage the broader international public on multiple climate regimes. Future concrete data collection could feature semi-structured telephone or personal interviews with finance experts representing a stakeholder range. Expert interviews will gain a stakeholder-specific definition of climate change, climate risk, climate mitigation and adaptation as well as climate change bond strategies in the finance sector. The acquired information will present stakeholder-specific contemporary notions of climate change, climate change mitigation and adaptation efforts as well as their interdependencies. Revealing the common sense, but also stakeholder-specific nuances of climate change risk perceptions with a special focus on climate change mitigation solutions of the finance sector offers an invaluable opportunity to highlight unknown climate implementation strategies. This working part will include a meta-analysis of risk and its various meanings held by different constituency groups in order to provide the basis for global governance and public policy recommendations on how to mitigate and adapt to global warming. A vital research exchange and scholar transfer between various stakeholder groups – featuring external quality control and results presentations – will help discuss risk definitions with colleagues prior to continuing to develop ideas and combine the lessons learned in approaches of the forming community around endeavors. The information retrieved will also help create a coherent set of papers on systemic climate change risks, mitigation and adaptation as well as policy briefings reflecting the different academic disciplines and viewpoints on the climate agenda. The data gathered should be quantitatively analyzed by descriptive and multivariate methods in order to scrutinize the international climate risk mitigation and adaptation means. Network analyses will capture climate mitigation and adaptation differences to derive climate justice implementation recommendations.

In order to unravel climate change risk mitigation and adaptation success factors of carbon divestiture, economic market data should be analyzed by descriptive and multivariate methods. For instance, network analysis will allow investigating risk mitigation factors and climate adaptation interdependencies following the greater goal to outline prescriptive public policies to enhance climate justice. The analysis of climate change risk mitigation means will help develop recommendations on regulatory schemes. Coupled with the study of climate change adaptation strategies through carbon divestiture by institutions, industry actors and policy makers, the results will lead to practical guidelines on how to implement environmental sustainability.

The gained insight on climate mitigation and adaptation as well as the expert discussions and scholarly exchange on how to prevent systemic risks through fossil fuel divestment will advance the climate change mitigation agenda. In addition, an open access interactive online climate change simulation should be released as an attempt to map the contemporary climate efforts and regimes on a global scale to provide a possible avenue for future work.

Overall, these outlined research avenues should innovatively develop new interpretations, understandings and concepts of averting climate risks through carbon divestiture but also help in deriving balanced approaches to implement climate justice and adapt to global warming through funding clean energy. In compiling scholarship and theories on risk mitigation strategies in the climate action domain as well as by bringing together experts on climate risk coupled with the financial sector insights on how to finance climate justice by a concrete divestiture plan, the planned research will help create a central reference point and resources on aggregate information on the implementation and sophistication of climate justice. The planned endeavors will elevate the importance of climate justice scholarship while deriving implications for climate stability. Emphasizing areas where to apply climate mitigation and where to promote climate adaptation strategies will help deriving practical implications for the private industry and public policy sector to fund specific causes. Understanding the different climate risk attitudes but also shedding light on previously unknown climate mitigation and adaptation interdependencies will aid environmental sustainability to ensure a future sustainable humankind.

For practitioners, the prospective results will help lowering institutional downfalls of increasingly interconnected and fragile global networks. For academia, the endeavors will spearhead interdisciplinary research on climate justice and lead to invaluable resources on systemic risk with short-term innovative and long-term historic value for this generation and the following.

As carbon divestiture serves many purposes and varies over time and by context, future comparative studies will help in defining political divestiture in the search for finding an overarching legal framework that unites disparate approaches. A definition of political divestiture will also help in drawing inferences about the impact of political divestiture on shareholder wealth. As political divestiture captures transnational foreign investment flows, becoming knowledgeable about the impact of political divestiture on shareholder wealth will help in crafting international standards for fiduciaries. Finding evidence for the effect of political divestiture on corporate endeavors will clarify to what degree political divestiture supports or infringes upon shareholder primacy rules and fiduciary responsibilities.

As of today, there are vast international differences in the legal interpretation of fiduciary responsibility – in Anglo-Saxon fiduciary, responsibility is more focused on return on investments, while Western European Roman Law-dominated

countries legally grant fiduciaries more leeway in considering the overall societal impact of the asset issuing entities. Prospective insights on the efficiency of
political divestiture to serve shareholder goals are a cornerstone in the conceptualization of a standardized international law on fiduciary responsibilities, which
appears necessary in a financially globalizing world that demands for ingraining
responsibility in market economies. For the international investment community,
shedding light on the impact of stakeholder pressure on investment decisions is
essential as for drawing inferences about the financial market stability.

On the global governance level, the prospective results may help in predicting future foreign investment flows and outcomes of contemporary political
frictions – such as, for example, humanitarian infringements in Burma, Iran's
nuclear proliferation and Sudan's humanitarian crisis in the Darfur region.
Insights on the effectiveness of political divestiture will also help in generating
public policies for international institutional assistance of political divestiture.
With the "U.S. Comprehensive Iran Sanctions, Accountability and Divestment
Act" having passed the House vote in April 2010, the downsides of sanctions and
political divestiture have been openly debated. Critics condemn sanctions as a
hostility breeding "act of war" and draw attention to unintended consequences
of insufficiently understood negative externalities that may eventually backfire.
Libertarians critiqued political divestiture as a misuse of financial markets that
undermines free trade and shareholder profit maximization goals. To contribute
to finding a fact-based solution for this political debate, a more sophisticated in-
depth understanding of the corporate implications of political divestiture that is
based on comparative results is needed. All these endeavors will aid in sophisti-
cating the idea of channeling funds toward renewable energy while improving the
ethical imperative of the corporate and financial worlds.

In conclusion, this chapter intended to help resolve the questions that emerge
from political divestiture's role in sustainable development. In the age of sustainable development, the demand for ingraining ethicality in financial decision making has reached unprecedented momentum. Overall, political activism in finance
releases innovative corporate and financial market potentials to create value for
society. A political divestiture for sustainable development framework portrayed
the manifold potentials of political divestiture to finance sustainable development
in a harmonious interplay of deregulated market systems and governmental control in ensuring market-driven social responsibility. Future research may address
ways how to better capture the effects of political divestiture on economic markets and societal systems in order to provide recommendations for a successful
rise of sustainable development solutions within modern market economies. All
these endeavors are aimed at fostering financial social responsibility as a future
guarantor of sustainable economic stability and societal progress throughout the
world.

2.4.20. Positive-screened SRI Ventures of the Future

Corporate and financial social responsibilities within market systems are enabled
under the auspice of international organizations with special attention to global

governance provision. As of today, social responsibility has emerged as an *en vogue* topic for corporate executives, governmental officials, international public servants and stakeholder representatives. Due to globalization, worldwide business mergers, but also as for international deficiencies beyond the scope of nation states; the call for CSR and SRI has reached unprecedented momentum (Ahmad, 2008; Beck, 1998; Levitt, 1983; Livesey, 2002, Scholte, 2000).

In the wake of the 2008 World Financial Recession, corporate social misconduct and financial fraud have steered consumers and investors to increasingly pay attention to democracy and social responsibility within market systems. Stakeholder pressure addressed the social responsibility of market actors and information disclosure of corporate and financial conduct. Legislative reforms enhance the accountability of financial market operations.

With the era of liberalization being halted by the 2008 financial crisis, the reinterpretation of the public-private sector roles in providing social services has leveraged social responsibility into a pressing topic of debate. The renaissance of attention to responsibility as a prerequisite for the functioning of economic systems portrayed CSR and SRI as windows of opportunity to re-establish trust in fallible market systems (Little, 2008; Livesey, 2002; Matten & Crane, 2005; Trevino & Nelson, 2004).

The new COVID-19 pandemic accounts for the most severe health and economic threat since about a century. The human, medical and economic shock with major fallout in social, humanitarian and international development domains is the most tragic event that has occurred since the Great Plagues of the medieval times, the Great Depression and the two World Wars. Yet, in every crisis and lasting economic, societal and humanitarian shock, there are always positive externalities as well.

A digitalization disruption with a particular focus on healthcare, preventive medicine and whole-rounded, ecofriendly lifestyles is perpetuated by COVID-19. The skyrocketing digitalization disruption in the wake of COVID-19 holds the potential for digital medical care.

Ethics of inclusion will become future key qualifications to succeed in international student pools and digitalized global careers. The future after the COVID-19 pandemic holds the potential of ethical imperatives of inclusion to ennoble our prospected future post-COVID-19 world to come. Overall, these trends aim at providing a glimpse of hope in despair and grievance over COVID-19 and allow to advocate for equal access or redistribution of the merits of the gains from COVID-19 for living the dream of a better, more beautiful society than COVID-19 has hit before.

A prospective post-COVID-19 New Age Renaissance will advance healthcare (Piper, 2020; Puaschunder, 2020e, 2020f). With the COVID-19 pandemic, the connection between preventive medicine, general health and prevalence has gained unprecedented attention. In the novel Coronavirus crisis, prevention and general, holistic medicine determine whether COVID-19 puts patients on a severe or just mild symptom trajectory. Lifestyle and the general status of the immune system are decisive in whether the Coronavirus becomes a danger for the individual. Due to a weakened immune system being significantly related to a severe COVID-19 disease trajectory propensity, preventive medical care has become more important for societal well-being and a precursor to avoid emergency medicine attention.

In light of the heightened health risks of COVID-19, in the corporate world, employers naturally select healthier workers (Gelter & Puaschunder, 2021). Already during the early onset of the pandemic, elder and chronic patients' passing and vulnerabilities risk estimates changed labor market demand toward favoring young, healthier and Corona-survivors, who may benefit from natural immunity and being more virus-resistant (The Schwartz Center for Economics Policy Analysis, 2020).

On the corporate level, those corporations that manage to build a healthy environment that is attentive to prevention will gain from COVID-19 in the long run. Corporations that invest in hygiene but also group learning and team skills of hygienic working conduct likely see a long-term labor-driven economic growth. In light of pre-existing conditions and obesity determining the likelihood of COVID-19 severity trajectory, corporations now also focus on fostering a healthy and ecological diet for their employees. Measures that can guarantee continued health in employment account for corporate success and economic growth. Corporate governance could also promote self-monitoring of the state of health of the employee and the comprehensive prevention in a holistic lifestyle. For instance, the German Prevention Act of 2015 of the German Federal Government compensates corporations to foster prevention in vigilant self-care but also team learning of healthy lifestyles in the workforce, acknowledging the power of preventive care for economic productivity. Focusing on collective health as a common good will in the long run make labor components more productive. All these means of a hygienic environment, healthy preventive care and workplace interactions may be summed up in learning-by-preventing economic growth potential. The expected economic growth potential should also be considered to be taxed and the extra fiscal space used to offset the socio-economic losses and social misery implied in inequalities in market selection.

As for outside working conditions, those corporations that are placed in benevolent health-promoting territories will have a competitive advantage and gain in terms of labor quality (Puaschunder & Beerbaum, 2020a, 2020b). Countries around the world are currently paying attention to preventive medical care in the wake of pandemic outbreak monitoring. Those nations that can offer technological advancements to monitor pandemic outbreaks but also medicine of the future that helps prevent diseases instead of just treating their consequences produce positive labor advantages (Salzburg Declaration, 2020).

The introduction of AI in our contemporary society imposes historically unique challenges for humankind. The emerging autonomy of AI holds unique potentials for eternal life of robots, AI and algorithms alongside unprecedented economic superiority, data storage and computational advantages.

The contemporary trend of slowbalisation, as the slowing down of conventional globalization of goods, services and FDI flows, and halted globalization due to COVID-19 lead to a continuous data transfer rising. These market trends of conventional globalization slowing and prospering AI-related industries are proposed as the first market disruption in the wake of the large-scale entrance of AI into our contemporary economy.

AI is "a broad set of methods, algorithms, and technologies that make software 'smart' in a way that may seem human-like to an outside observer" (Noyes, 2016). The "human-like" intelligence of machines derives from machines being created to think like humans but at the same time to also act rationally (Laton, 2016; Russell & Norvig, 1995; Themistoklis, 2018). AI is perceived as innovative technology or as the sum of different technological advances as the privilege of the private, technological sector with developing public regulation (Dowell, 2018).

The outbreak of the COVID-19 pandemic has exacerbated the rise of AI, robots and algorithms in the economy, which is expected to completely disrupt employment patterns. With the advancement of technologies, employment patterns will shift to a polarization between AI's rationality and humanness. Robots and social machines have already replaced people in a variety of jobs – for example, airports' smart flight check-in kiosks or self-check-outs instead of traditional cashiers but also in cleaning robotics and self-monitoring healthcare devices. Almost all traditional professions are prospected to be infused with or influenced by AI, algorithms and robotics in the future. For instance, robots have already begun to serve in the medical and healthcare profession, law and – of course – IT, transportation, retail, logistics and finance, to name a few. Social robotics may also be quasi-servants that overwhelmingly affect our relationships. Already now social robots are beginning to take care of our elderly and children (Alemi, Meghdari, & Saffari, 2017). Chat-GPT and Bard are additional market innovations that are expected to disrupt our workforce and way of living.

With the advancement of technology, social robots have found broader applications in the private and public sectors, such as educational and cultural affairs, games and entertainment, clinical and rehabilitation, nursing of children and/ or elderly, search and rescue operations, healthcare and hygiene management, to name a few (Meghdari, Alemi, Zakipour, & Kashanian, 2018). For example, social robots – such as ASIMO, Nao, iCub, ARASH and RASA – have been developed for "Edutainment" or "education-entertainment" purposes. They aid the study of cognition (both human and artificial), motion and other areas related to the advancement of robotics serving our society (Meghdari & Alemi, 2018). In addition, a few medical and healthcare toy-like robots, such as PARO, which looks like a baby seal, or ARASH, which is a humanoid, have been designed for therapeutic purposes, such as reducing distress, stimulating cognitive activity, teaching specific subjects and improving socialization (Meghdari, Shariati, Alemi, & Vossoughi, 2018). Similarly, Sharif University of Technology's socially assistive robot RASA has been developed to help coach and teach Persian Sign-Language to Iranian deaf children (Meghdari, Alemi, et al., 2018). Personal care and companion robots are increasingly being used to care for the elderly and children, such as RI-MAN, PaPeRo and CareBot (Meghdari & Alemi, 2018; Puaschunder, 2019c).

In recent years, robotics technology has extended its applications from factories to more general-purpose practices in society – for instance, such as the use of robots in clinical and rehabilitation, nursing and elderly care, search and rescue operations (Meghdari & Alemi, 2018). Social robots have become clinical and educational assistants for social interventions, treatment and education, such as language trainings but also assistance of children with disabilities like autism, down syndrome, cancer distress, hearing impairment, etc. (Meghdari, Alemi, et al., 2018; Meghdari, Shariati, et al., 2018; Taheri, Meghdari, Alemi, & Pouretemad, 2018). Initial investigations clearly indicate that social robots can play a positive role in the improvement of children's social performance, reduction of distress during treatments and enhancing their learning abilities (Meghdari & Alemi, 2018; Meghdari et al., 2018a,b; Veruggio, 2005).

Already now, about 28% of the workforce in modern economies are estimated to be based on AI or AI supported (Fraad-Wolff, in speech). First market disruptions of AI entering economies are currently speculated to cause a trend of slowbalisation – as a counter-trend to globalization. Globalization sprang from America's sponsorship of a new world order from the post-World Wars era, which allowed cross-border flows of goods and capital to recover after years of chaos (Centeno, Creager et al., 2013; Centeno & Tham, 2012). During the golden age of globalization from 1990 to 2010, the world became flat: immigration increased from 2.9% to 3.3% of the world's population and global trade grew from 39% of GDP in 1990 to 58% last year (*The Economist*, 2019). Asia became part of the globalized upon China's entry into the WTO in 2001, which created a model of offshoring manufacturing to countries based on cost efficiency variances, primarily labor costs (Profita, 2019). The Washington Consensus embraced the world and promised to bring prosperity to everyone around the globe (Rodrik, 2007). Open markets and free trade were praised to lift billions of people out of poverty in Asia, Latin America and Africa via economic growth (Held & McGrew, 2007).

With the collapse of the Soviet Union in 1989 and the end of the Cold War in 1991, the world became even more interconnected and global market economies integrated around the world. Trade and investment increased, while barriers to migration and cultural exchange lowered (Mohamed, 2016). The EU but also free trade agreements, such as the North American Free Trade Agreement – which the governments of the USA, Canada and Mexico signed in 1992 – removed barriers to the free flow of people, goods and services, thereby facilitating greater trade, investment and migration across borders to an unprecedented extent (Profita, 2019; Puaschunder, 2019a, 2019b; World Bank Group Migration and Development Brief 26, 2016).

From the turn of the millennium up until 2018, China increased its GDP from $1.2 trillion to $11 trillion, a sign of historically unprecedented growth for a country of this size (Profita, 2019). A similar phenomenon occurred in India, Vietnam and other countries. Globalization also supported the growth of large multinational companies that offshored production processes and consumers to access an endless number of products at competitive prices from around the globe. Commerce soared as the cost of shifting goods in ships and planes fell, phone calls got cheaper, tariffs were cut and finance liberalized. Business went gangbusters as subsidies opened production around the world, investors roamed and consumers shopped in supermarkets with goods from around the globe (Profita, 2019).

As never before in history, traveling had become available to the general populace at affordable prices. The number of refugees reached all-time highs. If not moving oneself, free data services provided on the "window to the world" of the internet, which allowed everyone to consume the globe anytime anywhere.

Yet, globalization also brought about negative consequences and unforeseen shadows of the invisible hand. Until the 1990s, studies report no connection between GDP and happiness – yet from the 1990s, there is a negative correlation found between GDP and happiness (Kirchler, 2011). This trend is attributed to the internet and access to information about other places on earth's living conditions creating emotionally hurtful comparisons in desolate places, also fueling migration trends, which have never been higher as of now.

When America took a protectionist turn in its 2016 Presidential election, the USA was, once again, first in sensing and acting on a contemporary detected, most novel worldwide trend: We currently live in the age of slowbalisation. Protectionism, trade wars, emerging economies' slowdown and the decrease in goods and services trade as well as a slump in transnational investments are all signs of the global trend of globalization that have come to a halt, even before COVID-19 contracted global efforts. UK followed shortly after the US presidential with voting for Brexit. Globalization has slowed in our current times of "slowbalisation," a term coined in 2015 by Adjiedj Bakas, who sensed first that globalization has given way to a new era of sluggishness.

Globalization has slowed in the past decade after the 2008 global recession. Trade has fallen from 61% of world GDP in 2008 to 58% now (*The Economist*, 2019). If these figures exclude emerging markets (of which China is one), it has been flat at about 60% (*The Economist*, 2019). The capacity of supply chains that ship half-finished goods across borders has shrunk. Intermediate imports rose fast in the 20 years to 2008, but since then have dropped from 19% of the world GDP to 17% (*The Economist*, 2019). The march of multinational firms has halted as the global corporate share of global profits of all listed corporations has dropped from 33% in 2008 to 31% (*The Economist*, 2019). Long-term cross-border investment by all firms, known as FDI, has tumbled from 3.5% of the world GDP in 2007 to 1.3% in 2018 (*The Economist*, 2019). As cross-border trade and companies have stagnated relative to the economy, so too has the intensity of financial links. Cross-border bank loans have collapsed from 60% of GDP in 2006 to about 36% (*The Economist*, 2019). Excluding rickety European banks, they have been flat at 17%. Gross capital flows have fallen from a peak of 7% in early 2007 to 1.5% (*The Economist*, 2019). Since 2008, the share of economies converging from emerging economies to catch up with the rich world in terms of output per person using purchasing-power parity has fallen from 88% to 50% (*The Economist*, 2019). So in fact, almost all conventional measures of global trade and market integration have fallen. Tariffs have reached the highest levels in the last 40 years and additional costs of trade have begun to be passed onto consumers (Profita, 2019). In the second half of 2018, the largest US companies lost about 6 billion – or 3% – in profits due to tariffs (Profita, 2019; *The Economist*, 2019). US and Chinese investments in Europe have fallen dramatically, for instance, China's investment by 73% in 2018 (*The Economist*, 2019). The global value of foreign investment by multi-nationals decreased by 20% in the same year (*The Economist*, 2019). As the service sector appears to continue to expand, relocation for the sake of consumption has stagnated or declined as it is harder to relocate services (Buera & Kaboski, 2012; Echevarria, 1997). Based on the post-2008–2009 World Financial Decade, *The Economist* (2019) already predicted a decline in exports from 28% to 23% of GDP over the next ten years, which would resemble a similar drop between 1929 and 1946, even before COVID-19 halted international export in an unprecedented way.

Slowbalisation speaks to the fact that since the 2008 World Financial Recession, Asia's growth rates are slowing, cross-border investments, trade, bank loans and supply chains have been shrinking or stagnating relative to world GDP (*The Economist*, 2019). While one of the main benefits of globalization was that between 1990 and 2010 most emerging countries were able to close some of the gaps with developed nations, a slowdown in globalization likely leads to a reversal in underdeveloped parts of the world catching up (*The Economist*, 2019). In addition to projected major political risks and the decline in socio-economic development, with the absence of a global cooperation, it will be more difficult to tackle and solve major coordination challenges – such as climate change and climate refugees, immigration and tax evasion (Baldwin, 2017; Profita, 2019). This predicament is crucial if we seem to trade off environmental degradation with international development opportunities – the two most pressing obstacles for contemporary humankind (World Bank, 2015).

Politically, where we seemed to have spent decades after two World Wars to break down walls and pacify Europe in a Union, we are now back to building barriers faster than before (Profita, 2019). Since 2009, the number of new free trade agreements between countries has plummeted and restrictions on trade have proliferated on duties, anti-dumping measures and on non-tariff barriers to trade. Bloomberg reports that the DHL monitor tracking shows that global trade is continuing to lose a little steam amid an escalating tariff battle between the world's biggest economies (Profita, 2019).[28] Media and news but also big data trends appear to have open gates to the world as never before while shrinking the number of local newspapers and media outlets (Hagey, Alpert, & Serkez, 2019; Puaschunder, 2019b, 2019c, 2019d). Corporate greed and politics of fear are partially argued as socio-political trends heating up slowbalisation (Profita, 2019). International remedies are called upon to ensure upholding the benefits of globalization in our commonly shared fragile world to ensure continuous economic prosperity, societal advancement and humane dignity for all (Banerjee & Moll, 2010).

Yet, this is not the end of the story, as some globalization features still show rising integration. Technological advances, including mobile phones and especially the internet, have contributed to globalization by connecting people all over the globe. Innovation spurs companies to substitute labor while technology shocks drive economic growth, especially when technologies progressively reduce

---

[28]www.bloomberg.com/news/articles/2018-09-27/global-trade-growth-slowly-losing-steam-as-business-feels-pinch

the physical work component (World Bank Report, 2008). While goods are not shipped around the globe in extensive global value chains, the consumers themselves have become yet more global. The World Wide Web links billions of people and devices, providing innumerable opportunities for the exchange of goods, services, cultural products, knowledge and ideas in the sharing economy. The internet connectivity and volume of data crossing borders have risen by 64 times, according to McKinsey, as people appear to enjoy experiences abroad and consume data. Building dreams and hope based on information shared online, migration to the rich world has risen over the past decade. International parcels and flights are growing fast, almost exponentially. In the beginning of 2019, *The Economist*[29] outlined that traditional globalization features have slowed while international parcel volume, data transfer and international air travel as well as migration to the developed world continues on a globalization course. At the same time, air travel was highest ever right before the outbreak of the Coronavirus pandemic, indicating that while goods do not travel around the globe anymore and emerging economies seem to become more versatile in producing on their own for their own needs, human did shop for experiences and service consumption to an extent and degree as never before in history.

Relocating production sights from global value chain offshore sights that were spread out during the golden years of globalization back to where goods and services are consumed is happening in the wake of slowbalization. High-end production has discovered the luxury of opening consumers' eyes for the entire production and ensuring that CSR is lived throughout the value change. Corporations appear to be focusing their production back to where they serve their customers and consumers have recently gained substantial interest in more local products. While companies around the globe featured an offshoring trend during the golden age of globalization, contemporary reshoring and "glocalization" in the increasing salience of local and regional levels occurs. With the ringing in of an ongoing AI revolution, technological development is bringing production and manufacturing closer to the end user. Reshoring will likely continue as domestic technology-enhanced production is favored over outsourcing to desolate low-skilled, low-income territories. 3D-printing techniques and nanotechnology that allow production to start at the molecular or even atomic level are fostering reshoring. Advances in 3D printers may soon make it possible to substitute large factories with much smaller ones, closer to the consumer, where the manufacturing process is simplified thanks to the reproduction of models (Aghion et al., 2017). New materials could be manufactured near the consumer, in order to substitute natural materials that need to be transported from distant mines and deposits (Tybout, 2000). Reshoring will bring back production to where goods and services are actually and finally consumed. The most obvious example is energy and a prospective attempt to decentralize renewable energy generation. A decentralized energy grid could be run on personal solar panels that

---

[29]https://www.economist.com/briefing/2019/01/24/globalisation-has-faltered

share energy among neighbors and thereby become more productive. Reshoring global production brought closer to where consumers are appears favorable in light of climate change and carbon emissions. Yet, shunning low-skilled labor in developing parts of the world from production for globally operating multinationals may revert international development (Banerjee & Duflo, 2005; Greenwood & Jovanovic, 1990; Moll, 2014; Mookherjee & Napel, 2007; Mookherjee & Ray, 2003). Slowbalisation appears to strengthen regional trade blocs, especially in Europe and Asia (Profita, 2019; *The Economist*, 2019).

This polarization between slowbalization of traditional goods and globalization of data is argued as the first sign of AI entering economic growth. Technological and political factors could indicate a market disruption that has already begun and currently echoes in globalization versus slowbalisation occurring parallel to each other. The trend of slowbalisation is therefore just seen as a forerunner of the AI revolution market disruption that exalted the world in the wake of the COVID-19 crisis, which will create a world of virtual opportunities very different from the one we had known before.

During the Fourth Industrial Revolution, robots are expected to become more efficient and affordable. With that, conventional globalization practices – such as offshoring manufacturing to cheap labor cost countries – will most likely decline. There is a projected impact of robotic development on international trade.

AI holds the potential to replicate human existence but live eternally. 24/7 working robots that can live eternally are expected to become the driver of industrialized economies and replace the majority of the human workforce (Lucas, 2004). Robots are expected to be more accurate and work 24/7, while being less demanding than human workers. Millions of employees in the East may lose their jobs over the next few decades, substituted by robots in the West. Trade links within regional blocs may increase and blocks become more homogenous, both in Europe and Asia.

When companies bring production back into their countries for AI, unskilled workers lose out in the domestic markets while leaving behind markets that flourished due to outsourcing companies (Birdsall, 2017). Reshoring means that former outsourced tasks are simply performed by AI in high-skilled interconnected countries with robotics, with whom low-skilled workers in the developing world now have to compete. The transition to the new globalization has caused the workers in developed markets to lose bargaining power as they now operate in the production phases that are most vulnerable to delocalization and automation, while the Western world will face competition with AI in wage-stagnating economies (Baldwin, 2017; Barseghyan & DiCecio, 2011; Profita, 2019). This trend will pit a 5G automated device against a low-skilled worker in a desolate place on earth with not even internet access, which allows learning and productivity gains (Lucas & Moll, 2014). Slowbalisation and reshoring are thereby expected to widen the gap between the rich and the poor. AI entering our economies may lead to a trend of reshoring and thereby shunning away international low-cost production sights from global production. The global gap between AI automated hubs and non-automated places on earth will therefore likely increase in the years to come. So while reshoring offers opportunities of more sustainable production in light of climate change, when we consider the environmental impacts of shipping goods around the globe until they reach the end user; in the end, it also bears the risk of restricting global economic development.

What all of this will do to standard economic growth, we do not have data-driven answers so far. Today's economies around the world are affected by the pandemic and health crisis. Future innovations in the medical field are predestined to be in the realm of digitized healthcare and self-monitoring with the help of electronic self-measuring devices and modern molecular genetic analyses. These can make the use of new active ingredients in the field of prevention of serious diseases more efficient.

As an addition to the current economic growth models, digitalization may be integrated into a future extension. In today's economy, robots and algorithms are taking over human decision-making tasks and entering the workforce. Most recently, big data has evolved to become a source of economic growth and governments in major economies are endeavoring to tax wealth creation from information transfer. Modern healthcare today is based on mobile monitoring and relies more than ever on AI by analyzing large amounts of data for prevention, diagnosis and healing. Future studies may empirically validate the proposed economic growth changes with attention to AI, big data insight, robotics and algorithms entering the medical profession (Puaschunder, 2019e, 2019j). This trend currently challenges conventional economic theory to capture growth based on purely capital and labor components (Puaschunder, 2019c, 2020f). Algorithms, machine learning and big data gains but also the shared economy do not seem to be represented accurately in conventional growth theory components of capital and labor (Alvarez, Buera, & Lucas, 2007). To this day, we do not have clear information on where to integrate AI and big data insight-derived economic gains into standard economic growth theory (Puaschunder, 2019i, 2019l, 2020a). It is not clarified whether these components are enhancing the production process, hence are considered as capital or aid as human enhancement more the labor component or are even imposing a burden on economic growth for set-up costs and litigation risks (Puaschunder, 2019i, 2019l, 2020a).

Future empirical validations of the proposed ideas should be tested cross-sectionally and by time series. Cross-sectional studies could differentiate between countries, while time series would allow to control for general economic trends. However, cross-sectional studies are often comparing countries at different stages of development and imply preference and technology parameters being identical for all countries in the sample. Differences in institutional conditions and social infrastructure are also to be expected in actuality, leading to the heterogeneity of estimated parameters of economic forecasting models (Brock & Durlauf, 2001). A time-series approach takes into account changes over time and stages of development. Drawbacks include the possibility of structural breaks and high data requirements. Time series are challenged by eventual non-stationarity that requires transformation into a stationary model. Time-series would require a high quality of data or curing unobservable variables' missing data to be replaced by observable lower-quality ones. Scale effects may occur as an increase in the level of state economic variables – such as human capital or knowledge capital imply-ing strong and lasting effects on the growth rate of the economy, which makes the introduction of non-linearities necessary. Including non-linearities into the empirical model helps to avoid scale effects which seem implausible due to dimin-ished forces of growth.

Contrary to the counter-globalization trends of the past, one area that grew globally and exponentially since 2010 is digitalized data transfer (*The Economist*, 2019). In the decade prior to COVID-19, an already ongoing digitalization dis-ruption heralded as big data allowed a set of innovative firms, including social media, online commercial platforms and search engines to reap skyrocketing profits that often remain untaxed (Puaschunder, 2021i). These economic gains are concentrated in areas such as big data hoarding, the sale of behavioral data about consumers and targeting online audiences with customized advertisement (Puaschunder, 2021i).

In contrast to earlier system-inherent economic turmoil resulting in finan-cial sector induced liquidity constraints, the external COVID-19 shock caused "social volatility" – a collectively depressed mood that largely dampened con-sumption. The difference to previous systemic recessions can be seen in the rapid recovery of well-managed financial funds – for example, the S&P 500 recovered 50% of its pre-COVID-19 value within the first three months after the crisis and reached an all-time high in August 2020. Deutsche Bank recorded rising earnings during the ongoing Coronavirus crisis, with its investment bank branch lead-ing with 43% or €2.4 billion revenue (DW, 2020). The clear distinction between COVID-19 profit and loss industries made it possible for today's highly flex-ible financial world to exchange underperforming market segments – such as oil, public transport and aviation, face-to-face service sectors such as interna-tional hospitality and gastronomy – with outperforming market options – such as pharmaceuticals and emergency devices for healthcare, digital technologies, fintech, AI and big data analytics industries, online retail, automotive and inte-rior design and architecture.

COVID-19 now not only created significant health and security risks, social dis-crimination and economic costs, but also brought about unanticipated opportuni-ties. Industries profiting economically from the pandemic are comprised of hygiene, pharmaceuticals and the medical professions (Agrawal et al., 2020; Lerner, 2020). From an economic perspective, COVID-19 is an external shock that has accelerated ongoing digitalization trends (Puaschunder, 2021a, 2021h). COVID-19 has per-petuated the online tech world. Physically distant, we became closer digitally than ever before. Worldwide data traffic exploded on a flat digitalized globe. Because of widespread lockdowns, "social distancing" and increased home office work in many industries, social scientists have observed a more widespread acceptance for instant communication tools, social engagement and entertainment platforms (Corlatean, 2020). We can thus say that certain firms and industries have benefited from the pandemic while many others have suffered from the expenses and bur-dens of COVID-19 (Aravanis, 2020; Arora, 2020; Dodd, 2020; Kumar & Haydon, 2020). Traditional small businesses appear to be particularly vulnerable (Bartik et al., 2020; Dua et al., 2020; Kwak, 2020; Price, 2020).

Today's economies around the world are affected by the pandemic and health crisis. Future innovations in the medical field are predestined to be in the realm of digitized healthcare and self-monitoring with the help of electronic self-measuring devices and modern molecular genetic analyzes. These can make the use of new active ingredients in the field of prevention of serious diseases more efficient.

In post-COVID-19 economies, digitalized hygiene and healthcare are likely to be further advanced as healthier workers around the world will have a competitive advantage (The World Economic Forum, 2021). The overall health status of employers will become a precious asset for determining the individual prevalence of a mild or severe COVID-19 disease trajectory. For another, the individual health conscientiousness will influence the likelihood of becoming a "superspreader" at work.

Employers may be more interested in what category their workforce may fall into in order to plan workplace safety precaution measures when building healthy working conditions (Ecowellness Group, 2020, 2021). More than ever before in the history of modern workforce do employers nowadays care about the overall well-being and physical interaction of their labor cadre in a hygienic environment. Respective preventive medical care of the workforce and community-building around monitoring of one's own and others' health but also group learning on how to enhance hygiene in teams will gain more attention in the COVID-19-struck workplace and will have lasting changes enacted (Ecowellness Group, 2020, 2021). Future responsible finance advancements may include attention to healthy capital and health wealth – the connection between financial prosperity and health as well as the overall productivity of a population based on the overall health level of nations.

In light of social distancing mandates and with the growth of scientific evidence derived from algorithms and big data, workers with better access to internet connectivity and AI–human compatibility (i.e., computer and AI literacy and related skills) have growing competitive advantages (Ecowellness Group, 2020, 2021). It may also become a matter of survival for large organizations to understand the health of their workers with the help of these novel technologies. On the one hand, employers will need to estimate whether workplace conditions are likely to produce mass outbreaks – such as the ones that, for instance, occurred in the meatpacking industry or luxury tourism cruise ships in several countries (Elliott, 2021; Foster, 2020). On the other hand, and maybe less benignly, employers will want to know whether workers' medical histories, genetic profiles, living arrangements and social habits are likely to result in COVID-19 infection risks and predict trajectory likelihoods based on genetic prevalence derived from big data analyses. With the entry of AI algorithms and big data insights from large data sets in the medical field, they may hope to maintain a healthy workforce through encouraging workers' self-monitoring, while also pro-actively caring for safety through mobile tracking of infected as a means of crowd control, as well as potentially through the use of predictive algorithms (Gelter & Puaschunder, 2021). Much like many employers require drug tests at the hiring stage or periodically, they may seek to use digitalization tools to predict health statuses and working conditions' outcomes to reduce the risk of being put out of business or severely harmed by a COVID-19 outbreak.

Arguably, firms that are better able to use technology to determine and track employees' health status will be the winners in the post-pandemic market. Already, however, it is becoming apparent that these novel digitalization opportunities come with the price of a heightened responsibility to protect privacy in retrieving big data inference, ensure access to information and healthcare democratically, secure individuals from discrimination against health status propensities and back those who are naturally hindered to compete in markets financially and socially (Puaschunder et al., 2020).

During the 2022 World Economic Forum address of US Secretary of the Treasury Janet Yellen, the post-COVID-19 economic growth was called for being inclusive and green.[30] In modern supply side economic growth, inclusion and diversity are meant to bring economic growth potential. Inclusion can breed social harmony and a diverse workforce allows diversification of potentials and complementary skills cross-pollination.

In its entirety, the presented futuristic outlook promises to hold novel insights for future success factors of economic growth calculus but also human resource management grounded on efficiency and ethics. Having parts of the world being AI-driven and others being human capital grounded in the future is prospected to increase the international development divide in the years to come. It is speculated that in the future, in the AI-hubs human will be incentivized to become more creative and humane while AI performs all rational tasks to a maximum productivity. Parts of the world without AI could then naturally fall back as for being stuck in spending human capital time on machine-outsourceable tasks and not honing humane skills, which are not replicable by machines.

Future research endeavors may therefore address inequality drawing on the future vision that central rational AI-hubs will outperform underdeveloped remote areas of the world even more in the digital age. Slowbalisation is projected to draw back outsourcing efforts and divide AI hubs from areas that are less connected. The following research should be concerned with the unprecedentedly high divide between skilled and unskilled labor and the diversion between AI hubs and non-AI territories. In the last four decades, the price of skilled labor has soared dramatically relative to that of unskilled labor despite a major uprise in the relative supply of skills. The notion of skill bias in growth theories has introduced the theoretical possibility that technological progress benefits only a sub-group of workers, placing technical change at the center of the income distribution debate (Goldberg & Pavcnik, 2007). Organizational changes have led to AI technologies reducing costs of communication, monitoring and supervision within the firm, which trigger a shift toward a new organizational design. The change toward AI induces an organizational shift toward skill-biased meritocracy. Endogenous technical progress leads to economic growth but also generates wage inequality between low- and high-skilled workers (Duarte & Restuccia, 2006; Murphy, Riddell, & Romer, 1998; Parente & Prescott, 1993). Faster technical change increases the return to ability and increases wage inequality between, and also within,

---

[30]https://home.treasury.gov/news/press-releases/jy0565

groups of high-skilled and unskilled workers (Galor & Moav, 2000, 2004). Future studies should integrate some of the contemporary inequality measurements such as the Palma ratio, financial development and wealth transfers in contemporary growth theories and measurement (Jacoby, 2008; Milanovic, 2013; Piketty, 2016). Wage inequality is only one way to assess inequality, but in order to get a richer picture of inequality derived from AI, future research may also consider inequality in wealth, health, status and within-group inequalities (Restuccia & Urrutia, 2001). Understanding the links between growth and inequality should also be placed in the different contexts of political, social and historical environments in order to derive inferences about the successful introduction of AI into today's workforce and society. Finally, more research is recommended to model and maximize the novel production function including AI and information sharing – especially in light of Chat-GPT, G5 and the internet of things leading to a further connection and benefits from technology. All these novel developments may lead to a potential polarization between more efficient AI hubs and low skill low labor cost areas that may be shunned from economic growth due to a predicted reshoring trend coupled with AI economic dominance and unprecedented technology gains (Aghion & Bolton, 1997; Matsuyama, 2000, 2011; Restuccia & Rogerson, 2017; Ventura, 1997).

Overall, the presented work captures AI's entrance into the workforce and our daily lives. The currently ongoing market transition of AI encroaching on conventional markets will likely lead to a re-ordering of the current global economic and political order. Depicting growth during this unprecedented time of economic change and regulatory reform of shaping a novel technology revolution in the wake of the COVID-19 pandemic holds invaluable historic opportunities for outlining technology-driven market changes' influence on the stability of economies and society.

As never before in history, automatization may enrich the world economy in very many novel ways regardless of national borders – but only if also been safeguarded by ethical imperatives. The presented research aims at the current creative destruction in the wake of AI entering the world economies being ennobled by a social face and lowering potential societal downfalls (Schumpeter, 1943/1976). The findings may also bestow global governance policy makers with ideas on how to better snapshot AI's potential in the digital age and market actors with future-oriented foresight on how to benefit from this new technology (Banerjee, 2008; Klenow, 2008).

Market and societal policy recommendations may aid global governance experts to strengthen society through AI but also overcome unknown emergent risks within globalized markets in the wake of the AI revolution. At the same time of acknowledging the potential of AI, ethical considerations appear necessary as we have to become aware of the risk imbued in the artificial age, such as legal regulatory gaps and crowding out humanness or reverting the past accomplishments of outsourcing helping nations to develop out of poverty. Conventional economic policies may therefore be coupled with a holistic vision that encompasses socio-economic and political values. Drawing attention to potential international development drawbacks and a further disparity of society based on skills and access to refined technology will offer market actors and governance bodies key insights – not only on how to benefit from a digitalizing world but also on how to administer the current market transition so the benefits get distributed equally around the world. Societies of tomorrow should therefore be built on AI ethics of inclusion in order to safeguard the transition to artificiality enhancing economies and ennoble society through a mutual understanding and exchange of putty and clay labor (Puaschunder, 2016d).

As for addressing heterodox aspects of economic business cycles, the role of socio-psychological online echo-chambers of information for financial markets may be addressed in the future. With the Coronavirus pandemic coming down on society in the age of digitalization, which exacerbated during lockdowns around the globe, market communication has shifted to online searchplaces. Constant information flows in the digital age and the unknown socio-psychologically effect induced by crisis communication make the project urgent to be started immediately to conserve the contemporary Zeitgeist and save society from social volatility market fallouts with strategic communication.

Economic fundamentals and mathematical formalizations in classic economics should be used to explain the mechanisms causing economic cycles missing out on the socio-psychological and behavioral group aspects of collective over- and underreaction in markets. While some information on euphoria is found in the animal spirits and behavioral finance literature describing overconfidence in markets leading to an overvaluation of assets, overleveraging and underestimation of risk; hardly any empirical studies explain collective panics from a socio-economic or social psychology angle.

The 2008–2009 World Financial Recession offered some data on the collective souls of economic crunches, yet the crisis emerged as an inherent feature in capitalism with the banking sector downfalls becoming the endogenous crunch factor. But how external influences can come down on society and materialize in an exogenous shock with drastic fallouts in the real economy due to new media coverage, we hardly have any economic model or empirical validation. No data existed prior to COVID-19 that were so rich in terms of instant communication, global interconnectivity and computational power to make sense of unprecedentedly big data capacity generated instantaneously and globally. At the same time, the constant informational bombardment of multi-faceted new media tools requires to conserve the fluidly growing "now"-driven information overload immediately.

Future research may aim at innovatively painting a novel picture of the mass psychological underpinnings of business cycles based on information flows with particular attention to digital communication. Concrete macro-economic research could specifically unravel how contemporary media communication produces certain types of expectations that form collective moods and how these change consumption patterns result in systemic global economic outcomes. After a thorough literature review on financial market theory with special attention to heterodox viewpoints, the history of economic cycle theories could lead to the analysis of the role of information in creating economic booms and busts. The concept of social volatility should be introduced and depicted in light of COVID-19. Social volatility adds to quantitative volatility any social aspects that influence and shape economic markets offering an innovative way to explain how and what information represented in the media creates economic ups and downs.

The core of research could investigate how online social mass media communication shapes individual decision making. Contrary to standard neoclassical ideas of time in discounting, a behavioral economic approach will be applied dividing time into past, present and future prospects. This fungibility of dependent moments adds temporal volatility. The highly fickle "now" present moment unmasked as a slippery reference point should be addressed in the theory of subjectivity and reflected upon behavioral economics' hyperbolic discounting present bias. Social online media fetishizing breaking news waves of concurrently presented similar information missing out on diversification potential but instead creating echo-chambers of alternative realities but also the crucial role of fast-paced uncensored social online platforms in perpetuating human present biases will be thematized. The media's untapped potential in setting potentially favorable or unfavorable anchors and building unknown economic choice architectures could become introduced.

As for social volatility, fat tail phenomena and robustness literature should be coupled with social systems' ideas. Affect theory, believes and desires theory would become the theoretical backbone to describe fallible likelihood estimations when the pains and joys over markets are felt collectively and social volatility waves break. How integrating indexicality, modality and subjectivity are related to intentionality should be explored. Reference point dependence on age and the "now" could be investigated in light of Prospect theory to see how losses and gains represented in the past or future may lead to biased decision-making patterns. The present bias potentially overinflating social volatility risks based on emotionality could be thematized.

Empirically, the current COVID-19 pandemic serves as an external shock coming down on society with a direct impact on societal moods and subsequently connected economic changes. Future studies could explore the role of communication and temporal foci in social media to create social volatility underlying economic downturns with attention to legally required public disclosure statements. The economic consequence of the endogenous crunch of the 2008 World Financial Recession could be compared to the external economic shock of the COVID-19 pandemic in order to retrieve crisis-specific recovery recommendations.

More concretely, a literature review on the history of economic cycle theories will lead to the analysis of the role of information in creating economic booms and busts. The concept of social volatility could be introduced in light of COVID-19. An empirical investigation could scrutinize what socio-psychological mechanisms potentially accelerate economic meltdowns with attention to collective moods to shape the daily choices and present behavior. The role of temporal foci could be explored – whether it makes a difference if information focuses on the past, present or future.

Empirically, the social media use of publicly traded firms during the COVID-19 pandemic could be studied. Social media communication about COVID-19 will be qualitatively analyzed and contrasted with legally required disclosure statements in the corporate sector. The analysis should cover the sharing rate (retweets) of Twitter postings about COVID-19 and contrast the temporal focus of Twitter tweets with Securities and Exchange Commission filings. A content analysis of retweet propensities will elucidate what moves information on social online media. Social representations theory and the core-and-periphery analysis content analysis based on word count could serve to categorize various approaches to introduce the external pandemic shock.

The qualitative exploration could target at showing economic cycles' natural complexity influenced by socio-historic trends and their representation. Addressing the different uses of the internet and modern communication tools with conventional market communication but also understanding how temporal foci and emotional prospects can shape echo-chambers of information and create collective moods offers to detect concrete media strategies and communication contents that stabilize economies during external shocks.

The operationalization could measure the retweet rate and content of corporate posts about COVID-19 in order to determine what moves a Twitter post. Why is one Twitter post more likely shared than another? What are the contents of shared posts? After determining what contents are more likely to be shared, backtesting is planned if there is any change in market pricing of the corporation under scrutiny if a COVID-19 post gets shared heavily. Lastly, this information could be compared to Securities and Exchange Commission filings about COVID-19 of the same corporations and tested if the Securities and Exchange Commission filings had a significantly more severe impact on corporate stock prices than the retweeted Twitter posts. The retweet likelihood could be measured by emotional content. The content and time focus of Twitter tweets could qualitatively be compared to Securities and Exchange Commission filings in relation to stock market movements and their release date.

Methodologically, linguistic text analyses of reports about the societal situation and the economy aim at depicting how social media versus legally required disclosure statement representations echo in economic correlates measured by the stock market of corporations retrieved online. Communication could be rated on being positive, negative, neutral based on polarity indices and having a past, present or future-oriented outlook based on Hofstede's cultural future-oriented versus past-tradition-oriented indicators.

Overall, such research projects could target at investigating whether social media information has a different impact on corporate stock market performance than conventional information about corporate performance in Securities and Exchange Commission filings. Prospective findings will have implications about the discussion culture of individuals and leaders as well.

All these qualitative analyses would pave the way for quantitative studies on temporal volatility, echo-chambers and framing online experiments. The results of the field experiment could be backtested with Amazon Mechanical Turk data, in which respondents are likely to see specific social media posts and their reposts. A behavioral economics experiment could backtest the results in an

Amazon Mechanical Turk (AMTURK) online survey enabled via Qualtrics. To investigate the role of social online media in cultivating human present biases or setting an anchor of favorable and unfavorable time prospects, different numbers of retweet cues could prime individuals into different perceptions of the truth. The number of posts and reposts could be varied between subjects. Different temporal perspectives and emotional contents could be varied between subjects to then decide on the accuracy and personal retweet likelihood. Demographic information could also help explain certain propensity differences between different societal groups.

Stringent hypothesis testing could clarify if "now" eliciting media information increases the present bias. Another hypothesis could outline if positive information triggers more consumption and investment in the domains of culture, economics, education, environment, foreign aid and infrastructure than negative information. Another hypothesis would be useful to see if "future" information triggers more consumption and investment in the domains of culture, economics, education, environment, foreign aid and infrastructure than "past" information. Further hypothesis testing could show if positive or negative emotions or forward-looking or past-ruminating temporal foci lead to a delay in consumption and investment in the domains of culture, economics, education, environment, foreign aid and infrastructure. Another hypothesis could target at elucidating that the more exposed individuals are to posts, the more likely they believe it is true. The final hypothesis could capture age dependent discounting preferences as an alternative reference point.

Overall, communication influences on market expectations and performance shaping economic cycles will reveal information contents that either cause social volatility bleeding into economic downturns or serve as crowd control stabilizers. Future research could acknowledge that human beings' communication and interaction online results in socially constructed volatility that echoes in economic correlates. Understanding how the social media forms economic outcomes promises to explain how market outcomes can be shaped by strategic communication with special attention to new media technologies.

The discussion could highlight the uniqueness and differences of social media communication versus legally required reportings during the COVID-19 pandemic economic fallout. The results promise to explain how an external shock can be fueled by social media communication and online interaction. The currently ongoing market communication about the pandemic serves as historic trace, whose conservation offers important insights into how the socio-psychological interpretation of an external shock echoes in economic fundamentals.

Implications could stress how communication can counterweight and alleviate the building of collective moods bleeding into disastrous mass movements causing turmoil in financial market and steering economic fallouts with negative implications for societies' weakest segments. Recommendations on how to build stable economic systems by avoiding emergent risks and communicating market prospects favorably may help in building the fundamental architecture of future more stable markets to be crafted by heterodox economists and off-mainstream public policy experts. A discussion of the mentioned topics could also address the contemporary divide between economic fundamentals, financial market performance versus the real economy fallout. The final remarks should also target at highlighting winning and losing industries only to follow the mandate to find creative strategies how to redistribute the gains of the crisis in order to offset the economic fallout losses in proposed inequality alleviation strategies. A prospective future research outlook and implications can be offered that aim at improving the economic future of healthcare, workforce, city planning and education based on strategic communication and emotional assets but also favorable time prospects in our post-COVID-19 world to come.

3

Discussion and Future Prospect

In today's finance literature, SRI has become a prominent term. The importance of financial markets in international development has grown. The current financial constraints and the largest-ever rescue and recovery aids granted in the aftermath of the COVID-19 pandemic external shock are leveraging the demand for transparency and accountability of finances. For the future, economists and trend analysts attribute the emergence of SRI the potential to lift entire market industries onto a more socially conscientious level.

Given the rising demand for social responsibility within market systems, the common body of knowledge on SRI is fairly limited. Empirical studies on SRI are rare with the current body of research primarily targeting at efficiency and financial correlates of SRI. The insights on socially responsible investors address demographic variables and lifestyle factors, but mainly neglect socio-psychological motives. While market studies foremost focus on economic fundamentals, the knowledge on socio-psychological components of socially responsible financial decision making is scarce. Mild attention has been paid to financial opinion leaders' view of SRI given their potential to support and advocate for innovative financial options. In addition, until today the contributing factors to the rise of SRI and success factors of financial social responsibility are unexplained.

Overall, future research may delineate the dynamics and implementation of social responsibility within markets in the interplay of the public and private sectors as well as financial markets. As a multi-stakeholder phenomenon, various actors' impact the management of financial social responsibility (Cuesta & Valor, 2007; Little, 2008; Rosen et al., 1991; Williams, 2005). As a novel topic under debate, multiple SRI constituents may lack a standardized SRI notion, which limits their understanding of social responsibility within financial market systems and hinders the overall communication on SRI (Bruyn, 1987). As investors differ in their social concerns, priorities and tactics to address financial social responsibility, SRI features a plethora of expression forms (Cooper & Schlegelmilch, 1993; Frankel, 1984; Pandey & Wright, 2006).

In order to promote a successful rise of SRI, an understanding of the essential stakeholders' perception of SRI and their attribution of success factors for

Responsible Investment Around the World: Finance after the Great Reset, 161–182
Copyright © 2023 by Julia M. Puaschunder
Published under exclusive licence by Emerald Publishing Limited
doi:10.1108/978-1-80382-851-020231006

financial social responsibility is key. Defining SRI in its various forms and foci could help explore motivational factors of financial social responsibility as well as gather information on success factors for SRI – with special attention to changes implied by the COVID-19 pandemic.

Paying attention to the ambiguity and complexity of the phenomenon, exploratory expert interviews on SRI will depict mutually shared contents of financial social investment. Understanding financial leaders' SRI notions serves as a first step to resolve societal losses imbued in the novelty, complexity and ambiguity of the phenomenon. Exploring the multi-faceted influences that attributed the SRI demand will outline success factors of financial social responsibility. Gaining a more sophisticated understanding of financial social responsibility will help in finding repeatable patterns and crafting policies to trigger SRI within financial markets. Describing key market agents' views on SRI will lead to managerial implications for the implementation of SRI. Being knowledgeable about socio-psychological facets of financial social responsibility may propel SRI to become a mainstream feature of financial decision making with the greater goal of fostering positive societal change.

Studying public and private actors' perceptions of CSR and SRI could help overcome information deficiencies within the stakeholder community and lower the complexity of these newly emerging phenomena. CSR and SRI stakeholder perceptions provide a sophisticated understanding of social welfare provision in the interplay of deregulated market systems and governmental control.

Depicting the implementation of corporate and financial social responsibility in global governance PPPs derives triggers, impact and success factors for the establishment of international networks to alleviate social deficiencies and improve societal conditions.

Research on political divestiture holds the potential for governments to reach corporations on political concerns (Steurer, 2010). Evaluating up-to-date research on political divestiture will increase the effectiveness of financial social responsibility and allow promoting SRI within the financial community. Addressing measurement deficiencies of political divestiture will help in generating alternative SRI measurement techniques.

Synthesizing the experience of key market actors with SRI will allow attributing success factors of financial social responsibility. Information on the socio-psychological motives of socially responsible investors may add behavioral insights to classic financial market theories. Research on SRI during the outbreak of the 2008 financial crisis helped in understanding SRI as a means to re-establish trust in financial global governance to foster financial market stability as a prerequisite for sustainable market economies.

Exploratory research may serve as the first step toward resolving conflicts embedded in the ambiguity of relatively newly emerging CSR and SRI phenomena. Academic discourse is targeted at a successful rise of social responsibility within modern market economies to become mainstream economic trends. Implications for corporate management, global governance as well as financial decision-making theory and practice may foster financial stability and sustainable market economies as future guarantors of sustainable societal progress.

In light of the contemporary post-pandemic era, COVID-19 accounts for the most widespread and large-scale complex external shock changing every sphere of human beings (Gelter & Puaschunder, 2021; Puaschunder & Gelter, 2021). The COVID-19 pandemic is likely to exacerbate existing inequalities between the finance world and the real economy given the financial market performance capabilities to exchange losing for winning industries during downturns and the real economy dependence on wages and trickle down economic effects (Puaschunder, 2021a, 2021c). In addition, homeownership and inflation-adjusted salary schemes become a driver of inequality in our longest-lowest-ever inflation regime (Puaschunder, 2021a, 2021c). COVID-19 also made apparent vast differences in healthcare provision around the world and the countries' quality care specificities (Puaschunder, 2020a, 2021h; Puaschunder & Beerbaum, 2020a, 2020b). Within workplace settings, digitalization will become essential and drive an already-existing gap between e-skilled and e-unskilled labor (Gelter & Puaschunder, 2021; Puaschunder, 2021a, 2021e; Puaschunder et al., 2020a, 2020b).

All these rising inequalities will drive the currently unfolding demand for ethics of inclusion as the spring feather of equality and social justice heralding in our post-pandemic renaissance (Puaschunder, 2022). Economic growth will be dependent on access to opportunities. Striving for excellence will only be justified if being pegged to the ethics of inclusive growth.

Despite the tremendous losses incurred in the COVID-19 pandemic, the crisis could also become a major turning point. The post-COVID-19 era could offer opportunities and long-lasting positive societal advancements that come out of the crisis. COVID-19 may have drawn attention to rising inequalities around the world, which heightened demand for alleviating gaps with inclusive growth. As a global pandemic, in which no one is safe before everyone is safe, the global interconnectedness in a common health crisis has become more blatant than ever before in the history of humankind. In addition, climate change not knowing any boundaries between countries but also over time in its gradual progression, is likely to further exacerbate the call for a fair and inclusive common solution plan within society, in between countries and over time.

Leadership on economic growth has started to acknowledge the need for creating a world, in which inclusion breeds social harmony. Striving for excellence has become essentially pegged to the need for redistribution and inclusion. Social justice is the excellence of our times. Law and economics mandates now – more than ever before – demand for employing disparate impact analyses in economic calculus to support those who are left behind.

Health and well-being underlying human workforce productivity can be introduced as a hidden driver of economic growth in the eye of a global pandemic risk. Digital healthcare can bring along access to affordable quality care around the world free from corruption (Puaschunder, 2021h). Digitalized healthcare information exchange has nowadays also proven as a means for the democratization of health and disease remedies when considering the role of online media forums to discuss COVID-19 long-haul issues (Puaschunder & Gelter, 2021). Ethics of inclusion in the future may advance online access to healthcare and fair and protected information exchange of vulnerable patients.

In the economics and finance sectors, inequality alleviation could bridge the performance gap between the finance world and the real economy with particular attention to inflation, low interest rate regimes and metropolitan versus rural areas. Disparate impact analyses will pave the way for a more diversified scheme of financial rescue and recovery aid. In the healthcare domain, equal access to medical care pledge in innovations – such as telemedicine and AI, robotics and big data insights – should be endeavored.

Our educational and workplace revolution in a truly digitalized economy will also drive novel inequalities and ethical dilemmas arising from digitalization. In addition, educational social transfer hubs with attention to online opportunities have transformed into a gateway of social justice access in the USA that also account for the most promising international development advancement of our times (Corlatean, 2020).

Environmental demands for a transition to a green economy are met in most novel economic attempts to stimulate the economy under the umbrella of sustainability and social inclusion – such as outlined in the GND and EGD including the Sustainable Finance Taxonomy (Puaschunder, 2020e, 2021b, 2021g). Future behavioral economics advancements and finance leadership will include the use of behavioral insights to improve the societal welfare under these novel frameworks. Behavioral insights for a greening of the economy will include micro-economic foundations but also build on a growing body of behavioral macro-economic findings of the unequal distribution of climate change gains and losses (Puaschunder, 2020a, 2020d).

As the shock of the pandemic had an immediate effect on all countries around the world, COVID-19 is likely to change the larger economic environment and societal structure of modern democracies for years to come. The longer COVID-19 long-haul symptoms persist and the more people get infected, the more direct and indirect effects COVID-19 will likely have on all our daily lives, families, workplaces and society now and in the future.

All measures during the onset of a lasting crisis point toward fundamental changes in society. Governments around the globe have therefore set out on a course to avert the negative impetus of the COVID-19 pandemic economic shock (Cassim et al., 2021, The White House of the United States of America, 2021a, 2021b, 2021c, 2021d). Having highlighted some of the major trends and developments in health, economics, finance, education, digitalization and the environment in the wake of the COVID-19 crisis was meant to aid in the determination of future-oriented policies and multi-faceted recovery aid (Brunnermeier Academy at the Princeton Bendheim Center for Finance, 2021).

Overall, the COVID-19 pandemic is the most massive exogenous shock that is likely to trigger subsequent policy changes. The pandemic may have drastic long-term health status shift of major parts of the productive workforce and society. COVID-19 also has the potential to change many aspects of the individual consumer, the family compound, societal care systems and economic incentives for market actors and industries. Paying attention to anticipated disruption fallouts will aid governments around the world in confronting the crisis but also to reinterpret the way we produce, consume and – most importantly – live our lives productively, healthily and within a fair society that acts in harmony with the environment.

Empirical knowledge on how to balance climate change benefits and burdens within society, between differently affected nation states and over time among overlapping generations will help in deriving novel policy strategies in the age of inclusive care. By learning from our crisis response resilience and deriving universal strategies for the future, we will hopefully emerge from COVID-19 stronger as a society in the long term and with gifts of better lives for future generations to come (Brunnermeier Academy at the Princeton Bendheim Center for Finance, 2021).

In the wake of ambitious bailout and recovery plans, a law and economics view could highlight necessary disparate impact facets of economic fallouts to a common crisis that should be considered when choosing capital transfer targets strategically and driven by fairness mandates and with a long-term view in mind (Puaschunder, 2021e, 2022). As for scientific advancements, generation COVID-19 long haul has the potential to imbue minimalism, rest and recovery as major axioms around which economic calculus is newly focused (Puaschunder, 2021d; Puaschunder & Gelter, 2021).

As for the continuous assessment of programs, diverse stakeholders should be included for the controlled evolution of a large-scale transformation to a more inclusive world. In the end, to the young and the diverse groups within society and around the world but also over time, the relevance, effectiveness, efficiency and impact of all these endeavors will matter the most on a grand scale and with a future-oriented discounting outlook. Future novel theories, methods and models could capture the dynamic interaction of behavioral nudges and economic incentives in the protection of humankind and the environment.

With the COVID-19 spreading around the world from the beginning of 2020 on accounting for the most challenging healthcare crisis of our lifetimes, calls have risen to find a common world solution to prevent future pandemics and overall healthcare crises. In order to prevent the world population from the transmission of a highly contagious, deadly virus, global concerted efforts and coordination of prevention and security on a global scale are required.

The United Nations Unequal World Conferences vividly outlined the inequality inherent in global healthcare provision (Puaschunder & Beerbaum, 2020a). COVID-19 on a global scale makes international differences in the approaches to combat global pandemics with technological solutions apparent (Puaschunder, 2021h; Puaschunder & Beerbaum, 2020a; Puaschunder & Gelter, 2021; Puaschunder, Mantl, & Plank, 2020).

During the pandemic, preventive medical care, reconnection with nature but also digitalization have gained unprecedented importance in our lives in a massive wave around the world. In macro-economic modeling, empirical research brought forward four indices shedding light on health inequality in the twenty-first digital century (Puaschunder & Beerbaum, 2020b). Internet connectivity and high GDP are likely to lead on AI-driven big data insights for pandemic prevention. On these dimensions, Europe, Asia and North America have optimal global healthcare leadership potential. International data on healthcare standards in relation to digitalization, economic prosperity, freedom from corruption and innovation market financialization revealed that Europe and North America feature excellent starting grounds for economic productivity, digitalized healthcare and relatively low levels of corruption.

Europe benefits from the highest standards on public preventive medical care, while the USA has the most prosperous market financialization to advance medical innovations and Asia appears to have the most sophisticated data tracking software in place. As future predictions, equal access to the internet and affordable preventive healthcare around the world would help as a future pandemic precaution.

As a future prospect in the healthcare domain, digitalization and big data insights for the healthcare sector appear as long-term future additional pandemic prevention aid. In the healthcare sector, the EU has a competitive edge as for a historically grown wealth of data of a homogenous population as European citizens pay for free universal healthcare by the automatic provision of data. Within Europe, potential exists to bundle the largest and most refined historic datasets on health of over 500 million European citizens in order to derive inferences for prevalences and tailored personal medical care.

In the corporate sector, the German *Präventionsgesetz*[1] or Prevention Act grants governmental funding to corporations for preventive self-care and team learning of healthy lifestyles. As never before in the history of industrialization, employers now watch out for creating a healthy workplace environment with hygienic interaction, constantly tracking workforce safety and requiring health self- and group monitoring. Home office flexibility outsources workplace health risks, as do newly erected office glass walls in interior designs. The Austrian *Sozialpartnerschaft* embraces stakeholder decision making in shaping an overall healthy workplace environment.

As for healthcare evolutions in the wake of the pandemic, changing lifestyles to achieve anti-depression and anti-obesity as well as anxiety control could create a collective environment for personal social change, involving the larger social network and our workplaces and living lastingly. The governmental, corporate and personal responsibility could target at providing oversight of the public good health whole-roundedly and precautiously.

The COVID-19 crisis turns out to be a crisis of rising inequality. Some features of inequality that persisted prior to the outbreak of the COVID-19 were exacerbated in the wake of the crisis, such as, for instance, access to affordable quality healthcare inequality around the world or income inequality within Western society (Gorz, 2003). Other inequality patterns that were not so obvious became accentuated by COVID-19 to a point that inequality became apparent to a broader population – for example, we saw rising inequality in the finance world

---

[1]Gesetz zur Stärkung der Gesundheitsförderung und der Prävention (Präventionsgesetz – PrävG) vom 17. Juli 2015, BGBl 2015, I/31. Retrieved from https://www.bgbl.de/xaver/bgbl/start.xav?startbk=Bundesanzeiger_BGBl&start=//*%255B@attr_id=%27bgbl115s1368.pdf%27%255D#__bgbl__%2F%2F*%5B%40attr_id%3D%27bgbl115s1368.pdf%27%5D__1643233416941.

versus real economy gap but also disparate effects of inflation and a low interest rate regime triggering a gap in socio-psychological propensity differences determined by industry classes.

At the same time, the COVID-19 pandemic has elements of an expurgatory catharsis and an opportunity for a reset to embark on a better, more just and equal world. In record speed, the world has seen drastic changes implemented in the healthcare, finance and economics sectors. The way we lived, worked and structured our days has changed dramatically since the outbreak of the crisis. In the aggregate, the modes of operation of corporations, governments and governance were challenged and redefined throughout the crisis as we go along with the recovery. Unprecedented policy shifts coupled with extraordinary rescue and recovery packages sprouted throughout the world. In most cases, these aids are pegged to noble causes and the wish to make the world a better place for this generation and the following. While it is still too early to tell whether the efforts in the aftermath of the crisis will become established and fruitful transitions to a better state, already now it is apparent that the rescue and recovery help offers a once-in-a-lifetime generational shift and a potential gateway to a new era. Throughout the history of humankind, very many different plagues and crises throughout the world have heralded betterment in the overall grand theme of developments that were adopted.

What will it take for the COVID-19 crisis to be remembered by historians as the beginning of a golden age or a new renaissance? Learning from the examples of previous pandemics, we can say that strong governmental support for productive causes has a history of transferring society to higher social welfare levels. The combination of economic stimulus in large-scale production and consumption coupled with educational and moral grounds appears to foster an extraordinarily vital societal development. Building growth on economic capital enhanced with human capital and strengthening the social glue is key to making something good out of a devastating crisis.

Today's society holds the largest levels of inequalities of which some are more obvious and blatant, whereas other inequalities are more implicit or just emerging. For instance, the finance–real economy gap opened somewhat surprisingly, while social justice pledges have risen steadily in the previous decades to culminate in an all-time-pressing demand during the pandemic that will shape decades to come. But also disparate effects of inflation and the low interest rate regime have become apparent in the wake of rescue and recovery packages floating economies with liquidity. Novel challenges arise in the disparate impact of inflation and the socio-psychological impetus of low interest rate regimes. Today's leadership in the public and the private spheres has to address these challenges and work toward contributing to causes such as inequality alleviation, social fairness and equal access to opportunities while protecting those who have the disadvantage to participate in markets.

In the future, social friction is expected due to the strong polarization of financial profits sponsored by low key interest rate policy in contrast to the real economy liquidity constraint pressures. The flexible substitutability of financial fund components in the exchange of loss segments for winning industries increases financial market profits, but at the same time reduces liquidity capacity and sustainability survival of small and medium-sized enterprises. In this sense, the generally low interest rate creates a situation that the financial world lives at the expense of the real economy.

Most recent developments indicate that there is also an increasingly affective quality of language online that turns the crisis communication into a hidden inequality accelerator. The general populace now faces a divide of affective differences in the perception of COVID-19 external shock communication that underlines the immaterial wealth of capital. Capital leverages as a shared skill that materializes in the everyday life decisions and grants peace of mind. But this feature in capital leads to a reduction of emotions and real economy experiences. The financial market hegemony therefore capitalizes on the real economy by creating security in making money from money and the exchange of non-profitable industries without creating wider cultural value or social capital. People's life choice in their profession they follow boils down to a rational versus emotional propensity state during external shock crises.

While the finance world features impersonal judgments with efficiency, the real-world consumption is based on personal judgment tainted with emotions. Intuitions guide both worlds in their choices, as do the personal networks and social reference groups. New hierarchies of statuses of affect arise based on the origins of wealth generation. Money skills in the finance world are pitted against life(style) skills acquired in the real economy. The laws of the creation of value determine a novel balance of power based on trust in the economy and gain prospects. Trust is established and reinforced together in networks and contexts that draft the social bubbles of information exchange. Fast-speeded digital media about market predictions connects us to uncertainty online.

For society, the question arises if the rational finance sector has an obligation to serve the higher societal progress and fund the real economy with the fruits of the spirit of capitalism (Boltanski, 1987). The instrumentalization of human beings and specifically human dimensions of life in the finance sector wears down the authenticity and individuality of daily life (Boltanski, 1987). Market actors of the future will have to align these two worlds. Legal scholars and law practitioners will be required to balance their powers to share benefits among themselves for the good of all society.

Governments' role in this appears to become the great equalizer and alleviate inequality via reset funding. Governments all over the world can advocate for a sustainable finance world and equally accessible economic growth benefits. Governmental leadership can bring back the financial world in the service of improving and stabilizing the real economy in a stricter separation between investment and consumer banks, which already began in the course of the regulations following the 2008–2009 recession. Central banks could offer diversified interest rates. Low key interest rates for driving innovation and economic growth in the financial sector that refunds higher interest rates for the real economy savings for consumers in order to avert socio-psychological fallouts of over-indebtedness in households. Online currencies, such as the currently planned European Central Bank digital currency, could help a transparent use of the currency over time to strictly divert interest rate profits and avoid arbitrage or interest rate swaps in diversified interest rate regimes. Mutual collateral insurance between the financial world and the real economy would also be possible in order to spread overall market risk. Throughout history, bonds have been used to finance long-term strategies with unknown outcome. Bonds are now discussed to enable innovations while repayments' interests should be redistributed to the real economy. In order to enact this diversified bonds effect, one could think of commitment bonds but also diversified interest rate regimes based on the professional starting ground or individual recipient's representing industry.

As an equalizer between financial market and real economy stability, taxing the COVID-19-profit industries, especially digitization winners, could create fiscal space for redistributing some of the economic gains to industries that clearly lose from COVID-19. Taxation of digitalized economic growth during our forced digitalization disruption could provide the necessary redistribution funds to back the liquidity-dried real economy sectors – such as the service industry, foremost in gastronomy and tourism.

In addition, the finance sector could be governmentally obliged or at least incentivized and encouraged to use the current profits for future large-scale investments that add societal long-term value. For example, large construction projects but also innovation in research and development, are valuable macro-economic multipliers that can benefit society as a whole in the short run and long term (Epstein, 2020; Keynes, 1936/2003). Governments and intergovernmental bodies, like the European Union, have the long-term vision and financial freedom to operate on deficits but also the regulatory means in legal frameworks to enact large-scale redistribution and long-term wealth creation in grand investments for the future. The COVID-19 pandemic could be used as a gateway of transition and become a major reset also offering exciting opportunities and long-lasting positive societal advancements. The potential focus of bailouts and recovery ranges from urban–local or national to even global and future-oriented beneficiaries, as pursued in public investments on climate stabilization in the GND or EGD.

On all the aspirational goals of these long-term investment projects, science and also implementation can benefit the most from learning from the young what future world they aspire to live in. Future research should couple macro-economic calculus with shedding light on economic disparate impacts of economic crises. Monetary policy to alleviate negative externalities of external shock crises could pay attention to the inequality pandemics impose on specific societal groups. Diversified research on the collective moods of certain societal groups and their propensity to certain kinds of affects triggering subsequent unfavorable behavioral patterns would allow to paint a deeper shadow of the invisible hand creating socio-psychological inequality.

Investigating the unprecedentedly described role of social online media information about markets driving inflation and/or debt could aid to understand the hidden behavioral dynamics that are constantly building and fueling economic booms and downturns. The future legal scholarship could also elucidate affectivity of events in order to provide group-specific modes of policy responses.

Different professional groups may feature different affective outfalls from crises given a certain propensity to face constraints, financial flexibility and differing opportunities to consume and invest. Attentive policy work may target certain affect propensities but also different affect stages during crises and through the individual lifespan. Affective fallouts may become a different layer of scrutiny on social stratification within society in order to highlight the different shades and alleviate the negative effects of inequality prevailing in society. Linking the world of feelings to the worlds of money and real economy will aid in capturing how catastrophes bleed into ordinary life in emotions that then guide consumption and life choices.

All these insights will offer the most novel ways on how to find the right communication and socio-psychological means to avert crises whole-roundedly and meaningfully. Pursuing the greater goal of deriving recommendations on how to stabilize economic markets in the instant communication century will add to purely economic calculus in finding an optimum balance of deregulated market systems and governmental control.

The future of the post-COVID-19 era holds difficult ethical challenges: With the planned post-COVID-19 bailouts representing more than 60% of the money ever issued in the history of the USA, should the finance float be pegged to an obligation to return to human well-being and promote the pursuit of sustainable growth? Can the finance sector lacking emotional fallouts return peace of mind to the real economy and soothe the hurtful anxieties of certain societal groups with heightened propensity to emotionally destructive states? Is there a moral sense or honor to put the finance world into service for the sake of human feelings that nurture the arts and culture of human progress? Should excellence in finance obligatorily be pegged to ethics of inclusion driving large-scale redistribution mandates within society, between countries and over time in between generations?

If handling all these challenges and efforts successfully based on values of justice, equity, ethics of inclusion and general trust, the COVID-19 pandemic and our generation hold the potential for becoming renown in the history of humankind as a great reset and ultimate driver of positive change for this generation and the following. This could become the post-COVID-19 renaissance and reformation of immaterial social capital, as in the end, life is about reality. The real present in the real conditions of existence. If we stop the real world social or the care for those around us, society loses itself in forgetting what life is about.

The currently ongoing COVID-19 crisis has challenged healthcare around the world. The pandemic has made already long existing healthcare inequality even more blatantly transparent as ever before (Puaschunder & Beerbaum, 2020a, 2020b). The common call for global solutions in international healthcare pandemic outbreak monitoring and crisis risk management has reached unprecedented momentum. The countries that score high on AI, anti-corruption and healthcare excellence are the ultimate innovative global pandemic alleviation leaders (Puaschunder & Beerbaum, 2020a, 2020b). Examining healthcare sector provision and combining the insights about global health with digitalization, GDP and levels of anti-corruption enabled to show the vast differences in medical sector performance around the globe (Puaschunder & Beerbaum, 2020a, 2020b). With the COVID-19 crisis imposing the most challenging healthcare crisis of the last century and the most worldwide spread pandemic that ever occurred in our contemporary society, the time is ripe to tackle the challenge to alleviate healthcare inequality around the world. COVID-19 can also be interpreted as a great reset advantage to use the potential of digitalization in order to spread access to global healthcare provision, foremost via telemedicine and healthcare apps.

Leadership and global governance of today can learn from bundling excellence in luxury as exhibited in the cultural and artistic worlds of the past. What insignia remained in the stress test of times, are often the product of luxury that can be shared and consumed by the many in their wonderfully practical and entertaining way. Cultural revolutions often entailed people driving a trend of inclusion and opening up of ideas, goods and cultures of being for the masses. To this day, the most relevant public leadership questions on innovation can be answered in the vital account of some items having stood the test of time in their endurance thanks to their universally beneficial character.

The main drivers of artistic excellence and acceptance of luxury in all cultures appear as the interplay of bundled excellence with inclusive access for all. Sociopsychological motives to cherish luxury and accept excellence lies in the elite sharing of opportunities to access that breeds harmony of inclusion within society. Luxury display and excellence striving are only acceptable by society when bestowing the notion of fairness to enjoy the benefits as a community. Innovations that transfer society widespread and sustainably are the ones carried by the many, which grants ethics of inclusion an eternal character.

Future booming industries may include luxury spending on health and prevention, which not only promotes general health in society but also drives economic growth. In the digital age of social media, luxury could force more comprehensive health prevention based on big data. In contrast to other types of consumption, large amounts of data enable exponential basic benefits to be generated. A bit more information therefore has exponentially grown added value, which in the medical field appears particularly helpful for finding connections and behavioral patterns in prevention (Schumpeter, 1934). Consumption of information is also not exclusive – reading information and learning from it does not diminish someone else's chances or diminish their consumption (Puaschunder, 2018a, 2018b, 2018e, 2019l).

In the digital age, information consumption on the internet could become an environmentally friendly luxury. The digital world truly opened up the world and access to information at one's fingertips. Future innovations in the medical field are predestined for digitized health care and self-monitoring with the help of electronic self-measuring devices. Self-monitoring devices and big data insights can provide uniquely valuable educational work for individuals who need to be encouraged to lead a holistic lifestyle focused on prevention. Coupled with insights derived from big data in the extrapolation and in relation to society, computational power in the digital age can become a preventive healthcare luxury moment.

As for the ongoing COVID-19 long-haul crisis, having individuals being capable and productive in one moment but potentially being debilitated and suffering in another, will likely breed a culture of tolerance for excellence in inclusion. Switching from productivity to disability within one's mind will likely hone skills to accept a spectrum of ability and further the embracement of a multitude of mental capacities in the educational sector. With COVID-19 long haulers being prone to mental capacity fluctuations, the post-pandemic era will be the time for opening up society to appreciate the range of mental states as a luxury of diversity.

The time has come to also rewrite economics in the cherishing of a multitude of maximization domains. Anti-discrimination efforts may protect excellence. But the sphere of excellence per se needs to be redefined and pegged to an appreciation for diversity and inclusion of different opinions. The economic concept of the multiplier may be broadened for a multitude of states and the acceptance of a diversity of receptions.

Digitalization can aid in the backing of individual's capacity, especially if people face fluctuations of productivity levels. Future ethics of inclusion in the digital domain may embrace AI and robotics informed by big data to fill in gaps, when long haulers exhaust. Digitalization can thus become complementary for filling in gaps in the human performance scheme. Ethics of inclusion could breed an acceptance of novel technologies taking over decision making. Diversity pledges may also embrace the integration of technology in our lives and human falling back on artificial devices.

Future inclusive growth endeavors may therefore support the most innovative AI, robotics and big data insights of our times. In the rescue and recovery aid but also in bold endeavors such as the GND, EGD and Sustainable Finance efforts, novel technologies could become subsidized to aid in the prevention of pandemics and their negative fallouts. Funds could target at deriving insights from big data, but also to enhance the human-technology blend in AI and robotics innovations to monitor and track pandemic outbreaks as well as the resource availability for human constant health status tracking. Funding could also allow for technological development of information and communication technologies for the low-cost generation of big data and patient-led monitoring on a more global scale. Telemedicine could bring access to affordable medical care via crowdsourcing of information to remote areas of the world.

In all these efforts to foster digitalization for the common social good, the post-pandemic aftermath could become the ultimate international development accelerator that offers easy and cheap access to decentralized information collection and inclusiveness in exchange of insights from data. Marginalized and remote communities could thereby benefit from equal, easy and cheap access to medical aid (Puaschunder, 2021a). Decentralized grids also open novel opportunities for monitoring and measuring information constantly and closely where health or diseases occur (Puaschunder, 2021a). Networking data sharing capacities have reached unprecedented density and sophistication (Puaschunder, 2021a). Novel mapping tools can display local search results and crowd media use into visible alert systems so it becomes more accessible in a broader way (Puaschunder, 2021a). Decentralized crisis management applications of AI and machine learning already range from data-driven assistance in pandemic outbreak control to battling hunger and poverty as well as forced migration (Puaschunder, 2021a).

One of the most powerful ways to enjoy luxury in the digital age is online education. The online digital opportunities to create truly international experience now elevate the envelope of cultural diversity to unprecedented heights. In online virtual luxury worlds, education can now benefit from the cross-pollination of many different cultural regions. The online educational wave will also likely lead to a downward adjustment in the price of education and thereby open up the spectrum range of opportunities for all sorts of income groups to gain knowledge. Online education thereby holds the potential for a truly diverse experience that lifts society to a more ethical and fair level playing field.

While all these digital innovations offer enormous potentials to improve our future world to come, at the same time, however, attention must be paid to ethics of inclusion for vulnerable populations. Especially when it comes to marginalized groups and/or vulnerable patient populations or minors, who have the longest time to discount and most uncertain future outcome prospects of their lives, heightened levels of privacy and dignity protection have to be called for. Ethical imperatives but also legal support must protect society from big data generation that is used in a harmful way. Data insight misuse at the expense of fair opportunities and equal access to chances must be avoided by all means. In this, again, the post-pandemic new renaissance offers the opportunity to flourish economic growth with respect for equality as well as fair and dignified treatment of all.

A warming earth under climate change is pressuring future generations' living conditions. Never before in the history of humankind have environmental concerns in the wake of economic growth heralded governance predicaments as we face today (Puaschunder, 2020d). Climate change presents societal, international and intergenerational fairness as challenge for modern economies and contemporary democracies. In today's climate change mitigation and adaptation efforts, high- and low-income households, developed and underdeveloped countries and overlapping generations are affected differently (Puaschunder, 2017c). Public policies and monetary aid appear as the most common and efficient transfer mechanisms to alleviate environmental injustice. Innovative GND strategies unleashing a sustainable economy in harmony with equity pledges for a healthy population have become the core of COVID-19 rescue and recovery aid.

The novel coronavirus SARS-CoV-2 imposes the most unexpected external economic shock on modern humankind. In order to alleviate unexpected negative fallouts from the crisis, global governance and governments around the globe engaged in bailouts and recovery packages of extraordinary size and scope. In confronting the crisis, economic bailout and rescue packages are currently also addressing widespread social inequality alleviation. In the eye of social inequality, governments around the world are therefore pegging bailout and recovery targets to social equality goals. As we are entering the age of corporate social justice and inclusive societies, governmental aid appears as a powerful force for alleviating discrimination or re-balancing a disparate impact toward creating a more right, just and fair allocation of economic gains. Governmental aid and rescue packages will have the extraordinary potential to fund anti-discrimination of unjust or prejudicial treatment of different categories of people or things. Long-standing, ample evidence of discrimination and most important attempts exist to legally abolish, economically counter-weight and societally alleviate the negative impacts of discrimination around the world. Yet to this day, there is hardly any description of discrimination of excellence against social justice. In the wake of the rising social justice movement, social justice plays a crucial role in pushing for positive societal change. Social justice striving is thus the excellence of our times that can be flourished by the GND.

Inspired by the economic success story of the New Deal reform of the USA to recover from the Great Depression of the 1920s, the so-called GND is the most advanced governmental attempt to secure a sustainable economic solution in harmony with the earth's resources. The GND advocates for using a transition to renewable energy and sustainable growth in order to stimulate economic growth (The United States Congress, 116th Congress, 1st Session, House Resolution 109, Introduced February 7, 2019).

The post-COVID-19 recovery era is also a time of blatant disparities and inequalities in terms of access to healthcare and social justice. In times of rising inequality, the GND has also become a vehicle to determine the COVID-19 economic bailout and recover aid targets. The GND thereby combines Roosevelt's economic approach with modern ideas of economic stimulus incentivizing industries for a transition to renewable energy and resource efficiency as well as healthcare equality and social justice pledges.

The GND is a governmental strategy to strengthen the US economy and foster inclusive growth. The GND is targeted at sharing economic growth benefits more equally within society. How to align economic interest with justice and fairness notions is the question of our times when considering the massive challenges faced in terms of environmental preservation, healthcare demands and social justice pledges.

In the currently implemented GND and EGD as the most widespread, large-scale and financially extensive programs, society will first have to define what the GND is, how the GND is implemented and why it matters in its multiple implementation facets and international angles. Ethics of inclusion and a diverse mindset with multiple stakeholders involved can thereby serve as a guiding post and beacon of hope that inclusion can bring positive change for everyone.

As an avenue of hope, the GND could be presented as a possibility to make the world and society more equitable in the domains of environmental justice, access to affordable healthcare and social justice excellence. Ethical imperatives and equity mandates lead the economic rationale behind redistribution in the GND as social peace, health and favorable environmental conditions are prerequisites for productivity. The GND offers unprecedented opportunities in making the world and society but also overlapping generations more equitable and thus bestowing peace and social harmony within society, around the world and over time. In answering the question if the GND is equitable, one has to acknowledge that the GND is a fairly novel phenomenon with international variations and diverse implementation strategies.

Implementing the social cost of carbon has already been part of US President Obama's administration plans for addressing climate change. The beginnings of the GND idea are attributed to Senator Edward Markey and Representative Alexandria Ocasio-Cortez pushing for transitioning the USA to use 100% renewable, zero-emission energy sources including investment into electric cars and high-speed rail systems (Puaschunder, 2021b). In January 2019, a letter signed by 626 organizations in support of a GND was sent to all members of the US Congress (Puaschunder, 2021b). The GND encourages to create jobs in green industries, thus boosting the world economy and curbing climate change at the same time (Puaschunder, 2021b). Economic foundations are grounded on John Maynard Keynes' (1936/2003) spending multiplier effect, which proves governmental spending to trickle down in the economy and ignite positive transformative change at the same time via innovation and social equity.

On the international level, emissions trading plays a role in order to incentivize corporations around the globe to reduce GHG emissions Braga, Fischermann, et al., 2020. Green bonds are another strategy in the wake of the environmental efforts of the GND in order to raise funds internationally and over time for green transition innovations but also to fund climate change mitigation and adaptation (Orlov et al., 2018). Within the country level, environmental pricing – foremost enabled via ecotaxation – curbs harmful emissions and sets incentives to reduce energy or transition to a renewable solution (Braga, Fischermann, et al., 2020). In the environmental sphere, the US GND fosters global governance efforts in fiscal policy strategies targeted at a carbon tax to fund climate change mitigation and adaptation efforts (Braga, Fischermann, et al., 2020). Monetary and credit policies – foremost enacted by the Federal Reserve and implemented by public policy officials – foster the financialization of climate change mitigation and adaptation while counterbalancing inflation rate rises in the eye of climate disasters and their recovery financing (Braga, Fischermann, et al., 2020). GND insurance policies are trying to back underserved communities' resilience that is challenged by ongoing environmental crises. The GND funding for R&D and governmental infant industry grants target at green market solutions, such as absorbing CO_2 or ecowellness solutions. Behavioral insights can be used to steer positive change and environmental conscientiousness during purchasing decisions and living choices (Puaschunder, 2020a). As such sustainability can become lived throughout working, leisure and healthcare activities. Examples include sustainable tourism, intergenerationally conscientious living as well as asset allocation styles in SRI. Portfolio managers and asset funds management executives have caught up on this emerging trend of a rise in interest to align financial goals with sustainability pledges (Braga, Semmler, et al., 2020; Puaschunder, 2013, 2015c, 2018d).

The results whether the environmental edge in economic stimulus will be successful or not will become visible long term. Most of the measures and changes implied are long-term goals that will not be easily captured with our contemporary stress test methodology or public policy monitoring and evaluation tools. In order to get a sense whether inequality is alleviated and the GND goals accomplishment plans are successful, it will be necessary to derive inference from two other major areas of change instigated by the GND and – of course – the passage of time. In order to structure the GND vigilantly, intergenerational decision making is recommended that embraces the opinions of younger generations, who likely will lead the future generations in the long run. The GND is like planting a tree to be fully grown in the future to come. Even if the elder know they will not be able to fully enjoy the grown up tree in the future anymore given their expected lifetime, the elder will naturally consult with the younger generation what kind of tree they want to enjoy in their future. The tree will be planted according to the wishes of the young. Future world inhabitants will be on the minds of the elders who are actually setting the seed and planting it for tomorrow's world inhabitants.

In the history of humankind, new ground-breaking trends but also striving for excellence survived throughout times if innovation ennobled society and advanced the general welfare. The current COVID-19 crisis brings about the largest-ever wave of effort to combat a disease, improve the general healthcare but also to alleviate inequality. New Deal efforts could draw from the strength of law and economics to fight discrimination and breed social equity. Excellence and luxury are nowadays found in a truly inclusive society that is built on the hallmarks of anti-discrimination. In the wake of the rising social justice sentiment all over the world, social justice is defined as multiplier luxury in offering the hope of a better, more equal society. Social justice pioneers are the heroes of our times and their excellence should be celebrated and gratified as luxury moment that needs to be protected to trickle down in society. Direct attempts to diminish inequality and foster social justice comprise increasing state-sponsored jobs to improve economic equality. A 10-year national mobilization targets at work security and uplifting working conditions by high-quality health care, affordable housing for all, economic security, access to clean water, air, healthy food and nature, education, clean, renewable, zero-emission energy, repairing of infrastructure, energy efficient smart power grids, improved living conditions by pollution elimination, clean manufacturing and positive work collaborations without discrimination.

More than ever before is leadership these days urged to set incentives against discrimination of excellence represented in the luxury of cultural diversity. Luxury may hold unprecedentedly captured easily implementable remedies against discrimination of excellence in inclusivity. We see these trends in the arts, where countercultures and diverse societies are often celebrated before the mainstream accepts them. The difference is celebrated as a novelty and the diverse representation praised as *en vogue* fortification of trends. In the GND, economics could come to life in combating economically suboptimal and societally hurtful discrimination of excellence in social justice.

Advances in the ethics of inclusion are likely to show these three speculative trends in the future and focus attention on: Ethics of inclusion in the wake of social justice pledges will demand a comparative approach to understand the most contemporary responsibility challenges of our time. With the COVID-19 pandemic having exacerbated existing inequalities and rising new gaps within society, inequality alleviation will become essential in the post-COVID-19 era in the domains of access to affordable healthcare, finance, education, digitalization and sharing the burden to protect the environment.

Law and economics developments may aid in envisioning a transition to a more inclusive society. The fields of law and economics are hallmarks of social sciences. Legal studies account for the oldest foundations of scholarly work and have ever since been at the heart of academic institutions. Since the inception of the science of economics, economic standardization of measuring utility enjoyed rising popularity. Surprisingly, the interdisciplinary discourse of law and economics has had a comparatively recent start but gained unprecedented urgency in today's world.

The time has come to acknowledge the power of integrating law and economics as one of the most important approaches to solve the most pressing contemporary societal predicaments of our times. Climate change, healthcare inequality and the exacerbated digitalization disruption require the bundled strength of law and economics to successfully harness positive advancement but also curb harmful threats to our society and future generations to come early on and wisely.

Law offers an ennobling humane-natural principle of ethicality, practical feasibility in governmental impetus but also historical adaptability to implement societal changes including a legal birds-eye view of comparative approaches around the world, an exemplary sensitivity to disparate impacts of external influences' impact on society but also clear guidelines how far the individual freedom and well-being can be granted in light of common security protection and societal welfare enhancement endeavors. Economics features the most advanced methods to discount future value, an exemplary formalization of societal welfare maximization over time, but also the most sophisticated ways to quantify societal gains and losses in often-overlooked and behaviorally unforeseen externalities.

Only in the harmonious combination of both disciplines will the most challenging contemporary predicaments of our time be solved and widespread inequalities be alleviated through disparate-impact-sensitive, fine-tuned redistribution mechanisms. While the legal analysis grants insights about the disparate impact of policies, the economic analysis allows to study efficiency of burden sharing over time and with consideration of externalities. Acknowledging unique interdisciplinary insights and cherishing an international field of law and economics can help bridge the gap between societal entities, politically divided nations and temporally distanced generations. Adopting an interdisciplinary study approach with a commonly understood language will promote a mutual understanding of multi-faceted insights in order to harvest the societal benefits of a fruitful law and economics *Gestalt* that is greater than its singular law and economics entities. Future education and scholarship may investigate how to apply state-of-the-art global interdisciplinary law and economics methods to help solve the most complex societal predicaments of our times.

Social justice pledges to create an inclusive world drawn from law, economics, sociology, psychology and cultural studies. Arts, fashion and lifestyle products are driven by luxury, another form of excellence only reachable by the elite. Artistic leadership in the luxury world appears somewhat resistant to discrimination of excellence. There is an implicit acceptance of excellence if coupled with artistic beauty, unique creativity in a transfer of ideas and deprecating endurance – all features that high-end luxury usually represents. Artistic excellence appears to be too beautiful and unique to fail and artists are often suffering anyhow.

Leadership against discrimination of excellence is proposed to learn from excellence represented by luxury in the cultural and artistic worlds. Luxury may hold unprecedentedly captured, cheap and easily implementable remedies against discrimination of excellence. In case studies and historical methods of research, future research projects should unravel the main drivers of excellence and what is unique in luxury in order to outline these features in social movements. Unique luxury features should be discussed to be proposed to lead academia but also economics in combating economically suboptimal and societally hurtful discrimination of excellence in social justice.

The success in the implementation of the current post-COVID-19 rescue and recovery aid will depend on a deeper understanding of the interaction and interdependence of economics within society. Longer term outcomes and impacts in the preventive healthcare provision around the world, environmental security and social justice will determine the living conditions and peace prospects of this generation and those to come.

In the future, social friction is expected due to the strong polarization of financial profits sponsored by low key interest rate policy. The flexible substitutability of financial fund components in the exchange of loss segments for winning industries increases financial market profits, but at the same time reduces liquidity capacity and sustainability survival of small and medium-sized enterprises. In this sense, the generally low interest rate creates a situation that the financial world lives at the expense of the real economy. Taxing the COVID-19-profit industries, especially digitization winners, could create fiscal space for redistributing some of the economic gains to industries that clearly lose from COVID-19. Taxation of digitalized economic growth during our forced digitalization disruption could provide the necessary redistribution funds to back the liquidity-dried real economy.

Governments can also bring back the financial world in the service of improving and stabilizing the real economy in a stricter separation between investment and consumer banks, which already began in the course of the regulations following the 2008–2009 recession. Central banks could offer diversified interest rates. Low key interest rates would drive innovation and economic growth in the financial sector, which could fund high key interest rates for real economy savings for consumers. This diversified interest regime could help avert psychosocial frictions between the finance world and the real economy. Online currencies, such as the currently planned European Central Bank digital currency, could help a transparent use of the currency over time to strictly divert interest rate profits and avoid arbitrage or interest rate swaps. Mutual collateral insurance between the financial world and the real economy would also be possible in order to spread risk. Bonds have also been discussed to enable innovations while repayments should be redistributed to the real economy. Bonds have been used throughout history to finance long-term strategies with unknown outcome (Puaschunder, 2021f). In addition, banks could be encouraged to use the current profits for future large-scale investments that add societal long-term value. For example, large construction projects but also innovation in research and development are valuable macro-economic multipliers that can benefit society as a whole in the short and long term (Epstein, 2020; Keynes, 1936/2003). Governments and intergovernmental bodies, like the European Union, have the long-term vision and financial freedom to operate on deficits but also the regulatory means to enact large-scale redistribution and long-term wealth creation in grand investments for the future.

Climate change heralded a call for a fair climate stabilization solution and burden sharing strategy *within society*, *between countries* and *over time*. Intergenerational equity to provide an at least as favorable standard of living to future generations as currently enjoyed challenges traditional economic utility discounting models. Trade-offs arise for today's consumers and taxpayers between individual profit maximization and future societal welfare improvement under the conditions of uncertainty and unperceivable outcomes for future beneficiaries.

In solving the climate change predicament, the law offers an ethically grounded climate justice justification of redistribution mechanisms *within society*, *around the world* and *between generations* in order to avert climate inequality. Intergenerational equity ethics back legal redistribution schemes to avert climate change-induced inequality. From a practical standpoint, legal foundations help global governance and governmental action to alleviate inequality. Sophisticated comparative legal analysis methods highlight regulatory peculiarities' impact on different living conditions on the societal, national and generational levels. Legal disparate impact analyses opening aggregate macro-economic calculus shed important light on the unequally distributed burden of external environmental shocks on specific societal groups, various world nations and different generations. Law and economics can address vulnerable groups on whom sustainability pledges place a disproportionate burden, which fosters the sustainable development goals on a granular but widespread level.

Long-term oriented economic prospect discounting and productivity measurement around the world can quantify climate change-induced inequalities. GDP prospect differences under climate change based on the optimum temperature for economic productivity and GDP sector composition per country reveal relative country differences on the economic climate change gains and loss spectrum (Puaschunder, 2020d). Climate flexibility – defined as the range of temperature variation per country – determines the future climate wealth of nations based on economic production and comparative trade advantages (Puaschunder, 2020d). The economic analysis of the economic gains and losses of a warming earth around the world but also an economic estimation of future trade prospects in light of global warming help quantify how to enact climate change burden sharing fairness in legally instigated redistribution and compensation schemes.

A law and economics analysis can dissect climate inequalities and provides viable means in order to enact climate justice via redistribution and compensation. First, *climate justice within a country* ensures that low- and high-income households carry a proportional burden in terms of disposable income enabled through a progressive carbon taxation. Consumption tax curbs harmful behavior. A corporate inheritance tax reaps benefits of past wealth accumulation that caused climate change. Second, fair *climate change burden sharing between countries* ensures those countries economically benefiting from a warmer environment also bear a higher responsibility regarding climate change mitigation and adaptation efforts. Third, *climate justice over time* can be enabled in climate bonds financed via debts that are paid back by future generations who inherit a favorable climate *in lieu*, which distributes the benefits and burdens of a warming earth Pareto-optimally among generations.

Direct law and economics-driven innovations to find economically feasible and judicially fair climate financialization methods are introduced in tax-and-bonds strategies. An international climate regime could feature countries to raise funds via taxation or become bond premium beneficiaries. A country's propensity to either grant the taxation-and-bonds solution via taxation or be a bonds payout recipient could be determined by a country's initial position on the climate change economic gains and losses spectrum, regular and consumption-based, trade-adjusted CO_2 emissions per country, climate flexibility as the range of temperatures within a national territory as future comparative trade advantage to other nations in the world, the willingness of countries to change CO_2 emissions and the historically determined banking lending regimes of a country. The idea of diversified tax-and-bonds is also extendable to sector-specific bond yield interest rate regimes. Within a country, the bonds could offer industry-specific diversified interest rate maturity bond yields based on the environmental sustainability of an industry, for example, as measured by the European Sustainable Finance Taxonomy. The bonds could also feature a long-time financialization via debt that can be repaid by future generations for inheriting a stable climate. All these law and economics-informed recommendations aim at sharing the burden but also the benefits of climate change within society in an economically efficient, legally equitable and practically feasible way now around the world and also between generations.

In the most recent decades, human decision-making heuristics were studied to show how nudging and winking can help citizens to make rational choices (Puaschunder, 2017f). Behavioral economics started with outlining human decision-making deviations from rationality, so-called heuristics or mental shortcuts. Heuristics were perceived as failures in the North American Behavioral Economics School, while the European tradition saw human decision making as a successful strategy to cope with an overly complex world (Puaschunder, 2020a, 2021j). Mental heuristics and biases were studied in field and laboratory experiments but also with the help of big data and online observations to retrieve powerful nudges to benefit from life and economic markets. Over time, a broad range of nudges and winks were developed to curb the harmful consequences of human decision making or improve human fitness to adapt to the environment. Some techniques were communicated openly, while other behavioral insights informed more subliminal change strategies. Since a bit more than 10 years, the behavioral economics approach was applied to political context in the behavioral insights revolution (Puaschunder, 2020a). Behavioral economics and finance leadership demonstrated how economics can be employed for the greater societal good. Most recently, leadership and followership directives on nudging in digitalized spaces emerged that appeal to scholars and policy makers interested in rational decision making and the use of nudging and winking in the digital age. Digitalization offers unprecedented human advancement and democratization potential free from corruption. At the same time, shifting marketplaces to online virtual spaces opens gates for misinformation and disinformation being used in a competitive sense. Ethics of inclusion, law and economics advocacy and interdisciplinary dialogue building but also human–AI algorithm compatibility are expected to become key advancements in behavioral economics and finance leadership of the future.

Advancements in the understanding of how AI, robotics and big data insights can aid society to come out stronger from the COVID-19 crisis will likely be grounded in behavioral insights. The COVID-19 pandemic also entailing a pandemic within the pandemic stemming from around 10% to over 30% of previously COVID-19-infected estimated to become suffering from long-haul symptoms, will likely open gates for AI, robotics and big data to become vital parts of our society. Like in ancient pandemics that drove mechanization to replace missing human-power, the currently estimated demographics of around 0.6–3.976 billion long haulers worldwide emerging, stresses the need for human-like creatures to replace weakened humanistic powers. With only 27–166 million US citizens expected to have continuous impairment of COVID-19 after an infection for more than 6–12 weeks, the need for autonomous self-learning entities filling in for gaps in human decision-making capability has leveraged into unprecedented momentum. While the causes and long-term lasting effects of long COVID-19 are unclear and to be investigated in the future, the impact of COVID-19 long haulers on democratization of healthcare information online and the economics of prevention, eHealth, and rest is without doubt. In the search for quick and easy access to information about a rising phenomenon, social online media forums have turned to cheap and easily accessible information portals as an alternative to overfilled hospitals. Social media self-help groups, such as Survivor Corps, offer quick remedies and information exchange for the masses on newly emerging healthcare problems in COVID-19 long-haul symptoms. Other foreseeable trends in light of generation long haulers, who face recurrent waves of debilitating symptoms and chronic illnesses, include preventive care self-measurement of health statuses in real-time but also the use of big data insights about virus spreads. Further, a heterodox economics case of attention to health, minimization, and rest in business, finance, and economics will likely emerge foremost driven by behavioral economics, which started to address cognitive overload and decision-making failures in a too complex world. In all these trends of attention to health, minimalism and rest, the COVID-19 long haulers generation has the potential to reboot economics and allow for an integration of AI to learn how to fill gaps of chronically or recurrently ill to assist us all in a phase of common rest and recovery.

Social justice pledges of our times have driven an awareness for rising inequality and demand for embracement of diversity. With COVID-19 long haulers facing waves of productivity being followed by unproductive debilitation, an appreciation for the necessity of attention to excellence in inclusion is prospected to be honed. Individuals who suffer from long COVID-19 will be prone to experience differences in productivity levels within themselves and thus be sensitized to the spectrum of capabilities – not only between people but also within themselves. This eye-opening awareness of differences in activation levels will hopefully breed trust in the empowering features of diversity and foster a culture of acceptance of differences. People are likely to become appreciative of ethics of compassion and empathic intelligence that respect variations on the productivity scales, which will likely elevate ethics of inclusion as a feature of modern growth theory.

The economic inequality exacerbated by COVID-19 implies that future economic policy research may take inspiration from the legal concept of disparate impact to channel the currently unprecedentedly large rescue and recovery aid wisely to alleviate inequality (Puaschunder, 2021a). Measuring a potentially disparately heavy impact of external shocks – such as COVID-19 but also climate change or racial disparities – on gender, race and other stratifying classifications that may lead to discrimination opens gates for targeted rescue and recovery aid with particular attention to empowering minorities and/or alleviating disadvantages. Already now we see a pegging of governmental rescue and recovery aid to socially uplifting causes to address inequality concerns and environmental causes (Puaschunder 2021a). Future efforts could directly investigate if there is a heavier load of the societal burden due to COVID-19 on particular groups that hinders a speedy, full and fair recovery. Legal excellence on how to detect disparate impacts could be coupled with behavioral insights on how to alleviate biases via taxation redistribution in an uncertain world in order to rescue, uplift and empower weaker societal segments in the age of our post-COVID-19 renaissance.

Law and economics interdisciplinary dialogue building and human–AI algorithm compatibility are expected to become key advancements in behavioral economics and finance leadership of the future. A comparative approach should be adopted to understand the most contemporary responsibility challenges of our time. The idea of fairness and social justice should be elucidated from an ethical perspective in our post-pandemic era. Ethics of inclusion and the economics of diversity management will embrace diversified potentials that overall empower society.

Disparate impact analyses of law and economics interdisciplinary endeavors account for the most cutting-edge novel advancements in behavioral sciences (Puaschunder, 2021a, 2021e). On the macro-level, the academic field of law and economics offers legal long-standing excellence in accounting for disparate impact, inequality and redistribution. The analysis of macro-economic aggregates benefits from a legal scholarship-led reflection of diversified and temporal views of social preferences, given patterns of differences based on age, gender, race and professional propensity risks.

Most recent law and economics developments should become the basis for solving practical ethical dilemmas arising in the fair distribution of healthcare, financial aid, education, digitalization and carrying the burden of climate stabilization. In the distribution of COVID-19 relief, a system change may be accomplished when being guided by the interdisciplinary insights of "law and economics" that in particular can address the disparate impact of the disease in order to derive targeted inequality alleviation strategies. Future economic policy research may be inspired by legal expertise on the measurement of disparate impact, which could open up neoclassical aggregate economic functions calculus as a measure of economic growth. The combined expertise of law and economics in their unique interaction may shed light on disparate impacts of diseases, public health and economic relief measures. This may lead to an interdisciplinary framework for crisis alleviation through redistribution that in combination can set the course for a better future in a more compassionate and inclusive world.

4

Conclusion

Global governance of corporate social conduct may advance corporate and financial social responsibility in the future. Based on stakeholder consensus, governance may set standards and support governments in subsidizing CSR frameworks that are backed up by institutional support. Global governance and stakeholder management on CSR standards in sync with universally agreed upon responsible finance principles may help corporate management to adopt social responsibility policies in business plans and financial asset management.

The implementation of sustainable finance should ideally be assisted by public and private efforts. Governments should provide information on societal challenges and advocate for the adoption of socially responsible corporate practices. The set-up of partnerships requires global governance to foster partnership-enhancing environments. In networking forums, multiple stakeholders can be encouraged to discuss social concerns and find consensus on commonly shared goals and network support. Regional initiatives can coordinate local action and govern the implementation of CSR.

Accountability and transparency are prerequisites for the advancement of CSR. Institutional efforts may also incentivize and sanction corporate social performance based on transparent quality control. Evaluations help assess and benchmark the transparent social impact of sustainable goal partners. Transparent goal accomplishment strategies will monitor the partners' contributions. Benchmarking and impact assessments will derive the best practice learning models for future PPPs.

Concerning financial social responsibility, securing a long-term sustainable market option trend will be key. Global governance on information disclosure about SRI options will help drive the trend toward sustainable investments. International financial institutions and governmental policies must work toward providing market actors with information on SRI. Financial institutions and experts are encouraged to consider environmental and social responsibility promoted by media reports, social rating criteria as well as social responsibility proxy voting strategies. SRI innovations will ensure concurrent economic market prosperity and societal advancement.

Responsible Investment Around the World: Finance after the Great Reset, 183–194
Copyright © 2023 by Julia M. Puaschunder
Published under exclusive licence by Emerald Publishing Limited
doi:10.1108/978-1-80382-851-020231008

In recent decades, CSR has emerged as for several trends. International organizations have strengthened CSR by providing guidelines and oversight on corporate social conduct. Concurrently governments have fostered social responsibility by legislative reforms and governmental regulations that raised corporate actors' awareness for social deficiencies.

With the rise of CSR, governmental entities have started to count on corporate resources and expertise in social welfare provision. At the same time, stakeholder pressure for information disclosure of corporate conduct has propelled CSR and let consumers increasingly pay attention to the social impact of corporate activities. As a consequence, corporations have integrated total responsibility management as an innovative corporate success factor.

PPPs have created win–win situations in addressing societal challenges by the combined forces of the public and private sectors. Given these trends, corporate social conduct is an *en vogue* phenomenon with the potential to steer entire market systems in a more socially conscientious direction.

International attention: The UN, World Bank and the Organization for Economic Cooperation and Development but also the European Commission and the US Congress play key roles in advancing social responsibility. International regulatory regimes must set CSR standards that harmonize corporate social endeavors in accordance with global responsibility legislations such as the UNGC, the ILO's labor regulations or the ISO guidelines. At the same time, international initiatives must create supportive environments for the adoption of socially responsible business practices and assist public policy makers in crafting CSR frameworks.

Governmental assistance: In a plethora of legislative requirements, best practice principles and implementation guidelines; governments may strive for stakeholder consensus on corporate social conduct. By raising awareness for social deficiencies, CSR stakeholders should be encouraged to administer corporate social conduct. Governmental networking forums can engage corporate actors, the media and NGOs to discuss societal concerns and find a common ground on social solution strategies. The invitation to social solution finding will convince corporations to contribute to social goals beyond legal requirements.

Based on a universal understanding of CSR, long-term focused governmental regulations and legislations set social responsibility standards. In a continuing dialogue on CSR standards, governments should promote an authentic adoption of social responsibility practices by outlining the economic, social and environmental impact corporations can have on society. The link between CSR, productivity and innovation will serve as an additional motivating factor for the consideration of social responsibility. Research focused on tangible and intangible CSR assets will portray CSR as a competitive advantage for corporations that mitigate social risks. Given administrative implementation costs, governments may strive for stakeholder consensus on corporate social conduct.

To close the gap between the theoretical planning and actual application of CSR, governments can administer the implementation of CSR. Governmental managerial guidelines that pay attention to international legal requirements, national laws and corporate constraints will set best practice standards. The corporate adoption of responsibility codes should be monitored by governmental control. In the implementation assistance of CSR, governments need to move from the qualitative expression of policy objectives to the quantitative measurement of results. Governments can also set up multi-stakeholder collaborative CSR networks as centers of expertise that constantly advance the social responsibility idea.

Governments should incentivize CSR. By steering capital and aid toward social and environmental attention, economic incentives encourage corporations to take on responsibilities. International export opportunities, credits and insurances based on the social performance can be coupled with internationally renowned accreditations, licenses to operate and CSR certifications. Positive governmental incentives feature tax and fee exemptions, credits, subsidies and loans. Public entities may also fall back on negative sanctions of taxation, penalties, litigations and charges to avert socially irresponsible corporate conduct. Implicit incentives comprise trade controls and outsourcing contracts for corporations that commit to social and environmental standards.

Corporate social engagement: Paying attention to strategic opportunities and risks of societal challenges, CSR departments should assign leaders to adopt social responsibility policies, integrate social responsibility in corporate mission plans and assist the implementation of ethical codes of conduct. Corporate leaders can promote a shared CSR vision and provide responsible leadership throughout the corporation and supply chain. At the operational level, the integration of CSR should be guidelined by action plans on day-to-day corporate social practices.

Accountability: Accountability refers to the expectation of having to justify actions to others (Lerner & Tetlock, 1999). Accountability provides an external quality control feedback by public and private actors periodically monitoring corporate social contributions. Civil society must maintain a watch-dog function on corporate social impacts and thereby implicitly supervise the CSR implementation.

Transparency: Transparent corporate conduct is ensured by governmental legal obligations (e.g., freedom of information legislation), the removal of industrial information transfer barriers, economic incentives, stakeholder campaigns and CSR reporting. Information disclosure will help in verifying the quality and accuracy of CSR conduct. As the basis for monitoring and benchmarking, transparent CSR information will help in identifying areas for improvement and grow the confidence of the stakeholder community and therefore secure investment capital.

Capacity building: Corporations and governments can educate socially responsible leaders. Academic institutions ingrain CSR in educational curricula to bestow future leaders with the ability to manifest and implement CSR codes of conduct at all hierarchical levels. CSR capacity building can be supported by trade unions and NGOs.

International standards: International CSR standards are the basis for the worldwide spread of corporate social conduct. Universal CSR standards leverage CSR from legal compliance and voluntary philanthropy to a state-of-the-art mainstream corporate practice. Corporate social standards guideline corporate social conduct and are essential for a harmonious CSR implementation.

The UNGC offers a framework that sets corporate social standards as an industrial "level playing field." The UNGC can be fortified by stakeholder management, implementation assistance and quality control. The UN SDGs provide a guideline on how to enact international development around the globe. European Sustainable Finance Taxonomy sets standards to address the sustainability impact throughout the range of industries on the market. The SDGs can also be seen as a nomenclature of international standardized goals to accomplish in the realm of CSR.

Stakeholder management: As CSR is not only a demand on the current agenda of multinational organizations operating in industrialized countries but also a concern for the developing world, the UNGC can approach global players entering international markets and embrace corporate professionals along the supply chain. In the international arena, inconsistent standards must be harmonized based on the international law. The UNGC framework should extend its range from legal constituents to offering coherent CSR codes of conduct and standardized best practices that are based on internationally agreed principles, formal requirements and contractual agreements. At the same time, the UNGC should remain applicable to national specificities and multi-stakeholder formations. A continued stakeholder dialogue on CSR can ensure that the UNGC implementation remains in accordance with societal demands and meets civic expectations.

The formulation of universal UNGC standards is hindered by differing missions, goal accomplishment time frames and expectations of the constituents who may have diverse motivations to engage in the UNGC. The UNGC global network can mediate conflicts between the UNGC partners by a variety of means. By fostering a mutual understanding of common societal goals, the UNGC works toward a universal consensus on CSR. Intercultural research projects must target at finding harmonization strategies that strengthen the UNGC's cooperation.

To foster the common understanding of CSR, the UNGC initiative should encourage participants to share information within the network and consult responsibility predicaments for the sake of harmonious CSR conduct. Additional value campaigns can decrease divergences among international constituents. Networking events should engage the corporate world, the public sector and civil society in expertise exchange on CSR. Internet platforms may store data on CSR information to create a common sense and best practice learning platform on corporate social conduct.

Implementation assistance: The UNGC should be integrated into corporate practices at the operational level. The UNGC participants are advised to change corporate policies in sync with the Ten Principles. The principles must further be ingrained in corporate conduct throughout all hierarchical levels. The UNGC and industrial CSR departments should coordinate and oversee the principles' implementation. Corporate executives' adoption of CSR can be assisted by respective action plans in accordance with the Ten Principles. The Ten Principles implementation should be advanced by concrete activities.

In the light of international corporate conduct, the enforcement of international *human rights* standards is challenged by differing national legal frameworks and public policy settings. As some countries have not codified international human rights, these governments are advised to comply with international standards. Transnational legal agreements and contractual CSR requirements ensure the codification of human rights. The implementation of basic human rights can be supported and monitored by international and national governance. Gaps in the legal codification and the actual application of human rights should be addressed by the UN and NGOs. International councils and national governments should be encouraged to exchange information and work closely on a joint human rights strategy before multinational corporations.

The improvement of *labor standards* and working conditions contributes to the efficiency of markets, socio-political stability and societal welfare. Governments should therefore promote compliance with labor standards and empower unions. The removal of legal, political and developmental barriers to the exercise of freedom of association will back up labor unions and protect workers' rights. Freedom of association and the right to collective bargaining have to be monitored by the UN – with a special focus on politically unstable countries. Forced and compulsory labor should be detected to overcome human exploitation and discrimination. Citizens can be educated on their rights by governmental and NGO information campaigns. Equal opportunities are ensured by legal frameworks, quota systems and structural empowerment featuring educational scholarships.

In the domain of CSR, interdisciplinary research can attribute the skills needed and motivational factors for socially responsible corporate conduct. UNGC education campaigns should foster CSR learning plans and training facilities advocating for the integration of CSR practices in daily operations. The UNGC's principles should be ingrained in university curricula and business management programs that train employees to consider the externalities of corporate conduct.

In terms of social responsibility toward the *environment*, corporate innovations are key. Environmental responsibility can be promoted as an innovative corporate conduct that attracts financial investment. Corporations and investors are incentivized for aligning corporate conduct with sustainability goals. The UNGC should create a database on environmental responsibility best practices to allow benchmarking and quality control.

The UNGC should engage private and public stakeholders in the set-up of a global governance framework on *anti-corruption*. In the international arena, anti-corruption standards bundle multi-stakeholder efforts. Backed up by regulatory reforms and legal codifications, anti-corruption codes of conduct should be established. Anti-corruption topics can be addressed by conferences, publications, newsletters and blogs that stress accountability, oversight and public scrutiny on corporate and financial social conduct as prerequisites of economic stability.

Quality control: A more sophisticated UNGC partner identification and selection based on the real commitment to the UN endeavors will foster the UNGC's credibility. As self-imposed goals and self-reporting on accomplishments give partners leeway to lower the bar of performance, the compliance with the UNGC standards should be enhanced by transparent goal setting and quality control. The UNGC can provide outcome, output and performance indicators that help in monitoring the participants' engagement and the overall effectiveness of the UNGC initiative.

CSR auditing will serve as a benchmarking for the improvement of CSR practices and basis for international legislative reforms. Accountability control will nurture the credibility and trust in the UNGC and therefore attract investments. In the international arena, successful UNGC goal accomplishments should be rewarded by governmental and national incentives as well as internationally renowned accreditations and certifications for CSR best practices. Failed CSR goals must be made transparent as for providing learning examples and allowing assistance for improvement. Goal accomplishment deficiencies should be sanctioned. Up to now, no immediate actions have been installed against corporations joining the UNGC and not meeting self-imposed goals. Current failures to provide an annual report on progress solely result in mild consequences. Corporations that do not meet self-set targets remain in the UNGC community, which negatively impacts the overall UNGC's credibility. Transparent and stringent warnings and sanction procedures will counterwork the partners' noncompliance with the UNGC.

In the wake of the 2008–2009 World Financial Recession, corporate scandals and the recapitalization of the finance sector have raised the demand for restoring public trust and credibility in corporate and financial markets. In the aftermath of the crisis, governmental and corporate actors bear unknown risks and face growing societal expectations of disciplined corporate conduct and responsible financial investments under conditions of heightened levels of public scrutiny. The recent trends have rebalanced social responsibility contributions in partnership models. Currently, PPPs feature responsibility restructuring between governance entities, the corporate world and the finance sector. In these challenging times of change, PPPs must meet social responsibility demands by attention to global governance, governmental assistance, stakeholder management and local networks.

Global governance: In the international arena, PPP-administered CSR should be backed up by international organizations. Global governance entities must create a partnership-enhancing institutional, political and judicial infrastructure. Legislative frameworks must be established that aim at corporate social value creation. International public policy makers should ratify social responsibility declarations that are in sync with societal goals and advocate for the adoption of social responsibility policies.

The UN plays a key role in advancing PPPs. The UNGC initiative must become an entry point for corporations to engage in social partnership projects featuring operational flexibility and focus on pragmatic solutions. In addition, the UNGC secretariat should promote CSR to the corporate world as a competitive advantage and PPP-administered social responsibility as a corporate success factor beyond the boundaries of legal compliance and philanthropy. Pro-active CSR reporting should be awarded by UN rewards that gain public recognition.

In networking events, public and private partners should be brought together to find a consensus on social responsibility. A fruitful dialogue between UNGC partners and stakeholders will guide a successful implementation of CSR partnerships.

International conferences must serve as CSR vision councils in which governmental representatives, business executives, financial professionals, NGO representatives and academics share insights on CSR success factors to advance PPPs. Summits will produce a constant stream of literature on PPP best practices that must be made accessible on the internet to further CSR in PPPs.

Governmental assistance: Apart from the social value created, PPPs engage multiple stakeholders in the policy dialogue and mobilize resources for societal welfare. Governments should create a CSR-fostering environment and assist the coordination of multi-stakeholder CSR partnerships. Based on international regulations, governments should build PPPs frameworks to mitigate social, environmental and political risks in the implementation of CSR. Governmental officials should advocate for the adoption of socially responsible corporate practices and encourage responsible leadership. Thereby governmental initiatives can inform corporate leaders about societal challenges and nurture an understanding of governmental priorities throughout the stakeholder community. Corporate executives' motivation can be enhanced by information on the positive economic, social and environmental advantages of CSR.

Stakeholder management: Partnerships are networking forums in which multiple stakeholders discuss topics of social concern in an atmosphere of trust and confidentiality. Mutual understanding of public and private partners is challenged by differing goals and time perspectives. Frictions may also stem from industry-specific expectations and individual motivations of the partners.

As for these challenges, partners must focus on common goals and determine their roles and responsibilities in their accomplishments. By raising awareness for shared endeavors, the confidence in the UNGC network will be strengthened. Actionable work agendas feature transparent timetables that pinpoint goal accomplishment strategies. Constant communication on the work in progress will allow for monitoring the partners' contributions. Transparency on local goal accomplishment strategies will identify and disseminate best practices for the UNGC implementation. Evaluations must assess the impact of partners and benchmark the partners' CSR practices. As a quality control, external audits will boost the overall efficiency of partnerships.

Local networks: To manage the UNGC's expansion, networks facilitate the local progress. As the impact of partnerships depends on coordinated action, local initiatives foster the implementation of the UNGC principles. Local stakeholder events will bring together CSR administrators for a common solution finding and create multi-stakeholder engagement opportunities. Local ownership of UNGC targets will help in rooting CSR in national and cultural contexts. National campaigns in local languages should also comprise seminars and workshops as for providing local learning possibilities. In addition, local meetings will give grassroot feedback opportunities to the UNGC leadership board and allow reflecting about future strategies and challenges for the development of partnerships.

The UN partnership network on the SDGs is the currently prevailing state-of-the-art international approach to foster social, ecologic and economic development. While the set-up of SDGs features positive results, such as the decentralized approach toward goal accomplishment, there are always areas for improvement identifiable.

The SDGs have been successful in leveraging their position as an UN-driven motivational standard that spans a worldwide network advocating for development on a global basis. The SDGs guide the international dialogue on development. Win–win combinations of the public and private sector expertise have advanced for development. Public and private actors have engaged in advocacy and policy dialogue, corporate social entrepreneurship and philanthropy on SDGs and their concrete targets.

On the partnership level, the UN can support building on existing networks and embrace new stakeholders in the SDGs. New partners may achieve a multitude of results, even though the SDGs are still in the start-up period. As vibrant parts of the UN network, the successful partnering of private and public sector entities can foster development on the regional, national and international levels. Under the UN umbrella, pre-existing partnerships can organize to streamline actions for the advancement of common endeavors.

Future endeavors may target at establishing a network in integrating individual partnerships and facilitating information exchange. Some pre-existing partnerships should be scrutinized for concrete goals attainment in improving sustainable development, stakeholder management, regional goal accomplishment strategies and accountability control.

Sustainable development: The SDG's long-term financial sustainability must be ensured by securing multi-year donations. By outlining the progress that has already been accomplished but also drawing attention to future needs, current donors must be motivated to contribute more extensively. In order to tap into new sources of funding, the UN should continuously build alliances with corporate professionals, trade unions, NGOs and academic communities. These entities must be asked for capital, in-kind contributions and collaborative support to develop the goals. Increasing the visibility of the SDGs will help to reach out for novel donors. Providing access to information on the status and benefits of contributing to the SDGs with capital and in kind by the use of innovative interaction tools – for example, e-newsletters, blogs and Facebook – will engage a broad audience. Internet information portals must position the UN as a network hub for information exchange that attracts funding streams for development, stakeholders' attention and raises the participants' commitment.

Stakeholder management: The UN plays an active role in the coordination of the partners' endeavors in accomplishing the SDGs and fortifying the networks' connectivity by launching stakeholder events. As UN-led networking forums, conferences will bring together executives from international organizations and corporations, government officials and the civil society to discuss funding for development interests. The agreement on common goals and creative financialization strategies will implicitly coordinate the partners' activities and fortify the impact of the entire UN SDG network. Social gatherings will build a mutual understanding about financing for development and promote a trust-based, supportive environment of integrity throughout the network. For the longer-term planning of the network, stakeholder meetings will also help in identifying emerging issues of concern and foster information exchange on future endeavors.

Regional goal accomplishment strategies: The SDG partners should be brought together in standards to agree on implementation strategies and align activities accordingly. By committing themselves to specific goal accomplishment strategies, the partners could specify how their activities will contribute to the overall SDG goals and targets on a constant basis. Transparency on goal accomplishment plans will help in monitoring the partners' contributions and work in progress. The degree to which partners feature standardized or local ownership of goals should be outlined to all stakeholders at the early stages of the partnering process. This will ensure that the SDG constituents work closely on implementing collectively shared endeavors. Corporate partners may incorporate the SDGs into business plans that become the basis for respective training programs. Local meetings may gather participants to coordinate and govern the implementation of developmental goals. Regional campaigns will root the SDGs for development in the cultural context and thereby support the network extension. Regional seminars and workshops can create learning experiences to foster the overall effectiveness of the SDGs in local networks. Regional dialogues will aid knowledge transfer on local success patterns and generate applicable problem-solving capabilities. Information share on SDG best practice standards will lead to contemporary developmental solutions and prepare for future challenges.

Accountability control: Accountability of the partners' commitments could include transparent activities and monitoring. Benchmarking of impact assessments will derive the best practice learning models for future endeavors. Accountability control should feature external goal accomplishment measurement. External audits should become the basis for rewarding positive results and providing assistance in case of defaults. Non-compliance with the goal accomplishment of the partners may include resilient financing options. Communication deficiencies of partners must feature contingency plans to make a reintegration possible to steer partner behavior into a favorable direction.

As for financial social responsibility trends of political divestiture and SRI, recent decades experienced a rise in stakeholder pressure on corporate and financial institutions as a means for spearheading socio-political change. Starting during the 1980s, political divestiture became a way to undermine politically incorrect market systems – such as the South African political regime during the Apartheid era. Since then, political divestiture has impacted economic markets in response to humanitarian crises around the world. After the steady rise of SRI in recent decades, stakeholder concerns for financial social responsibility have reached unprecedented momentum in the wake of the 2008 World Financial Recession, which changed the overall market oversight and responsible investment dynamics. In the course of the 2008 World Financial Recession, stakeholder pressure for financial social responsibility grew. Corporate social misconduct and fiduciary breaches have geared consumers and investors to increasingly pay attention to social responsibility within financial market. Citizens' attention to social responsibility has fostered information disclosure of financial market conduct. As a consequence, legislative reforms and governmental regulations currently promote transparent social responsibility in financial markets. The revitalized demand for transparency and accountability of financial market operations, sophisticated SRI into a mainstream feature of financial decision making (Ahmad, 2008).

In the aftermath of economic downturns of the COVID-19 crisis, SRI is once again a window of opportunity for fostering social progress while re-establishing trust in financial markets given rising inequality and inflationary disparate impact pressures. In the light of these occurrences, SRI appears as a window of opportunity for implementing financial social responsibility while re-establishing trust in financial markets.

Political divestiture appears as a viable means for steering socio-political change. In this light, corporate executives are advised to pay attention to political settings and respond to political infringements with ceasing operations in politically incorrect markets. Institutional investors and mutual funds managers should attribute political divestiture as an efficient market behavior.

Global governance: To leverage SRI from a niche market solution to a state-of-the-art financial practice, global governance on financial social responsibility coupled with governmental assistance in providing access to information on SRI is recommended. The interplay of heightened SRI supply of the financial community and demand for SRI options will innovate the financial social responsibility idea. International organizations can support long-term financial social responsibility. The UN should continue to promote SRI as a means of environmental and social governance. The World Bank Group, the IMF, the United States Green New Deal and the European Green Deal as well as the European Commission Finance Taxonomy and bilateral donors currently launch green bonds as an innovative financial practice to foster sustainable investment (European Commission, 2019). Transnational financial institutions now implement and oversee the implementation of SRI in green bonds in a systemic way.

Access to information: Information on SRI builds a shared understanding of social investment within the financial community. In line with the mere exposure effect, access to information on SRI fosters the integration of environmental and social governance in financial decision making and heightens the consumer confidence in markets (Frey & Irle, 2002). Information disclosure about the stability and effectiveness of SRI will promote financial social responsibility in times of crises. Information on SRI has the potential to concurrently stimulate the demand for SRI and vitalize the financial industry's efforts to further advance SRI innovations. The combined supply and demand increase will result in a quantitative and qualitative extension of SRI and advance the financial market social responsibility idea. In this light, transparency and accountability of financial social market operations will sophisticate SRI into a mainstream feature of financial decision making.

With the rising importance of transparent financial social responsibility and financial institutions integrating social, environmental and governance issues into investment analysis, social investment criteria will become part of the fiduciary duty of trustees, financial advisers, asset managers and intermediary institutions.

International financial institutions and governmental policy makers are major gateways to provide market actors with information on CSR for SRI screenings. International governance and intergovernmental entities, such as the UN, World Bank, IMF and the European Union but also Central Banks regulate financial social responsibility information disclosure to ensure the widespread availability of accurate, timely and comparable information about SRI. Freedom of information acts in the Anglo-Saxon world can set minimum disclosure standards on environmental and social financial practices. Governance entities can subsidize media industries and information service providers.

New media tools and instant online communication can be used to disseminate material on financial social performance in an easily accessible and standardized form. Web portals will help in promoting social responsibility as a state-of-the-art financial practice and provide internet-based SRI best practice standards. To this day, the relationship between cryptocurrencies and sustainability is not fully clear. On one hand, cryptocurrency mining and data storage are energy-intensive endeavors. On the other hand, paperless monetary transfers and the large-scale massive wealth direction cutting red tape appear as an interesting market strategy to imbue sustainability at the core of market activities. Decentralization of information and pegging social media to sustainable causes are other positive externalities of the digital millennium that lead the way to prospective SRI advancements.

Governmental assistance: SRI must also be backed up by governmental support. Governmental policy makers incentivize the integration of social responsibility into the agenda of financial institutions. Governmental control ensures that financial regulations are balanced with current societal needs, governmental obligations and market demands. Governmental regulatory frameworks set SRI standards for governmental agencies, financial institutions, self-regulatory bodies, accounting entities, rating agencies, index providers and NGOs. Governments encourage the integration of social responsibility in financial analyses by regulating fiduciary responsibilities. Concurrently governmental regulations foster accountability of socially responsible financial conduct by transparency guidelines for the retail of SRI funds. Governmental assistance provides information on how to adopt SRI-attentive regulations in order to achieve social responsibility goals. As a basis for improvements, governments reward CSR reporting based on monitoring and benchmarking financial institutions' social performance. In the USA, the Federal Trade Commission and the Securities and Exchange Commission have recently passed a line of regulations that favor the integration of social and environmental causes in relation to market and finance activities. The European Finance Taxonomy and the Next Generation EU are European pendants with similar impetus to steer market demand for sustainable and pro-social choices.

Financial market actors: Financial institutions and experts are encouraged to consider environmental and social responsibility in a variety of ways. Information on CSR and SRI becomes part of financial market operations, when media reports must inform asset managers and financial analysts about the link between CSR and SRI. Supervisory bodies can promote the inclusion of SRI criteria in financial management. Accounting entities, rating agencies and index providers should inform how to adopt environmental and social governance standards as a basis for evaluation criteria that guarantee the concurrent financial and ethical performance. Stock exchange advisors can communicate with listed corporations about the importance of environmental and social responsibility governance. Asset managers can encourage brokers to conduct SRI screenings. Investors are advised to request information on SRI and develop SRI proxy voting strategies. Pension fund trustees should consider environmental and social criteria in the formulation of investment mandates. Consultants and financial advisers are currently incentivized to incorporate environmental and social corporate governance in their portfolio allocation strategies and accept social responsibility as a state-of-the-art of fiduciary obligation. Financial analysts are increasingly under public pressure to assess market opportunities with respect to social contributions and actively participate in ongoing voluntary responsibility initiatives.

Innovations: The SRI community can ensure that financial social responsibility is constantly innovated. Analysts should work closely with policy makers in setting up SRI frameworks that reflect practitioners' needs. Financial experts are key to sophisticate financial social responsibility measurement models and contribute to research on environmental and social investments. Novel SRI options that fulfill unmet responsibility needs will open the market for socially responsible economic growth while bringing societal change. Academic institutions can nurture the financial community's ethical sense. Business schools and think tanks can support SRI research and offer financial ethics education. Financial economists are more and more interested in integrating socio-economic factors into standard economic profit maximization models. Behavioral economics has delved into human decisions-making fallibility in responsibility considerations and ethicality perceptions to now apply their findings in behavioral insights on a global scale. Profound research findings are the basis for stimulating SRI innovations that promise to lead to harmonious economic prosperity in sync with societal advancement and sustainable ecological care.

References

Aaker, D. J. (1996). *Building strong brands.* New York, NY: Free Press.

Aaker, D. J., & Joachimsthaler, E. (2000). The brand relationship spectrum: The key to the brand architecture challenge. *California Management Review, 42,* 8–23.

Aaronson, S. A. (2002). How the Europeans got a head start on policies to promote global corporate responsibility. *Corporate Environmental Strategy, 9*(4), 356–367.

Abe, S. (2020, March 5). Prime Minister of Japan, Statement at Council on Investments for the Future. Retrieved from https://japan.kantei.go.jp/98_abe/actions/202003/_00009.html

Abramson, L., & Chung, D. (2000). Socially responsible investing: Viable for value investors? *Journal of Investing, 9*(3), 73–81.

Aghion, P., & Bolton, P. (1997). A theory of trickle-down growth and development. *Review of Economic Studies, 64*(2), 151–172.

Aghion, P., & Howitt, P. (1992). A model of growth: Through creative destruction. *Econometrica, 60*(2), 323–351.

Aghion, P., & Howitt, P. (1998). *Endogenous growth theory.* Cambridge, MA: Massachusetts Institute of Technology Press.

Aghion, P., Jones, B. F., & Jones, C. I. (2017, October). *Artificial intelligence and economic growth.* Working Paper 23928, National Bureau of Economic Research. Retrieved from https://www.nber.org/chapters/c14015; doi:10.3386/w23928

Agrawal, G., Ahlawat, H., & Dewhurst, M. (2020, April 15). Winning against COVID-19: The implications for biopharma. McKinsey & Co. Retrieved from https://www.mckinsey.com/industries/pharmaceuticals-and-medical-products/our-insights/winning-against-covid-19-the-implications-for-biopharma#the-implications-for-biopharma

Agritecture. (2021, June 17). The Agrihoods are coming. Retrieved from https://www.agritecture.com/blog/2021/6/17/the-agrihoods-are-coming

Ahmad, M. (2008, January 24). *Global CEOs at World Economic Forum cite sovereign wealth funds as the new power broker.* BI-ME.

Aiken, M., & Hage, J. (1971). The organic organization and innovation. *Sociology, 5,* 63–82.

Ait-Sahalia, Y. (2004). Disentangling diffusion from jumps. *Journal of Financial Economics, 74,* 487–528.

Aizenman, N., Carlsen, A., & Talbot, R. (2021, February 6). Coronavirus by the numbers: Why the pandemic is 10 times worse than you think. NPR. Retrieved from https://www.npr.org/sections/health-shots/2021/02/06/964527835/why-the-pandemic-is-10-times-worse-than-you-think

Akerlof, G. A., & Shiller, R. J. (2009). *Animal spirits: How human psychology drives the economy, and why it matters for global capitalism.* Princeton, NJ: Princeton University Press.

Alemi, M., Meghdari, A., & Saffari, E. (2017, November 2017). RoMa: A hi-tech robotic mannequin for the fashion industry. *Lecture Notes in Computer Science (LNCS): Social Robotics, 10652,* 209–219.

Alperson, M., Tepper-Marlin, A. T., Schorsch, J., & Wil, R. (1991). The better world investment guide: One hundred companies whose policies you should know about before you invest your money. *From the Council on Economic Priorities.* New York, NY: Prentice Hall.

Alpert, G. (2021, May 26). International COVID-19 stimulus and relief: International fiscal and monetary stimulus and relief efforts. Investopedia. Retrieved from https://www.investopedia.com/government-stimulus-and-relief-efforts-to-fight-the-covid-19-crisis-5113980

Alvarez, F., Buera, F., & Lucas, R. E. (2007). *Idea flows, economic growth, and trade.* Working Paper No. 19667, National Bureau of Economic Research. Retrieved from https://www.nber.org/papers/w19667

Anderson, J., Bergamini, E., Brekelmans, S., Cameron, A., Darvas, Z., Domínguez Jiménez, M., ... Midões, C. (2020, November 24). The fiscal response to the economic fallout from the coronavirus. Bruegel Datasets. Retrieved from https://www.bruegel.org/publications/datasets/covid-national-dataset/

Andreoni, J. (1989). Giving with impure altruism: Applications to charity and Ricardian equivalence. *Journal of Political Economy, 97,* 1447–1458.

Andreoni, J., & Miller, J. (2002). Giving according to GARP: An experimental test of the consistency of preferences for altruism. *Econometrica, 70,* 737–753.

Appelbaum, B., & Herszenhorn, D. H. (2010, July 15). Financial overhaul signals shift on deregulation. *The New York Times.* Retrieved from https://www.nytimes.com/2010/07/16/business/16regulate.html

Aravanis, J. (2020, April 7). Five industries set to outperform due to COVID-19. IBISWorld. Retrieved from https://www.ibisworld.com/industry-insider/coronavirus-insights/five-industries-set-to-outperform-due-to-covid-19/

Armour, J., Enriques, L., & Wetzer, T. (2021, July 2). Corporate carbon reduction pledges: Beyond greenwashing. Oxford Business Law Blog. Retrieved from https://www.law.ox.ac.uk/business-law-blog/blog/2021/07/corporate-carbon-reduction-pledges-beyond-greenwashing

Armstrong, Ph., Glyn, A., & Harrison, J. (1991). *Capitalism since 1945.* Oxford: Blackwell.

Armstrong, St., & Sotala, K. (2012). How we're predicting AI – Or failing to. In J. Ramportl (Ed.), *Beyond AI: Artificial dreams* (pp. 52–65). Pilsen: University of West Bohemia.

Arora, R. (2020, June 30). Which companies did well during the Coronavirus pandemic? *Forbes.* Retrieved from https://www.forbes.com/sites/rohitarora/2020/06/30/which-companies-did-well-during-the-coronavirus-pandemic/?sh=5036e6a87409

Arrow, K. (1962). The economic implications of learning by doing. *Review of Economic Studies, 29*(3), 155–173.

Asimov, I. (1942). *Runaround.* London: Grafton Books.

Asimov, I. (1950). *I, Robot.* New York, NY: Bantam Dell.

Asimov, I. (1978). My own view. In R. Holdstock (Ed.), *The encyclopedia of science fiction* (pp. 6–7). New York, NY: St. Martin's.

Asimov, I. (1985). *Robots and empire.* New York, NY: Doubleday.

Auhagen, A. E., & Bierhoff, H. W. (2001). *Responsibility: The many faces of a social phenomenon.* London: Routledge.

Ayache, E. (2008, June). I am a creator. *Wilmott Magazine,* pp. 36–46.

Aydalot, Ph., & Keeble, D. (1988). *High technology industry and innovative environments: The European experience.* Routledge: London.

Ayres, I., & Abramowicz, M. (2011). Commitment bonds. *Georgetown Law Journal, 100,* 605–656.

Ayres, M. (2020, March 16). Brazil government to inject $30 billion into economy to combat coronavirus hit. Reuters. Retrieved from https://www.reuters.com/article/us-brazil-economy-budget-idUSKBN213411

Bagnoli, M., & Watts, S. (2003). Selling to socially responsible consumers: Competition and the private provision of public goods. *Journal of Economics and Management Strategy, 12*(3), 419–445.

Baldwin, R. (2017). *The great conversion: Information technology and the new globalization.* Cambridge, MA: Harvard University Press.

Baldwin, R., & Weder di Mauro, B. (2020). Economics in the time of COVID-19. Retrieved from https://cepr.org/sites/default/files/news/COVID-19.pdf

Banerjee, A. (2008). Big answers for big questions: The presumption of growth policy. In Brookings Institute (Ed.), *What works in development? Thinking big and thinking small* (pp. 207–231). Washington, DC: Brookings Institute.

Banerjee, A., & Duflo, E. (2005). Growth theory through the lens of development economics. In P. Aghion & S. Durlauf (Eds.), *Handbook of economic growth* (pp. 473–552). Amsterdam: Elsevier.

Banerjee, A., & Moll, B. (2010). Why does misallocation persist? *American Economic Journal: Macroeconomics, 2*(1), 189–206.

Banerjee, A., & Newman, A. F. (1993). Occupational choice and the process of development. *Journal of Political Economy, 101*(2), 274–298.

Bank of Canada. (2020a, March 4). *Bank of Canada lowers overnight rate target to 1 ¼ percent* [Press release]. Retrieved from https://www.bankofcanada.ca/2020/03/fad-press-release-2020-03-04/

Bank of Canada. (2020b, March 13). *Bank of Canada lowers overnight rate target to ¾ percent* [Press release]. Retrieved from https://www.bankofcanada.ca/2020/03/bank-of-canada-lowers-overnight-rate-target-to-%C2%BE-percent/

Bank of Canada. (2020c, March 27). *Bank of Canada lowers overnight rate target to ¼ percent* [Press release]. Retrieved from https://www.bankofcanada.ca/2020/03/press-release-2020-03-27/

Bank of Canada. (2020d, May 6). *COVID-19: Actions to support the economy and financial system* [Press release]. Retrieved from https://www.bankofcanada.ca/markets/market-operations-liquidity-provision/covid-19-actions-support-economy-financial-system/

Bank of Canada. (2020e, June 3). *Bank of Canada maintains target for the overnight rate, scales back some market operations as financial conditions improve* [Press release]. Retrieved from https://www.bankofcanada.ca/2020/06/fad-press-release-2020-06-03/

Bank of England. (2020a, March 11). Bank of England measures to respond to the economic shock from Covid-19. Retrieved from https://www.bankofengland.co.uk/news/2020/march/boe-measures-to-respond-to-the-economic-shock-from-covid-19

Bank of England. (2020b, March 11). Term funding scheme with additional incentives for SMEs (TFSME): Market Notice. Retrieved from https://www.bankofengland.co.uk/markets/market-notices/2020/term-funding-scheme-market-notice-mar-2020

Bank of England. (2020c, March 17). HM Treasury and the Bank of England launch a Covid Corporate Financing Facility (CCFF). Retrieved from https://www.bankofengland.co.uk/news/2020/march/hmt-and-boe-launch-a-covid-corporate-financing-facility

Bank of England. (2020d, March 19). Monetary policy summary for the special Monetary Policy Committee meeting on 19 March 2020. Retrieved from https://www.bankofengland.co.uk/monetary-policy-summary-and-minutes/2020/monetary-policy-summary-for-the-special-monetary-policy-committee-meeting-on-19-march-2020

Bank of England. (2020e, April 9). HM Treasury and Bank of England announce temporary extension to ways and means facility. Retrieved from https://www.bankofengland.co.uk/news/2020/april/hmt-and-boe-announce-temporary-extension-to-ways-and-means-facility

Bank of England. (2020f, June 5). Asset purchase facility (APF): Pricing of CBPS eligible securities: Market Notice. Retrieved from https://www.bankofengland.co.uk/markets/market-notices/2020/apf-pricing-of-cbps-eligible-securities-june-2020

Bank of England. (2020g, June 18). Bank rate maintained at 0.1%. Retrieved from https://www.bankofengland.co.uk/monetary-policy-summary-and-minutes/2020/june-2020

Bank of England. (2020h, June 19). Update on the contingent term repo facility (CTRF): Market Notice. Retrieved from https://www.bankofengland.co.uk/markets/market-notices/2020/update-on-the-contingent-term-repo-facility

Bank of England. (2020i, November 5). Bank rate held at 0.1% and asset purchases increased by £150bn. Retrieved from https://www.bankofengland.co.uk/monetary-policy-summary-and-minutes/2020/november-2020

Bank of Japan. (2020, June 16). BOJ's measures in response to COVID-19. Retrieved from https://www.boj.or.jp/en/announcements/release_2020/k200616b.pdf

Bank of Korea. (2020a, February 7). *Ceiling on the bank intermediated lending support facility raised by 5 trillion won to provide financial support to SMEs affected by COVID-19* [Press release]. Retrieved from https://www.bok.or.kr/eng/bbs/B0000308/view.do?nttId=10057411&menuNo=400380&pageIndex=2

Bank of Korea. (2020b, March 16). *Bank of Korea announces 50bp base rate cut and measures to stabilize economic and financial conditions* [Press release]. Retrieved from https://www.bok.or.kr/eng/bbs/E0000627/view.do?nttId=10057024&menuNo=400022&pageIndex=1

Bank of Korea. (2020c, March 26). *Bank of Korea implements financial stability measures including adoption of unlimited liquidity support facility* [Press release]. Retrieved from http://www.bok.or.kr/eng/bbs/B0000308/view.do?nttId=10057418&menuNo=400380&pageIndex=1

Bank of Korea. (2020d, April 9). *Bank of Korea broadens securities eligible for open market operations* [Press release]. Retrieved from http://www.bok.or.kr/eng/bbs/B0000308/view.do?nttId=10057612&menuNo=400380&pageIndex=1

Bank of Korea. (2020e, April 16). *BOK to launch corporate bond-backed lending facility* [Press release]. Retrieved from https://www.bok.or.kr/eng/bbs/E0000634/view.do?nttId=10057756&menuNo=400069

Bank of Korea. (2020f, May 28). *Monetary policy decision* [Press release]. Retrieved from http://www.bok.or.kr/eng/bbs/E0000634/view.do?nttId=10058434&menuNo=400069

Bank of Russia. (2020a, March 27). *Additional measures to support lending to small and medium-sized enterprises* [Press release]. Retrieved from http://www.cbr.ru/eng/press/PR/?file=27032020_204520eng2020-03-27T20_45_02.htm

Bank of Russia. (2020b, April 3). *Bank of Russia approves additional measures to support lending and protect people's interests* [Press release]. Retrieved from https://www.cbr.ru/eng/press/pr/?file=06042020_193737eng2020-04-06T19_37_06.htm

Bank of Russia. (2020c, April 24). *Bank of Russia reduces key rate within SME lending support programme* [Press release]. Retrieved from https://www.cbr.ru/eng/press/pr/?file=24042020_174619eng_dkp2020-04-24T17_45_47.htm

Bank of Russia. (2020d, April 24). *The Bank of Russia cuts the key rate by 50 bp to 5.50% p.a.* [Press release]. Retrieved from http://www.cbr.ru/eng/press/pr/?file=24042020_133000Key-eng.htm

Bank of Russia. (2020e, June 19). *Bank of Russia reduces interest rate within programmes to support lending to SMEs and for urgent needs* [Press release]. Retrieved from https://www.cbr.ru/eng/press/pr/?file=22062020_185309pr_eng_20200619_03.htm

Bank of Russia. (2020f, June 19). *The Bank of Russia cuts the key rate by 100 bp to 4.50% p.a.* [Press release]. Retrieved from https://www.cbr.ru/eng/press/pr/?file=19062020_133000Key_eng.htm

Bank of Russia. (2020g, July 24). *The Bank of Russia cuts the key rate by 25 bp to 4.25% p.a.* [Press release]. Retrieved from http://www.cbr.ru/eng/press/PR/?file=24072020_133000Key_eng.htm

Barbier, E. (2009). *A global Green New Deal*. Report prepared for the Green Economy Initiative of UNEP. United Nations Environmental Programme. Retrieved from https://sustainabledevelopment.un.org/index.php?page=view&type=400&nr=670&menu=1515

Barkemeyer, R. (2007). Beyond compliance – Below expectations? Cross-border CSR, development and the UN Global Compact. In *Corporate responsibility research conference*, University of Leeds, July 15–17.

Barnett, M. L. (2005). Stakeholder influence capacity and the variability of financial returns to corporate social responsibility. In L. Ryan & J. Logsdon (Eds.), *Proceedings of the sixteenth annual meeting of the International Association for Business and Society* (pp. 16:287–16:292).

Barnett, M. N., & Sikkink, K. (2011). From international relations to global society. In R. Goodin (Ed.), *The Oxford handbook of political science* (pp. 748–765). Oxford: Oxford University Press.

Barney, J. (1991). Firm resources and sustained competitive advantage. *Journal of Management, 17*, 771–792.

Baron, J. (2000). *Thinking and deciding*. Cambridge: Cambridge University Press.

Baron, J., & Spranca, M. (1997). Protected values. *Organizational Behavior and Human Decision Processes, 70*(1), 1–16.

Barro, R. J. (1991). Economic growth in a cross section of countries. *The Quarterly Journal of Economics, 106*(2), 1, 407–444.

Barseghyan, L., & DiCecio, R. (2011). Entry costs, industry structure, and cross-country income and TFP differences. *Journal of Economic Theory, 146*(5), 1828–1851.

Bartik, A. W., Bertrand, M., Cullen, Z., Glaeser, E. L., Luca, M., & Stanton, Ch. (2020). How are small businesses adjusting to COVID-19? Early evidence from a survey. Working Paper No. 26989, National Bureau of Economic Research, Cambridge, MA.

Batson, C. D. (1991). *The altruism question: Toward a social psychological answer*. Hillsdale, NJ: Erlbaum.

Bauer, R., Koedijk, K., & Otten, R. (2005). International evidence on ethical mutual fund performance and investment style. *Journal of Banking and Finance, 29*, 1751–1767.

BBC News Scotland. (2020, March 2). '50–80% of population' could be affected by coronavirus. Retrieved from https://www.bbc.com/news/av/uk-scotland-51711747

Beck, U. (1998). *Politik der Globalisierung*. Frankfurt am Main: Suhrkamp.

Becker, G. S. (1976). *The economic approach to human behavior*. Chicago, IL: The University of Chicago Press.

Becker, G. S. (2008). Is corporate altruism viable in a competitive environment? Retrieved from http://www.huffingtonpost.com/gary-becker/is-corporate-altruismvia_b_110726.html

Becker, G. S., & Murphy, K. M. (2000). *Social economics: Market behavior in a social environment*. Cambridge, MA: Harvard University Press.

Beerbaum, D., & Puaschunder, J. M. (2018). A behavioral economics approach to digitalisation: The case of a principles-based taxonomy. In *Proceedings of the 10th international RAIS conference on social sciences and humanities* (Vol. 211). ASSEHR Series. Amsterdam: Atlantis Press. ISSN: 2352–5398.

Beinhocker, E. D. (2007). *The origin of wealth: The radical remaking of economics and what it means for business and society*. Cambridge, MA: Harvard Business School.

Bekefi, T. (2006). *Business as a partner in tackling micronutrient deficiency: Lessons in multisector partnership*. Report of the Corporate Responsibility Initiative. Cambridge, MA: Harvard University Press.

Benoit, B., & Fairless, T. (2020, August 26). Germany boosts already hefty Coronavirus stimulus. *The Wall Street Journal*. Retrieved from https://www.wsj.com/articles/germany-boosts-already-hefty-coronavirus-stimulus-11598440184

Bergson, H. (1911). *Matter and memory*. London: Allen and Unwin.

Bergson, H. (1913). *Time and free will: An essay on the immediate data of consciousness*. New York, NY: Dover.

Berlant, L. G. (2011). *Cruel optimism*. Durham, NC: Duke University Press.

Berman, S. L., Wicks, A. C., Kotha, S., & Jones, T. M. (1999). Does stakeholder orientation matter? The relationship between stakeholder management models and firm financial performance. *Academy of Management Journal, 42*(5), 488–506.

Bernstein, P. W., & Swan, A. (2007). *All the money in the world: How the Forbes 400 make – and spend – their fortunes*. New York, NY: Knopf.

Bhattacharya, C. B., & Sen, S. (2003). Consumer-company identification: A framework for understanding consumers' relationships with companies. *Journal of Marketing, 67*, 7688.

Biermann, F., & Siebenhüner, B. (2009). *Managers of global change: The influence of international environmental bureaucracies.* Cambridge, MA: MIT Press.

Biller, A. (2007). Socially responsible investing now part of the landscape. *Benefits & Compensation Digest, 44,* 12.

Birdsall, N. (2017). *Middle class: Winners or losers in a globalized world?* Center for Global Development. Retrieved from https://www.cgdev.org/publication/middle-class-winners-or-losers-globalized-world

Bishop, N. (2019). Green bond governance and the Paris Agreement. *New York University Environmental Law Journal,* 377–411. Retrieved from https://www.nyuelj.org/wp-content/uploads/2019/10/Bishop_Green-Bond-Governance-and-the-Paris-Agreement.pdf

Blanchard, O. (2017). Public debt and low interest rates. *American Economic Review, 109*(4), 1197–1229.

Blanchard, O. (2021, February 18). *In defense of concerns over the $1.9 trillion relief plan.* Peterson Institute for International Economics. Retrieved from https://www.piie.com/blogs/realtime-economic-issues-watch/defense-concerns-over-19-trillion-relief-plan

Blank, H. D., & Carty, C. M. (2002). The eco-efficiency anomaly. Working Paper, Innovest. Retrieved from http://www.sristudies.org/Blank+and+Carty+(2002)?

Bollen, N. P. B., & Cohen, M. A. (2004). Mutual fund attributes and investor behavior. Unpublished Working Paper, Vanderbilt University.

Boltanski, L. (1987). *The making of a class: Cadres in French society.* Cambridge: Cambridge University Press.

Bolton, P., Despres-Luiz, M., Pereira, A., Silva, D. A., Samama, F., & Svartzman, R. (2020). *The green swan central banking and financial stability in the age of climate change.* Bank for International Settlements Climate Change International Central Banks Sustainability Project. Retrieved from https://www.bis.org/publ/othp31.pdf

Boutin-Dufresne, F., & Savaria, P. (2004). Corporate social responsibility and financial risk. *Journal of Investing, 13*(1), 57–66.

Boyle, A. D., Leggat, G., Morikawa, L., Pappas, Y., & Stephens, J. (2021). Green New Deal proposals: Comparing emerging transformational climate policies at multiple scales. *Energy Research & Social Science, 81,* 1–8.

Braga, J. A., Fischermann, T., & Semmler, W. (2020, March 5). Ökonomie und Klimapolitik: So könnte es gehen. *Die Zeit.* Retrieved from https://www.zeit.de/zustimmung?url=https%3A%2F%2Fwww.zeit.de%2F2020%2F11%2Feuropaeischer-green-deal-emissionshandel-wirtschaft-klimaschutz

Braga, J. A., Semmler, W., & Grass, D. (2020). De-risking of green investment through a green bond market: Empirics and a dynamic model. Working Paper WP-20-014, International Institute of Applied Systems Analysis, Laxenburg, Austria. Retrieved from http://pure.iiasa.ac.at/id/eprint/16666/

Bragdon, J. H., & Marlin, J. A. T. (1972). Is pollution profitable? *Risk Management, 19*(4), 918.

Brammer, S., Brooks, C., & Pavelin, S. (2006). Good reputations can be bad investments: Corporate reputation and stock returns: Are good firms good for investors? *Professional Investor, 10,* 21–25.

Brammer, S., Williams, G. A., & Zinkin, J. (2005). *Religion and attitudes to corporate social responsibility in a large cross-country sample.* Nottingham: Nottingham University Business School.

Brenner, R. (2003). *The boom and the bubble: The US in the world economy.* New York, NY: Verso.

Britt, R. R. (2020, August 14). Long-lasting COVID symptoms: Early research helps quantify coronavirus long-hauler' experiences. *Elemental.* Retrieved from https://elemental.medium.com/new-survey-identifies-98-long-lasting-covid-symptoms-87935b258a3e

Broadhurst, D., Watson, J., & Marshall, J. (2003). *Ethical and socially responsible investment. A reference guide for researchers.* München: Saur.

Broccardo, E., Hart, O., & Zingales, L. (2020). *Exit. v. voice.* Finance Working Paper No. 694/2020, European Corporate Governance Institute. Retrieved from https://ssrn.com/abstract=3671918

Brock, W. A., & Durlauf, St. N. (2001). Discrete choice with social interactions. *Review of Economic Studies, 68*, 235–260.

Brooks, A. (2008, Spring). *Social entrepreneurship* (Course reader). Syracuse, NY: Maxwell School of Citizenship and Public Affairs, Syracuse University.

Brown, T. L., Potoski, M., & Van Slyke, D. M. (2006). Managing public service contracts: Aligning values, institutions, and markets. *Public Administration Review, 66*(3), 323331.

Brunnermeier Academy at the Princeton Bendheim Center for Finance. (2021). Retrieved from https://bcf.princeton.edu/markus-academy/

Bruyn, S. T. (1987). *The field of social investment.* Cambridge: Cambridge University Press.

Buera, F. J., & Kaboski, J. P. (2012). The rise of the service economy. *American Economic Review, 102*(6), 2540–2569.

Burke, M., Hsiang, S. H., & Miguel, E. (2015). Global non-linear effect of temperature on economic production. *Nature, 527*, 235–239.

Butz, Ch. (2003, September). *Decomposing SRI performance: Extracting value through factor analysis.* Pictet Quants.

Camagni, R. (1991). *Innovation networks.* Routledge: London.

Canada Mortgage and Housing Corporation. (2020, March 26). CMHC expands insured mortgage purchase program. Ottawa: Canada Mortgage and Housing Corporation. Retrieved from https://www.cmhc-schl.gc.ca/en/media-newsroom/news-releases/2020/cmhc-expands-insured-mortgage-purchase-program

Čapek, K. (1921/2004). *Rossum's universal robots.* New York, NY: Penguin.

Carroll, A. B. (1979). A three-dimensional model of corporate social performance. *Academy of Management Review, 4*, 497–505.

Carroll, A. B. (1991). The pyramid of corporate social responsibility: Toward the moral management of organizational stakeholders. *Business Horizon, 34*, 39–48.

Carroll, A. B. (1999). Corporate social responsibility: Evolution of a definitional construct. *Business & Society, 38*(3), 268–295.

Carswell, A. (2002). Crisis of conscience. *Australian CPA, 72*, 26–27.

Case, A., & Deaton, A. (2020). *Death of despair and the future of capitalism.* Princeton, NJ: Princeton University Press.

Caselli, F., & Feyrer, J. (2007). The marginal product of capital. *The Quarterly Journal of Economics, 122*(2), 535–568.

Cassim, Z., Handjiski, B., Schubert, J., & Zouaoui, Y. (2020, June). *The $10 trillion rescue: How governments can deliver impact governments have announced the provision of trillions of dollars in crisis relief, but translating that into sustained recovery will not be easy.* McKinsey Public Sector Practice Report. Retrieved from https://www.mckinsey.com/~/media/McKinsey/Industries/Public%20Sector/Our%20Insights/The%2010%20trillion%20dollar%20rescue%20How%20governments%20can%20deliver%20impact/The-10-trillion-dollar-rescue-How-governments-can-deliver-impact-vF.pdf

Cellan-Jones, R. (2014, December 2). Stephen Hawking warns artificial intelligence could end mankind. BBC News. Retrieved from www.bbc.com/news/technology-30290540

Centeno, M. A., Cinlar, E., Cloud, D., Creager, A. N., DiMaggio, P. J., Dixit, A. K., ... Shapiro, J. N. (2013, April). *Global systemic risk.* Unpublished manuscript for research community. Princeton Institute for International and Regional Studies, Princeton University, Princeton, NJ.

Centeno, M. A., & Cohen, J. N. (2010). *Global capitalism*. Hoboken, NJ: Wiley

Centeno, M. A., Creager, A. N., Elga, A., Felton, E., Katz, St. N., Massey, W. A., & Shapiro, J. N. (2013). *Global systemic risk: Proposal for a research community*. Working Paper, Princeton University, Princeton Institute for International and Regional Studies, Princeton, NJ.

Centeno, M. A., & Tham, A. (2012). *The emergence of risk in the global system*. Working Paper, Princeton University, Princeton, NJ.

Central Bank of Brazil. (2020, March 26). Central Bank of Brazil announces BRL 1.2 trillion in liquidity to support the economy. Retrieved from https://www.bcb.gov.br/en/pressdetail/2321/nota

Chang, H.-J. (2002). *Kicking away the ladder: Development strategy in historical perspective*. London: Anthem.

Chetty, R., & Brunnermeier, M. (2020, June 17). Raj Chetty on the economic impacts of COVID-19: Real-time evidence from private sector data. Princeton University Bendheim Center for Finance. Retrieved from https://bcf.princeton.edu/events/raj-chetty-on-the-economic-impacts-of-covid-19-real-time-evidence-from-private-sector-data/

Chichilnisky, G. (1996). Development and global finance: The case for an international bank for environmental settlements. New York, NY: United Nations Development Programme, Office of Development Studies.

Chichilnisky, G., Heal, G., & Vercelli, A. (1998). *Sustainability: Dynamics and uncertainty*. Dordrecht: Kluwer.

Chua, A. (2003). *World on fire: How exporting free market democracy breeds ethnic hatred and global instability*. New York, NY: Anchor.

Clancy, E. (1998). The tragedy of the global commons. *Indiana Journal of Global Legal Studies, 5*(2), 601–619.

Clark, R. (1986). *Corporate law*. Boston: Little, Brown & Company.

Clarkson, M. B. E. (1995). A stakeholder framework for analyzing and evaluating corporate social performance. *Academy of Management Review, 20*, 92–117.

Cohen, M., Fenn, S. A., & Konar, S. (1997). Environmental and financial performance: Are they related? Unpublished Working Paper, Vanderbilt University.

Colby, A., & Damon, W. (1992). *Some do care: Contemporary lives of moral commitment*. New York, NY: Free Press.

Coleman, J. (1990). *Foundations of social theory*. Cambridge, MA: Harvard University Press.

Coleman, J. (2021, April 23). CDC study on COVID-19 long-haulers: Two-thirds of non-hospitalized patients receive new diagnoses. *The Hill*. Retrieved from https://thehill.com/policy/healthcare/549950-cdc-study-on-covid-19-long-haulers-two-thirds-of-non-hospitalized-patients

Comin, D., & Hobijn, B. (2004). Cross-country technology adoption: Making the theories face the facts. *Journal of Monetary Economics, 51*(1), 39–83.

Commission of the European Communities Report. (2001). *Green paper: Promoting a European framework for corporate social responsibility*. Brussels: European Union Commission.

Congressional Research Service. (2020, July 13). Unemployment rates during the COVID-19 pandemic. Retrieved from https://crsreports.congress.gov/product/pdf/R/R46554

Congressional Research Service. (2021, July 9). Global economic effects of COVID-19. Retrieved from https://fas.org/sgp/crs/row/R46270.pdf

Connaker, A., & Madsbjerg, S. (2019, January 17). The state of socially responsible investing. *Harvard Business Review*. Retrieved from https://hbr.org/2019/01/the-state-of-socially-responsible-investing

Cooper, C., & Schlegelmilch, B. (1993). Key issues in ethical investment: *Business ethics: A European approach*. Hemel Hempstead: Prentice Hall.

Copeland, J. (2000, May). What is artificial intelligence? Retrieved from www.alan-turing.net/turing_archive/pages/Reference%20Articles/what_is_AI/What%20is%20AI02.html

Corfield, A. (1998). The stakeholder theory and its future in Australian corporate governance: A preliminary analysis. *Bond Law Review, 10*(2), 213–232.

Corlatean, T. (2020). Risk, discrimination and opportunities for education during the times of COVID-19 pandemic. In *Proceedings of the 17th Research Association for Interdisciplinary Sciences (RAIS) conference on social sciences and humanities*, June 1–2, pp. 37–46. Retrieved from http://rais.education/wp-content/uploads/2020/06/004TC.pdf

Cornell, B., & Shapiro, A. (1987). Corporate stakeholders and corporate finance. *Financial Management, 16*, 5–14.

Coulson, A. (2002). *A benchmarking study: Environmental credit risk factor in the panEuropean banking sector.* London: ISIS Asset Management.

Cox, J. (2021, June 10). Consumer prices jump 5% in May, fastest pace since the summer of 2008. *CNBC News*. Retrieved from https://www.cnbc.com/2021/06/10/cpi-may-2021.html

Cox, J., & Haven, T. (2003). *Corporations.* New York, NY: Aspen.

Coy, P. (2021, February 12). Summers and Krugman debate stimulus: Here's a blow-by-blow account. *Bloomberg Businessweek*. Retrieved from https://www.bloomberg.com/news/articles/2021-02-12/summers-and-krugman-debate-stimulus-here-s-a-blow-by-blow-account

Crane, A., & Livesey, S. (2002). Are you talking to me? Stakeholder communication and the risks and rewards of dialogue. In J. Andriof, S. Waddock, S. Rahman, & B. Husted (Eds.), *Unfolding stakeholder thinking*. Sheffield: Greenleaf.

Crane, A., & Livesey, S. (2003). Are you talking to me? Stakeholder communication and the risks and rewards of dialogue. In J. Andriof, S. Waddock, B. Husted, & S. Sutherland Rahman (Eds.), *Unfolding stakeholder thinking 2: Relationships, communication, reporting and performance* (pp. 39–52). London: Routledge.

Crane, A., Matten, D., & Moon, J., McWilliams, A., & Siegel, D. S. (2007), The Oxford handbook of corporate socially responsible stocks. *Business and Society, 1*, 71–75.

Crane, A., Matten, D., & Moon, D. (2004). Stakeholder as citizens? Rethinking rights, participation and democracy. *Journal of Business Ethics, 53*, 107–122.

Crawford, N., & Klotz, A. (1999). *How sanctions work: A framework for analysis: Lessons from South Africa.* New York, NY: St. Martin's.

Crescat Capital. (2021, May 19). May research letter: The 3 pillars of inflation. Retrieved from https://www.crescat.net/may-research-letter/

Crowther, D., & Rayman-Bacchus, L. (2004). *Perspectives on corporate social responsibility.* Burlington, VT: Ashgate.

Csikszentmihalyi, M. (1990). *Flow: A psychology of optimal experience.* New York, NY: Harper.

Csikszentmihalyi, M. (2003). *Good business: Leadership, flow, and the making of meaning.* New York, NY: Viking.

Cuesta González de la, M., & Martinez, C.V. (2004). Fostering corporate social responsibility through public initiative: From the EU to the Spanish case. *Journal of Business Ethics, 55*, 275–293.

Cui, C. (2008, March 6). Social investing soars amid more options. *The Wall Street Journal*. Eastern Edition.

Cummings, L. A. (2000). The financial performance of ethical investment trusts: An Australian perspective. *Journal of Business Ethics, 25*(3), 167–177.

Cushman, F. (2008). Crime and punishment: Distinguishing the roles of causal and intentional analyses in moral judgment. *Cognition, 108*(2), 353–380.

D'Urbino, L. (2019, January 24). The steam has gone out of globalisation. *The Economist.* Retrieved from https://www.economist.com/leaders/2019/01/24/the-steam-has-gone-out-of-globalisation

Damon, W., Menon, J., & Bronk, K. C. (2003). The development of purpose during adolescence. *Applied Developmental Science, 7*(3), 119–128.

Darley, J. M., & Latane, B. (1968). Bystander intervention in emergencies: Diffusion of responsibility. *Journal of Personality and Social Psychology, 8*, 377–383.

Dasgupta, S., Laplante, B., & Mamingi, N. (1998). Capital markets responses to environmental performance in developing countries. Policy Research Working Paper 1909, The World Bank, Washington, DC.

Davis, K. (1973). The case for and against business assumptions of social responsibilities. *Academy of Management Journal, 16*, 312–317.

De Sam, M., Dougan, B., Gordon, J., Puaschunder, J., & St. Clair, C. (2008). *Building a globally competent citizenry in the United States.* Washington, DC: United States Department of Education.

De Silva, S., & Amerasinghe, F. (2004). *Corporate social responsibility: Issues, problems and challenges.* Colombo: Lake House.

De Soto, H. (2000). *The mystery of capital: Why capitalism triumphs in the west and fails everywhere else.* New York, NY: Perseus Books.

De Woot, A. (2005). *Should Prometheus be bound? Corporate social responsibility.* London: Palgrave Macmillan.

Deegan, C., & Blomquist, C. (2006). Stakeholder influence on corporate reporting: An exploration of the interaction between WWF-Australia and the Australian minerals industry. *Accounting, Organizations and Society, 31*, 343–372.

Deleuze, G., & Guattari, F. (1987). *A thousand plateaus: Capitalism and schizophrenia.* Minneapolis, MN: University of Minnesota Press.

Derwall, J., & Koedijk, K. (2006). *Socially responsible fixed-income funds.* Unpublished Working Paper, Erasmus University.

DeThomasis, L., & St. Anthony, N. (2006). *Doing right in a shrinking world: How corporate America can balance ethics and profit in a changing economy.* Austin, TX: Greenleaf.

Dhrymes, P. J. (1998). Socially responsible investment: Is it profitable? The investment research guide to socially responsible investing. In *The colloquium on socially responsible investing.* Retrieved from http://www.columbia.edu/~pjd1/

Dietz, S., Rising, J., Stoerk, Th., & Wagner, G. (2021). Economic impacts of tipping points in the climate system. *Proceedings of the National Academy of Sciences, 118, 34*, 1–9.

Dixon, F. (2002). *Financial markets and corporate environmental results.* Working Paper, Innovest.

Dockser Marcus, A. (2021, January 30). Covid-19 patients are doing their own research: To advance scientific knowledge of the disease, lay people are organizing to generate data about their experiences. *The Wall Street Journal.* Retrieved from https://www.wsj.com/articles/covid-19-patients-are-doing-their-own-research-11611982860

Dodd, D. (2020, June 22). COVID 19's corporate casualties. *Financial Times.* Retrieved from https://www.ft.com/content/eb6efc36-bf99-4086-a98a-7d121738b4b4

Dodd, E. M. (1932). From whom are corporate managers trustees? *Harvard Law Review, 45*(7), 1145–1163.

Donaldson, T., & Preston, L. E. (1995). The stakeholder theory of the corporation: Concepts, evidence and implications. *Academy of Management Review, 20*, 65–91.

Dowell, R. (2018). Fundamental protections for non-biological intelligences or: How we learn to stop worrying and love our robot Brethren. *Minnesota Journal of Law, Science & Technology, 19*(1), 305–336.

Dray, M., & Thirlwall, A. P. (2011). The endogeneity of the natural rate of growth for a selection of Asian countries. *Journal of Post Keynesian Economics, 33*(3), 451–468.

Drbeen Medical Lectures. (2021, June 24). Spike proteins in immune cells: Dr. Bruce Patterson discusses COVID Long Haul. Retrieved from https://www.youtube.com/watch?v=JwjJs5ZHKJI

Drucker, P. F. (1985). *Innovation and entrepreneurship: Practice and principles.* New York, NY: Harper Business.

Dua, A., Ellingrud, K., Mahajan, D., & Silberg, J. (2020, June 18). Which small businesses are most vulnerable to COVID-19: And when. McKinsey & Co., 2020. Retrieved from https://www.mckinsey.com/featured-insights/americas/which-small-businesses-are-most-vulnerable-to-covid-19-and-when

Duarte, M., & Restuccia, D. (2006). The productivity of nations. *Federal Reserve Bank Richmond Economic Quarterly, 92*(3), 195–223.

Duchac, J. (2008, December 15). The perfect storm: A look inside the 2008 financial crisis. WU talks special notes, Vienna University of Economics and Business, Vienna, Austria, European Union.

Dupré, D., Girerd-Potin, I., & Kassoua, R. (2004). Adding an ethical dimension to portfolio management. *Finance, 18*, 625–641.

DW. (2020, October 28). Deutsche Bank überrascht mit hohem Gewinn. Retrieved from https://www.dw.com/de/deutsche-bank-%C3%BCberrascht-mit-hohem-gewinn/a-55417971

Earthworks. (2019, January 10). Group letter to Congress urging Green New Deal passage. Retrieved from https://www.earthworks.org/publications/group-letter-to-congress-urging-green-new-deal-passage/

Echevarria, C. (1997). Changes in sectoral composition associated with economic growth. *International Economic Review, 38*(2), 431–452.

Economy, Eurostat. (2020). Economy: COVID-19, Eurostat. Retrieved from https://ec.europa.eu/eurostat/web/covid-19/economy

EcoWellness Group. (2020, July 14–15). Salzburg declaration: Interdisciplinary conference on 'system change?! The chance of transformation of the healthcare system: Analysis and chances of the coronavirus crisis. Retrieved from https://www.oekowellness.de/laenderuebergreifende-konzerenz-zum-thema-system-change-die-chance-der-transformation-des-gesundheitswesens-14-07-2020/

EcoWellness Group. (2021, July 14–15). Salzburg European declaration from the Gasteinertal: Interdisciplinary conference on 'system change?! The chance of transformation of the healthcare system. Retrieved from https://www.oekowellness.de/wp-content/uploads/2021/07/Final-Stand-5.7.-2021.07.04_Programm-14.7.-und-15.07.2021-2.pdf

Ehrlich, C. (2005). Is business ethics necessary? *DePaul Business & Commercial Law Journal, 4*(3), 55–67.

Elkington, J. (1998). *Cannibals with forks: The triple bottom line of 21st century business.* Gabriola Island: New Society.

Elliott, Ch. (2021, February 5). When will it be safe to cruise again? These signs that will help you decide when to sail. *USA Today.* Retrieved from https://www.usatoday.com/story/travel/advice/2021/02/05/covid-when-will-it-be-safe-to-cruise/4386762001

Epstein, G. (2020, March 2020). The coronavirus consensus: "Spend, spend, spend." *Dollar & Sense: Real World Economics.* Retrieved from http://dollarsandsense.org/archives/2020/0320epstein–spend.html

Erosa, A., Koreshkova, T., & Restuccia, D. (2010). How important is human capital? A quantitative theory assessment of world income inequality. *The Review of Economic Studies, 77*(4), 1421–1449.

Espitia, A., Rocha, N., & Ruta, M. (2020, April 2). Database on COVID-19 trade flows and policies, Washington, DC: World Bank. Retrieved from https://www.worldbank.org/en/data/interactive/2020/04/02/database-on-coronavirus-covid-19-trade-flows-and-policies

EU Committee on Legal Affairs. (2016, May 31). Draft report with recommendations to the Commission on Civil Law Rules on Robotics.

European Central Bank. (2020a, March 15). *Coordinated central bank action to enhance the provision of global US dollar liquidity* [Press release]. Retrieved from https://www.ecb.europa.eu/press/pr/date/2020/html/ecb.pr200315˜1fab6a9f1f.sv.html

European Central Bank. (2020b, April 30). *ECB announces new pandemic emergency longer-term refinancing operations* [Press release]. Retrieved from https://www.ecb.europa.eu/press/pr/date/2020/html/ecb.pr200430_1˜477f400e39.en.html

European Central Bank. (2020c). Monetary policy decisions. Retrieved from https://www.ecb.europa.eu/press/govcdec/mopo/html/index.en.html

European Central Bank. (2020d, June 25). *New Eurosystem repo facility to provide euro liquidity to non-euro area central banks* [Press release]. Retrieved from https://www.ecb.europa.eu/press/pr/date/2020/html/ecb.pr200625˜60373986e5.en.html

European Commission. (2002). Communication from the commission concerning corporate social responsibility: A business contribution to sustainable development. COM. Retrieved from https://op.europa.eu/en/publication-detail/-/publication/6e2c6d26-d1f6-48a3-9a78-f0ff2dc21aad/language-en

European Commission. (2006). Implementing the partnership for growth and jobs: Making Europe a pole of excellence on corporate social responsibility: Communication from the Commission. COM. Retrieved from https://eur-lex.europa.eu/legal-content/EN/TXT/?uri=celex%3A52006DC0136

European Commission. (2019). A European Green Deal. Retrieved from https://ec.europa.eu/info/strategy/priorities-2019-2024/european-green-deal_en

European Investment Fund. (2022, January 21). *State Investment Management Agency and European Investment Bank launch first support for Lithuanian mid-caps under European Guarantee Fund* [Press release]. Retrieved from https://www.eib.org/en/press/all/2022-016-state-investment-management-agency-and-european-investment-bank-launch-first-support-for-lithuanian-mid-caps-under-european-guarantee-fund

European Union Technical Expert Group on Sustainable Finance. (2020, March). *Financing a sustainable European economy: Technical report.* Taxonomy: Final report of the Technical Expert Group on Sustainable Finance. Retrieved from https://ec.europa.eu/info/sites/default/files/business_economy_euro/banking_and_finance/documents/200309-sustainable-finance-teg-final-report-taxonomy_en.pdf

Fanto, J. A. (1998). The role of corporate law in French corporate governance. *Cornell International Law Journal, 31,* 31–45.

Farzad, R. (2007, January 22). A bigger voice for small investors. *Business Week.*

Federal Reserve Bank of St. Louis. (2015). The origins of unconventional monetary policy in the U.S. Retrieved from https://www.stlouisfed.org/annual-report/2015/the-origins-of-unconventional-monetary-policy-in-the-us

Federal Reserve Bank of St. Louis. (2021, April 10). Real gross domestic product. Retrieved from https://fred.stlouisfed.org/series/GDPC1#0

Federal Reserve of the United States. (2020a, March 15). Federal Reserve actions to support the flow of credit to households and businesses. Retrieved from https://www.federalreserve.gov/newsevents/pressreleases/monetary20200315b.htm

Federal Reserve of the United States. (2020b, March 19). Federal Reserve announces the establishment of temporary U.S. dollar liquidity arrangements with other central banks. Retrieved from https://www.federalreserve.gov/newsevents/pressreleases/monetary20200319b.htm

Fernandes Maia, C. M., Pereira Marques, N., Gomes de Lucena, E. H., Fernandode Rezende, L., Barbosa Martelli, D. R., & Martelli-Júnior, H. (2021). Increased number of Herpes Zoster cases in Brazil related to the COVID-19 pandemic. *International Journal of Infectious Diseases, 104,* 732–733.

Fernando, F. (2021, June 17). What is inflation? Investopedia. Retrieved from https://www.investopedia.com/terms/i/inflation.asp

Finnemore, M., & Sikkink, K. (1998). International norm dynamics and political change. *International Organization, 52*(4), 887–917.

Fisch, J. E. (2006). Robert Clark's corporate law: Twenty years of change: Measuring efficiency in corporate law: The role of shareholder primacy. *The Iowa Journal of Corporation Law, 31*(3), 637.

Fitzgerald, N., & Cormack, M. (2007). The role of business in society: An agenda for action. Retrieved from http://www.hks.harvard.edu/mrcbg/CSRI/publications/report_12

Flaherty, M., Gevorkyan, A., Radpour, S., & Semmler, W. (2017). Financing climate policies through climate bonds: A three stage model and empirics. *Research in International Business and Finance, 42,* 468–479.

Flavelle, Ch. (2021a, December 3). Billions for climate protection fuel new debate: Who deserves it most. *The New York Times.* Retrieved from https://www.nytimes.com/2021/12/03/climate/climate-change-infrastructure-bill.html

Flavelle, Ch. (2021b, December 8). The climate bill includes billions in funding: Will it be spent fairly? *The New York Times.* Retrieved from https://www.nytimes.com/2021/12/03/climate/climate-change-infrastructure-bill.html

Fogler, H. R., & Nutt, F. (1975). A note on social responsibility and stock evaluation. *Academy of Management Journal, 18,* 155–160.

Fombrun, C. (1996). *Reputation: Realizing value from the corporate image.* Cambridge, MA: Harvard Business School.

Foster, A. D., & Rosenzweig, M. R. (2010). *Microeconomics of technology adoption.* Discussion Paper 984, Yale University Economic Growth Center, New Haven, CT.

Foster, V. (2020, June 21). Is eating meat from meatpacking plants with Covid-19 Coronavirus outbreaks safe? *Forbes.* Retrieved from https://www.forbes.com/sites/victoriaforster/2020/06/21/is-eating-meat-from-meatpacking-plants-with-covid-19-coronavirus-outbreaks-safe/?sh=5d2d5bcb7089

Fowler, S. J., & Hope, C. (2007). A critical review of sustainable business indices and their impact. *Journal of Business Ethics, 76*(3), 243–252.

Frankel, T. (1984). Decision making for social investing. In D. M. McGill (Ed.), *Social investing* (pp. 131–162). Homewood, IL: Irwin.

Freeman, R. E. (1984). *Strategic management: A stakeholder approach.* Mashfield, MA: Pitman.

Frey, B. S. (2008). *Happiness: A revolution in economics.* Cambridge, MA: MIT Press.

Frey, B. S., & Stutzer, A. (2007). *Economics and psychology: A promising new cross-disciplinary field.* Cambridge, MA: MIT Press.

Frey, D., & Irle, M. (2002). *Theorien der Sozialpsychologie.* Bern: Hans Huber.

Friedman, M. (1970). The social responsibility of business is to increase its profits. *New York Times Magazine, 13,* 33–38.

Friedman, M. (2002). *Capitalism and freedom.* Chicago, IL: Chicago University Press.

Fromhold-Eisebith, M. (2004). Innovative milieu and social capital: Complementary or redundant concepts of collaboration-based regional development? *European Planning Studies, 12*(6), 747–765.

Fukuyama, F. (1995). *Trust: The social virtues and the creation of prosperity.* New York, NY: Free Press.

Fullerton, D., & Henderson, Y. K. (1989). The marginal excess burden of different capital tax instruments. *Review of Economics and Statistics, 71*(3), 435–442.

Gabaldon, T. A. (2006). Like a fish needs a bicycle: Public corporations and their shareholders. *Maryland Law Review, 65,* 538–578.

Galeon, D., & Reedy, Ch. (2017, October 5). Kurzweil claims that the singularity will happen by 2045. *Futurism.* Retrieved from futurism.com/kurzweil-claims-that-the-singularity-will-happen-by-2045/

Galor, O., & Moav, O. (2000). Ability biased technological transition, wage inequality and growth. *Quarterly Journal of Economics, 115,* 469–498.

Galor, O., & Moav, O. (2004). From physical to human capital accumulation: Inequality in the process of development. *Review of Economic Studies, 71,* 1001–1026.

Gamauf, R. (2009). Slaves doing business: The role of Roman law in the economy of a Roman household. *European Review of History, 16*(3), 331–346.

Garden Destinations. (2021). Agrihoods: A new trend in lifestyle living. Retrieved from https://www.gardendestinations.com/agrihoods-a-new-trend-in-lifestyle-living/

Gardner, H. (2007). *Responsibility at work: How leading professionals act (or don't act) responsibility*. San Francisco, CA: Jossey-Bass.

GBD 2016 Healthcare Access and Quality Collaborators. (2018). Measuring performance on the healthcare access and quality index for 195 countries and territories and selected subnational locations: A systematic analysis from the global burden of disease study 2016. *Lancet, 391*, 2236–2271.

Gebert, D., & Rosenstiel, L. v. (1996). *Organisationspsychologie: Personen und Organisationen*. Stuttgart: Kohlhammer.

Geczy, Ch. C., Stambaugh, R. F., & Levin, D. (2003). *Investing in socially responsible mutual funds*. Philadelphia, PA: The Wharton School.

Geist-Benitez, C., Valenzuela, J., & Walsh, J. (2020, June 25). COVID-19: Survey of Latin America's regulatory response to COVID-19. JD Supra. Retrieved from https://www.jdsupra.com/legalnews/covid-19-survey-of-latin-america-s-53792/

Gelter, M. (2021). Is economic nationalism in corporate governance always threat?. *Ohio State Business Law Journal, 16*(1), 1–36.

Gelter, M., & Puaschunder, J. M. (2021). COVID-19 and comparative corporate governance. *Journal of Corporation Law, 46*(3), 557–629.

Georgieva, K., & Tshisekedi, F. (2021, December 17). Africa cannot confront climate change alone. Project Syndicate. Retrieved from https://www.project-syndicate.org/commentary/supporting-climate-adaptation-in-africa-by-kristalina-georgieva-and-felix-tshisekedi-2021-12?utm_source=Project+Syndicate+Newsletter&utm_campaign=488625a940-sunday_newsletter_19_12_2021&utm_medium=email&utm_term=0_73bad5b7d8-488625a940-105014969&mc_cid=488625a940&mc_eid=8e5e2229bb

German Federal Ministry for Economic Affairs and Energy. (2020, March 27). *Minister Altmaier: "Unprecedented support programme for employees and enterprises"* [Press release]. Retrieved from https://www.bmwi.de/Redaktion/EN/Pressemitteilungen/2020/20200327-altmaier-unprecedented-support-programme-for-employees-and-enterprises.html

German Federal Ministry of Finance. (2020, March 23). *Federal government takes large-scale measures to tackle crisis fallout* [Press release]. Retrieved from https://www.bundesfinanzministerium.de/Content/EN/Pressemitteilungen/2020/2020-03-23-supplementary-budget.html

Gerson, K. (2002). Moral dilemmas, moral strategies and the transformation of gender: Lessons from two generations of work and family change. *Gender and Society, 16*(1), 8–28.

Gertz, G. (2020, July 24). How to deglobalize. *Foreign Policy*. Retrieved from https://foreignpolicy.com/2020/07/24/how-to-deglobalize

Gevorkyan, A., & Semmler, A. (2016). Oil price, overleveraging and shakeout in the shale energy sector: Game changers in the oil industry. *Economic Modeling, 54*, 244–259.

Ghilarducci, T. (2021, August 14). Are firms causing people to quit? Quits rate increasing to 2.7%. *Forbes*. Retrieved from https://www.forbes.com/sites/teresaghilarducci/2021/08/14/are-firms-causing-people-to-quit-quits-rate-increasing-to-27/?sh=3a18e42d35d0

Gill, A. (2001). *Saints and sinners: Who's got religion?* Hong Kong: Credit Lyonnais Securities Asia Report.

Goldberg, K., & Pavcnik, N. (2007). The distributional effects of globalization in developing countries. *Journal of Economic Literature, 45*(1), 39–82.

Goleman, D. (2006). *Social intelligence: The new science of human relationships*. New York, NY: Bantam.

Gompers, P., Kovner, A., Lerner, J., & Scharfstein, D. (2005). Venture capital investment cycles: The impact of public markets. Working Paper 11385, National Bureau of Economic Research, Cambridge, MA.

Goodpaster, K. E., & Matthews, J. B. (2003). Can a corporation have a conscience? In *Harvard business review on corporate responsibility*. Cambridge, MA: Harvard Business School.

Gore, A. (1992). *Earth in the balance*. Boston: Houghton-Mifflin.

Gorz, A. (2003). *The immaterial: Knowledge, value and capital*. London: Seagull.

Gössling, St., Scott, D., & Hall, M. (2020). Pandemics, tourism and global change: A rapid assessment of COVID-19. *Journal of Sustainable Tourism, 29*(1), 1–20.

Government of Brazil. (2020, June 2). Economic measures aimed at reducing the impacts of Covid-19 (Coronavirus) – Timeline. Retrieved from https://www.gov.br/economia/pt-br/centrais-de-conteudo/publicacoes/boletins/covid-19/timeline

Graff-Zivin, J., & Small, A. (2005). A Modigliani–Miller theory of altruistic corporate social responsibility. *Journal in Economic Analysis and Policy, 5*(1), 1–19.

Graves, S. B., Rehbeim, K., & Waddock, S. (2001). Fad and fashion in shareholder activism: The landscape of shareholder resolutions 1988–1998. *Business and Society Review, 106*, 293–314.

Greening, D. W., & Turban, D. B. (2000). Corporate social performance as a competitive advantage in attracting a quality workforce. *Business & Society, 39*, 254–280.

Greenspan, A. (2007). *The age of turbulence: Adventures in a new world*. New York, NY: Penguin.

Greenwood, J., & Jovanovic, B. (1990). Financial development, growth, and the distribution of income. *Journal of Political Economy, 98*(5, Part 1), 1076–1107.

Griffin, J. J., & Mahon, J. F. (1997). The corporate social performance and corporate financial performance debate: Twenty-five years of economic and organizational factors. *Strategic Management Journal, 10*, 399–411.

Grossman, G. M., & Helpman, E. (1991a). *Innovation and growth in the global economy*. Cambridge, MA: MIT Press.

Grossman, G. M., & Helpman, E. (1991b). Quality ladders in the theory of growth. *Review of Economic Studies, 58*(1), 43–61.

Guenster, N., Derwall, J., Bauer, R., & Koedijk, K. (2005). *The economic value of corporate eco-efficiency*. Unpublished Working Paper, Erasmus University.

Hagey, K., Alpert, L. I., & Serkez, Y. (2019, May 4). In news industry, a stark divide between haves and have-nots: Local newspapers are failing to make the digital transition larger players did and are in danger of vanishing. *The Wall Street Journal*. Retrieved from https://www.wsj.com/graphics/local-newspapers-stark-divide/

Haidt, J. (2001). The emotional dog and its rational tail: A social intuitionist approach to moral judgment. *Psychological Review, 1089*(4), 814–834.

Hall, P. A., & Soskice, D. (2001). An introduction to varieties of capitalism. In P. A. Hall & D. Soskice (Eds.), *Varieties of capitalism: The institutional foundations of comparative advantage* (pp. 8–9). Oxford: Oxford University Press.

Hamilton, S., Hoje, J., & Statman, M. (1993). Doing well while doing good? The investment performance of socially responsible mutual funds. *Financial Analysts Journal, 49*(6), 62–66.

Hana, L. (2020, April 23). KRW 85T budget added to stabilize key sectors, employment. Korea Culture and Information Service. Retrieved from https://m.korea.net/english/NewsFocus/policies/view?articleId=184852

Handy, Ch. (2006). What's a business for? In *Harvard business review on corporate responsibility*. Cambridge, MA: Harvard Business School.

Harris, W. V. (2000). Trade. In *The Cambridge ancient history: The high empire A.D. 70–192* (p. 11). Cambridge: Cambridge University Press.

Harrison, A. (2021, April 27). 70% of COVID long haulers have impaired organs up to 4 months after infection, study finds. KuTv. Retrieved from https://kutv.com/news/local/70-of-long-haulers-have-impaired-organs-up-to-4-months-after-covid-19-infection

Harrod, R. F. (1939). An essay in dynamic theory. *The Economic Journal, 49* (193), 14–33.

Hart, R. (2021, July 15). Long Covid has over 200 symptoms and leaves 1 In 5 unable to work, study finds. *Forbes.* Retrieved from https://www.forbes.com/sites/roberthart/2021/07/15/long-covid-has-over-200-symptoms-and-leaves-1-in-5-unable-to-work-study-finds/?sh=7f71338e5eb2

Hart, S. L. (1995). A natural resource-based view of the firm. *Academy of Management Review, 20,* 986–1014.

Harvey, C. (2008). Campbell R. Harvey's hypertextual finance glossary. Retrieved from http://www.duke.edu/~charvey/Classes/wpg/bfglosa.htm

Hausmann, R., Pritchett, L., & Rodrik, D. (2005). Growth accelerations. *Journal of Economic Growth, 10*(4), 303–329.

Hayek, F. A. (1944/2007). *The road to serfdom.* London: The University of Chicago Press.

Hayes, A. (2018). *Decentralized banking: Monetary technocracy in the digital age.* Working Paper, Social Science Research Network. Tenth Mediterranean Conference on Information Systems (MCIS), Paphos, Cyprus, September 2016. Retrieved from https://papers.ssrn.com/sol3/papers.cfm?abstract_id=2807476

Hayes, A. (2020, August 23). Fisher effect definition. Investopedia. Retrieved from https://www.investopedia.com/terms/f/fishereffect.asp

Hayes, A. (2021, June 27). *Why didn't quantitative easing lead to hyperinflation?* Investopedia. Retrieved from https://www.investopedia.com/articles/investing/022615/why-didnt-quantitative-easing-lead-hyperinflation.asp

Hayes, J. (2001). The greater good: How ethical investment pays off. *Australian Financial Review, 26*(8), 29–31.

Heine, D., Semmler, W., Mazzucato, M., Braga, J. P., Flaherty, M., Gevorkyan, A., … Radpour, S. (2019, August). Financing low-carbon transitions through carbon pricing and green bonds. Working Paper 8991, World Bank Policy Research, Washington, DC.

Held, D., & McGrew, A. G. (2007). *A new world economic order? Global markets and state power: Beyond globalization/anti-globalization: Beyond the great divide.* New York, NY: Polity.

Helper, S., & Soltas, E. (2021, June 17). Why the pandemic has disrupted supply chains. The White House of the United States. Retrieved from https://www.whitehouse.gov/cea/written-materials/2021/06/17/why-the-pandemic-has-disrupted-supply-chains/

Hennigfeld, J., Pohl, M., & Tolhurst, N. (2006). *The ICCA handbook on corporate social responsibility.* West Sussex: Wiley.

Hermann, M. (2008, Spring). Political leadership (Course reader). Syracuse, NY: Maxwell School of Citizenship and Public Affairs, Syracuse University.

Hofmann, E., Hoelzl, E., & Kirchler, E. (2008). A comparison of models describing the impact of moral decision making on investment decision. *Journal of Business Ethics, 82*(1), 171–187.

Holgaard, J. E., & Jørgensen, T. H. (2005). A decade of mandatory environmental reporting in Denmark. *European Environment, 15*(6), 362–373.

Holman, W. R., New, J. R., & Singer, D. (1985). The impact of corporate social responsiveness on shareholder wealth. In L. Preston (Ed.), *Research in corporate social performance and policy* (pp. 265–279). Greenwich, CT: JAI.

Hong, H., & Kacperczyk, M. (2006). *The price of sin: The effects on social norms on markets.* Unpublished Working Paper, Princeton University.

Huberman, B. A., Loch, Ch. H., & Önçüler, A. (2002). Status as a valued resource. Unpublished Working Paper. Retrieved from www.ssrn.com

Hyunjung, B. (2020, April 8). S. Korea unveils another massive stimulus package against coronavirus. *The Korea Herald*. Retrieved from http://www.koreaherald.com/view. php?ud=20200408000825

Inglehart, R. (1999). *Trust, well-being and democracy: Democracy and trust*. Cambridge: Cambridge University Press.

International Monetary Fund. (2020a, June). A crisis like no other: An uncertain recovery. Retrieved from https://www.imf.org/en/Publications/WEO/Issues/2020/06/24/ WEOUpdateJune2020

International Monetary Fund. (2020b). Policy responses to COVID-19. Retrieved from https://www.imf.org/en/Topics/imf-andcovid19/Policy-Responses-to-COVID-19

International Monetary Fund. (2020c). The IMF's response to COVID-19. Retrieved from https://www.imf.org/en/About/FAQ/imf-response-to-covid-19

Jacoby, H. G. (2008). Food prices, wages, and welfare in rural India. *Economic Inquiry*, *54*(1), 159–176.

Jahan, S. (2021, December 8). Inflation targeting: Holding the line. Washington, DC: International Monetary Fund. Retrieved from https://www.imf.org/external/pubs/ft/ fandd/basics/target.htm

Janis, I. L., & Mann, L. (1977). *Decision making: A psychological analysis of conflict, choice, and commitment*. New York, NY: Free Press.

Jenkins, B. (2007). *Expanding economic opportunity: The role of large firms*. Economic Opportunity Series. Cambridge, MA: Harvard Kennedy School.

Jonas, H. (1979). *Das Prinzip Verantwortung: Versuch einer Ethik für die technische Zivilisation*. Suhrkamp: Frankfurt am Main.

Jones, H., & Milliken, D. (2020, March 20). Bank of England cancels stress test of banks over coronavirus. Reuters. Retrieved from https://www.reuters.com/article/us-health-coronavirus-britain-regulation/bank-of-england-cancels-stress-test-of-banks-over-coronavirus-idUSKBN2170QI

Jones, I., & Pollitt, M. (1998). *The role of business ethics in economic performance*. London: Macmillan.

Jones, L., Palumbo, D., & Brown, D. (2020, June 30). Coronavirus: A visual guide to the economic impact. BBC News. Retrieved from https://www.bbc.com/news/business-51706225

Jones, S., van der Laan, S., Frost, G., & Loftus, J. (2008). The investment performance of socially responsible investment funds in Australia. *Journal of Business Ethics*, *80*(2), 181–203.

Jones, T. M., & Wicks, A. C. (1999). Convergent stakeholder theory. *Academy of Management Review*, *24*, 206–221.

Kahn, M. E., Mohaddes, K., Ng, R. N. C., Pesaran, M. H., Raissi, M., & Yang, J.-Ch. (2019). Long-term macroeconomic effects of climate change: A cross-country analysis. Working Paper WP/19/215, International Monetary Fund. Retrieved from https://www.imf.org/-/media/Files/Publications/WP/2019/wpiea2019215-print-pdf. ashx

Kahneman, D., & Tversky, A. (1974). Judgment under uncertainty: Heuristics and biases. *Science*, *185*(4157), 1124–1131.

Kahneman, D., & Tversky, A. (1979). Prospect theory: An analysis of decision under risk. *Econometrica*, *47*(2), 263–291.

Kahneman, D., & Tversky, A. (2000). *Choices, values, and frames*. Cambridge: Cambridge University Press.

Kaldor, N. (1961). Capital accumulation and economic growth. In F. A. Lutz & D. C. Hague (Eds.), *The theory of capital* (pp. 177–222). New York, NY: St. Martin's Press.

Kant, I. (1783/1993). *Grounding for the metaphysics of morals*. Cambridge: Hackett.

Kant, I. (1787/1974). *Kritik der reinen Vernunft*. Frankfurt am Main: Suhrkamp.

Kant, I. (1788/1974). *Kritik der praktischen Vernunft*. Frankfurt am Main: Suhrkamp.

Kanter, R. M. (2003). From spare change to real change. In *Harvard business review on corporate responsibility*. Cambridge, MA: Harvard Business School.

Karp, P. (2020, March 30). Australian economic stimulus package: How much governments have committed to coronavirus crisis. *The Guardian*. Retrieved from https://www.theguardian.com/australia-news/2020/mar/31/australian-economic-stimulus-package-how-much-governments-have-committed-to-coronavirus-crisis

Kashyap, R. K., & Iyer, S. I. (2006). *Who are socially responsible investors?* Unpublished Working Paper, University of Massachusetts at Amherst.

Kato, M., Mittnik, St., Samaan, D., & Semmler, W. (2014). Employment and output effects of climate policies. In L. Bernard & W. Semmler (Eds.), *The Oxford handbook of the macroeconomics of global warming* (pp. 445–476). Oxford: Oxford University Press.

Kazmin, A. (2020, October 12). India unveils 'underwhelming' $10bn stimulus for pandemic-hit economy. *Financial Times*. Retrieved from https://www.ft.com/content/c0d23498-e91f-4f58-bebb-4237ed2d5398

Keller, K. L. (2003). Brand synthesis: The multidimensionality of brand knowledge. *Journal of Consumer Research, 29*, 595–600.

Kempf, A., & Osthoff, P. (2007). The effect of socially responsible investing on portfolio performance. *European Financial Management, 13*(5), 908–922.

Kettl, D. F. (2006). *The global public management revolution*. Washington, DC: The Brookings Institution.

Keynes, J. M. (1936/2003). *The general theory of employment, interest and money*. Cambridge, MA: Harvard University Press.

Kirchler, E. M. (2011). *Wirtschaftspsychologie: Individuen, Gruppen, Märkte, Staat*. Göttingen: Hogrefe.

Klenow, P. (2008). Discussion of 'Big answers for big questions: The presumption of growth policy' by A. V. Banerjee. In Brookings Institute (Ed.), *What works in development? Thinking big and thinking small* (pp. 207–231). Washington, DC: Brookings Institute.

Knack, St., & Keefer, Ph. (1997). Does social capital have an economic payoff? A cross-country investigation. *Quarterly Journal of Economics, 112*, 1251–1288.

Knoll, M. S. (2008). *Socially responsible investment and modern financial markets*. Unpublished Working Paper, University of Pennsylvania Law School.

Konrad, A., Martinuzzi, A., & Steurer, R. (2008). When business associations and a Federal Ministry jointly consult civil society: A CSR policy case study on the development of the CSR Austria guiding vision. *Corporate Social Responsibility and Environmental Management, 15*, 270–280.

Kortum, S. S. (1997). Research, patenting, and technological change. *Econometrica, 65*(6), 1389–1420.

Kose, A., & Sugawara, N. (2020, June 15). Understanding the depth of the 2020 global recession in 5 charts. World Bank. Retrieved from https://blogs.worldbank.org/opendata/understanding-depth-2020-global-recession-5-charts

Kotler, Ph., & Lee, N. (2005). *Corporate social responsibility: Doing the most good for your company and your cause*. Hoboken, NJ: Wiley.

Kowert, W. (2017). The foreseeability of human–artificial intelligence interactions. *Texas Law Review, 96*, 181–204.

Kramer, R. (1999). Trust and distrust in organizations: Emerging perspectives, enduring questions. *Annual Review of Psychology, 50*, 569–598.

Kramer, R., & Tyler, T. (1996). *Trust in organizations*. Thousand Oaks, CA: Sage.

Kumar, N., & Haydon, D. (2020, April 7). Industries most and least impacted by COVID-19 from a probability of default perspective: March 2020 update. S&P Global Market Intelligence. Retrieved from https://www.spglobal.com/marketintelligence/en/news-insights/blog/industries-most-and-least-impacted-by-covid-19-from-a-probability-of-default-perspective-march-2020-update

Kwak, J. (2020, July 9). The end of small business. *The Washington Post*. Retrieved from https://www.washingtonpost.com/outlook/2020/07/09/after-covid-19-giant-corporations-chains-may-be-only-ones-left/?arc404=true

LaPorta, R., Lopez-de-Silanes, F., Shleifer, A., & Vishny, R. W. (1997). Trust in large organizations. *American Economic Review, 87*, 333–338.

Larson, D. A. (2010). Artificial intelligence: Robots, avatars, and the demise of the human mediator. *Ohio State Journal on Dispute Resolution, 25*, 105–164.

Laton, D. (2016). Manhattan_Project.Exe: A nuclear option for the digital age. *Catholic University Journal of Law & Technology, 25*(4), 94–153.

Law, J., & Smullen, J. (2008). *A dictionary of finance and banking*. Oxford: Oxford University Press.

Lea, R. (2002). *Corporate social responsibility: Institute of Directors (IoD) member opinion survey*. London: IoD.

Lee, B. (2021). Volatility. In C. Borch & R. Wosnitzer (Eds.), *Routledge handbook of critical finance studies* (pp. 54–68). New York, NY: Routledge.

Lee, B., & Martin, R. (2016). *Derivatives and the wealth of societies*. Chicago: IL: University of Chicago Press.

Lenk, H., & Maring, M. (1992). *Wirtschaft und Ethik*. Stuttgart: Reclam.

Lennick, D., & Kiel, F. (2007). *Moral intelligence: Enhancing business performance and leadership success*. Upper Saddle River, NJ: Wharton School Publishing.

Lerner, J. S., & Tetlock, P. E. (1999). Accountability for the effects of accountability. *Psychological Bulletin, 125*(2), 255–275.

Lerner, S. (2020, March 13). Big pharma prepares to profit from the Coronavirus: Pharmaceutical companies view the Coronavirus pandemic as a once-in-a-lifetime business opportunity. *The Intercept*. Retrieved from https://theintercept.com/2020/03/13/big-pharma-drug-pricing-coronavirus-profits

Levitt, T. (1983). The globalization of markets. *Harvard Business Review, 61*, 2–11.

Lewis, A., & Mackenzie, C. (2000). Morals, money, ethical investing and economic psychology. *Human Relations, 53*, 179–191.

Lexology. (2019, July 17). Emerging legal issues in an AI-driven world. Retrieved from https://www.lexology.com/library/detail.aspx?g=4284727f-3bec-43e5-b230-fad2742dd4fb

Lichtenberger, A., Braga, J. P., & Semmler, W. (2022). Green bonds for the transition to a low-carbon economy. *Econometrics, 10*(1), 11. https://doi.org/10.3390/econometrics10010011

Lighthizer, R. E. (2020, May 11). The era of offshoring U.S. jobs is over. *The New York Times*. Retrieved from https://www.nytimes.com/2020/05/11/opinion/coronavirus-jobs-offshoring.html

Lin, P., Abney, K., & Bekey, G. A. (2012). *Robot ethics: The ethical and social implications of robotics*. London: The MIT Press.

LiPuma, E., & Lee, B. (2004). *Financial derivatives and the globalization of risk*. Durham, NC: Duke University Press.

Little, K. (2008). *Socially responsible investing: Put your money where your values are*. New York, NY: Penguin.

Livesey, S. (2002). The discourse of the middle ground: Citizen Shell commits to sustainable development. *Management Communication Quarterly, 15*, 313–349.

Lomborg, B. (2021, September 16). Climate change saves more lives than you'd think: Eight times as many people die from cold as heat, and the fix for both is access to cheap fuel. *The Wall Street Journal*. Retrieved from https://www.wsj.com/articles/climate-change-heat-cold-deaths-medical-journal-health-risk-energy-cost-fossil-fuels-11631741045?st=w4h947wjnxd6iio&reflink=article_email_share

Lucas, R. E. (1988). On the mechanics of economic development. *Journal of Monetary Economics, 22*, 3–42.

Lucas, R. E. (2004, May). *The industrial revolution: Past and future*. Annual report of the Federal Reserve Bank of Minneapolis (pp. 5–20). Retrieved from https://www.minneapolisfed.org/article/2004/the-industrial-revolution-past-and-future

Lucas, R. E. (2009). Ideas and growth. *Economica, 76,* 1–19.

Lucas, R. E., & Moll, B. (2014). Knowledge growth and the allocation of time. *Journal of Political Economy, 122*(1), 1–51.

Luf, G. (2009). Grundfragen der Rechtsphilosophie und Rechtsethik. *Einführung in die Rechtswissenschaften und ihre Methoden.* Wien: Manz.

Lydenberg, S. (2002). Envisioning socially responsible investing: A model for 2006. *Journal of Corporate Citizenship, 7,* 57–77.

Lynch-Fannon, I. (2007). The corporate social responsibility movement and law's empire: Is there a conflict? *Northern Ireland Legal Quarterly, 58*(1), 1–22.

MacDonald, F. (2016, June 23). Harvard scientists think they've pinpointed the physical source of consciousness. *Science Alert.* Retrieved from http://www.sciencealert.com/harvard-scientists-think-they-ve-pinpointed-the-neural-source-of-consciousness

Mackey, A., Mackey, T. B., & Barney, J. B. (2004). Corporate social responsibility and firm performance: Investor preferences and corporate strategies. *The Academy of Management Review, 32*(3), 817–835

Mandavilli, A. (2021, July 21). Coronavirus infections much higher than reported cases in parts of U.S., study shows. *The New York Times.* Retrieved from https://www.nytimes.com/2020/07/21/health/coronavirus-infections-us.html

Mansbridge, J. (1999). Altruistic trust. In M. E. Warren (Ed.), *Trust and democracy* (pp. 290–307). Cambridge: Cambridge University Press.

March, J., & Simon, H. (1958). *Organizations.* New York, NY: Wiley.

Margolis, J., Elfenbein, H., & Walsh, J. (2007). *Does it pay to be good? A meta-analysis and redirection of research on the relationship between corporate social and financial performance.* Ann Arbor, 1001, 48109–1234. https://doi.org/10.2139/ssrn.1866371

Marinov, B., & Heiman, B. (1998). Company law and corporate governance renewal in transition economics: The Bulgarian dilemma. *European Journal of Law and Economics, 6*(3), 231–262.

Marra, W., & McNeil, S. (2013). Understanding "The loop": Regulating the next generation of war machines. *Harvard Journal of Law & Public Policy, 36,* 1139–1187.

Martin, S. (2020, March 11). What the Australian government's $17bn coronavirus stimulus package means for you. *The Guardian.* Retrieved from https://www.the-guardian.com/business/2020/mar/12/what-australian-governments-coronavirus-stimulus-package-means-for-you-explainer

Massumi, B. (1995). The autonomy of affect. *Cultural Critique: The Politics of Systems and Environment, 31,* 83–109.

Massumi, B. (2015). *Politics of affect.* Cambridge: Polity.

Mathiason, J. (2007). *Invisible governance: International secretariats in global politics.* Bloomfield, CT: Kumarian.

Mathieu, E. (2000). *Response of UK pension funds to the SRI disclosure regulation.* London: UK Social Investment Forum.

Mathis, A. (2008). *Corporate social responsibility and public policy-making: Perspectives, instruments and consequences.* Twente: University of Twente.

Matsuyama, K. (2000). Endogenous inequality. *Review of Economic Studies, 67*(4), 743–759.

Matsuyama, K. (2008). Structural change. In S. Durlauf & L. E. Blume (Eds.), *The new Palgrave dictionary of economics* (pp. 52–55). London: Palgrave-Macmillan.

Matsuyama, K. (2011). Imperfect credit markets, household wealth distribution, and development. *Annual Review of Economics, 3,* 339–362.

Matten, D., & Crane, A. (2005). Corporate citizenship: Toward an extended theoretical conceptualization. *Academy of Management Review, 30,* 166–179.

Matten, D., & Moon, J. (2004). "Implicit" and "explicit" CSR: A conceptual framework for understanding CSR in Europe. In *20th EGOS colloquium,* Ljubljana, Slovenia, July 1–3.

Mauss, M. (1979). A category of the human mind: The notion of the person, the notion of 'self', In M. Mauss (Ed.), *Sociology and psychology* (pp. 81–103). London: Routledge.

Maux, J., & Saout, E. (2004, April 1). The performance of sustainability indexes. Finance India.

Mayhaw, K., & Anand, P. (2020). COVID-19 and the UK labour market. *Oxford Review of Economic Policy, 36*(1), 217–221.

Mazzucato, M. (2013). *The entrepreneurial state: Debunking public vs. private sector myths.* New York, NY: Anthem.

McCann, L., Solomon, A., & Solomon, J. F. (2003). Explaining the growth in U.K. socially responsible investment. *Journal of General Management, 28*(4), 15–36.

McDonald, J. (2020, June 29). Companies prodded to rely less on China, but few respond. AP NEWS. Retrieved from https://apnews.com/bc9f37e67745c046563234d-1d2e3fe01

McPhillips, D. (2021, January 5). Study estimates US COVID-19 infections may be 4 times higher than reported. *CNN.* Retrieved from https://www.cnn.com/world/live-news/coronavirus-pandemic-vaccine-updates-01-05-21/h_833be27384fd892bf390e72fe3f3 4b1e

McWilliams, A., & Siegel, D. (1996). The use of event studies in management research. In S. Taneja (Ed.), *Academy of management best papers proceedings* , Cincinnati, OH (pp. 338–342).

McWilliams, A., & Siegel, D. (2000). Corporate social responsibility and financial performance: Correlation or mis-specification? *Strategic Management Journal, 21,* 603–609.

McWilliams, A., & Siegel, D. (2001). Corporate social responsibility: A theory of the firm perspective. *Academy of Management Review, 26,* 117–127.

McWilliams, A., Siegel, D., & Teoh, S. W. (1999). Issues in the use of the event study methodology: A critical analysis of corporate social responsibility studies. *Organizational Research Methods, 2,* 340–365.

Meghdari, A., & Alemi, M. (2018). Recent advances in social and cognitive robotics and imminent ethical challenges. In *Proceedings of the 10th international RAIS conference on social sciences and humanities.* Organized by Research Association for Interdisciplinary Studies (RAIS) at The Erdman Center at Princeton University, Princeton, New Jersey, United States, August 22–23. Cambridge, MA: The Scientific Press.

Meghdari, A., Alemi, M., Zakipour, M., & Kashanian, S. A. (2018). Design and realization of a sign language educational humanoid robot. *Journal of Intelligent & Robotic Systems, 95,* 3–17.

Meghdari, A., Shariati, A., Alemi, M., & Vossoughi, G. R. (2018). Arash: A social robot buddy to support children with cancer in a hospital environment. *Journal of Engineering in Medicine, 232*(6), 605–618.

Merriam Webster Dictionary. (2008). Retrieved from https://www.merriam-webster.com/

Meyer, R. E., & Höllerer, M. A. (2005). From value management to values management: Contrasting views or just two sides of the same coin: Shareholder value and corporate social responsibility in Austrian publicly listed corporations. In *NFF 2005 conference: The 18th Scandinavian Academy of Management (NFF) meeting,* Aarhus, Denmark, August 18–20.

Meyers, J. G., & Nakamura, L. (1980). Energy and pollution effects on productivity: A putty-clay approach. In J. Kendrick (Ed.), *New developments in productivity measurement and analysis* (pp. 463–506). Chicago, IL: University of Chicago Press.

Meznar, M. B., Nigh, D., & Kwok, C. C. (1994). Effect of announcements of withdrawal from South Africa on stockholder wealth. *Academy of Management Journal, 37,* 1633–1648.

Michelson, G., Wailes, N., van der Laan, S., & Frost, G. (2004). Ethical investment processes and outcomes. *Journal of Business Ethics, 52,* 1–10.

Micklethwait, J., & Wooldridge, A. (2003). *A future perfect: The challenge and promise of globalization*. New York, NY: Crown Business Press.

Midttun, A. (2005). Policy making and the role of government: Realigning business, government and civil society. *Corporate Governance, 5*, 159–174.

Milanovic, B. (2013). Global income inequality in numbers: In history and now. *Global Policy, 4*(2), 198–208.

Milanovic, B. (2016). *Global inequality: A new approach for the age of globalization*. Cambridge, MA: Harvard University Press.

Mitchell, R. K., Agle, B. R., & Wood, D. J. (1997). Toward a theory of stakeholder identification and salience: Defining the principle of who and what really counts. *Academy of Management Review, 22*, 853–888.

Mohamed, A. M. I. (2016). *Globalization and new international public works agreements in developing countries: An analytical perspective*. London: Routledge.

Mohr, L. A., & Webb, D. J. (2005). The effects of corporate social responsibility and price on consumer responses. *Journal of Consumer Affairs, 39*(1), 121–147.

Mohr, L. A., Webb, D. J., & Harris, K. E. (2001). Do consumers expect companies to be socially responsible? The impact of corporate social responsibility on buying behavior. *Journal of Consumer Affairs, 35*(1), 45–72.

Moll, B. (2014). Productivity losses from financial frictions: Can self-financing undo capital misallocations? *American Economic Review, 104*(10), 3186–3221.

Monck, A. (2020, June 3). The great reset: A unique twin summit to begin 2021. *World Economic Forum*. Retrieved from https://www.weforum.org/press/2020/06/the-great-reset-a-unique-twin-summit-to-begin-2021/

Mookherjee, D., & Napel, S. (2007). Intergenerational mobility and macroeconomic history dependence. *Journal of Economic Theory, 137*(1), 49–78.

Mookherjee, D., & Ray, D. (2003). Persistent inequality. *Review of Economic Studies, 70*, 369–393.

Moon, J. (2002). The social responsibility of business and new governance. *Government and Opposition, 37*(3), 385–408.

Moon, J. (2004). Government as a driver of corporate social responsibility: The UK in comparative perspective. Research Paper Series. Nottingham: International Centre for Corporate Social Responsibility.

Moon, J. (2005). An explicit model of business–society relations. In A. Habisch, J. Jonker, M. Wegner, & R. Schmidpeter (Eds.), *Corporate social responsibility across Europe* (pp. 51–65). Berlin: Springer.

Moon, J. (2007). The contribution of corporate social responsibility to sustainable development. *Sustainable Development, 15*, 296–306.

Moon, J., Crane, A., & Matten, D. (2003). Can corporations be citizens? Corporate citizenship as a metaphor for business participation in society. *Research Paper Series of ICCSR, 4*, 2–17.

Moskowitz, M. (1972). Choosing socially responsible stocks. *Business and Society, 1*, 71–75.

Murnighan, J. K., Cantelon, D. A., & Elyashiv, T. (2001). Bounded personal ethics and the tap dance of real estate agency. *Advances in Qualitative Organization Research, 3*, 1–40.

Murphy, K. (2020, March 21). Scott Morrison to announce $66bn stimulus, including income support for workers. *The Guardian*. Retrieved from https://www.theguardian.com/business/2020/mar/22/scott-morrison-to-announce-66bn-stimulus-including-income-support-for-workers

Murphy, K. M., Riddell, W. C., & Romer, P. M. (1998). *Wages, skills, and technology in the United States and Canada*. Working Paper 6638, National Bureau of Economic Research (NBER), Cambridge, MA. Retrieved from https://www.nber.org/papers/w6638.pdf

Myers, St. (1984). The capital structure puzzle. *Journal of Finance, 39*, 575–592.

Nagarajan, S. (2020, May 30). The European Union's \$826 billion stimulus plan to battle the coronavirus is 'too small and too late,' analysts say. *Business Insider*. Retrieved from https://www.businessinsider.com/what-eu-826-billion-covid-19-stimulus-package-means-2020-5

Nani, B., & Beyoud, L. (2022, April 4). Shareholders up climate, social demands after SEC policy shift. Bloomberg Law. Retrieved from https://news.bloomberglaw.com/esg/shareholders-up-climate-social-demands-after-sec-policy-shift

Nassif-Pires, L., de Lima Xavier, L., Masterson, T., Nikiforos, M., & Rios-Avila, F. (2020, April 2). We need class, race, and gender sensitive policies to fight the COVID-19 crisis. Multiplier effect: The Levy Economics Institute Blog. Retrieved from http://multiplier-effect.org/we-need-class-race-and-gender-sensitive-policies-to-fight-the-covid-19-crisis/

National Bureau of Economic Research. (2021a, July 19). Business Cycle Dating Committee announcement. Retrieved from https://www.nber.org/news/business-cycle-dating-committee-announcement-july-19-2021

National Bureau of Economic Research. (2021b, July 19). US business cycle expansions and contractions. Retrieved from https://www.nber.org/research/data/us-business-cycle-expansions-and-contractions

Nelson, J. (2004). *Leadership, accountability and partnership: Critical trends and issues in corporate social responsibility*. Report of the Corporate Responsibility Initiative. Harvard University, Cambridge, MA.

New Hope Village & Farm (2021, December 8). What is an Agrihood? Retrieved from https://www.newhopevillagefarm.com/what-is-an-agrihood

Newton, L. H., & Ford, M. M. (2008). *Taking sides: Clashing views on controversial issues in business ethics and society*. New York, NY: McGraw-Hill.

Ngai, S. (2020). *Theory of the Gimmick: Aesthetic judgment and capitalist form*. Cambridge, MA: Harvard University Press.

Ngassam, C. (1992). *An examination of stock market reactions to U.S. corporate divestitures in South Africa*. Newark, DE: University of Delaware.

Nikiforos, M. (2020). When two Minskyan processes meet a large shock: The economic implications of the pandemic. *The Levy Economics Institute of Bard College Policy Note, 29*, 1. Retrieved from http://www.levyinstitute.org/pubs/pn_2020_1.pdf

Nikulin, D. (2021). Responsibility and hope. Bollettino della Società Filosofica Italiana, Carocci editore Roma, Nuova Serie n. 232, Gennaio/Aprile 2021.

Noh, J., & Danuser, G. (2021). Estimation of the fraction of COVID-19 infected people in the U.S. states and countries worldwide. *PLoS ONE, 16*, 2. https://doi.org/10.1371/journal.pone.0246772

Nordhaus, W. D. (1994). *Mapping the global commons: The economics of climate change*. Cambridge, MA: MIT Press.

Nourick, S. (2001). *Corporate social responsibility: Roundtable conference partners for progress: Towards a new approach*. Washington, DC: Brookings Institution Press.

Noyes, K. (2016, March 3). 5 things you need to know about A.I.: Cognitive, neural and deep, oh my! *Computerworld*. Retrieved from www.computerworld.com/article/3040563/enterprise-applications/5-things-you-need-toknow-about-ai-cognitive-neural-anddeep-oh-my.html

O'Callaghan, B. J., & Murdock, E. (2021). Are we building back better? Evidence from 2020 and pathways for inclusive green recovery spending. United Nations Environment Programme. Retrieved from https://wedocs.unep.org/bitstream/handle/20.500.11822/35281/AWBBB.pdf

Omarova, S. T. (2020, August). The climate case for a national investment authority. Data for Progress. Retrieved from https://www.filesforprogress.org/memos/white-paper-nia.pdf

O'Neil, R. F., & Pienta, D. A. (1994). Economic criteria versus ethical criteria toward resolving a basic dilemma in business. *Journal of Business Ethics, 13,* 71–78.

Organisation for Economic Co-operation and Development. (2020). OECD economic outlook. https://doi.org/10.1787/16097408

Organisation for Economic Co-operation and Development. (2021). OECD economic outlook. Retrieved from https://www.oecd-ilibrary.org/economics/oecd-economic-outlook_16097408

Orlitzky, M., Schmidt, F. L., & Rynes, S. L. (2003). Corporate social and financial performance: A meta-analysis. *Organization Studies, 24*(3), 403–441.

Orlov, S., Rovenskaya, E., Puaschunder, J. M., & Semmler, W. (2018). *Green bonds, transition to a low-carbon economy, and intergenerational fairness: Evidence from an extended DICE model.* Working Paper WP-18-001, International Institute for Applied Systems Analysis, IIASA, Laxenburg, Austria, European Union.

Osnabrugge, M. V., & Robinson, R. J. (2000). *Angel investing: Matching start-up funds with start-up companies: The guide for entrepreneurs, individual investors, and venture capitalists.* San Francisco, CA: Jossey-Bass.

Ostrom, E., & Walker, J. (2003). *Trust and reciprocity.* New York, NY: Russel Sage.

Palazzo, G. (2002). *Die Mitte der Demokratie.* Baden-Baden: Nomos.

Pandey, S. K., & Wright, B. E. (2006). Connecting the dots in public management: Political environment, organizational goal ambiguity and public manager's role ambiguity. *Journal of Public Administration Research and Theory, 16*(4), 511–532.

Parente, St., & Prescott, E. (1993). Changes in the wealth of nations. *Quarterly Review of Economics, 17*(2), 3–16.

Pargendler, M. (2020). *The rise of international corporate law.* Legal Working Paper No. 555/2020, European Corporate Governance Institute. Retrieved from https://ssrn.com/abstract=3728650

Passy, J. (2021, June 11). An inflation storm is coming for the U.S. housing market. MarketWatch. Retrieved from https://www.msn.com/en-us/money/realestate/an-inflation-storm-is-coming-for-the-u-s-housing-market/ar-AAKWtdx?ocid=msedgntp

Pearlman, A. (2021). Biophilic homes prove nature is the best medicine: Living design elements create a serene, multisensory, healing experience. Retrieved from https://neo.life/2020/12/biophilic-homes-prove-nature-is-the-best-medicine/

Peterson, P. P. (1989). Event studies: A review of issues and methodology. *Quarterly Journal of Business and Economics, 28*(3), 37–50.

Pharma IQ. (2019, June 11). Excellence in the era of precision medicine. Retrieved from https://www.pharma-iq.com/business-development/articles/excellence-in-the-era-of-precision-medicine

Piketty, Th. (2016). *Capital in the twenty-first century.* Cambridge, MA: Harvard University Press.

Piper, N. (2020, April 10). Die Ökonomie des Todes. Süddeutsche Zeitung. Retrieved from https://www.sueddeutsche.de/wirtschaft/pest-coronavirus-wirtschaft-1.4873813

Porter, M. E. (1991). America's green strategy. *Scientific American, 264*(4), 168.

Porter, M. E., & Kramer, M. R. (2003). The competitive advantage of corporate philanthropy. In *Harvard business review on corporate responsibility.* Cambridge, MA: Harvard Business School.

Posnikoff, J. F. (1997). Disinvestment from South Africa: They did well by doing good. *Contemporary Economic Policy, 15,* 1, 76–86.

Powell, B. (2008). *Making poor nations rich: Entrepreneurship and the process of economic development.* Stanford: Stanford Economics and Finance and the Independent Institute.

Prahalad, C. K., & Hammond, A. (2003). Serving the world's poor profitably. In *Harvard business review on corporate responsibility.* Cambridge, MA: Harvard Business School.

Price, L. (2020, April 29). *Impact of COVID-19 on small businesses: Where is it worst?* Small Business Trends. Retrieved from https://smallbiztrends.com/2020/04/impact-of-coronavirus-on-small-businesses.html

Profita, S. (2019). *Slowbalization and its risks*. Working Paper, Columbia University.

Puaschunder, J. M. (2006). *Vom symbolischen Markennutzen: Interkulturelle Darstellung der Markenwahl als Beziehung von Persönlichkeiten*. [*On symbolic brand equity: Intercultural brand management as a relation management strategy.*] Vienna: Vienna University of Economics and Business.

Puaschunder, J. M. (2011a). *On the emergence, current state and future perspectives of socially responsible investment*. Working Paper, Harvard University Weatherhead Center for International Affairs. Retrieved from http://www.wcfia.harvard.edu/node/6552

Puaschunder, J. M. (2011b). *Socio-psychological motives of socially responsible investors*. Working Paper, Harvard University Weatherhead Center for International Affairs. Retrieved from http://www.wcfia.harvard.edu/node/7416

Puaschunder, J. M. (2013). Ethical investing and socially responsible investing. In K. H. Baker & V. Ricciardi (Eds.), *Investor behavior* (pp. 515–532). New York, NY: John Wiley & Sons Finance Series.

Puaschunder, J. M. (2015a). On the social representations of intergenerational equity. *Oxford Journal of Finance and Risk Perspectives, 4*(4), 78–99.

Puaschunder, J. M. (2015b). Trust and reciprocity drive social common goods allocation norms. In *Proceedings of the Cambridge business and economics conference*. Cambridge: Cambridge University. *Proceedings of the 6th international conference of the Association of Global Management Studies at Columbia University*. New York, NY: The Association of Global Management Studies.

Puaschunder, J. M. (2015c). When investors care about politics: A meta-synthesis of political divestiture studies on the capital flight from South Africa during Apartheid. *Business, Peace and Sustainable Development, 5*(24), 29–52.

Puaschunder, J. M. (2016a). Intergenerational climate change burden sharing: An economics of climate stability research agenda proposal. *Global Journal of Management and Business Research: Economics and Commerce, 16*(3), 31–38.

Puaschunder, J. M. (2016b). Mapping climate justice. In *Proceedings of the 2016 young scientists summer program conference*. Laxenburg: International Institute for Applied Systems Analysis (IIASA).

Puaschunder, J. M. (2016c). On eternal equity in the fin-de-millénaire: Rethinking capitalism for intergenerational justice. *Journal of Leadership, Accountability and Ethics, 13*(2), 11–24.

Puaschunder, J. M. (2016d). Putty capital and clay labor: Differing European Union capital and labor freedom speeds in times of European migration. *The New School Economic Review: A Journal of Critical Economics at The New School, 8*(3), 147–168.

Puaschunder, J. M. (2016e). The call for global responsible intergenerational leadership in the corporate world: The quest for an integration of intergenerational equity in contemporary Corporate Social Responsibility (CSR) models. In D. Jamali (Ed.), *Comparative perspectives in global corporate social responsibility* (pp. 275–288). Advances in Business Strategy and Competitive Advantage Book Series. Hershey, PA: IGI Global.

Puaschunder, J. M. (2016f). The role of political divestiture for sustainable development. *Journal of Management and Sustainability, 6*(1), 76–91.

Puaschunder, J. M. (2017a). Climate in the 21st century: A macroeconomic model of fair global warming benefits distribution to grant climate justice around the world and over time. In *Proceedings of the 8th international RAIS conference on social sciences and humanities*. Organized by Research Association for Interdisciplinary Studies (RAIS) at Georgetown University, Washington, DC, United States, March 26–27 (pp. 205–243).

Puaschunder, J. M. (2017b). *Global responsible intergenerational leadership: A conceptual framework and implementation guidance for intergenerational fairness.* Wilmington: Vernon Press.

Puaschunder, J. M. (2017c). Mapping climate in the 21st century. *Development, 59*(3), 211–216.

Puaschunder, J. M. (2017d). Nudging in the digital big data era. *European Journal of Economics, Law and Politics, 4*(4), 18–23.

Puaschunder, J. M. (2017e). Nudgital: Critique of behavioral political economy. *Archives of Business Research, 5*(9), 54–76.

Puaschunder, J. M. (2017f). Nudgitize me! A behavioral finance approach to minimize losses and maximize profits from heuristics and biases. *International Journal of Management Excellence, 10*(2), 1241–1256.

Puaschunder, J. M. (2017g). Socio-psychological motives of socially responsible investors. *Global Corporate Governance: Advances in Financial Economics, 19*, 209–247.

Puaschunder, J. M. (2017h). The climatorial imperative. *Agriculture Research and Technology, 7*(4), 1–2.

Puaschunder, J. M. (2017i). The nudging divide in the digital big data era. *International Journal of Research in Business, Economics and Management, 4*, 11–12, 49–53.

Puaschunder, J. M. (2018a). Dignity and utility of privacy and information sharing in the digital big data age. *International Journal of Commerce and Management Research, 5*(4), 62–70.

Puaschunder, J. M. (2018b). Gifts without borders: Intergenerational glue connecting over distance and time as pure international development in the age of migration. In J. M. Puaschunder (Ed.), *Intergenerational responsibility in the 21st century* (pp. 143–174). Wilmington, DE: Vernon.

Puaschunder, J. M. (2018c). *Intergenerational responsibility in the 21st century.* Wilmington: Vernon Arts & Science.

Puaschunder, J. M. (2018d). Nudgitize me! A behavioral finance approach to minimize losses and maximize profits from heuristics and biases. *Journal of Organizational Psychology, 18*(1), 46–66.

Puaschunder, J. M. (2018e). Towards a utility theory of privacy and information sharing and the introduction of hyper-hyperbolic discounting in the digital big data age. *International Journal of Strategic Information Technology and Applications, 10*(1), 1–22.

Puaschunder, J. M. (2019a). Artificial diplomacy: A guide for public officials to conduct artificial intelligence. *Journal of Applied Research in the Digital Economy, 1*, 39–45.

Puaschunder, J. M. (2019b). *Artificial intelligence, big data, and algorithms in healthcare.* Report on behalf of the European Parliament European Liberal Forum in cooperation with The New Austria and Liberal Forum. Retrieved from https://papers.ssrn.com/sol3/papers.cfm?abstract_id=3472885

Puaschunder, J. M. (2019c). Artificial intelligence evolution: On the virtue of killing in the artificial age. *Journal of Sociology, 3*(1), 10–29.

Puaschunder, J. M. (2019d). Artificial intelligence market disruption. In *Proceedings of the 13th international RAIS conference on social sciences and humanities.* Organized by Research Association for Interdisciplinary Studies (RAIS) at Johns Hopkins University, Montgomery County Campus, Rockville, MD, United States, June 10–11 (pp. 1–8).

Puaschunder, J. M. (2019e). *Big data, artificial intelligence and healthcare: Developing a legal, policy and ethical framework for using AI, big data, robotics and algorithms in healthcare.* Report on behalf of the European Parliament European Liberal Forum in cooperation with The New Austria and Liberal Forum Lab. Vienna, Austria, European Union.

Puaschunder, J. M. (2019f). Big data ethics. *Journal of Applied Research in the Digital Economy*, *1*, 55–75.

Puaschunder, J. M. (2019g). *Corporate and financial intergenerational leadership.* Lady Stephenson, Newcastle upon Tyne: Cambridge Scholars Publishing.

Puaschunder, J. M. (2019h). *Intergenerational equity: Corporate and financial leadership.* Cheltenham: Edward Elgar.

Puaschunder, J. M. (2019i). On artificial intelligence's razor's edge: On the future of democracy and society in the artificial age. *Journal of Economics and Business*, *2*(1), 100–119.

Puaschunder, J. M. (2019j). *Stakeholder perspectives on artificial intelligence (AI), robotics and big data in healthcare: An empirical study.* Report on behalf of a European Parliament Agency. New York, NY. Retrieved from https://papers.ssrn.com/sol3/papers.cfm?abstract_id=3497261

Puaschunder, J. M. (2019k). *The legal and international situation of AI, robotics and big data with attention to healthcare.* Report on behalf of the European Parliament European Liberal Forum in cooperation with The New Austria and Liberal Forum. Retrieved from https://papers.ssrn.com/sol3/papers.cfm?abstract_id=3472885

Puaschunder, J. M. (2019l). Towards a utility theory of privacy and information sharing and the introduction of hyper-hyperbolic discounting in the digital big data age. In E. Idemudia (Ed.), *Handbook of research on social and organizational dynamics in the digital era* (pp. 157–200). Hershey, PA: IGI Publishing.

Puaschunder, J. M. (2020a). *Behavioral economics and finance leadership: Nudging and winking to make better choices.* Cham: Springer Nature.

Puaschunder, J. M. (2020b). *Big data, algorithms and health data.* Report on behalf of the European Liberal Forum of the European Parliament, Brussels and Vienna, European Union. Retrieved from https://lab.neos.eu/_Resources/Persistent/4fc7244 4cbd9d26dbc0b55d3efee2a8f93355fc2/NEOS-Lab-AI_Health-ELF-online.pdf

Puaschunder, J. M. (2020c). Economic growth in times of pandemics. In *Proceedings of the ConScienS conference on science and society: Pandemics and their impact on society, September 28–29* (pp. 1–9).

Puaschunder, J. M. (2020d). *Governance and climate justice: Global South and developing nations.* New York, NY: Palgrave Macmillan.

Puaschunder, J. M. (2020e). The future of the city after COVID-19: Digitionalization, preventism and environmentalism. In *Proceedings of the ConScienS conference on science and society: Pandemics and their impact on society*, September 28–29 (pp. 125–129).

Puaschunder, J. M. (2020f, October 30). *The Green New Deal: Historical foundations, economic fundamentals and implementation strategies.* The FinReg Blog: Global Financial Markets Center Duke University School of Law Blog. Retrieved from https://sites.law.duke.edu/thefinregblog/author/julia-m-puaschunder/

Puaschunder, J. M. (2021a). Alleviating COVID-19 inequality. In *ConScienS conference proceedings*, January 17–18 (pp. 185–190).

Puaschunder, J. M. (2021b). Equitable Green New Deal (GND). In *Proceedings of the 22nd Research Association for Interdisciplinary Studies (RAIS) conference*, June 21 (pp. 27–32).

Puaschunder, J. M. (2021c). Focusing COVID-19 bailout and recovery. *Ohio State Business Law Journal*, *16*(1), 91–148.

Puaschunder, J. M. (2021d). Generation COVID-19 long haulers. In *Scientia Moralitas conference proceedings*, April 19 (pp. 99–104).

Puaschunder, J. M. (2021e). Law and economics. In *Proceedings of the 24th Research Association for Interdisciplinary Studies (RAIS) conference*, October 17 (pp. 18–21).

Puaschunder, J. M. (2021f). Long-term investments. In W. L. Filho, A. M. Azul, L. Brandli, A. L. Salvia, & T. Wall (Eds.), *Partnerships for the goals: Encyclopedia of the UN sustainable development goals* (pp. 721–730). Cham: Springer Nature.

Puaschunder, J. M. (2021g). Monitoring and Evaluation (M&E) of the Green New Deal (GND) and European Green Deal (EGD). In *21st Research Association for Interdisciplinary Studies (RAIS) conference proceedings*, March 1 (pp. 202–206).

Puaschunder, J. M. (2021h). The future of Artificial Intelligence in international health-care: An index. In H. Nagl-Docekal & W. Zacharasiewicz (Eds.), *Proceedings of the Transatlantic dialog conference on artificial intelligence and human enhancement: Affirmative and critical approaches in the humanities from both sides of the Atlantic Conference* (pp. 181–208). De Gruyter: Austrian Academy of Sciences.

Puaschunder, J. M. (2021i). The nudging divide in the digital big data era. *International Journal of Research in Business, Economics and Management, 4*(11–12), 49–53.

Puaschunder, J. M. (2021j). *Verhaltensökonomie und Verhaltensfinanzökonomie: Ein Vergleich europäischer und nordamerikanischer Modelle.* Cham: Springer Gabler.

Puaschunder, J. M. (2022). *Ethics of inclusion: The cases of health, economics, education, digitalization and the environment in the post-COVID-19 era.* Bury Saint Edmunds: Ethics International.

Puaschunder, J. M., & Beerbaum, D. (2020a). Healthcare inequality in the digital 21st century: The case for a mandate for equal access to quality medicine for all. In *Proceedings of the 1st unequal world conference: On human development, United Nations, New York, New York*, September 28–29.

Puaschunder, J. M., & Beerbaum, D. (2020b). The future of healthcare around the world: Four indices integrating technology, productivity, anti-corruption, healthcare and market financialization. In *Proceedings of the 18th Research Association for Interdisciplinary Studies Conference at Princeton University, Princeton, New Jersey, United States*, August 17–18 (pp. 164–185).

Puaschunder, J. M., & Gelter, M. (2019). On the political economy of the European Union. In *Proceedings of the 15th international RAIS conference on social sciences and humanities*. Organized by Research Association for Interdisciplinary Studies (RAIS) at Johns Hopkins University, Montgomery County Campus, Rockville, MD, United States, November 6–7 (pp. 1–9).

Puaschunder, J. M., & Gelter, M. (2021). The law, economics and governance of generation COVID-19 long-haul. *Indiana Health Law Review, 19*(1), 47–126.

Puaschunder, J. M., Gelter, M., & Sharma, S. (2020a). Alleviating an unequal COVID-19 world: Globally digital and productively healthy. In *Proceedings of the 1st unequal world conference: On human development, United Nations, New York, New York*, September 28–29.

Puaschunder, J. M., Gelter, M., & Sharma, S. (2020b). COVID-19 shock: Considerations on socio-technological, legal, corporate, economic and governance changes and trends. In *Proceedings of the 18th International Research Association for Interdisciplinary Studies conference on social sciences and humanities*, August 22 (pp. 82–93). Retrieved from http://rais.education/wp-content/uploads/2020/08/011JPB.pdf

Puaschunder, J. M., Mantl, J., & Plank, B. (2020). Medicine of the future: The power of artificial intelligence (AI) and big data in healthcare. *Research Association for Interdisciplinary Studies Journal for Social Sciences, 4*(1), 1–8.

Puaschunder, J., & Schwarz, G. (2012). *The future is now: How joint decision-making curbs hyperbolic discounting but blurs social responsibility in the intergenerational equity public policy domain.* Working Paper, The Situationist, Harvard University Law School Project on Law and Mind Sciences. Retrieved from https://thesituationist.wordpress.com/2012/12/17/thesituation-of-intergenerational-equity/

Putnam, R. D. (2000). *Bowling alone: The collapse and revival of American community*. New York, NY: Simon & Schuster.

Putnam, R. D., Leonardi, R., & Nanetti, R. Y. (1993). *Making democracy work: Civic traditions in modern Italy*. Princeton, NJ: Princeton University Press.

Rajan, R. G., & Zingales, L. (1998). Financial dependence and growth. *American Economic Review, 88*(3), 559–586.

Ramani, A., & Bloom, N. (2021). The donut effect of Covid-19 on cities. Working Paper No. 28876, National Bureau of Economic Research. Retrieved from https://www.nber.org/papers/w28876

Rawls, J. (1971). *A theory of justice*. Cambridge, MA: Harvard University Press.

Ray, P., & Anderson, S. R. (2000). *The cultural creatives: How 50 million people are changing the world*. New York, NY: Three Rivers Press.

Reinhardt, F. L. (2000). Sustainability and the firm. *Interfaces, 30*(3), 26–41.

Reinhardt, F. L., Stavins, R. N., & Vietor, R. H. (2008). Corporate social responsibility through an economic lens. *Review of Environmental Economics and Policy, 2*, 219–239.

Renneboog, L. D. R., Horst, J. R. T., & Zhang, C. (2007). *Socially responsible investments: Methodology, risk and performance*. Discussion Paper 2007-2031, Tilburg University Center for Economic Research, Tilburg, The Netherlands.

Reserve Bank of Australia. (2021, March 2). *Statement by Philip Lowe, Governor: Monetary policy decision* [Media release]. Retrieved from https://www.rba.gov.au/media-releases/2021/mr-21-03.html

Reserve Bank of India. (2020, May 20–22). *Monetary policy statement, 2020–21: Resolution of the Monetary Policy Committee (MPC)* [Press release]. Retrieved from https://www.rbi.org.in/Scripts/BS_PressReleaseDisplay.aspx?prid=49843

Restuccia, D., & Rogerson, R. (2017). The causes and costs of misallocation. *Journal of Economic Perspectives, 31*(3), 151–174.

Restuccia, D., & Urrutia, C. (2001). Relative prices and investment rates. *Journal of Monetary Economics, 47*(1), 93–121.

Reuters. (2020, June 3). Factbox: Germany's stimulus package helps consumers and companies. Retrieved from https://www.reuters.com/article/us-health-coronavirus-germany-stimulus-p/factbox-germanys-stimulus-package-helps-consumers-and-companies-idUSKBN23A3IN

Risse-Kappen, T. (1995). *International relations: Theory and the end of the cold war*. New York, NY: Columbia University.

Rivoli, P. (2003). Making a difference or making a statement? Finance research and socially responsible investment. *Business Ethics Quarterly, 13*(3), 271–288.

Roberts, A. S. (2006). *Blacked out: Government secrecy in the information age*. Cambridge: Cambridge University Press.

Rockness, J., Schlachter, P., & Rockness, H. O. (1986). Hazardous waste disposal, corporate disclosure and financial performance in the chemical industry. In M. Neimark (Ed.), *Advances in public interest accounting* (pp. 167–191). Greenwich, CT: JAI.

Roddick, A. (2001). *Take it personally: How to make conscious choices to change the world: A globalization action guide*. Great Britain: Bath Press.

Rodrik, D. (2007). *One economics, many recipes*. Princeton, NJ: Princeton University Press.

Romer, P. M. (1986). Increasing returns and long-term growth. *The Journal of Political Economy, 94*(5), 1002–1037.

Romer, P. M. (1990). Endogenous technological change. *Journal of Political Economy, 98*(5), 71–102.

Rosen, B. N., Sandler, D. M., & Shani, D. (1991). Social issues and socially responsibility investment behavior: Preliminary empirical investigation. *Journal of Consumer Affairs, 25*(2), 221–234.

Roston, E., Kaufman, L., & Warren, H. (2022, March 24). How the world's richest people are driving global warming. Bloomberg. Retrieved from https://www.bloomberg.com/graphics/2022-wealth-carbon-emissions-inequality-powers-world-climate/

Rothkopf, D. (2008). *Superclass: The global power elite and the world they are making.* New York, NY: Farrar, Straus & Giroux.

Rubin, R. (2020). As their numbers grow, COVID-19 "long haulers" stump experts. *Journal of the American Medical Association, 14,* 1381–1383.

Ruckelshaus, W. (1996). Trust in government: A prescription for restoration. Webb Lecture Series. Washington, DC: National Academy of Public Administration.

Ruggie, J. (2008). *Promotion and protection of all human rights, civil, political, economic, social and cultural rights, including the right to development: Protect, respect and remedy: A framework for business and human rights.* Report of the Special Representative of the Secretary-General on the issue of human rights and transnational corporations and other business enterprises. Presented at the Eighth Session of the Human Rights Council. Retrieved from http://www.businesshumanrights.org/Documents/RuggieHRC2008

Russell, St., & Norvig, P. (1995). *Artificial intelligence a modern approach.* New York, NY: Simon & Schuster.

Russo, M. V., & Fouts, P. A. (1997). A resource-based perspective on corporate environmental performance and profitability. *Academy of Management Journal, 40,* 534–559.

Ryan, P. (2019, July 11). Multinational companies are adjusting to shorter supply chains. *The Economist.* Retrieved from https://www.economist.com/special-report/2019/07/11/multinational-companies-are-adjusting-to-shorter-supply-chains

Sachs, J. D. (2007). *Common wealth: Economics for a crowded planet.* London: Penguin.

Sachs, J. D. (2021, November 17). *Fixing climate finance.* Social Europe: Politics, Economy and Employment & Labor.

Sachs, J. D., Horton, R., Bagenal, J., Amor, Y. B., Karadag Caman, O., & Lafortun, G. (2020). *The Lancet* COVID-19 commission, *The Lancet, 396,* 454–455.

Saffari, E., Meghdari, A., Vazirnezhad, B., & Alemi, M. (2015, October). Ava (a social robot): Design and performance of a robotic hearing apparatus. *LNCS: Social Robotics, 9388,* 440–450.

Saha, M. (2020, May 18). Stimulus to cost only about 1% of GDP. *The Hindu.* Retrieved from https://www.thehindu.com/business/stimulus-to-cost-only-about-1-of-gdp/article31617629.ece

Schmelzing, P. (2020, January). *Eight centuries of global real interest rates, R-G, and the 'suprasecular' decline, 1311-2018.* Staff Working Paper No. 845, Bank of England. Retrieved from https://www.bankofengland.co.uk/working-paper/2020/eight-centuries-of-global-real-interest-rates-r-g-and-the-suprasecular-decline-1311-2018

Schneider, H. (2021, February 12). Friendly fire erupts as economists spar over U.S. stimulus. Reuters. Retrieved from https://www.reuters.com/business/friendly-fire-erupts-economists-spar-over-us-stimulus-2021-02-12/

Scholte, J. A. (2000). *Globalization: A critical introduction.* Basingstoke: Palgrave.

Schroeder, M. (2003, March). *Socially responsible investments in Germany, Switzerland, and the United States.* Discussion Paper 03-10, Centre for European Economic Research.

Schueth, S. (2003). Socially responsible investing in the United States. *Journal of Business Ethics, 43,* 189–194.

Schuller, A. (2017). At the crossroads of control: The intersection of artificial intelligence in autonomous weapon systems with International Humanitarian Law. *Harvard National Security Journal, 8,* 379–425.

Schumpeter, J. A. (1934). *The theory of economic development.* Cambridge, MA: Harvard University.

Schumpeter, J. A. (1943/1976). *Capitalism, socialism and democracy.* London: Allen & Unwin.

Schumpeter, J. A. (1949). Economic theory and entrepreneurial history. In R. R. Wohl (Ed.), *Change and the entrepreneur: Postulates and the patterns for entrepreneurial history* (pp. 131–142). Cambridge, MA: Harvard University Press.

Schumpeter, J. A. (1951/1989). *Essays on entrepreneurs, innovations, business cycles, and the evolution of capitalism*. Piscataway, NJ: Transaction.

Schumpeter, J. A. (1989). *Essays on entrepreneurs, innovations, business cycles, and the evolution of capitalism*. London: Routledge.

Searing, L. (2021, November 15). 50 percent of people who survive Covid-19 face lingering symptoms, study finds. *The Washington Post*. Retrieved from https://www.washingtonpost.com/health/long-covid-50-percent-lingering-symptoms/2021/11/12/e6655236-4313-11ec-9ea7-3eb2406a2e24_story.html

Semmler, W. (2021). Economics of climate change. *Lecture notes*. New York, NY: The New School for Social Research.

Semmler, W., Braga, J. A., Lichtenberger, A., Toure, M., & Hayde, E. (2021). *Fiscal policies for a low-carbon economy*. World Bank Report, Washington, DC. Retrieved from https://documents1.worldbank.org/curated/en/998821623308445356/pdf/Fiscal-Policies-for-a-Low-Carbon-Economy.pdf

Sennett, R. (1998). *Der flexible Mensch. Die Kultur des Kapitalismus*. Berlin: Berlin. Verlag

Shaikh, A. (2016). *Capitalism: Competition, conflict, and crises*. Oxford: Oxford University Press.

Shalal, A., Alper, A., & Zengerle, P. (2020, May 18). U.S. mulls paying companies, tax breaks to pull supply chains from China. Reuters. Retrieved from https://www.reuters.com/article/us-usa-china-supply-chains/u-s-mulls-paying-companies-tax-breaks-to-pull-supply-chains-from-china-idUSKBN22U0FH

Sheehy, B. (2005). Screening the reluctant stakeholder: Theoretical problems in the shareholder–stakeholder debate. *University of Miami Business Law Review, 14*(3), 193.

Shilon, N. (2011). *Illusory equity holding policies*. Unpublished Working Paper, Harvard Law School.

Shilon, N. (2013). *Stock ownership policies: Rhetoric and reality*. Discussion Paper No. 49, John M. Olin Center for Law, Economics, and Business Fellows.

Sichler, R. (2006). *Autonomie in der Arbeitswelt. Psychologie und Beruf*. Göttingen: Vandenhoeck & Ruprecht.

Siegel, D. S., & Vitaliano, D. F. (2006). *An empirical analysis of the strategic use of corporate social responsibility*. Working Paper, Rensselaer Polytechnic Institute.

Siegel, D. S., & Vitaliano, D. F. (2007). An empirical analysis of the strategic use of corporate social responsibility. *Journal of Economics & Management Strategy, 16*, 773–792.

Simon, H. A. (1957). *Models of man: Social and rational*. New York, NY: Wiley.

Simon, Th. (2004). *Gute Policey: Ordnungsbilder und Zielvorstellungen politischen Handelns in der Frühen Neuzeit*. Frankfurt am Main: Klostermann.

Simons, J. G., Powers, Ch. W., & Gunnemann, J. P. (1972). *The ethical investor: Universities and corporate responsibility*. New Haven, CT: Yale University Press.

Smialek, J., & Irwin, N. (2020, March 5). Fed slashes rates to near-zero and unveils sweeping program to aid economy. *The New York Times*. Retrieved from https://www.nytimes.com/2020/03/15/business/economy/federal-reserve-coronavirus.html

Smith, A. (1759/1976). *The theory of moral sentiments*. Oxford: Clarendon.

Smith, A. (1761/2014). Theory of moral sentiments. Retrieved from https://matej.ceplovi.cz/cizi/moral.pdf

Smith, A. (1776/1976). *An inquiry into the nature and causes of the wealth of nations*. Oxford: Clarendon.

Smith, C. (2003). The new corporate philanthropy. *Harvard business review on corporate responsibility*. Cambridge, MA: Harvard Business School.

Smith, E. (2020, October 28). Deutsche Bank swings back to profit in third quarter, beats expectations. CNBC Earnings. Retrieved from https://www.cnbc.com/2020/10/28/deutsche-bank-q3-earnings-2020.html

Social Investment Forum Report. (2006, January 24). *Report on socially responsible investing trends in the United States*. Social Investment Forum Industry Research Program 10-year Review.

Sofge, E. (2015). Bill Gates fears A.I., but A.I. researchers know better. *Popular Science*. Retrieved from www.popsci.com/ bill-gates-fears-ai-ai-researchers-know-better

Solomon, J. F., Solomon, A., & Norton, S. D. (2002). Socially responsible investment in the UK: Drivers and current issues. *Journal of General Management, 27*(3), 1–13.

Solum, L. (1992). Legal personhood for artificial intelligences. *North Carolina Law Review, 70*(4), 1231–1287.

Soros, G. (1995). *Jan Patocka memorial lecture: A failed philosopher tries again*. Unpublished notes. New York, NY: The Open Society Institute.

Soros, G. (1997). *The capitalist threat*. Tbilisi: Open Society Georgia Foundation.

Soros, G. (1998). *The crisis of global capitalism: Open society endangered*. New York, NY: PublicAffairs.

Soros, G. (2000). *Open society: Reforming global capitalism*. New York, NY: PublicAffairs.

Soros, G. (2003). *The alchemy of finance*. New York, NY: Wiley.

Soros, G. (2008). *The new paradigm for financial markets: The credit crisis of 2008 and what it means*. New York, NY: Public Affairs.

Soskice, D. (1978). Strike waves and wage explosions, 1968–1970: An economic interpretation. In C. Crouch & A. Pizzorno (Eds.), *The resurgence of class conflict in Western Europe since 1968* (pp. 221–245). London: Macmillan.

Sparkes, R. (2002). *Socially responsible investment: A global revolution*. Cronwall: Wiley.

Sparkes, R., & Cowton, Ch. J. (2004). The maturing of socially responsible investment: A review of the developing link with corporate social responsibility. *Journal of Business Ethics, 52*, 45–57.

Spicer, B. H. (1978). Investors, corporate social performance and information disclosure: An empirical study. *Accountability Review, 53*, 94–111.

Springer, J. (1999). Corporate law, corporate constituency statues: Hollow hopes and false fears. *Annual Survey of American Law*, 85.

Sproles, G. B. (1985). From perfectionism to faddism: Measuring consumers' decision-making styles. In *Proceedings of the American Council on Consumer Issues* (pp. 79–85) Retrieved from https://www.consumerinterests.org/proceedings.

Sproles, G. B., & Kendall, E. L. (1986). A methodology for profiling consumers' decision-making styles. *Journal of Consumer Affairs, 20*, 267–279.

Starr, M. (2008). Socially responsible investment and pro-social change. *Journal of Economic Issues, 42*(1), 51–73.

Statista. (2021). Monthly unemployment rate in the United States from April 2020 to April 2021 (seasonally-adjusted). Retrieved from https://www.statista.com/statistics/273909/seasonally-adjusted-monthly-unemployment-rate-in-the-us/

Statman, M. (2000). Socially responsible mutual funds. *Financial Analysts Journal, 56*(3), 3039.

Statman, M. (2007). *Socially responsible investors and their advisors. Journal of Investment Consulting, 9*(1), 15–26.

Statman, M. (2008). *The expressive nature of socially responsible investors*. SSRN Working Paper 1094068, Santa Clara University. Retrieved from www.ssrn.com

Steurer, R. (2010). The role of governments in corporate social responsibility: Characterising public policies on CSR in Europe. *Policy Science, 43*, 49–72.

Steurer, R., Margula, S., & Martinuzzi, A. (2008). Socially responsible investment in EU member states: Overview of government initiatives and SRI experts' expectations towards governments. *Analysis of national policies on CSR, in support of a structured exchange of information on national CSR policies and initiatives.* Final report to the EU high-level group on CSR provided by the Research Institute for Managing Sustainability. Vienna University of Economics and Business.

Stevis-Gridneff, M. (2020, December 10). E.U. Adopts groundbreaking stimulus to fight Coronavirus recession. *The New York Times.* Retrieved from https://www.nytimes.com/2020/07/20/world/europe/eu-stimulus-coronavirus.html

Stiglitz, J. E. (2003). *Globalization and its discontents.* New York, NY: Norton.

Stone, B. K., Guerard, J. B., Gületkin, M. N., & Adams, G. (2001). *Socially responsible investment screening: Strong evidence of no significant cost for actively managed portfolios.* Invested Interests Working Paper. Retrieved from https://investedinterests.com/wp-content/uploads/2018/03/Socially_Responsible_Screening_-_Strong_Evidence_of_No_Significant_Cost_for_Actively_Managed_Portfolios_-_Stone_Guerard_Gultekin__Adams1.pdf

Strebel, H. (1980). *Umwelt und Betriebswirtschaft: Die natürliche Umwelt als Gegenstand der Unternehmenspolitik.* Berlin: Schmidt.

Strupczewski, J., & Abnett, K. (2020, December 9). EU leaders unblock 1.8 trillion euro budget, recovery fund, eye climate goals. Reuters. Retrieved from https://www.reuters.com/article/us-eu-summit/eu-leaders-unblock-1-8-trillion-euro-budget-recovery-fund-eye-climate-goals-idUSKBN28J37L

Szmigiera, M. (2021, May). Value of COVID-19 stimulus packages in the G20, as share of GDP 2021. Statista. Retrieved from https://www.statista.com/statistics/1107572/covid-19-value-g20-stimulus-packages-share-gdp/

Taheri, A. R., Meghdari, A., Alemi, M., & Pouretemad, H. R. (2018). Human–robot interaction in autism treatment: A case study on three pairs of autistic children as twins, siblings, and classmates. *International Journal of Social Robotics, 10*(1), 93–113.

Taylor, Ch. (1988). *Negative Freiheit? Zur Kritik des neuzeitlichen Individualismus.* Frankfurt am Main: Suhrkamp.

Teoh, S. H., Welch, I., & Wazzan, C. P. (1999). The effect of socially activist investment politics on the financial markets: Evidence from the South African boycott. *Journal of Business, 72*(1), 35–89.

Thaler, R. H., & Sunstein, C. R. (2008). *Nudge: Improving decisions about health, wealth, and happiness.* New Haven, CT: Yale University Press.

The Economist. (2008, January 17). How good should your business be?. *The Economist.* Retrieved from https://www.economist.com/leaders/2008/01/17/how-good-should-your-business-be

The Economist. (2019, January 26). The steam has gone out of globalisation: Slowbalisation (pp. 17–20). *The Economist.* Retrieved from https://www.economist.com/leaders/2019/01/24/the-steam-has-gone-out-of-globalisation?utm_medium=cpc.adword.pd&utm_source=google&ppccampaignID=17210591673&ppcadID=&utm_campaign=a.22brand_pmax&utm_content=conversion.direct-response.anonymous&gclsrc=ds&gclsrc=ds

The Economist. (2020a October 8). The pandemic has caused the world's economies to diverge. *The Economist.* Retrieved from https://www.economist.com/leaders/2020/10/08/the-pandemic-has-caused-the-worlds-economies-to-diverge?utm_medium=cpc.adword.pd&utm_source=google&ppccampaignID=17210591673&ppcadID=&utm_campaign=a.22brand_pmax&utm_content=conversion.direct-response.anonymous&gclsrc=ds&gclsrc=ds

The Economist. (2020b, October 8). The peril and the promise. *The Economist.* Retrieved from https://www.economist.com/special-report/2020/10/08/the-peril-and-the-promise

The Economist. (2021a, October 8). Changing places: The pandemic will not end globalization, but it will reshape it. *The Economist*. Retrieved from https://www.economist.com/special-report/2020/10/08/changing-places

The Economist. (2021b, April 29). Post-COVID syndrome researchers are closing in on long Covid: The results are alarming. *The Economist*. Retrieved from https://www.economist.com/science-and-technology/2021/04/29/researchers-are-closing-in-on-long-covid

The Hindu. (2020, June 30). PM extends free foodgrains scheme till November. *The Hindu*. Retrieved from https://www.thehindu.com/news/national/coronavirus-lockdown-prime-minister-narendra-modi-addresses-nation-on-june-30-2020/article31953944.ece

The Moscow Times. (2020, June 2). Russia prices economic recovery plan at $70Bln. *The Moscow Times*. Retrieved from https://www.themoscowtimes.com/2020/06/02/russia-prices-economic-revery-plan-at-70bln-a70456

The Schwartz Center for Economics Policy Analysis. (2020, August 5). Older workers report: Over half of unemployed older workers at risk of involuntary retirement. Retrieved from https://www.economicpolicyresearch.org/jobsreport/over-half-of-older-workers-unemployed-at-risk-of-involuntary-retirement

The Straits Times. (2020, March 4). South Korea unveils $13.7b stimulus package to fight coronavirus. *The Straits Times*. Retrieved from https://www.straitstimes.com/business/economy/south-korea-unveils-137b-stimulus-package-to-fight-coronavirus

The United States Congress. (2019). Recognising the duty of the Federal Government to create a Green New Deal. Retrieved from https://www.congress.gov/bill/116th-congress/house-resolution/109/text

The United States Congress, 116th Congress, 1st Session, House Resolution 109. (2019, February 7). Recognizing the duty of the Federal Government to create a Green New Deal, Washington, DC. Retrieved from https://www.congress.gov/116/bills/hres109/BILLS-116hres109ih.pdf

The White House. of the United States of America (2009, January 21). President Barack Obama's inaugural address. Retrieved from https://obamawhitehouse.archives.gov/blog/2009/01/21/president-Barack-obamas-inaugural-address

The White House of the United States of America. (2021a, July 26). Fact sheet: Biden–Harris administration marks anniversary of Americans with Disabilities Act and announces resources to support individuals with long COVID, 2021. Retrieved from https://www.whitehouse.gov/briefing-room/statements-releases/2021/07/26/fact-sheet-bidenharris-administration-marks-anniversary-of-americans-with-disabilities-act-and-announces-resources-tosupport-individuals-with-long-covid/

The White House of the United States of America. (2021b). President Biden and G7 leaders launch build back better world (B3W) partnership. Retrieved from https://www.whitehouse.gov/briefing-room/statements-releases/2021/06/12/fact-sheet-president-biden-and-g7-leaders-launch-build-back-better-world-b3w-partnership/

The White House of the United States of America. (2021c). President Biden announces American rescue plan. Retrieved from https://www.whitehouse.gov/briefing-room/legislation/2021/01/20/president-biden-announces-american-rescue-plan/

The White House of the United States of America. (2021d, March 31). The American jobs plan. Retrieved from https://www.whitehouse.gov/briefing-room/statements-releases/2021/03/31/fact-sheet-the-american-jobs-plan/

The White House of the United States of America. (2021e). The build back better agenda. Retrieved from https://www.whitehouse.gov/build-back-better/

The World Economic Forum. (2021). The World Economic Forum great reset. Retrieved from https://www.weforum.org/great-reset/

Themistoklis, T. (2018). Artificial intelligence as global commons and the "international law supremacy" principle. In *Proceedings of the 10th international RAIS conference on social sciences and humanities.* Organized by Research Association for Interdisciplinary Studies (RAIS) at The Erdman Center at Princeton University, Princeton, New Jersey, United States. Cambridge, MA: The Scientific Press.

Theodosopoulos, V. (2020, July). The geopolitics of supply: Towards a new EU approach to the security of supply of critical raw materials? Institute for European Studies Policy Brief. Retrieved from https://brussels-school.be/publications/other-publications/geopolitics-supply-towards-new-eu-approach-security-supply-critical

Thomasson, L., & Hirai, J. (2021, August 21). The cost of saving global economy: $834 million an hour for 18 months. Bloomberg. Retrieved from https://www.business-standard.com/article/international/the-cost-of-saving-global-economy-834-million-an-hour-for-18-months-121082100048_1.html

Thomson, J., & Wheeler, D. (2004). *Human capital-based investment criteria for total shareholder returns: A Canadian and international perspective.* Phase I Report to SSHRC. Toronto: York University.

Tippet, J. (2001). Performance of Australia's ethical funds. *Australian Economic Review, 34*(2), 170–178.

Tippet, J., & Leung, P. (2001). Defining ethical investment and its demography in Australia. *Australian Accounting Review, 11*(3), 44–55.

Tocqueville, A. (1835/1959). Über die Demokratie in Amerika. Stuttgart: Deutsche Verlagsanstalt.

Trevino, L. K., & Nelson, K. A. (2004). *Managing business ethics: Straight talk about how to do right.* Hoboken: Wiley.

Trivers, R. (1971). The evolution of reciprocal altruism. *Quarterly Review of Biology, 46,* 3557.

TU The Top Alumni Club Event (2020, May 8). Panel on digi-disruption & New Age Renaissance. TU The Top Alumni Club. Retrieved from https://tuthetop-alumni.at/digidisruption/

Tumpel-Gugerell, G. (2009, June 15). *Monetary policy challenges in the light of the current financial market development.* Notes to the speech delivered at the Vienna Alpbach Talks.

Tversky, A., & Kahneman, D. (1974). Judgment under uncertainty: Heuristics and biases. *Science, 185,* 1124–1131.

Tybout, J. R. (2000). Manufacturing firms in developing countries: How well do they do, and why? *Journal of Economic Literature, 38*(1), 11–44.

UNICEF. (2020 September 16). *150 million additional children plunged into poverty due to COVID-19* [Press release]. UNICEF, Save the Children Say. Retrieved from https://www.unicef.org/press-releases/150-million-additional-children-plunged-poverty-due-covid-19-unicef-save-children

United Nations. (2020). Climate change and COVID-19: UN urges nations to 'recover better.' Retrieved from https://www.un.org/en/un-coronavirus-communications-team/un-urges-countries-%E2%80%98build-back-better%E2%80%99

United Nations Conference on Trade and Development. (2020, October 27). Investment Trends Monitor, UNCTAD/DIAE/IA/INF/2020/4. Retrieved from https://unctad.org/system/files/official-document/diaeiainf2020d4_en.pdf

United Nations Conference on Trade and Development Committee for the Coordination of Statistical Activities. (2020). How COVID-19 is changing the world: A statistical perspective (pp. 14–31). Retrieved from https://unstats.un.org/unsd/ccsa/documents/covid19-report-ccsa.pdf

United Nations Department of Economic and Social Affairs. (2017). Will robots and AI cause mass unemployment? Not necessarily, but they do bring other threats. Retrieved from https://www.un.org/development/desa/en/news/policy/will-robots-and-ai-cause-mass-unemployment-not-necessarily-but-they-do-bring-other-threats.html

United Nations Environment Programme. (2009). Global Green New Deal Policy Brief. Retrieved from https://www.unep.org/resources/report/global-green-new-deal-policy-brief-march-2009#:~:text=UNEP%20outlines%20a%20GGND%20with,carbon%20dependency%20and%20environmental%20destruction

United Nations General Assembly. (2020). Comprehensive and coordinated response to the Coronavirus Disease (COVID-19) pandemic. Retrieved from https://www.un.org/pga/74/wp-content/uploads/sites/99/2020/09/Omnibus_Final-clean.pdf

United States Bureau of Labor Statistics. (2020, May 13). Unemployment rate rises to record high 14.7 percent in April 2020. Retrieved from https://www.bls.gov/opub/ted/2020/unemployment-rate-rises-to-record-high-14-point-7-percent-in-april-2020.htm?view_full

United States Centers for Disease Control and Prevention (CDC). (2020, December 17). Newsroom Releases, Overdose deaths accelerating during COVID-19: Expanded prevention efforts needed. Retrieved from https://www.cdc.gov/media/releases/2020/p1218-overdose-deaths-covid-19.html

USASpending.Gov. (2020, October 1). The federal response to COVID-19. Retrieved from https://datalab.usaspending.gov/federal-covid-funding/#fn1

Uzawa, H. (1965). Optimum technical change in an aggregative model of economic growth. *International Economic Review, 6*(1), 18–31.

Van Maanen, J., & Laurent, A. (1993). The flow of culture: Some notes on globalization and the multinational corporation. In S. Ghoshal & D. E. Westney (Eds.), *Organization theory and the multinational corporation* (pp. 276–298). New York, NY: St. Martin's.

Van Slyke, D. M. (2003). The mythology of privatization in contracting for social services, *Public Administration Review, 63*(3), 296–315.

Veblen, T. (1899/1994). *The theory of the leisure class: An economic study of institutions.* New York, NY: Dover.

Ventura, J. (1997). Growth and interdependence. *The Quarterly Journal of Economics, 112*(1), 57–84.

Veruggio, G. (2005). The birth of roboethics. In *IEEE international conference on robotics and automation (ICRA 2005): Workshop on robo-ethics*, Barcelona, April 18.

Vitek, F. (2017). *Policy, risk and spillover analysis in the world economy: A panel dynamic stochastic general equilibrium approach.* Washington, DC: International Monetary Fund.

Vivid Economics. (2021). Greenness of stimulus index. Retrieved from https://www.vivideconomics.com/casestudy/greenness-for-stimulus-index/

Vlassopoulos, K. (2009). *Politics antiquity and its legacy.* Oxford: Oxford University Press.

Voorhes, M. (1999). *The US divestment movement: How sanctions work: Lessons from South Africa.* New York, NY: St. Martin's.

Waddock, S. A., & Graves, S. B. (1997). The corporate social performance-financial performance link. *Strategic Management Journal, 18*, 303–319.

Waldman, D. A., Siegel, D., & Javidian, M. (2004, January). *Transformational leadership and corporate social responsibility.* Working Paper. Retrieved from http://www.sristudies.org/Waldman+et+al+(2004)

Waldman, D. A., Siegel, D., & Javidian, M. (2006). Components of CEO transformational leadership and corporate social responsibility. *Journal of Management Studies, 43*(8), 1703–1725

Weber, W. G. (1997). *Analyse von Gruppenarbeit: Kollektive Handlungsregulation in soziotechnischen Systemen.* Bern: Huber.

Weber, W. G., Pasqualoni, P., & Burtscher, Ch. (2004). *Wirtschaft, Demokratie und soziale Verantwortung. Psychologie und Beruf.* Göttingen: Vandenhoeck & Ruprecht.

WebMD. (2020, April 1). How scientists predict how many people will get COVID-19. WebMD. Retrieved from https://www.webmd.com/lung/news/20200401/how-scientists-predict-how-many-people-will-get-covid-19#1

Webster, F. E. (1975). Determining the characteristics of the socially conscious consumer. *Journal of Consumer Research, 12*(2), 188–196.

Weinreb, E. (2004, March 22). Top talent looks beyond bottom line. Letter to the editor. *Financial Times.*

Werther, W. B., & Chandler, D. (2006). *Strategic corporate social responsibility: Stakeholders in a global environment.* Thousand Oaks, CA: Sage.

Wetzel, W. E., & Freear, J. (1996). Promoting informal venture capital in the United States: Reflections on the history of the venture capital network. In R. T. Harrison & C. M. Mason (Eds.), *Informal venture capital: Evaluating the impact of business introduction services* (pp. 61–74). Hemel Hempstead: Woodhead-Faulkner.

Whelan, R. (2021, August 30). High pay for Covid-19 nurses leads to shortages at some hospitals: Some hospitals pay signing bonuses of up to $40,000; 'We're desperate for nurses'. *The Wall Street Journal.* Retrieved from https://www.wsj.com/articles/high-pay-for-covid-19-nurses-leads-to-shortages-at-some-hospitals-11630253483

Whitley, R. (1997). Business systems. In A. Sorge & M. Warner (Eds.), *The IEBM handbook of organizational behaviour* (pp. 173–186). London: Thomson Business Press.

Williams, C. A., & Aguilera, R. V. (2006). *Corporate social responsibility in a comparative perspective.* Working Paper. Retrieved from http://www.business.uiuc.edu/aguilera/pdf/Williams%20Aguilera%20OUPfinal%20de c%202006.pdf

Williams, C. A., & Aguilera, R. V. (2008). Corporate social responsibility in a comparative perspective. In A. Crane, D. Matten, A. McWilliams, J. Moon, & D. S. Siegel (Eds.), *Oxford handbook of corporate social responsibility* (pp. 452–472). Oxford: Oxford University Press.

Williams, G. (2005). *Are socially responsible investors different from conventional investors? A comparison across six countries.* Unpublished Working Paper, University of Bath.

Wilson, E. O. (1975). *Sociobiology.* Cambridge, MA: Harvard University Press.

Windsor, D. (2001). Corporate citizenship: Evolution and interpretation. In J. Andriof & M. McIntosh (Eds.), *Perspectives on corporate citizenship* (pp. 39–52). Sheffield: Greenleaf.

Winship, C., & Rein, M. (1999). The dangers of 'strong' causal reasoning in social policy. *Society, 36*(5), 38–46.

Wolff, M. (2002). Response to "Confronting the critics." *New Academy Review, 1,* 230–237.

Woo, A. (2021, April 16). *Environmental fascism and the zero waste movement.* Panel on Monitoring and Evaluation in Environmental Economics, The New School New York.

World Bank. (2015). *Report 2015.* Washington, DC: World Bank.

World Bank. (2020, April 22). *World Bank predicts sharpest decline of remittances in recent history* [Press release]. Retrieved from https://www.worldbank.org/en/news/press-release/2020/04/22/world-bank-predicts-sharpest-decline-of-remittances-in-recent-history

World Bank. (2021). Global economic prospects. Retrieved from https://www.worldbank.org/en/publication/global-economic-prospects

World Bank. *World Bank Group announces up to $12 billion immediate support for COVID-19 country response* [Press release]. Washington, DC: World Bank. Retrieved from https://www.worldbank.org/en/news/press-release/2020/03/03/world-bank-group-announces-up-to-12-billion-immediate-support-for-covid-19-country-response#:~:text=WASHINGTON%2C%20March%203%2C%202020%20%E2%80%94,impacts%20of%20the%20global%20outbreak

World Bank. *World Bank Group increases COVID-19 response to $14 billion to help sustain economies, protect jobs* [Press release]. Washington, DC: World Bank. Retrieved from https://www.worldbank.org/en/news/press-release/2020/03/17/world-bank-group-increases-covid-19-response-to-14-billion-to-help-sustain-economies-protect-jobs

World Bank Group. (2020, March 17). *100 countries get support in response to COVID-19 (Coronavirus)*. Washington, DC: World Bank. Retrieved from https://www.worldbank. org/en/news/press-release/2020/05/19/world-bank-group-100-countries-get-support-in-response-to-covid-19-coronavirus

World Bank Group Migration and Development Brief 26. (2016, April). Migration and remittances: Recent development and outlook. Washington, DC: International Bank for Reconstruction and Development, World Bank Group.

World Bank Report. (2008). *Technology diffusion in the developing world: Global economic prospects Report*. Washington, DC: World Bank.

World Development Report. (2005). *A better investment climate for everyone*. Washington, DC: The World Bank.

World Investment Report. (2015). *Reforming international investment governance*. United Nations Conference on Trade and Development Report, United Nations, New York, NY.

World Trade Organisation. (2020). Communication on trade and environmental sustainability. Retrieved from https://docs.wto.org/dol2fe/Pages/SS/directdoc.aspx?filename= q:/WT/CTE/W249.pdf&Open=True

World Trade Organisation. (2021). Members review draft MC12 declaration on trade and environmental sustainability. Retrieved from https://www.wto.org/english/news_e/ news21_e/tessd_21jul21_e.htm

Worldometer Coronavirus Cases. (2021). Retrieved from https://www.worldometers.info/ coronavirus/

Wright, P., & Ferris, S. (1997). Agency conflict and corporate strategy: The effect of divestment on corporate value. *Strategic Management Journal, 18*(1), 77–83.

Yamagishi, T., & Yamagishi, M. (1994). Trust and commitment in the United States and Japan. *Motivation and Emotion, 18*(2), 129–166.

Zak, P. J. (2008). *Moral markets: The critical role of values in the economy*. Princeton, NJ: Princeton University Press.

Zak, P. J., & Knack, St. (2001). Trust and growth. *Economic Journal, 111*, 295–321.

Zeff, E., & Pirro, E. (1999). *Redistribution of authority: The South African case*. Washington, DC: International Studies Association.

Zhang, S. (2021, August 17). The Coronavirus is here forever: This is how we live with it. *The Atlantic*. Retrieved from https://www.theatlantic.com/science/archive/2021/08/ how-we-live-coronavirus-forever/619783/

Zheng, L. (2020, June 15). We are entering the age of corporate social justice. *Harvard Business Review*. Retrieved from https://hbr.org/2020/06/were-entering-the-age-of-corporate-social-justice

Ziegler, A., Rennings, K., & Schröder, M. (2002). *Der Einfluss ökologischer und sozialer Nachhaltigkeit auf den Shareholder Value europäischer Aktiengesellschaften*. Diskussionspapier 02-32, Zentrum für Europäische Wirtschaftsforschung.

Zoellick, R. (2009, January 25). Time to herald the age of responsibility. *Financial Times*. Retrieved from https://www.ft.com/content/1348d34e-eb0d-11dd-bb6e-0000779fd2ac

Index